ROOSEVELT'S
WARRIOR

The Johns Hopkins University Press   Baltimore and London

ROOSEVELT'S
WARRIOR

HAROLD L. ICKES AND THE NEW DEAL

Jeanne Nienaber Clarke

© 1996 Jeanne Nienaber Clarke
All rights reserved. Published 1996
Printed in the United States of America on acid-free paper
05 04 03 02 01 00 99 98 97 96   5 4 3 2 1

The Johns Hopkins University Press
2715 North Charles Street
Baltimore, Maryland 21218-4319
The Johns Hopkins Press Ltd., London

Published in cooperation with The Center for American Places,
Harrisonburg, Virginia

Library of Congress Cataloging-in-Publication Data will be found at the
end of this book.
A catalog record for this book is available from the British Library.

ISBN 0-8018-5094-0

To Steven and Mary Nienaber,

who have been there for the duration.

The White House
Washington (Feb'y 7, 1940)

We—you & I, were married "for better, for worse"—and it's
too late to get a divorce & too late for you to walk out of the
home—anyway, I need you! Nuff said. Affec. FDR

Feb. 8, 1940

You are a hard man to deal with, especially when anyone ad-
mires and loves you as I do. Your letter quite touched me. I am
yours to command . . . of my devotion there can be no doubt.

Harold L. Ickes, to FDR

CONTENTS

PREFACE

The idea for this book came to mind a decade ago. I was then completing a book that examined, among other things, the administrative history of resource management in the United States. In the course of that research I kept coming across references to a secretary of the interior with the odd name of Ickes. He appeared to have shaped significantly conservation policy during his long tenure in Franklin D. Roosevelt's cabinet. And he did it with élan. Here, it seemed, was an unusual type, a "charismatic bureaucrat." After finishing that other book I went back to the library.

It was a surprise to learn that there existed at the time no comprehensive study of Interior Secretary Harold L. Ickes, an official who held that position longer than anyone else has. At about the same time as I discovered how little had been written about him, the historian William Leuchtenburg came to the University of Arizona to deliver a lecture on Franklin D. Roosevelt and his impact on modern politics. My interest in the New Deal period was piqued, and I decided to write about Ickes.

Harold Ickes is best known for his numerous contributions to the cause of conservation. He was well ahead of his time when, as secretary of the interior, he created a soil erosion service, worked toward conserving domestic energy resources, pushed grazing reform on the public lands of the West, moved to make the national park system a truly national entity, and proclaimed that the nation needed a congressionally designated wilderness system.

But Ickes also was an unusually versatile executive who worked in a fluid political environment. He was able to move well beyond the traditional boundaries of the Interior Department to make his presence felt in a number of policy areas. Although during his thirteen years in office he strayed virtually all over the map of major issues, his most noteworthy accomplishments beyond conservation were linked to the jobs President Roosevelt gave him at the outset of the New Deal: administrator of public works (PWA) and oil administrator under the National Recovery Administration (NRA). With FDR's concurrence, and sometimes without it, Ickes also was a force in the presidential campaign of 1936, the Supreme Court fight of 1937, the congressional elections of 1938, and the struggle for equal rights for minorities that spanned the decade.

This book covers a particular period in Harold Ickes's life, one marked by dramatic changes in both his public career and in his personal life. It was probably the most tumultuous and exciting time of his life. An introductory chapter provides an overview of his early career as an attorney in Chicago and as a municipal reformer. Subsequent chapters cover the period from February 1933, when FDR appointed him secretary of the interior, to December 1939, when he and the rest of the nation watched the unfolding tragedy in Europe. By then the New Deal had run its course. The book is organized chronologically and substantively, with separate chapters focusing on his official responsibilities and his political activities. I made every effort, however, to capture the kaleidoscopic nature of the New Deal and of Ickes's participation in it, for that was, in my opinion, one of the outstanding features of the man and the era. Ickes, like Roosevelt and others working in this chaotic environment, was a "juggler."

My purpose in this book is to describe and evaluate Harold Ickes's role in fashioning the New Deal. Although presidents usually get most of the credit, or blame, for what occurs under their watch, they don't work "in splendid isolation." The administrative presidency, itself a product of the Roosevelt era, is a collective institution, and political executives besides the chief can make or break an adminstration. FDR understood this as well as anyone ever has, and no chief executive in the twentieth century has surpassed his talent for getting other people to do what he wanted them to do.

Ickes's contributions to the New Deal must be understood in this context. A special relationship with FDR began when the president-elect plucked him from relative obscurity and made him Interior secretary. Ickes realized that Roosevelt had given him, in 1933, the opportunity of his lifetime. He never forgot it. Although their friendship was severely tested on several occasions, it endured. It endured because of the mutual affection that developed between them, and also because the president found Ickes's fighting spirit on behalf of reform to be indispensable. "All presidents need a whipping post," Roosevelt once remarked to Ickes, "and you have become mine since Hugh Johnson resigned."

If Harold Ickes performed the function of being FDR's lightning rod during much of the New Deal, he also succeeded in *his* overall political objective—to push the president's agenda toward liberalism. Ickes was no sycophant. He demonstrated his independence time and again by taking principled stands irrespective of their popularity. Whether it was ordering the racial integration of the Interior Department's public facilities in 1933—without asking Roosevelt's permission—or in refusing to sell helium to Hitler's Germany in 1938—over FDR's objections—Harold Ickes earned himself the reputation of being the boldest and most outspoken Interior secretary in the history of that department. Most of the time, in my view, he was right.

Ickes said and did many memorable things, but the one I think best summarizes his New Deal accomplishments is a comment he made in 1937. When the court-packing fight was at its most intense, and when motives were being questioned on both sides of the conflict, Ickes cut through to the heart of the matter. "Some southern leaders," he wrote, "affect to believe that an enlarged and more liberal court would lift from the southern Negro some of the weight of oppresssion that he has carried since the Civil War."

No one said it better. His words resonate with clarity of thought and constancy of principle. So did his actions.

ACKNOWLEDGMENTS

The research and writing of this book spanned nearly ten years. Much of my time during that period was spent sitting, reading, and taking notes in libraries; then, more sitting, writing, and rewriting on the word processor in my office. Although it looked like a solitary endeavor akin to torture to my gregarious teenaged son, I found it anything but that. The activity that went into this book not only involved an ongoing dialogue in my mind with Harold L. Ickes and his fellow New Dealers (whom I've gotten to know very well), but dialogues with friends, family members, students, colleagues across the country, and individuals who personally knew Harold Ickes.

This book has benefited substantially from those conversations and interviews. It has been improved as well from the advice and suggestions, both solicited and unsolicited, that I have received from fellow scholars. Others have helped by providing me with room, board, and companionship while I was doing the research, and still other people have read early drafts of the manuscript. Institutional support came in the form of a travel grant from the American Council of Learned Societies in 1987, from the National Endowment for the Humanities' Travel to Collections Program in 1989, and from the Social and Behavioral Sciences Research Institute at the University of Arizona in 1992. A one-semester research professorship gave me time for uninterrupted writing. I am grateful not only for the financial support I received from these organizations but for the moral support that comes from knowing that someone else, besides myself, thought that this was a worthwhile project.

I wish to thank the following individuals for their help: Grace Collier, Hanna and Richard Cortner, John Crow, Paul Culhane, James C. Davies, Vine Deloria Jr., Hazel Desjardins, Leonard Dinnerstein, Brian Flagg, Perry Hagenstein, Helen Ingram and David Laird, Henry and Margaret Kenski, William Leuchtenburg, Margaret Lundgren, Clifford Lytle, Daniel McCool, William Warne, and Allen and Alice Whiting. Staffs at the Library of Congress, the National Archives, the Franklin D. Roosevelt Library, the Department of the Interior, the

University of Arizona, and Glacier National Park were very helpful. To my good friends who put me up during my many research trips, and put up with me, I owe a special debt: Susan and Wendell Fletcher, Suzanne and Richard Linford, Judy May, Beryl Radin, and Dwight and Harriet Simpson. Scott Ryerson and Shoshana Green made a useful organizational suggestion a few years ago and it is a pleasure to thank them for their advice and friendship.

I wish also to acknowledge the research assistance of several graduate students: John All, Mohammed Bahramzadeh, Anwara Begum, Stan Wonn, and especially Andrea Gerlak. My department's staff, Denise Allyn, Becky Evans, and Trisha Morris, have been supportive and helpful in many ways.

Harold Ickes's three children, Raymond, Harold, and Elizabeth, were most gracious in granting me interviews and access to their family documents. Raymond and Janet Ickes have been especially kind, and I now count them among my friends. Having spent so many years researching their father's contributions to the New Deal I have come to feel as though I am some distant relative of theirs. I hope they don't mind.

Reading initial drafts of a manuscript and then not telling its author to find something else to do calls for a special kind of person. I have been fortunate indeed to have a husband, James Clarke, who willingly read the entire manuscript and provided me with valuable editorial advice. He even read parts of it more than once. A former student who is now a friend, Michael Keith, also critiqued drafts of several chapters. The late Aaron Wildavsky showed himself to be the special friend and mentor that he was to me for nearly twenty-five years. He, too, read and critiqued the first draft of the project that he called my "Moses of the Interior Department." Fortunately for me, I expect that I always will be influenced by Aaron. He loved scholarship and I wish he were still with us to see this work, which he influenced so significantly, in print.

I wish to thank Gloria Stern, my agent, for encouraging this work and assisting in getting it published. George F. Thompson, president of the Center for American Places and my liaison with the Johns Hopkins University Press, has been involved for nearly the duration of this project. He initially expressed interest in it in 1987, and continued to be supportive. Each fall when I wrote him my annual letter outlining my progress and predicting that I would have it done the following year, George patiently wrote back a lovely letter of encouragement. I suspect that he knew better than I did how long it would take. I am also indebted to Therese Boyd, whose editorial skills have substantially improved this book.

My deepest appreciation and affection, however, go to my husband and son, Jim and Michael. They have helped me with this labor of love in countless ways, from not complaining about having to fend for themselves in the kitchen to listening to an endless stream of New Deal anecdotes. They must be given credit for whatever contributions this book makes to scholarship. Its defects are, of course, my responsibility.

PART ONE

THE MAKING OF A REFORMER

CHAPTER I

THE GREAT TRANSFORMATION

FROM ALTOONA TO

THE NATION'S CAPITAL

"MAY YOU LIVE in interesting times." For a man who loved Chow dogs, shopped at Gump's in San Francisco for Ming vases, and ran the Interior Department for thirteen years "like a Chinese warlord," the oriental proverb is particularly fitting. Harold LeClair Ickes was born in a Pennsylvania farmhouse on the ides of March in the year 1874. He passed away seventy-eight years later, on February 3, 1952, in a hospital near his elegant Headwaters Farm in Olney, Maryland. Ickes thus witnessed the great transformation of America, from a society of small farmers and artisans wherein regional distinctions were of paramount importance while national power and international distinction were fragile at best, to a nuclear-armed, urbanized, unified world power. By the time Harold Ickes died, the United States had become what his foremost political hero and dear friend Franklin D. Roosevelt announced that it would be: The world's arsenal of democracy.

Not only was Harold Ickes witness to this vast change, however; throughout his adult life he helped make it happen. His most significant contributions to the processes of social change and political reform occurred rather late in his life, after President-elect Roosevelt surprised many people by offering the obscure 58-year-old Ickes a cabinet post and before an exasperated and elderly secretary of the interior handed his resignation to Pres. Harry Truman some ten months after Roosevelt's death.

Harold Ickes came into this world during lean years. The phenomenal growth in industry and business activity, centered in the nation's burgeoning cities, and which characterized the immediate post–Civil War period, took a downturn in 1873 that lasted until about 1879. While the rural sector, farmers and their families, and the small businesses that served them in towns of 500 or 1,000, were particularly hard-hit, the cities did not escape the effects of this country's first industrial-based depression either. Laborers who had descended upon the cities in the previous decade now found themselves out of work, the competition for jobs exacerbated by a constant stream of new immigrants, from both the countryside and abroad, to these islands of economic opportunity. By 1877 strikes had broken out in all of the country's major cities; the violence climaxed in Pittsburgh, where twenty-five people were killed by local authorities during a hot and tense summer. The assumption of America as unquestionably the land of opportunity, for rich and poor, black and white, new arrival and old aristocrat, began to find critics during this decade of economic distress.

Residents of the small town of Altoona, in central Pennsylvania, where the Ickeses and the McCunes went back for many generations, felt the ripples of economic insecurity like everyone else. Harold was the second of seven children born to Martha Ann McCune Ickes and Jesse B. W. Ickes. His memories of childhood in this fertile, forested land of rolling hills and nearby streams make clear that the Ickes family was no exception; making ends meet was a continual struggle, from the time Harold was born in 1874 until he reluctantly left home in 1890.

In part due to his own nature, in part due to the times, Harold's father, Jesse, was a barely adequate provider for his large family. Although the previous generation of McCunes and Ickes—Harold's grandparents, of whom the boy was very fond—lived in "better than comfortable circumstances," Jesse managed to fritter away that secure middle-class existence which, the son points out in his autobiography, was rooted in the land. "A respectable number of us," Harold wrote, "loved books and read whatever came to hand. Here and there were a few professional men—doctors and preachers—but generally speaking, we were of the soil and proud of it." [1]

Jesse, by contrast, loved "the city," and although Altoona could hardly be considered cosmopolitan, it, like many other small towns in America after the Civil War, showed impressive growth. Because Jesse's father had had the foresight to buy up some real estate in downtown Altoona before the boom, Jesse was set up in a tobacco store that sold not only tobacco but a number of other modest luxuries of life. In harmony with his gregarious, carefree nature, Jesse whiled away his days and evenings in conversation and socializing. After a fire destroyed the store, Jesse worked as a clerk in a local industry connected with the dominant economic activity in Altoona—the railroads—and again eked out a living for his family of nine. But, as Harold remembered, his mother was under a constant strain to make ends meet. She did so with a lot of help from her children, especially from her favorite child, Harold, and with just a minimum of help from her husband.

The period during which Harold Ickes came of age was characterized by ambivalence about the newly emerging society. On the one hand, Americans' faith in material progress and individual advancement based on hard work was only slightly shaken as a result of the economic slump of the 1870s (which, for the agricultural sector, only got worse in the 1880s). The profound demographic changes, immigration from overseas and inmigration from countryside to city, continued unabated. America, and especially its cities, remained the land of opportunity. But reform was in the air. Some Americans began questioning the economic system, which moved inexorably toward larger and larger enterprises while forcing many wage-earners and their families to live at a bare subsistence level. Others noted the stench of political corruption wafting through corridors of power in city halls, state houses, and even in the nation's capital. That great general, Union hero, and admirable citizen Ulysses S. Grant was proving to be an utter embarrassment as president of the United States; the one saving grace of the Grant administration was that it at least pointed the way others had to go in their efforts to reform politics. And in social life, decent Americans worried about an erosion of morals among the younger generation and among the many newcomers to America. Especially in the nation's growing urban centers, a traditional America witnessed alarming behavior while social reformers vowed to clean things up.

The reform movement gained momentum through those decades. In 1872, at a convention of dissident Republicans (and some Democrats) held in Cincinnati, Ohio, the word "liberal" was tacked onto "Republican," and thus liberalism was launched in American politics. Its meaning was clear: anti-Grantism, implying anticronyism, antimonopoly, anticorruption.[2] Liberal reformers simply believed that government, at all levels, should not be for sale.

Seven years after the Cincinnati convention, a young San Franciscan named Henry George published a scholarly critique of the economy; *Progress and Poverty,* a homegrown version of Marxism, was widely read in the 1880s, while its author became nationally recognized as a leader in the reform movement. His suggestions for reform, such as heavily taxing profits made from land speculation, began appearing in party platforms. In the 1884 election, reform Democrat Grover Cleveland captured the White House. During his administration Congress passed a historic piece of legislation aimed at regulating the powerful railroad industry—the Interstate Commerce Act (ICA) of 1887. Although the act, and the commission it created, were largely ineffective at the time, they did become the model for future regulatory action by the federal government. Cleveland's presidency thus became linked in the minds of Americans with reform.

After the country returned to four more years of Republican rule under Benjamin Harrison, during which time he and Congress proceeded to give away the store, "Grover the Good" was reelected in the 1892 presidential election. By then Congress had passed another regulatory statute—the Sherman Anti-Trust Act of 1890—and it, like the ICA, stood on the books awaiting implementation. In the meantime President Cleveland added to his reputation as a strong chief executive by zealously creating national forest reserves in the West—without congressional consent—and by flexing federal muscle during the infamous Pullman Strike of 1894.

But the year 1892 was significant for another reason. Far to the west, the reform movement reached a new plateau of power when its adherents met in Omaha, Nebraska, and nominated James B. Weaver to be the People's, or Populist, Party candidate for president. The newly formed Populists hoped to speak for the millions of disgruntled Americans who still lived on farms, who saw their economic status get worse, not better, during the decades in which capital became increasingly concentrated in America, and who felt that they had no voice within either the Democratic or Republican Party. Weaver's strong showing—over one million votes in the 1892 election—made possible a genuinely serious run for the presidency by William Jennings Bryan in the 1896 election.

THE SPIRIT OF REFORM, which so animated Harold Ickes throughout his entire adult life, came to him naturally. It was present in his family and in the volatile, questioning era in which he lived. Although he derived his Republicanism from both sides of the family, it was primarily his mother's values that the young boy assumed. Martha Ickes, or "Mattie" as she was called, was not only a faithful Republican but also a devout Presbyterian. The family's social life thus revolved principally around the church, and although the Ickes children, like most children, complained loudly about being dragged to church so often, nevertheless some Christian-based humanitarian values took hold. In Harold's eyes, his mother was a good, hard-working, long-suffering woman; as a practicing Christian, she was concerned about poverty and suffering, about issues of justice and fairness. These values she imparted to her son Harold, who in later life became well known for acting on them. Her concern for others, and his concern for her, was a cornerstone in his developing liberalism.

Overall Harold Ickes grew up in an era of optimism tempered by the recognition that gross inequities existed in society, that poverty was too present in the midst of plenty, that outdated barriers to opportunity stifled many talented people, and that utter profligacy was common in the use of the nation's wealth and resources. Harold Ickes's nature encompassed these attitudes. He was simultaneously an optimist, a firm believer in the Protestant ethic that hard work and unstinting effort pay off, while also evidencing a dark, pessimistic strain about the present and future. He could be hypercritical and was inclined to see catastrophe in the offing. He usually preferred, as he put it, to be "swimming against the current,"[3] on the attack rather than on the defense, defending the underdog rather than running with the pack. Every time that Franklin Roosevelt ran for reelection, for instance, Ickes predicted disaster, even prior to the landslide election of 1936. Good fortune and good outcomes were never taken for granted by this man who chose to title his memoirs *The Autobiography of a Curmudgeon*. Harold Ickes's childhood had been too uncertain emotionally, too marginal economically, to have made him simply an optimist.

MOVEMENT WAS EVERYWHERE in *fin-de-siècle* America. Earlier in the century the Colorado journalist and politician Horace Greeley uttered his famous advice to Americans: "Young man, go West and grow up with the country." They did so. In fact, settlers sprawled all across the continent so swiftly that the historian Frederick Jackson Turner boldly proclaimed, about 1890, that the frontier was all but gone. Nevertheless, Americans continued the migration, both to the West and to the cities that were sprouting up on the frontier during the last few decades of the nineteenth century. The life history of the great American novelist Theodore Dreiser was representative of that generation; Dreiser, full of ambition and anxious for excitement, left his stolid little hometown of Terre Haute, Indiana, and the suffocating religiosity of his large, working-class family for the growing metropolises of St. Louis, Chicago, and New York City. As he wrote in his first and finest book, *Sister Carrie,* young people were drawn to the cities "like moths to the light." And it was there, in the cities, that another reform movement, termed Progressivism, was born.

In 1890, just after Harold's sixteenth birthday, his world was torn apart. His beloved mother came down with a severe cold that, over the space of two months, developed into pneumonia. She was strong and only 38 years old as she struggled to overcome the illness, but in early June it proved fatal. Harold was devastated. He had lost the most important person in his life just as he verged on manhood. Compounding his grief was the decision, made by Mattie and her sister Ada Wheeler just before Mattie's death, to send Harold and his younger sister, Mary, to live with Aunt Ada and Uncle Felix in Englewood, a suburb of Chicago. So in July, with rural Pennsylvania in full bloom and looking its best, Harold and nine-year-old Mary boarded the train in Altoona that took them the few hundred miles west to Chicago, and to a new life with their aunt and uncle.

Although Harold grieved over the loss of his mother, and was desperately homesick, his new situation could have been much worse. Having no children of their own, the Wheelers provided a decent enough home for their nephew and niece. Like most young people his age, Harold went to work, in this instance in the couple's drugstore. But Aunt Ada also determined that he should continue his studies beyond the eighth grade. He enrolled in Englewood High School, threw himself into his schoolwork, became senior class president, and was graduated in 1893 with honors. It was not a carefree transition to manhood, but, thanks to his aunt's insistence on schooling, Harold discovered that he had a formidable intellect.

The 1890s were part of what is referred to as the Gilded Age, an era remembered for its extremes, when the captains of industry flaunted their wealth by throwing lavish parties and by building family mansions out of the most expensive materials on Long Island, in Grosse Point, or on Chicago's Gold Coast. The grumpy but brilliant economist Thorstein Veblen defined the period in his book, *The Theory of the Leisure Class,* published in 1899. He coined the term "conspicuous consumption" to describe the behavior that so disgusted him, and it has since remained part of America's political vocabulary. All the while, the Sister Carries of America crowded into small flats with their relatives on the cities' west and south sides and worked ten-hour days in shoe factories in order to earn $4.50 for a six-day work week. Such inequities necessarily fed the flames of liberal reform, so that by the 1896 presidential election there was a real chance that the "Great Commoner," the Nebraskan William Jennings Bryan, would gain the White House.

Ickes was 22 in the summer of 1896 when the Democrats joined with the Populists to hold their national convention in Chicago. By then he was working his way through the newly opened University of Chicago. College was a liberating experience for the young man, and although there is more than a trace of resentment in his memoirs— directed primarily at his father for ignoring his few requests for financial help—nevertheless the educational experience was a profound and generally positive one. In college, Ickes wrote, "My spirit began to throw off the shackles of blind partisanship, although I still accounted myself a Republican with the seed of the unborn Progressive in me."[4] Ickes's elder son, Raymond, also believed that his father's profound liberalism deepened as a result of his university experiences.[5] Both father and son were University of Chicago alumni.

That liberal seed began to germinate when the young man attended the Democratic National Convention and was in the audience when

Bryan made history with his "Cross of Gold" speech. "The campaign," Ickes remembered,

> was hard-fought and very exciting. Bryan set the country on fire, but he had no money. Mark Hanna had plenty of money for McKinley. Never had money flowed so freely. The precedent set by Hanna in 1896 was a bad one that has had a malevolent effect upon American politics ever since. . . . He corrupted states that have been corrupt ever since. I have never doubted that if the Democrats had been able to raise enough money, even for legitimate purposes, Bryan would have been elected.[6]

Not all historians agree with Ickes's assessment, although the contest was in fact a close one: Bryan came within 600,000 votes of equaling McKinley's 7 million. Eric Goldman, for example, summarized the defining 1896 election this way:

> The huge slush funds spent by the Republicans and the intimidation of industrial workers practiced by many employers had something to do with the result, but these were hardly the essential story. The essential story was that reform associated with shaggy agrarianism could not carry a swiftly industrializing, swiftly urbanizing nation.[7]

Had William Jennings Bryan won the presidency it would not have been with Harold Ickes's support, however. This was the first election in which the young college student was eligible to vote, and it held, as it does for many citizens, a special significance. Although Ickes was inspired by Bryan, who became one of his first political heroes, he stayed true to his Republican upbringing and voted unenthusiastically for William McKinley.

But by this time Ickes also had been influenced by the progressivism of the Democratic governor of Illinois, John P. Altgeld. Altgeld was well known not only for his reform politics but for being a "modern" criminologist. With the publication of *Our Penal Machinery and Its Victims* in 1884, the affluent Chicagoan stirred up the debate between environmentalists and geneticists over the root causes of crime. The book was widely read during the decade; perhaps its greatest contribution was that it inspired Clarence Darrow to leave Ashtabula, Ohio, for the "City with Broad Shoulders" in order to meet Altgeld, and then to go on to make his reputation as one of the greatest lawyers of his generation.

John Altgeld, Ickes wrote, "stood about where I wanted to stand on social questions. . . . I started my active political life by voting at the same election for a conservative Republican candidate for President and a radical Democratic candidate for Governor. Thus I was well launched upon the *independent* political career that I have ever since followed."[8] Altgeld lost his bid for reelection in 1896.

If Bryan came close in 1896 to merging all the strands of local and regional reformism into a unified, national movement, the country did not have to wait long until Progressivism found its genuine voice in the slightly high-pitched, yet piercing vocal cords of the young Theodore Roosevelt. Catapulted into the presidency in September of 1901 by fate and Leon Czolgosz's hatred of the ruling class, the 43-year-old patrician proceeded to lead America, with style, wit, passion, and elegance of expression, into the twentieth century. Not everyone was amused. Mark Hanna had thought that the New York reform governor was safely stashed away in the vice-presidency, never to be heard from again. Hanna and many other Republican Party regulars gasped at the reality of this rambunctious former cowboy, former Rough Rider, and thoroughly cultured man in the White House—the mansion that had been the domain of the Republican Party's special interests, except for Cleveland's two stays, since Ulysses S. Grant set up camp in the 1860s.

Working like a human dynamo, which he was, President Roosevelt had time enough, in eight years, to do what he felt needed to be done to steer America in a new direction. In doing so he secured for his family a permanent place in the history of enlightened reform. Whereas populism had been too radical for the majority of Americans, and too much associated with their agrarian past, the progressivism of the urbane Theodore Roosevelt, who was born and raised in New York, and who sprang out of one of the country's most respectable families—but who also had more than a trace of the maverick in him—perfectly matched the temper of the times.

Initiatives tumbled out of the White House and the Capitol in record numbers. Under Theodore Roosevelt's administration antitrust laws were strengthened and even enforced. Pure food and drug laws were enacted; the meatpacking industry, made notorious by Upton Sinclair's 1906 novel, *The Jungle,* became subject to federal inspection; the railroad's practice of granting rebates was outlawed; a Bureau of Reclamation was created to bring irrigated family farming to the parched West; a reassertion of the Monroe Doctrine was effected, as was an Open Door trade policy with Asia. The president personally intervened to end racial segregation of Asians in San Francisco's public schools; he spoke out against the persecution of Jews in Russia, although noting that America must also put its own house in order with respect to racial issues; he invited Booker T. Washington to dine with him at the White House; and he made history by appointing Oscar Straus, a Jew, to the cabinet post of secretary of commerce and labor. His militarism notwithstanding, Theodore Roosevelt was awarded the Nobel Peace Prize in 1907 for his efforts to resolve the conflict between Russia and Japan, the first American so honored.

Finally, Roosevelt made giant strides in bringing the country to accept the doctrine of resource conservation. Perhaps his greatest legacy was in the area that was so close to his heart—nature and the great outdoors. After having remade his own frail body as a youth, Roosevelt remained committed all of his life to strenuous physical exercise, to revitalizing himself through contact with nature. In 1884 when his young wife Alice died suddenly after childbirth—just a few hours after Theodore's dearly beloved mother died—the grieving young man set out for his ranch in the badlands of South Dakota. There, "like a lion obsessively trying to drag a spear from its flank, Roosevelt set about dislodging Alice Lee from his soul." [9] In time, living the gentleman cowboy's life on the high plains in full contact with the elements, Roosevelt was able to accept losing both his wife and his mother. At age 36 Theodore was still young, and nature had assisted, as he had hoped it would, in healing the wounds.

As president, with the invaluable assistance of conservationists such as Gifford Pinchot, Roosevelt boldly moved forward in creating a national forest system and a system of wildlife reserves. "Is there any law that will prevent me from declaring Pelican Island [in Florida] a Federal Bird Reservation?" he asked. "Very well, then I so declare it!" [10] Utilizing the Antiquities Act of 1906, which gave the president considerable power to protect unusual natural sites, Roosevelt set aside a score of national treasures, including Devil's Tower in Wyoming, the first to be set aside under this law, the Petrified Forest and Montezuma's Castle in Arizona, and Muir Woods in northern California. Operating on the utilitarian principle of the greatest good for the greatest number, the conservation movement, under the president's invigorating leadership, managed to preserve millions of acres of public lands from despoliation. "Wise use, sustained yield" became the battle-cry of progressive conservationists all across the country as they warred with the private interests that until then had laid waste to much of America's natural heritage.

Drawing strength and inspiration from the enormously popular president, local reformers redoubled their efforts at cleaning up city halls, city streets, state houses, and much else during this first decade of the twentieth century. Now in his mid- to late twenties, Harold Ickes was already established as a member of Chicago's reform circle when Roosevelt reigned in the White House. Only once a candidate in his own right, but invariably a campaigner, Ickes was initiated into electoral politics during John Maynard Harlan's several bids for the mayor's office. Harlan was the son of the famous Supreme Court Justice who made history as the "Great Dissenter" on the noxious 1896 *Plessy v. Ferguson* case, among others. Harlan ran for mayor of Chicago in 1897, 1903, and 1905 and lost all three elections, but for Ickes that didn't in the least tarnish him, a man very much like Theodore Roosevelt. After listening to one of his campaign speeches, Ickes wrote words that would have just as well described the effect that the president had on his audiences: "How I envied Harlan his power, which was the power of sincerity and truth—the power to advocate boldly the just cause—in strong, forceful speech, expressed in brilliant phrases and beautiful English." [11]

During Harlan's last attempt at the Chicago mayoralty in 1905, Harold Ickes, who took a leave of absence from his studies at the University of Chicago's law school to work full time on the campaign, met a number of people who would prove to be important to him later in life. These included the railroad magnate and city planner Frederic A. Delano, who happened to be not only a "fine, public-spirited citizen," but who was also the uncle of a young man named Franklin Delano Roosevelt. Ickes also met Raymond and Margaret Robins, social workers originally from New York City, who joined the Chicago reform circle during the 1900s and who became two of Ickes's closest friends.

That circle also included Jane Addams, the cofounder of Hull House, and a University of Chicago history professor named James Thompson and his wealthy wife, Anna Wilmarth Thompson. While Harold Ickes had been acquainted with Anna for about a decade— they met when both were undergraduates at the University of Chicago—the casual relationship intensified in 1903 when he was invited to live with them at their spacious home on Washington Street. At the time Harold was a nearly broke law student struggling to make ends meet but still trying to remain involved in reform politics. He accepted their invitation, an arrangement that would last for several years and would have profound ramifications on the lives of the entire household.

The year before ex-president Theodore Roosevelt bellowed out against the corrupt Republican Party, which had the impertinence to refuse to endorse him as its candidate in the 1912 presidential election, Harold Ickes was at it again in Chicago. In the 1911 campaign for mayor he persuaded his friend Charles Merriam, an alderman and a professor of political science at the University of Chicago, to challenge Fred Busse for the Republican nomination. Ickes managed the campaign. By 1911 the 37-year-old Ickes had a reasonably successful law practice in downtown Chicago, he had earned a local reputation as a liberal reformer, and he was now married. In September, a year or so after she divorced James, Anna Wilmarth Thompson married Harold Ickes at a small ceremony held at her family's vacation home on Lake Geneva in southeastern Wisconsin. The marriage culminated several years of a tumultuous courtship that, to no one's surprise, had originated in the Thompson-Ickes living arrangement. A tumultuous twenty-four-year marriage was in the making. Anna and Harold were both independent, ambitious, intelligent, and strong-willed. As a consequence of being too much alike, their marriage was one long and largely miserable power struggle.

Ickes was anxious to have Charles Merriam run in the mayor's race because Fred Busse and his cronies were among Ickes's first political enemies. He despised their machine politics. When Busse won the 1905 mayor's race against the clearly superior John Harlan, Ickes noted in his autobiography that he, Ickes, became "distinctly *persona non grata* at the City Hall." He added that "Yerkes, Busse, and Insull helped to sharpen my teeth for Mussolini, Hirohito, and Hitler." So when his candidate wrested the Republican nomination from the Busse machine, it was sweet revenge for campaign manager Ickes. That fall he threw himself into the task of getting Merriam elected but once again had to accept defeat: The Democrats ran the popular Carter Harrison III, several times Chicago's mayor, who again emerged victorious. From Ickes's perspective, the reason was to be found in the odoriferous politics within his own party: "I had reason, based on experience," Ickes wrote, "to expect that if they were licked in the primaries, the Republican 'regulars' would rock on their fat bellies into the Democratic tent as they had done when Harlan was a candidate." [12]

Harold Ickes celebrated two births during the summer of 1912. The first was the birth of his and Anna's son, Raymond, on June 24. The baby was named after their good friend, Raymond Robins. His arrival brought to three the number of children in the Ickes household, since Anna's two children from her first marriage, Wilmarth and Frances, stayed with their mother. The second birth was of the Progressive Party, founded by Theodore Roosevelt after he and his followers walked out of the Republican National Convention that summer, only to return to Chicago two months later with a bold new idea. Ickes wrote that he leapt aboard Roosevelt's bandwagon: "The moment it was decided to hold a Progressive National Convention at the Coliseum in August, I became active." [13]

By 1912 Ickes was no novice to politics; nevertheless, the occasion when he first met the legendary Theodore Roosevelt could not have been other than memorable. The two men were heading to Chicago by train, and Ickes was invited to breakfast with the president. He related the event:

> All through the meal he talked politics in his vivacious and eager way. It was a great occasion for me. I was reminded, when his breakfast was served, of the rumors of excessive drinking on his part. Fruit, a large order of oatmeal, an extra allotment of specially cooked whitefish, a man's portion of bacon and fried potatoes, large quantities of toast, and two cups of coffee—I reflected that no heavy drinker could stow away a breakfast like that. [14]

The third-party candidate whom Ickes admired so much roared his way through a full-blown campaign in which he promised a "square deal" to the American people, a platform that included a more thorough taming of the trusts, the direct election of U.S. senators, extending suffrage to women, child labor laws, and resource conservation. He even survived an assassin's bullet fired into him in Milwaukee, Wisconsin, an experience that earned him the nickname "Bull Moose." In a three-way race, Roosevelt came in second, not far behind another reform candidate who had been selected on the 46th ballot at the Democratic National Convention. That was Woodrow Wilson. With not one but two liberals running against him, Pres. William Howard Taft accepted the fact that he had no choice but to play the role of the conservative in the fall campaign and go down in dignified defeat.

Wilson in the White House took the wind out of the sails of the Progressive Party. He proceeded to enact much of Theodore Roosevelt's, and his own, liberal platform. And although reformers throughout the country missed the Roosevelt *élan*—for the excitement of a circus, one historian wrote, the granite-faced son of a Virginia minister substituted "the dedication of a sunrise service" [15]— nevertheless Wilson *was* implementing reform. Ickes thus observed that many of his colleagues in the Progressive Party proceeded to desert the party, moving like the proverbial rat to Wilson after the November election. But Ickes didn't. He preferred, instead, to stick to his principles and the party he helped to create to the end. "After all," Ickes wrote, "*guts* and an *appetite for punishment* are implicit in a curmudgeonish character."

The end came soon enough. After the passage of the seventeenth amendment in 1916, the Progressives in Illinois and Pennsylvania put up two candidates to run in that historic race for the U.S. Senate. For years reformers had urged the direct election of senators; now that they had it, they proceeded to make the most of it. Ickes, as chairman of the Progressive Party in Illinois, met with Theodore Roosevelt and a few other men who decided on running Raymond Robins in the Illinois election and Gifford Pinchot in his native state of Pennsylvania. Both candidates lost.

The decline of the Progressive Party during Wilson's first term in the presidency paralleled its founder's physical decline. Just as the dynamic Theodore Roosevelt had lost much of his strength, and nearly his life, when he went off in a huff to explore the jungles of Brazil after losing the election of 1912, so too did his party collapse shortly after its leader returned to America. A distressed Ickes observed that "there was no doubt that the Brazilian jungles had left an indelible mark upon the man." [16] The 54-year-old legend was not the same man after he had pitted himself against the steamy, malaria-infected Amazon. But Harold Ickes remained devoted to Theodore Roosevelt through thick and thin, for he had found in him a political hero with whom he could completely identify. The qualities that mattered most to Ickes—intelligence, oratorical skill, liberalism, virility, courage, and Victorian manners—were all present in the man who addressed his protégé simply as "Ickes."

Naturally there were many causes for the Progressive Party's collapse in 1916 or thereabouts, but Ickes, characteristically, placed most of the blame on an individual. In his autobiography and elsewhere Ickes accused the powerful Republican business tycoon George W. Perkins of betraying TR and the Progressive Party through the usual back-room machinations. A tendency toward a Manichean view of the world—the political world especially, which substituted for religious belief in Harold Ickes's life—was becoming evident in the maturing curmudgeon. He needed political devils just as much as he needed saints. It was a feature of his personality that made him the colorful, iconoclastic, and quixotic public official that he became under Franklin Roosevelt. It made him interesting.

THE OUTBREAK OF the Great War in Europe split modernizing America right down the middle. The war itself was a classic muddle, as E. M. Forster might have said. It started with an accident and proceeded to escalate into civilization's first Total War. Spanning some four years, it became the most costly, in lives lost and resources expended, in recorded history. Eventually, the German nation-state bore most of the blame for having caused the war, but at the time the situation was not so clear. The famous Austrian psychiatrist Sigmund Freud, for example, initially supported Germany in its battle against such imperialist powers as Great Britain.[17] Many other thoughtful members of Europe's Jewish minority feared a revolutionary Russia in the East much more than they did a confident and cultured Germany that had given the world the likes of Bach, Beethoven, Mozart, Dürer, Goethe, and Kant.

In the United States people drew up sides as well, but the major rift was between interventionists and isolationists. The question was whether or not America would be dragged into a foreign war, not whose side we would take, since that question had been decided by history. In the 1916 presidential election the major issue for the voters naturally was this momentous one; but according to Ickes, who described himself as an interventionist, neither the incumbent Woodrow Wilson, nor his Republican challenger Charles Evans Hughes, was willing to declare himself so. This left many voters guessing as to the course America would take and it left others, including the bellicose Theodore Roosevelt, disgusted. He, like Ickes in 1916, returned to the Republican fold and reluctantly campaigned for Hughes, but he remarked to his fellow Progressive that "there wasn't any difference between Wilson and Hughes except a set of whiskers."[18]

When in April 1917 the reelected president went before Congress to ask for a declaration of war, the reception he received underscored the strong opposition progressive reformers felt over the issue. Senators

George Norris and Robert LaFollette, the latter in a four-hour oration, railed against the hypocrisy they saw in phrases like America's "duty to humanity," and proceeded to offer a very different explanation of why America was being asked to go to war: The war sentiment, they argued, had been whipped up by "munitions manufacturers, stockbrokers, and bond dealers," who stood to make tremendous profits on the war.[19]

Reformers in the House of Representatives continued the opposition against the war resolution, but it was beginning to appear as a lost cause; only seven senators ultimately voted "no" before the issue was addressed in the House. Nevertheless, Congressman William La-Follette of Washington State, Jeannette Rankin of Montana, and Claude Kitchin of North Carolina were among those who voted their pacifist consciences. It was reported that when the first woman elected to Congress stood up to cast a "no" vote, she was not alone in choking back tears; the young congressman from New York City, Fiorello La Guardia, who voted for war, also had tears in his eyes.[20]

Theodore Roosevelt and Harold Ickes, however, desperately wanted to get into the war. When the former president, who loved combat, asked the incumbent president to allow him to lead a band of Rough Riders and gallop off to Europe, he was livid when Wilson said "no." "That damned Presbyterian hypocrite," Roosevelt growled. Ickes was a little more sensible on the subject, in that he realized that he was 43 (TR was then 58!), that he had a wife, a four-year-old son, and Anna's other children to consider. Moreover, he was almost deaf in his left ear. Nevertheless, primarily because he was caught up in an awful marriage, Ickes was determined to get to Europe in one capacity or another. So, while Theodore was sidelined at Oyster Bay on Long Island, and Theodore's distant cousin, the handsome Franklin Roosevelt, had a role to play in the world war—in 1913 President Wilson appointed the young Democrat to the position of assistant secretary of the Navy—Harold in Chicago was scouring the noncombatant organizations for a position that would take him abroad.

Ickes finally found one. Joining the YMCA early in 1918, Harold Ickes was sent to France to assist the U.S. Army in various capacities. Although he spent less than a year in Europe it was an exciting experience for him to be in the midst of an actual war; he laconically claimed that it was more or less a continuation of his seventeen years in the "front-line trenches" of Chicago politics, but it really was much more than that. It was liberating, in that he was free, temporarily, from Anna and the terribly unhappy home life. It also was educational in that it opened his eyes to what modern warfare was all about. Ickes was in Paris when the armistice was declared and was part of the crowd that greeted a triumphant President Wilson when he came to make peace. "The French threw their hearts in front of Wilson's carriage," Ickes wrote. "He was their hope of the future. Important avenues had already been named for him in every Allied capital. All of Europe, excepting only Germany and Austria, was at his feet." [21]

Harold Ickes arrived in New York City on the first day of January, 1919. He had heard that Theodore Roosevelt was ailing and tried to see him, but no visitors were allowed in his hospital room. A few days later Ickes learned that his friend and political hero had died. Never given to gushing sentimentality, Harold Ickes later wrote simply, "I don't mind saying that something went out of my life that has never been replaced." [22] Some people said that it was the death of Roosevelt's son, Quentin, in combat, that the father could not bear. All four of his sons fought in the Great War, but his second youngest didn't return. Theodore Roosevelt was only 59 when his heart stopped beating.

With the end of the war, with Wilson crippled by a stroke and Theodore Roosevelt dead, the pendulum of politics swept back toward conservatism. For progressives such as Ickes, it looked suspiciously as if another period of Grantism was in the making. Americans turned unself-consciously inward, to the pursuit of wealth and personal pleasure, to electing a government promoting the interests of the entrepreneurial class while ignoring the fact that over two-thirds of all families struggled to get by with an annual income below what today is called the poverty line.

A few people tried to keep the reform movement going during the 1920 presidential election, but they recognized that they were fighting a rear-guard battle. When the Republicans met in Chicago that summer to nominate their candidate, Harold Ickes was there to help put forward the name of the progressive senator from California, the "reform bulldozer" Hiram Johnson. But the Republican Old Guard turned instead to Warren G. Harding, a "typical small-bone Ohio politician," [23] completely lacking, according to Ickes, in character and integrity. It was a stinking affair, he recalled, and when the convention met to make the Harding nomination unanimous, as was customary, Ickes was down in front of the coliseum in order to yell *"No!"* at the top of his lungs. Hiram Johnson then refused to compromise his principles by accepting the vice-presidential slot under Harding—though if he had, he would have been president in 1923, and his friend Harold Ickes may have been in the administration.

The 1916 election was the last time Harold Ickes voted for a Republican for president. After having his stomach turned by the smell of the Republican smoke-filled rooms, Ickes talked with a friend in the Democratic Party named George Brennan. He obviously was not the only one to suggest that the Democrats would do well—especially in the West, where the Roosevelt name was revered—by putting Theodore's young cousin, Franklin, on the ticket. Ickes supported the Cox-Roosevelt ticket in 1920, although he knew "in his heart" that it had no chance of beating the Harding-Coolidge duo. There was the future to consider, however.

With the establishment Republicans making a clean sweep of the presidency for twelve straight years, Harold Ickes was relegated to keeping a low profile on the national political scene. With the election of Coolidge in 1924, Ickes quipped that the nation had returned not to "normalcy" but to "sub-normalcy," and Herbert Hoover, whom he had met in 1917 and who had snubbed him at the meeting, didn't excite him in the least. "Hoover," he said, "was, well, always Hoover." This left local politics to muck around in, during a decade when Ickes's emotions were overwhelmingly negative; he said he felt alternately depressed, unenthusiastic, cynical, not caring whether he lived or died, and, perhaps worst of all, a has-been. He was always prone to exaggerate how terrible he felt.

Nevertheless, Ickes, who was now in his fifties, stayed the course. In between his work as an attorney and playing the stock market, largely with his wife Anna's considerable wealth, he managed to add to his reputation as a reformer during the Roaring '20s. In 1923 he formed the Independent Republican Committee to back the Democratic candidate for mayor, William Dever, and happily found himself on the winning side for once. Dever, Ickes claimed, gave Chicago "one of the best administrations it ever had." [24] Ickes also assumed briefly the presidency of the Chicago chapter of the recently formed National Association for the Advancement of Colored People, and he helped form the People's Traction League to continue his long-standing battle against the city's transportation and utilities magnates. The public ownership of these essential municipal services was an issue that Ickes cared deeply about and fought for—against such powerful men as Samuel Insull, John Hertz, and Charles Yerkes (the latter being the inspiration for Dreiser's trilogy on the life and times of a turn-of-the-century capitalist). He usually lost these battles, too.

Anna Ickes was very much a reformer in her own right, and over the years she developed an intense interest in the culture and condition of the American Indians. This particular interest appears to have developed as an unintended result of her frequent bouts with asthma. Around 1915, often accompanied by Harold and the children, she began seeking relief from the suffocating humidity of Chicago's summers by vacationing in northern New Mexico. At the same time as other Easterners discovered this land of great beauty, clear air, and indigenous peoples, the Ickeses built a simple adobe home near Gallup, close to the border of the Navajo reservation. The plight of the Indians touched Anna deeply, and for the rest of her life she was a passionate spokeswoman in Chicago and in Washington, D.C., on their behalf. She also became a self-taught expert on Indian culture; she learned to speak Navajo and wrote *Mesa Land,* a book published in 1933 detailing the rugged land and its original peoples. Anna's humanitarian concern for others less fortunate than herself was one of her best qualities.

With his innate concern for the underdog, Harold also developed an interest in the Indians. Largely through his wife's circle of friends and her membership in organizations like the Cliff Dwellers' Club and the General Federation of Women's Clubs, Ickes began to move comfortably in the Indian rights reform movement of the 1920s. Spearheading the movement was the rail-thin dreamer and idealist, originally from Georgia, John Collier. Others active included a number of influential businessmen, artists, social workers, and attorneys who had come of age during the Progressive Era of Roosevelt and Wilson— such as the Indian law expert Felix Cohen, San Francisco attorney and philanthropist Charles de Young Elkus, artists Georgia O'Keeffe and Alfred Steiglitz, the eccentric Mabel Dodge, Judge Richard Hanna, and Nathan Margold.

The Ickeses first met Collier in 1923 when he led a band of Pueblo Indians from New Mexico on a long lobbying expedition that wound up in the Senate's hearing chambers to argue against the infamous Bursum bill. The proposed legislation was another attempt to take lands away from the Indians.[25] En route to Washington Collier and his colorful group, dressed in traditional clothing, stopped off in Chicago and

New York City to speak before sympathetic audiences about this latest outrage. It was at a meeting of the Cliff Dwellers' Club that a long and mutually rewarding association between John Collier and Harold Ickes was launched. After listening to Collier and to the Indian activists, Ickes came to believe that no minority group, Negroes included, had been so mistreated by the white majority than had the Indians. His deep reservoir of moral indignation gushed forth and he proceeded to create the Chicago Indian Rights Association. Among other activities, over the next ten years Harold and Anna Ickes pushed forward on this battlefront, too.

WITH THE STOCK-MARKET crash on October 29, 1929, Black Tuesday, history came full circle. "It started like 1873," the historian Eric Goldman wrote, but the depression proceeded quickly to assume far grimmer lines.[26] America was considerably more urbanized and industrialized in 1929 than it had been in 1873; thus millions more workers found themselves out of work and with no other means, like tilling the soil, of sustaining themselves and their families. Moreover, the once-fertile agricultural lands of America's heartland were depleted and overutilized to a greater extent than they had been in the 1870s. A period of drought, combined with the short-term mentality of the cash crop, which led to intensive farming and ranching, produced the condition known as the Dust Bowl. The land was dried up, gone, blown away, just as were wage-earners' jobs in America's cities. The economic catastrophe that began in 1929 soon became labeled the Great Depression.

In the 1870s Ickes had been a child whose family's marginality during that economic slump made a lasting impression on him. During the recession of the 1890s, which brought on another round of class warfare epitomized by the Haymarket Riot and the Pullman Strike, Harold was a young man struggling on one fifteen-cent meal of ham a day to get through college. But in 1929, he was a wealthy attorney living with his family, the children now nearly grown, in a sumptuous Winnetka estate called Hubbard Woods. Despite their wealth, the Ickeses' life, like that of the vast majority of Americans, was shaken severely by this latest economic cycle. By the summer of 1930, Ickes estimated that he had lost his paper profit of a quarter of a million dollars: "It was fortunate for me that I had this very large margin or I would have been utterly ruined," Ickes admitted. He also learned a bitter lesson about speculation: "I had my fill of the stock market . . . in 1929 and '30," he wrote some ten years later, "and I want no more of it." [27]

Harold Ickes thus lived through another cycle of economic insecurity, but this time it was far worse and more prolonged than the preceding ones. He and his family were among the most fortunate ones. Millions of Americans were unemployed, hungry, homeless, or all of that. They looked to the government for help, but too little was forthcoming. In Washington, D.C., the president and Congress were stalemated; Hoover refused to put people on "the dole," and Congress refused to pass his emergency relief measures. Fear, uncertainty, and anger spread over America as year by year the Depression deepened.

In the election year of 1932, hope was in very short supply. But the American people were desperate for change, and the man who emerged the victor after a big battle at the Democratic National Convention was speaking words of hope. Ickes, who had been relatively inactive for years in national politics, sensed a good fight shaping up between the conservative and colorless Hoover, whom he couldn't stand, and the liberal New York governor whose family name of Roosevelt held so much meaning for him. He was, he said, head over heels for the nomination of Franklin D. Roosevelt. When two of his friends, Basil Manley and Roscoe Fertich, asked him to get involved in the fall campaign there was nothing to consider. Ickes organized the "Western Independent Republican Committee for Roosevelt," and this time his efforts were rewarded almost beyond his wildest dreams.

AN INDIVIDUAL'S LIFE in retrospect displays a pattern that is usually not discernible at the time. In 1932, Harold Ickes was 58, trapped in an agonizing marriage, only moderately successful in his chosen career as a lawyer, and sensing that his time had come and gone. Only after Roosevelt's historic victory over Hoover in November of 1932 did Ickes dare to think that he might be able to play some small role in the New Deal Administration. But he was enough of a realist to know that his political aspirations were not likely to be fulfilled.

CHAPTER 2

"IS MR. ICKES HERE?"

THE APPOINTMENT

WITH LESS THAN two weeks remaining before his inauguration, President-elect Franklin Roosevelt needed to find a secretary of the interior, a position that by tradition went to a westerner. Roosevelt initially considered appointing Utah's former governor, George Dern. In October, the Democratic candidate had told his campaign manager, James Farley, that if elected he had decided definitely on only three appointments: "Louis [Howe] for my secretary, George Dern for Secretary of the Interior, and you for Postmaster General." [1] But this offhand remark wasn't the last word on such an important decision as cabinet appointments. After the victory the president-elect spent two months talking with people and making up lists of likely candidates which were subsequently discarded for new lists, a process Brains Truster Raymond Moley described as pretty haphazard. By the middle of January 1933, when Roosevelt actually began filling cabinet positions, he offered Dern the position of secretary of war rather than interior. The Utah Democrat was in the mining business, and Roosevelt, who otherwise thought highly of Dern's qualifications, did not wish to appoint anyone to that position who could be labeled "anticonservationist." Dern, therefore, ended up in War as the president reconsidered the Interior appointment.

Roosevelt decided that he needed a western progressive Republican to fill the slot, someone in the tradition—and ideally with the style— of his late cousin Theodore. This narrowed the field down considerably. On the afternoon of January 19 the president met at Washington's Mayflower Hotel with a small group of senators which included the nationally prominent Californian Hiram Johnson. An ideal choice, he was the first senator to be offered any cabinet position. He cordially but firmly refused the offer, telling Roosevelt he'd been born a "natural rebel" and was too old to accept the political constraints that came with a top-level executive position.[2] FDR's second choice was Sen. Bronson Cutting of New Mexico. Bronson wavered for weeks, but in the end decided, like Johnson, not to trade his influential and independent position in the U.S. Senate for the opportunity to run one of the less prestigious and more scandal-prone executive departments of the federal government.

Although disappointed by these refusals Roosevelt, with time running out, was aware of a third possibility for the job—a man who seemed to have the necessary credentials. He was a westerner of sorts, having spent a lifetime in Chicago as a reform-minded lawyer, and had been a progressive in the Theodore Roosevelt tradition since the turn of the century. Most significantly, he had been FRBC—For Roosevelt Before Chicago. After Roosevelt won a difficult battle for the Democratic Party's nomination at the Chicago convention, this individual headed the "Western Independent Republicans for Roosevelt."[3] These activities naturally made him very attractive to the man who had to fight for the Democratic nomination and then go on to beat an incumbent president. The man was, of course, Harold L. Ickes, and Roosevelt decided that he needed to meet, for the first time, this loyal supporter of his.

Once the Roosevelt victory was assured, Harold Ickes began an intense lobbying campaign for a position in the new administration. He wanted the Interior post but his problem, as he saw it, was getting his name put before Roosevelt. So he called on virtually everyone he knew who either knew the president or knew those close to him— people like Louis Howe, Raymond Moley, Rexford Tugwell, Bernard

Baruch, and James Farley—to suggest him for the position. Ickes himself raced back and forth between Chicago and Washington to talk with friends who might have access to Roosevelt and his advisors. By January Ickes's old friend Hiram Johnson was well aware of Ickes's ambition, as were Charles Merriam, John Collier, Charles de Young Elkus, Gifford Pinchot, Nebraska's progressive senator George Norris, and many others.

The frenetic activity paid off. About the middle of February Ickes received a telephone call from Raymond Moley, inviting him to attend a small meeting with the president at his New York City home to be held on the twenty-first. Although he didn't hesitate to accept, Ickes, by this late date, considered a cabinet position yet another of his many lost causes. As far as he knew, Bronson Cutting was still deliberating, and besides, the president had already chosen two Republicans to fill cabinet positions: William Woodin was to hold the important position of secretary of the treasury, and Henry Wallace, a midwestern progressive Republican whose politics were very similar to Ickes's, had just been named secretary of agriculture. He thought the president would not reach out for a third Republican, liberal or otherwise, should Cutting decline the Interior position. The Democrats, out of power for what seemed like an interminable twelve years, felt they deserved these prestigious offices; they would be fighting for what remained. A stoic Ickes thus considered the invitation to come to New York a consolation prize, but at least he would finally meet the man whom he first had supported in the 1920 presidential race and again in 1932.[4]

At 10:30 A.M. on a chilly Tuesday morning Harold Ickes arrived at the president's unpretentious brownstone home at 49 East 65th Street. Along with about ten other people, including Frances Perkins, who was about to make history as the first woman to be appointed to a cabinet position, Ickes was ushered into the front drawing room. Soon after everyone was seated, Roosevelt was wheeled into the room, and several of those in attendance had their first look at the 51-year-old president-elect. James Warburg who, like Ickes, had never met Roosevelt, found him impressive; he had, Warburg wrote, "massive shoulders surmounted by [a] remarkably fine head, the gay smile with which he greeted his guests, and the somewhat incongruous, old-fashioned pince-nez eyeglasses that seemed to sit a little uncertainly on his nose."[5]

Looking at a list in his hand, the first question the president asked was "Is Mr. Ickes here?"[6] Ickes indicated that he was present. The president then addressed some pressing economic issues, but all the while Roosevelt kept eying Ickes. The real purpose of the meeting, it appears, was to look over Mr. Ickes. The gathering was brief and Ickes said nothing because, as he frequently admitted, he had little interest in or knowledge of economic policy. Frances Perkins, who was seated not far from Ickes in the president's drawing room, described her first impression of the Chicago reformer as a "plump, blond, be-spectacled gentleman" who ignored her presence. He "didn't have any of that flip style about him that a New York City person has," she noted, "none of the New York elegance, nor the Bowery or Broadway style." She assumed that he was a friend of Roosevelt's from upstate New York.[7]

When the meeting was over, Ickes, along with the others in attendance, shook the president's hand and offered him their congratulations. As Ickes headed for the doorway, he must have felt deep disappointment at having come so close to power, only to find it eluding him once again. But, as if a character in a theatrical drama, before Ickes was out of the door Rexford Tugwell caught up with him and said that the president wished to see him alone, as soon as he'd finished talking with Bernard Baruch. Ickes was brought back into the drawing room and this time he sat directly across from the new president. He heard Roosevelt tell him what he thought he would never get to hear:

> Mr. Ickes, you and I have been speaking the same language for the past twenty years, and we have the same outlook. I am having difficulty finding a Secretary of the Interior. I want a man who can stand on his own feet. I particularly want a Western man. Above all things, I want a man who is honest, and I have about come to the conclusion that the man I want is Harold L. Ickes of Chicago.[8]

Roosevelt then asked him to stay overnight to give him a bit more time to make a final decision on the Interior post, and Ickes replied that he could be reached, naturally, at the Roosevelt Hotel not far away from the president's home.

After the interview, Ickes floated downtown to meet two of his friends who also were in New York City that day. Ickes was ebullient; at long last his dream of being at the center of power and influence was almost a reality. John Collier recalled that he, Charles Merriam, and a buoyant Ickes met "over generous drinks" at a speakeasy to discuss what looked to be a major turnaround in his political fortunes. FDR's near-decision surprised all three men; Collier, for example, thought that since Ickes was "not nationally prominent," it was most unlikely that Roosevelt would name him to his cabinet.[9] That was the commonly accepted wisdom.

Ickes remained in a state of nervous excitement until Moley called him back that evening. When he arrived at Roosevelt's home he found it vibrating with activity; people, most of whom he didn't know, were coming and going. Moments later Ickes was again in the presence of the president-elect, who, with Frances Perkins at his side, warmly greeted him. In his casual but gracious manner, Ickes recalled, the president said, "It is nice to have the Secretary of Labor meet the Secretary of the Interior tonight." [10]

"Harold who?" most people asked, while others scrambled to take credit for having put Ickes's name before Roosevelt. Few people outside of Chicago had heard of the liberal, scrappy Ickes, who had the carefully groomed appearance of a bank vice-president but the instincts, when crossed, of a pit bull. Several explanations surfaced as to Roosevelt's choice. A reporter for the *New York Times* claimed that it was the friend of Nebraska's Sen. George Norris, Arthur Mullen, who was responsible for bringing Mr. Ickes to the attention of the president. The president's son, Elliott, who later edited his father's personal letters, said that Ickes's name was brought up at a dinner meeting by Senator Norris himself sometime in January of 1933.[11] Others gave Ickes's close friend Hiram Johnson the credit, although Johnson denied that it was he. He was very much in favor of the appointment, but felt it impolitic to suggest Ickes after he had turned down the offer. "Luck finally did for a man what he was breaking his heart for," Johnson whimsically explained.[12] Indeed, it was lucky for Ickes that Johnson and Cutting turned down FDR's offer.

In his memoirs, John Collier took credit for Ickes's great good fortune. He wrote that "through Raymond Moley . . . I arranged for an interview in New York between Ickes and Roosevelt, and accompanied Ickes to New York." Rexford Tugwell, an economist and a member of Roosevelt's "transition team," as it is called today, observed that since time was running out, FDR did what he often did in such circumstances: he made a "blind choice" and hoped for the best. For his part, the president gave only this simple, cryptic one-liner: "I liked the cut of his jib." [13]

Actually it was not an unlikely choice at all. Roosevelt relied on his considerable talent to size up people quickly, and coupled that with a knowledge of Harold Ickes's long history as a liberal reformer to conclude that this was a reasonable choice. No doubt Ickes's name was mentioned to FDR more than once during those crucial months between November and March, and he would have assigned one of his assistants to find out more about him. It is likely that the president-elect discovered that Harold Ickes had broken, loudly and publicly, with the Republican Party in 1920 and had supported the Cox-Roosevelt Democratic ticket in that election. The maverick Republican proceeded to vote for Democratic presidential candidates in every election thereafter. Thus, while it took more than twelve years to reap the benefits of this decision, Harold Ickes's principled stand in 1920 definitely marked a turning-point in his political career.

As Roosevelt told Ickes in their initial meeting, the two men had been on parallel ideological and political tracks for twenty years, most recently in Ickes's noisy fight in Chicago over the public transportation issue. But above all, Roosevelt said that he wanted someone who was honest at the helm of the scandal-prone Interior Department, someone "who can stand on his own two feet." There is a poignancy, of course, in Roosevelt's choice of words to describe the necessary qualifications; ever since he contracted polio in 1921 he could, only with great strain and an enormous expenditure of energy, stand on his own two feet. However Roosevelt came by the information, he discerned in Harold Ickes the very qualities that came to distinguish him as a political executive: Honesty, a tremendous capacity for work, and the courage to stand up for his principles. In the twelve years he served with Roosevelt, no one ever accused Secretary Ickes of not standing his ground.

The solution to this "mystery" appointment thus was revealed by the president himself: Roosevelt appointed Ickes Interior secretary precisely for the reasons he gave him on February 21.

WITH ICKES'S APPOINTMENT the president's first cabinet was complete. The tall, dignified former senator from Tennessee, Cordell Hull, was Roosevelt's secretary of state. For the critical position of secretary

of the treasury—especially critical due to the economic collapse—
Roosevelt selected the Republican businessman William Woodin.
Tom Walsh, the liberal Democratic senator from Montana who helped
uncover the "Teapot Dome" scandal during the Harding administration, was appointed attorney general. Unfortunately, he died just
before inauguration day and Homer Cummings of Connecticut, a
Democratic Party politico, was appointed in his stead. Daniel Roper,
the commissioner of internal revenue under Woodrow Wilson, came
aboard as secretary of commerce, while Henry Wallace carried on his
family's tradition by heading up the Agriculture Department; Wallace's father had served in that capacity under presidents Harding and
Coolidge.

George Dern was named secretary of war, and Virginia's elderly
senator Claude Swanson assumed the position of secretary of the Navy.
As originally contemplated by FDR, James Farley was given the postmaster generalship. Frances Perkins, a long-time friend and associate
of the president's, became secretary of labor. And finally, there was the
relatively unknown Chicagoan, Harold L. Ickes, as secretary of the
interior. Interestingly, only Perkins and Ickes were with Roosevelt for
the twelve years from his inauguration on March 4, 1933, until his
death at Warm Springs, Georgia, on April 12, 1945. At the time they
were the two most controversial and difficult appointments that Roosevelt made.

ON FEBRUARY 22 Harold Ickes returned home from New York City
as the newly designated secretary of the interior. There was much to
do before taking the oath of office on March 4. He had to close down
his law practice, leaving his long-time personal secretary, May B. Conley, in charge until he had time to sort things out. This proved relatively easy because Miss Conley was both experienced and efficient,
and Ickes was confident that she could take over in his absence.

The more difficult task was to get his family affairs in order. Harold
and Anna Ickes's family life was, in many respects, some fifty years
ahead of its time. Coping with what are called today a "blended
family" and a "commuter marriage" has become fairly commonplace.
But in 1933 the Ickes ménage was unusual, to say the least, and it took
a lot of negotiating to get it to work. First of all, when Harold married
Anna, she brought with her the children of her first marriage to James

Thompson; they had had a son, Wilmarth, born in 1899, and an adopted daughter, Frances, three years older than Wilmarth. After Anna divorced James, he completely faded out of the family picture; he married another woman and eventually left Chicago to take a job as a history professor at the University of California in Berkeley. Anna and Harold thus raised Wilmarth and Frances.

Their son, Raymond, was born in 1912. A few years later Anna insisted on bringing into the family another child, a four-year-old named Robert, to be a companion for Raymond. Robert, who was about the same age as Raymond, grew up in the Ickes household but, unlike Frances, was never formally adopted, a situation never explained. The result of all this was, as Ickes once described it, a fairly conglomerate family, with two sets of children from two unions.

By the time Ickes's political fortunes made their 180-degree turn, the two older children, Wilmarth and Frances, were married and living on their own. Frances Thompson became Mrs. ReQua Bryant of Evanston, and Wilmarth married a Milwaukee girl named Betty Dahlman. With their children, Wilmarth and Betty Ickes (Wilmarth having taken his stepfather's name) lived near Anna and Harold in the fashionable Chicago suburb of Winnetka.

The two younger boys, Raymond and Robert, were about 20 years old in 1933. Although both were enrolled in school—Raymond at the University of Chicago and Robert at Lake Forest College—they still needed a place to call home. Anna had been elected to the Illinois legislature initially in 1928, reelected in 1930 and again in 1932. While she was in Springfield Harold held down the fort at Hubbard Woods. But with his appointment to Roosevelt's cabinet, he could no longer do that, so the two parents coped as best they could for the next few years, juggling family and professional responsibilities.

As far as his marital situation was concerned, the move to Washington, D.C., did not bother Harold Ickes. In fact, he saw his new position as a welcome opportunity to alter fundamentally both his public career and his private life. In the power struggle that defined their marriage Harold too often found himself beaten into a state of bitter resignation. After some twenty years of living under Anna's domination, he sensed that personal liberation, along with the fulfillment of his life's ambition to be at the center of power, awaited him in Washington. Franklin Roosevelt became his savior. The feelings he previously had for Theodore Roosevelt were transferred to Franklin, and although their long relationship was severely tried on occasion, Harold Ickes never forgot who had given him the chance of a lifetime.

MARCH 1933 CAME IN like a lion. As the new president and the members of his New Deal Administration trooped into Washington, they were met with not only the gloom and chill of a late winter sleet storm but the prospect of the collapse of the nation's banking industry.[14] Two days before the inauguration, the Roosevelts checked into the Mayflower Hotel, as did the secretary of the interior and his family—Anna and the two boys, Raymond and Robert, having accompanied Harold to the capital not only to witness their first presidential inauguration, but also to participate in the activities as part of the official family. Although Harold and Anna were accustomed to traveling in rarefied social circles—at least compared with the average American of the time—nevertheless, this was heady stuff. Their time prior to the inauguration was spent in such pleasurable activities as meeting other members of the incoming administration and getting acculturated to Washington.

March 4 fell on a Saturday. An overcast sky and a chilling wind greeted the president-elect, his entourage, and the thousands of spectators gathered in front of the Capitol and along Pennsylvania Avenue to watch the historic changing of the guard. The gloom of the day, and the downcast demeanor of the outgoing chief executive, Herbert Hoover, contrasted sharply with the buoyant, smiling, spirited Franklin Delano Roosevelt. As he gave his memorable inaugural address it was as if he were inflating a balloon, someone remarked. The audience palpably reacted to his words, "The only thing we have to fear is fear itself," and they seemed eager to accept his challenge to attack the Great Depression with as much vigor and dedication as if it were a war. When Roosevelt said that, if necessary, he would ask Congress for "broad executive power to wage a war against the emergency, as great as the power that would be given to me if we were in fact invaded by a foreign foe," the bold message was greeted by the greatest applause given to any passage in his address.[15]

President and Mrs. Roosevelt then made their way by limousine up Pennsylvania Avenue, followed by members of the cabinet and a five-hour-long inaugural parade. Because of the crisis confronting the country, Roosevelt asked the Senate to confirm his cabinet members without the usual lengthy hearings, which it did. About dusk on March 4, 1933, all ten members took the oath of office, administered by Supreme Court Justice Benjamin Cardozo, in the Oval Room of the White House. With these formalities concluded, Roosevelt presided briefly over his "little family party" before going off to greet a group of crippled children who had been invited from Warm Springs to attend the inauguration.[16]

Harold Ickes and his cabinet colleagues left the White House knowing that they would be returning the next day—Sunday, March 5—to meet in emergency session. Eleven days later Harold Ickes would turn 59.

PART TWO

THE FIRST TERM

CHAPTER 3

"FORM YOUR RANKS AND FIGHT!"

THE 100 DAYS

THE MEN AND WOMEN called to Washington by Franklin Roosevelt in March of 1933 were there to begin the long, hard task of lifting an entire country out of the recesses of a monumental crisis. Appropriately termed the Great Depression, it had many faces: A barely functioning system of production in which one-quarter of the nation's labor force could not find work; an ecological disaster of drought, grasshopper plagues, and dust storms that affected at least one-third of America's interior land mass; psychological despair written on the weathered, angular faces of millions of ordinary Americans as they saw their material security draining away; and, finally, political stalemate in the nation's capital as neither the president nor Congress found themselves capable of pulling together to exercise leadership. Herbert Hoover, after having met with Roosevelt just before the inauguration, gloomily assessed the situation and said to his advisers, "We're at the end of our string. There's nothing more we can do." [1]

Roosevelt thought differently. He had spent the previous

several months putting together a Brains Trust and a New Deal administration that was poised for action. The heavily Democratic Congress
that had been returned to Washington was anxious for leadership. On
his first full day in office—Sunday, March 5—Roosevelt called on the
73rd Congress to convene in emergency session on Thursday the
ninth. He held his first cabinet meeting and, with its concurrence, issued a presidential proclamation on Monday, March 6, declaring a
"bank holiday." When Congress convened on Thursday, it approved
the president's emergency actions. And on national radio the following
Sunday evening, March 12, Roosevelt explained to the American
people what he had done with respect to the financial crisis, and why.
The American people listened to the president's first Fireside Chat and
approved: FDR was delighted to learn that once the banks reopened,
more deposits were made than were monies withdrawn. "Those of us
who heard that first speech," the writer Robert Sherwood recalled,
"will never forget the surge of confidence that his buoyant spirit
evoked. It was all the more thrilling after the hair-shirted carping and
petulance that we had been hearing from Hoover." [2]

Executive initiative, a Sunday cabinet meeting, a serious discussion
with the American people about the crisis and the government's response to it—Roosevelt's actions that first week in office formed a
pattern that broke with tradition. Emphasizing that pattern, on
Wednesday, March 8, FDR ignored Hoover's advice about presidential
protocol; he left the White House to pay an afternoon visit to former
Chief Justice Oliver Wendell Holmes at his Georgetown home. The
occasion was the Justice's 92nd birthday, and Roosevelt's thoughtful-
ness pleased the old man enormously. During their chat, the president
asked Holmes what he ought to do about the emergency. The Civil
War veteran responded, "Form your ranks and fight!" [3]

The military metaphor was apt. Frenetic, dedicated activity characterized the first few months of Roosevelt's presidency, as the president himself set the tone and pace for his assistants. Roosevelt obviously did not have all of the answers to solving the national calamity
confronting him, but he did understand that it was extraordinarily
complex, and that to find solutions he needed to be surrounded by
diversity and differences of opinion. He also needed his people to
make decisions and take action as swiftly as possible. The composition
of his cabinet and his other key appointments reflected his pluralistic
and pragmatic bent. Some of FDR's cabinet members were old-timers
to Washington—having served in Congress or in previous administra-

tions—while others were novices. Some were liberal and a few conservative. Many were young, and with the exuberance of youth willing to work night and day. But several also were middle-aged, like the president himself, and his associate Harry Hopkins. Only a few were over 60. Secretary of the Navy Claude Swanson was born during the Civil War, in 1862, and Bernard Baruch, the millionaire businessman and adviser to many presidents, was born in 1870.

They came from all parts of the country. Harold Ickes and Frances Perkins, for instance, came to Washington from the nation's cities, where the sight of men and women rummaging in garbage cans or waiting in long soup lines at the Salvation Army was commonplace. Others, such as Henry Wallace, hailed from America's breadbasket, where the typical scene in the 1930s was the long and lonely parade of jalopies heading West, their occupants choking on dust while their abandoned dogs trailed after their masters until they passed from sight. Still other appointees, George Dern and Roosevelt's young budget director, Lewis Douglas, came from the Rocky Mountains and the West, where the ravages of the Depression possibly hit hardest that group least able to cope with it, the American Indians. Living on the brink of starvation through most of the Depression years, the Hill Indian Tribe of Montana, for example, found shelter under "teepees" made of a few poles on which they nailed flattened tin cans.[4] Together, the kaleidoscopic experiences and backgrounds of Roosevelt's team produced a remarkably accurate collage of the nation in distress.

The pace couldn't have suited Harold Ickes any better, for he had been a compulsive worker throughout his life. He began his first full day in office, Monday, March 6, however, attending a funeral: The president and his cabinet attended the services of their colleague, Thomas J. Walsh of Montana, who would have served as attorney general had he lived. Afterwards, the president asked his Interior secretary to sit in on a conference of state governors which he had called. It was only after the meeting at the White House, at about 12:30, that Ickes entered the Interior Department building and went to his office. There, he related in his diaries, "I met the heads of the various bureaus and departments and during the afternoon I attended to routine matters until four o'clock, when all of the employees in the building were asked to come up to be introduced to me. They filed past me about twenty-five hundred strong." [5]

Like any incoming executive, Ickes began by looking for people to help him run his small army of 2,500 bureaucrats. He needed a solicitor for the department's top legal position, a personal assistant, and at least one new bureau chief. He wanted the best people, irrespective of whether they were Republican or Democrat, but they had to be committed to reform and be willing to work as hard as he did. For the top legal position, Ickes sought the advice of two well-known jurists, Felix Frankfurter of Harvard University, and the legendary "Isaiah" of the Supreme Court, Louis Brandeis. Ickes tracked down Frankfurter at Washington's fashionable Cosmos Club on March 10, and the two men briefly discussed possible appointees for the solicitor's position. Frankfurter also agreed to help set up an appointment for Ickes with his friend on the Supreme Court. On Sunday, the secretary called on Brandeis at his home and had "a most delightful talk with him on Government policies. . . . I felt as if I were sitting at the feet of one of the fine old prophets." [6]

Both Brandeis and Frankfurter advised Ickes that he couldn't find a better man than Nathan N. Margold, a brilliant 33-year-old graduate of Harvard Law School, for the solicitor's job. Margold already had earned a reputation as a champion of the rights of blacks and American Indians; he was active in the NAACP and had done *pro bono* work for the Pueblo Indians in their struggle with whites over land in the 1920s. Given such credentials, Ickes immediately offered Margold the solicitor's job, and he was sworn in at the end of March.

The secretary continued the search for legal talent. With the changes in policy and procedure that were being contemplated by the New Deal administration in those first hundred days, Ickes knew he needed a critical mass of top-rate lawyers. On March 27, 1933, he wrote Dean Harry A. Bigelow of his alma mater, the University of Chicago Law School, asking him to suggest the names of some young lawyers who might be interested in coming to work for him:

> There are likely to be some vacancies and for those vacancies I wish we might be in a position to choose young men . . . who have real legal minds and who like to work. More than this, I want men who have a progressive outlook on our political and social institutions. While I want to choose men on the basis of their character and ability, it would make it easier for me, other things being equal, to put in Democrats, and I would like to have them from some of the Western States. [7]

Shortly thereafter, two young attorneys with liberal credentials, Charles Fahy and Felix Cohen, were hired to assist Margold in the solicitor's office.

While he looked for lawyers, Ickes also lobbied strenuously for the appointment of his friend John Collier to head the Office of Indian Affairs—the bureau within the Interior Department which then had jurisdiction over 50 million acres of land and which served as a trustee for 300,000 "Native Americans."[8] It was an important, even critical, appointment, for the person Roosevelt and Ickes selected would determine whether the New Deal would extend to the original inhabitants of America, whom Ickes believed to be society's most destitute group.

Several names had been given to the president for his consideration in February and March. In the running were a number of strong candidates, including Lewis Meriam, director of the Washington-based Institute for Government Research. Among other accomplishments Meriam (who was not related to Ickes's good friend Charles Merriam of the University of Chicago) was noted for his 1928 report, *The Problem of Indian Administration*. The report took Congress to task for being so penurious when funding Indian welfare and relief programs.[9] Felix Frankfurter initially lobbied FDR on behalf of Nathan Margold, but Margold dropped out of the competition when Secretary Ickes appointed him solicitor for the entire department. There was also Edgar B. Meritt, whose most powerful backer was the Senate's majority leader, Joseph T. Robinson of Arkansas. Meritt had not only been assistant commissioner of Indian affairs from 1913 to 1929, but in 1933 he held the position of assistant solicitor in the Interior Department. He also happened to be Robinson's brother-in-law. Thus there were several good reasons why Senator Robinson, and Robinson's ally from Oklahoma, Elmer Thomas, pushed strongly for Meritt's appointment.

John Collier, Ickes's choice for the commissionership, was backed by most of the Indian rights organizations. Collier, who had dedicated his life to the cause, claimed that he had supported Harold Ickes in his quest for the secretaryship; Ickes never discussed whether there was some reciprocity operating here, but what is not in doubt is the fact that Ickes was determined to get Collier appointed to the Indian Affairs post. He went so far as to tell the Senate that he would not send up any further nominations for positions in his department until it made this one.[10] At the same time Ickes tried to convince the president that John Collier, although considered a fanatic or a radical by people he had crossed swords with in the conservative 1920s, was the best person for the job.[11]

Roosevelt was caught between Senator Robinson's nominee and

Harold Ickes's choice. On April 11 he broke the deadlock by calling Robinson and Ickes to a meeting in his study where Ickes got his first glimpse of the president's ability to charm people into acquiescence, a political skill for which he later became well known. Over tea, Roosevelt initiated the discussion by talking generally about governmental policies and pending legislation; only after "everyone was feeling very well," Ickes wrote, did he bring up the question of the commissionership. First the majority leader spoke briefly on behalf of Meritt, after which the president asked Ickes for his views. FDR and Senator Robinson then got their first glimpse of the secretary's *modus operandi.* "I went prepared with documentary proofs tending to show the total disqualification of Meritt for this job," Ickes related in his diaries. "I made my points, telling the President and Senator Robinson that every statement I was making was one of fact which I could substantiate . . . , mostly in the handwriting of Meritt himself."

After a tactful digression, the president turned to Robinson and in a light, friendly way, said, "Well, Joe, you see what I am up against. Every highbrow organization in the country is opposed to Meritt, and Secretary Ickes, under whom he would have to work, doesn't want him."[12]

John Collier got the appointment, and at the end of April Ickes wrote to a mutual friend of theirs telling him that he was pleased indeed by this coup: "It wasn't easy going, but I knew that was one thing that I particularly wanted and it was magnificent the way the President stood by me and put the thing over for me, in spite of powerful opposition which in the end did not appear on the surface."[13]

One more bureau appointment remained, that of assistant commissioner of Indian affairs. The position went to an Indianapolis businessman named William Zimmerman, who was known to both Ickes and Collier, and whose liberal stands included his advocacy of the ownership of corporations by workers.[14] With Harold Ickes at the helm, with John Collier and William Zimmerman heading the Office of Indian Affairs, and with Nathan Margold, Charles Fahy, and Felix Cohen in the solicitor's office—all men who had worked in the Indian rights movement—the personnel was in place to launch the "Indian New Deal."

In fact, Commissioner Collier and his group, which "looked more like a cabal than a happy circumstance of appointments," wasted no time in getting to work. They drafted the Pueblo Relief bill and secured its passage during Congress's celebrated 100 Days Session. At the same time, Collier announced several changes in administrative policy, which included the right to religious freedom for Indians "without fear of harassment from the bureau" and the cancellation of debts against tribal treasuries that had been incurred without tribal approval; he also secured President Roosevelt's consent to abolish the foot-dragging Board of Indian Commissioners.[15]

In August Collier wrote a memo to Ickes calling his attention to scandalous conditions at an Indian mental asylum in Canton, South Dakota, apprising him that "we are conducting an institution so outrageously cruel and injurious that we would deserve to be 'blown out of the water' if we continued it. . . . Canton should be abolished entirely and its personnel discharged." Three days later Secretary Ickes inquired of the superintendent of St. Elizabeth's Hospital in Washington whether the Indian patients could be transferred there.[16]

Finally, during their first summer in Washington, the New Dealers in Interior began drafting a comprehensive reform bill that, when passed in 1934, even in it's watered-down version, planted the seeds of Indian sovereignty in America. This was the Indian Reorganization Act, one of the most important pieces of legislation affecting Native Americans ever passed by Congress.

Another disadvantaged group was concerned with the question, "Would there be a New Deal for Negroes?" Roosevelt had not been elected in 1932 with the support of the Negro electorate, and there was very little in his record to indicate that as president he would give much consideration to the minority occupying—along with Indians—the lowest rungs of the economic and social ladder. Nevertheless, as soon as the new president took office NAACP leaders Walter White and Roy Wilkins began pressuring him to pay some attention to their concerns. At the same time the liberally inclined Julius Rosenwald Fund (a private philanthropic organization headquartered in New York) suggested that the president establish an executive position on the status of blacks vis-à-vis the national recovery program.

Roosevelt knew he had to be cautious; he was fearful of losing Democratic support in the South, on which the entire emergency recovery plan depended. Harold Ickes, however, felt no such constraints and offered his Department of the Interior as the appropriate place to house such a position. In 1933, after all, Interior not only had responsibilities for Indians, territories, and island possessions, but it also managed the few programs and institutions that had been created over the years to benefit blacks. The agency helped run, for example, Howard University in Washington, D.C., as well as the Freedmen's Hospital and St. Elizabeth's Hospital for mentally disturbed indigents. Interior's primary responsibilities focused on the management of natural resources, but because these other "people" programs had found their way into the department, in Ickes's day it was often referred to as the "Department of Things in General."

Roosevelt approved the position after the Julius Rosenwald Fund agreed to pay the salary of Secretary Ickes's "special assistant on the economic status of Negroes." The peculiar funding situation arose in part because of the president's strenuous efforts, during these first months of his presidency, to cut ongoing federal spending in order to make room for emergency spending. Ickes, for example, was told he must reduce the Interior Department's budget by nearly half, a cut which amounted to a whopping $14 million! [17] Other executives were ordered to do much the same thing. Roosevelt even told his wife, Eleanor, that the White House budget had to be cut by 25 percent. It was an action, however, with which Mrs. Roosevelt wholeheartedly concurred, and her economizing methods became well publicized through her "My Day" newspaper column. The other reason for turning to the Rosenwald Fund was political; the president did not want to run the risk of alienating the congressional "boll weevils" by even so minor a move (by contemporary standards) as paying the salary of a special assistant for Negro affairs. Such was the racial situation in the United States circa 1933.

For the new position Ickes moved quickly and selected Clark Foreman, who was young, liberal, religious, Southern, and white. Roy Wilkins of the NAACP immediately wrote the secretary a letter in which he stated that Negroes "bitterly resent having a white man designated by the government to advise them of their welfare." [18] The criticism was well taken; Ickes realized he had made a mistake, although it was commonplace at the time to have white males run minority group organizations, as he himself did in Chicago. Nevertheless, to rectify this error Ickes returned to the public-spirited Rosenwald trough and with its financial assistance created two more positions—one for a Negro secretary and one for Robert Weaver, a young black man who recently earned a doctorate in economics from Harvard University, and whose status would be on a par with Foreman's.

With these appointments, and with Harold Ickes at the top, the civil rights ball "started to roll." [19] Without getting President Roosevelt's approval, Ickes took the tremendously bold step of desegregating the public facilities of the Department of the Interior. Through executive order, the "whites" and "colored" signs for restrooms, drinking fountains, and cafeterias that had been condoned in the United States since the 1896 *Plessy v. Ferguson* decision were torn down and consigned to the trash barrel. After Ickes took the first step, other liberally inclined members of the cabinet followed suit, although such action was by no means universal. The nation's capital was still very much a Southern town with Southern mores until the Second World War transformed it, along with the rest of the country, into a more liberal place.

HAROLD ICKES BROUGHT into Interior several new faces in these first few months, but he recognized that he needed some insiders around him as well. He therefore retained the department's first administrative assistant, 48-year-old Ebert K. Burlew. Burlew had been with the department since 1923 and was known to be hard-working and a dedicated civil servant. Louis Glavis was another old hand whom Ickes selected to run the Division of Investigations—a "necessary evil," whose function was to keep an eye on the activities of the department's 2,500 employees.

Glavis, 50 years old in 1933, seemed to be the kind of person Ickes needed to head this widely despised surveillance operation. His reputation went back to the Taft administration when, as a newly hired agent in the Interior Department, he uncovered some questionable transactions concerning coal fields in Alaska. The affair became known as the "Pinchot-Ballinger" dispute and resulted in, among other things, President Taft's firing of Chief Forester Gifford Pinchot for insubordination. After Glavis became *persona non grata* in the Interior Department for his whistle-blowing, he worked for the Senate's Indian Affairs Investigating Committee; there he continued to guard the public interest. Glavis was tough, thick-skinned, and competent, a good combination of qualities for the position in which Ickes put him. Moreover, like his boss, he was sympathetic toward minority rights.

Occupying the governor's office in Harrisburg, Pennsylvania, in 1933 was Ickes's old friend and fellow Bull Moose Progressive Gifford Pinchot. Few people could boast of having done more for the conservation cause than this imperious former chief forester, who sported a bushy, turn of the century–style moustache and who could freeze a person in his or her tracks with a piercing look. And few people appreciated his contributions more than Pinchot himself. In his correspondence with the new president, who just happened to be the distant cousin of Pinchot's intimate friend, the late Theodore Roosevelt, the governor invariably opened his letters with "Dear Franklin," and proceeded to offer his invaluable advice to the younger man.

His intellect was legendary, making him the most formidable of opponents (as Ickes soon discovered). At 68 he'd lost none of his faculties, and he was anxious to be a part of the action in Washington. As soon as he learned of Ickes's appointment Governor Pinchot wrote him (naturally addressing him as "Dear Harold") to suggest that "the best man in Washington to give you . . . information [on the history of the Interior Department] is Harry Slattery." [20] He went on to sing Slattery's praises by pointing out that this man was a Washington insider *par excellence,* having been involved with matters pertaining to the department since before the Ballinger days. Slattery, moreover, knew "intimately all the older Senators who are at all on our side of the fence" and was on good relations with the newspaper men. Finally, Pinchot wrote, this "animated guide book to public life in Washington" was devoted to the public interest, just as he and Ickes were. Harry Slattery was subsequently hired as the secretary's personal assistant.

PERSONNEL WAS ONE matter occupying Ickes's time in these first few months in Washington; policies were another. Ickes knew very well that the Department of the Interior was as conservative and hidebound as any in existence in 1933, and that it was ripe for reform. It seemed as if the department either languished in public indifference as to what it was or was not doing, or else its officials were making sensational headlines about giveaways, conflicts of interest, and general mismanagement of the country's resources. The most recent scandal had been Teapot Dome during the Harding administration, and Secretary of the Interior Albert Fall's ignominious departure from public service was still, in 1933, quite fresh in people's minds. "Honest Harold," as he came to be called, intended from the outset to do something about both the sorry state of Interior's reputation and the thrust, or direction, of its programs. He was determined to get his department in the limelight of public interest—but under his administration it had better be for the right reasons.

In this regard, one of Ickes's bureau chiefs provided him with an idea for one of his first policy initiatives. Horace Albright, who was the second director of the National Park Service and about to retire from government service, wrote his new boss a memo late in March suggesting that the time was ripe for "reform on the range." Albright was referring to the proper management and control of 173 million acres of federal land administered, up to that time, by the Interior Department's notoriously lax General Land Office. For decades debate had raged over what to do with the public domain lands of the West, whether to dispose of them or keep them in federal hands and, if the latter, how best to manage them.

During his presidency Theodore Roosevelt and his Interior secretary, Ethan Allen Hitchcock, had tried to wrest a reform-minded leasing provision from Congress without success. The western congressmen, ably protecting their livestock industries, blocked governmental efforts to limit the number of cattle and sheep roaming the range. The result was the continued deterioration, during the 1910s and 1920s, of rangeland conditions. Mercilessly combining with overgrazing on the public lands were drought and grasshopper plagues, so that by the late 1920s all that kept cattle from starvation in many areas was an unsavory nonnative bush called Russian thistle—commonly known as tumbleweed.[21]

In its turn the Hoover administration wrestled with the politically thorny problem of the public range. A presidential commission headed by former Interior Secretary James Garfield recommended in 1930 that the federal government cede these residual lands to the states in which they lay, thereby handing over the problem to those governmental entities for resolution. But this original Sagebrush Rebellion proposal was not very popular at the time, as a number of state officials were uninterested in acreage "on which a jack rabbit could hardly live."[22] Thus, in the midst of a serious economic collapse, Congress decided to do nothing; it shelved the Garfield Report.

By 1933 the situation was desperate. One historian described the West of the 1930s as an "underdeveloped region paralyzed by the economic collapse that followed the boom of the mid-1920s." With a conservation-minded president now occupying the White House, National Park Service Director Albright felt the time had come for action. So did Ickes. On April 19, in response to the memo from Albright, Ickes thanked the director for his suggestion: "I am strongly impressed with your recommendation that we ask for legislation at this time that will make it possible to husband the resources of the public domain not already under management, and to regulate the use of these resources." [23]

As soon as Ickes had Roosevelt's approval he put his staff to work drafting a bill. On June 7, Secretary Ickes went to the Capitol to testify in support of H.R. 2835, a bill "to stop injury to the public grazing lands by preventing overgrazing and soil deterioration, to provide for their orderly use, improvement and development, to stabilize the livestock industry dependent upon the public range, and for other purposes." In addition to pointing out the long overdue nature of the legislation and the need to restore the productivity of the land, the secretary threw in an added benefit:

> The passage of this bill at this time is particularly desired because it would dovetail with present national policy. Great projects are underway to furnish employment, to rehabilitate industries of all kinds, to extend relief to States and individuals. To stop the ravages against these grazing lands . . . would add to employment at a time when such employment would fulfil the double need of the land itself and of our unemployed citizens. [24]

With more pressing problems, Congress did not pass the legislation in what became known as its 100 Days Session. But the Taylor Grazing Act, named for Edward Taylor of Colorado who had fought for such legislation for years, was passed in 1934. It was one of the earliest New Deal contributions to the conservation cause, and its importance was profound, for it marked the end of the era of the federal government's free, or nearly free, land disposal policy. The legislation also created a new agency within the Interior Department, called the Grazing Service, which Secretary Ickes used to effect additional public land reforms, while the scandal-prone General Land Office was gradually phased out.

But Ickes moved toward reforming the situation on the public domain even as Congress debated the bill. Knowing that the legislative branch usually moved at a glacier-like pace, Ickes pushed for changes through administrative action—doing precisely what FDR wished his cabinet members to do during the national emergency. In July 1933 he asked his solicitor's office to find out what right, if any, the department had to regulate grazing on the public domain. He had learned that a land-managing agency in the Agriculture Department, the U.S. Forest

Service, had for years charged fees to ranchers for the privilege of grazing on federal lands under its jurisdiction. He asked his lawyers, "I understand that the Forest Service fences in its land and charges fees for grazing. Has it any broader rights of ownership than we have?" [25]

At the same time Ickes made a frontal assault on that powerful symbol of the West, the barbed wire fence. Although the practice of fencing in public domain land by the big ranchers was technically illegal, they had been doing it for decades. Range wars were fought when one cattleman cut down the fences of his neighbor, who was as often as not his competitor, given the marginality of the land. And the homesteaders who tried to eke out a living among the ranchers were often the biggest losers of all, sometimes paying with their lives for the privilege of attempting dry farming where the cattle roamed free. By executive order the secretary instructed the General Land Office to begin removing fences on the public domain lands in Arizona and New Mexico.

By midsummer the new policy was receiving support from the small ranchers and homesteaders but was hotly contested by the powerful cattlemen's association, their financial backers, and some southwestern congressmen. In July, the president of the State National Bank of El Paso, Texas, C. N. Bassett, wrote an acquaintance in Douglas, Arizona, asking him to bring pressure to bear on Secretary Ickes to rescind the order. Bassett noted that "undoubtedly Lewis Douglas [Roosevelt's director of the Bureau of the Budget] understands the situation and might be of considerable help to us." A few weeks later Lewis Douglas's office responded by telling S. P. Applewhite of Douglas, Arizona, that the director's position did not allow him to take "an active personal interest in this matter," but that "Senator Hayden [of Arizona] . . . has taken the matter up with the Secretary of the Interior and is making every effort to have the order rescinded." [26]

In this conflict President Roosevelt sided with Ickes and the order was not rescinded. It proved difficult to enforce, however. The General Land Office was extremely short-handed, as it had been throughout its nearly 100-year existence. In 1933 the GLO was not up to the task of removing all illegal fences in a land mass the size of Arizona and New Mexico. Enforcement was further complicated when ranchers told government officials just where to put their new order. Despite implementation problems, however, the order definitely constituted a start at rangeland reform. And Secretary Ickes doggedly stuck with it by asking his colleagues at the Justice Department to vigorously pursue and prosecute "flagrant cases [of noncompliance]."[27]

THE RESPONSIBILITIES OF office during the national emergency left Harold Ickes with little time to do more than keep his head above water. Indeed, as the popular, young newcomer to Washington, Tom Corcoran, commented, the New Dealers that first year were behaving just like "rabbits dodging the lightning."[28] Ickes spent his first few weeks staying at the Mayflower Hotel, but in early April he found a comfortable rowhouse to rent at 1327 33rd Street in Georgetown, just a few doors away from Frances Perkins and her husband. It was not only located in a fashionable part of the city but, more important for the clock-watching Ickes, it was convenient to his office; it took his chauffeur, Carl Witherspoon, fewer than fifteen minutes to get the secretary to 19th and E streets Northwest, and to his office in the old Interior building.

When his six-month lease was up in September Ickes moved again, this time to a house a little further away, at 4880 Glenbrook Road Northwest. The Pinchots had offered their Washington house to him at a reasonable rent, but after considering it, Ickes decided not to accept the offer. The governor and Mrs. Pinchot were known to be quite domineering, and Ickes no doubt didn't want to feel beholden to them. Because he was a newcomer to Washington he was particularly anxious to establish his independence vis-à-vis old friends and political allies. He politely declined the invitations to the Pinchots' annual Fourth of July celebrations in 1933 and again in 1934, pleading that he simply was too busy, but one suspects that the underlying reason was again to keep some distance in their relationship.

Ickes's old friends from the Bull Moose Days, the Pinchots, weren't the only ones whom he wished to keep at arm's length during his acculturation period to Washington. During most of 1933 Harold and his wife Anna lived apart. In March he wrote a friend that she had come for the inaugural "but was compelled to return to Illinois . . . and will not be with me in Washington for the time being."[29] The ostensible reason was Anna's position in the Illinois legislature, which she held through 1934. She also chose to spend the summer of 1933 at their vacation home in New Mexico rather than to suffer the heat and humidity of Washington, which would have aggravated her asthma.

But the underlying reason was that this was how Harold, and perhaps Anna as well, wanted their relationship. With the backdrop of years of an unhappy and tortured union, neither of them seemed anxious to spend a lot of time together. Ickes, in fact, was very relieved by being on his own this first year in Washington. He could concentrate more fully on his work, and he set out to establish a social life that was independent of Anna.

The two youngest Ickes children, son Raymond and foster child Robert, presented some logistical problems that summer, inasmuch as both parents were very much occupied with work and didn't want the boys hanging about the house in Winnetka with nothing to do. The secretary solved half of the problem by asking National Park Service Director Albright to find summer jobs for Raymond and a friend. Ickes also found employment in the parks for the son of Secretary of Agriculture Henry Wallace; Ickes thought Mrs. Wallace, who became his favorite cabinet wife, to be "charming, delightful and personable," and thus was happy to do this favor for them. In April, Director Albright informed the secretary that Raymond and his friend would be employed as rangers in Wyoming's rugged Grand Teton National Park.[30] Harold and Anna asked Wilmarth, Anna's oldest son, to keep an eye on Robert. He and his family lived near Hubbard Woods so presumably they could make sure Robert didn't tear down the family estate in his parents' absence.

Anna was in New Mexico, the children were away, and Harold, on his own and with family responsibilities settled, worked his way through the dog days of summer in the national capital, which President Washington, back in 1790, decided to locate on top of a swamp. Ickes suffered from the heat and the humidity during that first summer; his offices, like most in Washington, had no air conditioning. The White House in 1933 was about the only building that had installed the newly invented refrigeration system, and so the secretary never minded going to the White House for cabinet and other meetings; it was about his only respite from the suffocating heat, he said. Air conditioning probably helped him establish his near-perfect attendance record for cabinet meetings, for which he was proud.

However the heat was on in other, more ominous ways that summer. In his personal life things were becoming sticky, and Ickes felt that there was a sub-rosa attempt on the part of his political enemies to, as he put it, "break my morale."[31] First, he learned that Anna was receiving anonymous letters charging her husband with infidelity while she was vacationing in New Mexico. After she received several of these letters, Anna understandably became disturbed. She confronted her husband over the long-distance wires, but Ickes denied them convincingly enough that Anna did not come rushing to Washington.

Ickes then learned that the scurrilous letters were being sent to newspaper publishers and editors around the country! Fortunately for him, all those receiving the letters took the same position as did the legendary William Randolph Hearst, who personally decided that none of the papers in his vast chain would dignify the dirt.

That the press in the 1930s had certain standards of conduct as to what it considered newsworthy was a real break for Harold Ickes, because the allegations were in fact true. Just one week after he arrived in Washington he embarked on a long-term affair with Marguerite Moser Brumbaugh.[32] In 1933 she was a divorcée, considerably younger than Harold, the mother of two children, and was in the process of moving to Washington from Pittsburgh. Ickes had known her family since his childhood; therefore, he had known her since she was a youngster and had seen her occasionally over the years. It was during his first week in Washington that Marguerite called him at the Mayflower Hotel and asked to see him. They agreed to meet in his room on Sunday, March 12.

Marguerite, Ickes related in his unpublished memoirs, came to the hotel looking lovely. He was immediately taken with her. The reason for her visit, she told him, was to ask whether he could find a job for her fiancé in the Interior Department. He said he would look into it. Their initial meeting was brief but as she stood up to leave, Ickes said he was overcome with desire. He took her in his arms, kissed her passionately, and wrested a commitment from her to come back the following Sunday.

"It is funny what sex can do to a man," Ickes later wrote about this affair.[33] By his third week in Washington Ickes was deeply involved with Marguerite, or "X" as he referred to her in his memoirs, and enjoying sex as he had never before. She was totally without inhibitions, Ickes observed, using her petite and still youthful body to full effect. "I became quite mad about X and very reckless," he admitted, adding that he "had to have her" even if it meant losing his job.

Although it was fortunate for Ickes that President Roosevelt was quite tolerant of his aides' personal indiscretions—perhaps because his own behavior was not above reproach—nevertheless Ickes acted with extraordinary abandon in his first months in Washington. He behaved like a teenager who had just discovered the pleasures of the flesh. To reduce the chances of being seen too often together at the Mayflower or, later, at his Georgetown home, the couple would go for long drives at night in the Virginia and Maryland countryside. With Ickes's faithful chauffeur silently commandeering the secretary's car, the couple groped and groaned in the backseat as the car wound its way over darkened country roads. "He had known every occasion that we had been together," Ickes wrote with unintended humor about his driver, "but I was confident that no one would wring any admission from his loyal throat."

Although Anna conveniently was away most of the spring and all of the summer, there was Marguerite's fiancé, a man named Thornton Bonneville, to contend with. To get him out of town, Ickes hired him for a job in the Interior Department that had responsibilities in the Midwest. Reluctantly, the fiancé left Washington, thus leaving Harold and his mistress with relatively little to worry about—or so they thought. Harold put Marguerite on the payroll and even hired her female roommate, who needed a job, for some minor position in the department. This was hardly behavior worthy of the man who had a reputation for integrity, but it is testimony to the degree of emotional and sexual deprivation he had endured for years in his marriage.

The affair became public when Bonneville, who obviously hadn't been born yesterday, began sending anonymous letters to Marguerite and to Anna Ickes in New Mexico. At first, Harold and his mistress had no idea who was writing the letters; they "were mailed in Washington and completely non-plussed us," he wrote. But at the same time as he was writing the letters, Bonneville was demanding to be returned to Washington. So Ickes had him brought back. At one point that summer practically everyone involved was working under the same roof in the Interior Department: Ickes, Marguerite, Marguerite's roommate, and Bonneville. Only Anna was elsewhere.

But with Bonneville's return, the flow of letters to Marguerite and Anna not only increased but were sent to newspaper offices. This genuinely alarmed Ickes; the affair was becoming exceedingly untidy, embarrassing, and potentially threatening to his career. He recognized that he had to do something, although that "something" did not include giving up the relationship that was so satisfying to him. Instead, in August he went to FDR's closest adviser, Louis Howe, to tell him about the letters and to ask him for his help in tracking down the letter-writer—though by this time Ickes was rather sure that it was Bonneville. Howe, an old pro in the political arena, turned out to be sympathetic. Ickes said he told him "that I was only getting my turn."

Howe also called in a Captain Moran of the Secret Service, who assigned a man named Burns to the case. "Burns turned out to be a dumb-bell," Ickes noted with disgust. He worked side by side with the fiancé in Interior, yet was unable to get any evidence that would incriminate him. Ickes, however, discovered the identity of the letter-writer by other means, had it out with Bonneville, and then fired him.[34] That at least ended the flow of letters, if not the affair, which the two continued, with the usual stops and starts, for several more years.

RECOGNIZING THAT HE had made himself vulnerable in his personal affairs, Ickes thus set about making sure that no scandal attached to his official duties. At about the same time that he spoke with Louis Howe, he wrote his stepson Wilmarth that his Chicago firm, the General Printing Company, ought not to bid on any government work. This represented a reversal from what he had told Wilmarth in May, which was that he thought that his printing company could bid on the contract to print National Park Service brochures. Ickes explained to Wilmarth that "a well organized effort is already being made to discredit me and make my position here untenable."[35]

In his August letter to Wilmarth, Ickes frankly told him that he was being attacked on personal and political fronts simultaneously: The affair with Marguerite, although he didn't give Wilmarth the details about that problem, and a political attack, which involved the threat of a lawsuit against him brought by a Chicago judge named Lucius Malmin. Malmin claimed that Ickes had promised him a sinecure in the Division of Islands and Territories, an agency within Interior which, for obvious reasons, held much appeal for persons wanting a patronage position. Ickes said that not only had he not offered Malmin a position, but that Malmin was blackmailing him by threatening to bring charges against him about an estate case he had handled several years earlier in Chicago. "If I am guilty of any unprofessional conduct or of committing any crime or misdemeanor in handling the Saunders' estate case," Ickes wrote, "I don't know what it is. The whole thing was clean as a whistle."[36]

Malmin persisted. Early in September he wrote FDR and asked to see the president at Hyde Park. He was interested, he said, in "preventing unfavorable publicity" which reflected on the administration. Roosevelt handled him peremptorily. He refused to see him, and instead wrote a letter in which he said, as Ickes paraphrased it, that "he would not enter into any scheme to cover up anything affecting a member of the Administration, for if any member of the Administration had done what was not right, he should stand the consequences, and if he had not, he would doubtless know how to protect his good name."[37]

A few days later Ickes discussed the Malmin affair with the president and Attorney General Homer Cummings at the White House. Neither FDR nor Cummings believed there was any basis to the charges made by the judge, whom Ickes said was "off his balance," but in order to clear up Ickes's name it was decided that the whole matter would be turned over to the Justice Department for investigation.

On Wednesday, September 13, the young director of the FBI, J. Edgar Hoover, came to the secretary's office to retrieve the written correspondence between Ickes and Malmin. In a July meeting in his office with Malmin, Ickes had tried to verbally entrap him, "but without success." With Louis Glavis and Ickes's stenographer hiding behind a partly opened door, Ickes related that "I talked to him for some twenty minutes . . . and tried to get him to threaten me,"[38] but the clever judge didn't rise to the bait. So Director Hoover took only the written record and promised to get right on the case.

Malmin soon learned he had pressured the wrong man. Ickes described a basic feature of his character in a letter written to a friend in 1933: "As you know only too well, my first disposition is always to hit back and put a little more behind my blow than was back of the blow that was leveled at me." Not content to let the matter rest with the FBI, Harold Ickes initiated proceedings against Malmin, and three years later, in 1936, the Illinois Supreme Court disbarred Judge Lucius Malmin. He died in January of 1941, just after he was reinstated.[39]

ALTHOUGH HAROLD ICKES worked far better than most people under pressure, the strain nevertheless was enormous. In September a diary entry read:

Pressure continues unabated. I would welcome even a half-hour's letup. I feel like the man who tried to sweep the ocean back. There is a never-ceasing avalanche of mail, communications, memoranda, telephone calls, and visitors. So far I have reasonably well kept my poise, although I am conscious of my nerves getting on edge pretty frequently. I realize that it might be fatal if I should once allow myself to feel overwhelmed.[40]

By the time he wrote this, Ickes had had to parry attacks on both his personal and professional lives. But equally important for his nervous state was the fact that Harold Ickes no longer had just one job to do; he had three. In addition to running the Interior Department, the president proceeded in June to add the Public Works Administration to his charge, and then, in late August, the Oil Administration. Even for a man who thrived on being in the center of things, holding down three full-time jobs was an enormous undertaking.

Ickes turned to his trusted friend Charles Merriam of the University of Chicago for organizational advice, and Merriam wrote him in August a detailed and sympathetic letter about how to handle his extraordinary position in government, that of being a "super Cabinet officer." The professor urged him to delegate responsibilities:

> Hon. Harold L. Ickes is taking over powers and responsibilities *such as no Cabinet officer has ever held* in time of peace, and if we are to preserve your health and usefulness, you must be relieved of too much detail and placed in a position where only the most important decisions must be made by you. . . . You need strong deputies whom you can absolutely trust, and who relieve you of responsibility for the minutiae, and free for the bigger questions which come out of your new [PWA] position; otherwise your health will crack, and your power of clear and fast thinking weaken.[41]

So, after just three months of experience with being a high-ranking federal official, Super Cabinet Member Harold Ickes found himself with some unexpected priorities. He took Merriam's advice and delegated responsibilities for running the Interior Department to his assistants, while he spent most of his time that summer and fall setting up two new organizations, a Public Works Administration and an Oil Administration. Further reform of the Interior Department could wait; putting desperate people back to work, and stabilizing the powerful but fractured oil industry, could not.

CHAPTER 4

"TO RIVAL CHEOPS"

THE NEW PUBLIC WORKS ADMINISTRATOR

ONE MONTH BEFORE Roosevelt gave Harold Ickes his second full-time job, the secretary glimpsed the types of problems he would encounter in running the Public Works Administration (PWA). The Interior Department's principal construction agency, the Bureau of Reclamation, was in the process of building one of the engineering marvels of the century, Hoover Dam on the Colorado River.[1] Diverting a mighty river in order to construct a mightier arched gravity structure kept the engineers of the Reclamation Service occupied for years, but other problems of a nontechnical nature had to be resolved before the dam could be built. One of them involved the price of cement.

"I am receiving many telegrams and letters from manufacturers of cement uttering loud wails and protesting their high virtues," Ickes's May 8, 1933, diary entry read, "all as a result of the newspaper article that was running last Saturday in which I commented on the fact that we had to reject bids for 400,000 barrels of cement for the Boulder [alias Hoover] Dam project because, except for a variation due to different freight rates, all the bids were identical." [2]

The secretary's public criticism of the cement industry, which was carried on the front page of the *New York Times* as well as in hundreds of other papers across the country, may have drawn curses from the manufacturers. However, it was warmly welcomed by those who wanted to see the monopoly broken, a group that included the chief executives of several states who found themselves frustrated in implementing their recovery programs by the industry's behavior. In June, just after the National Industrial Recovery Act was passed and after FDR designated Harold Ickes administrator of public works, Ickes received letters from Illinois's Gov. Henry Horner, Governor Pinchot of Pennsylvania, and other individuals regarding the need to lay down the law to the industry. Pinchot wrote him confidentially that "a friend of mine, Colonel R. H. Bruce, one of the old rough riders, has information concerning the Cement Trust which I believe would be very valuable to you." Governor Horner informed Ickes that the State of Illinois was able recently to buy two million barrels of cement at $1.44 per barrel, "as against the combination's price of $1.62." He went on to suggest how Ickes could effect similar savings in his new federal works program. [3]

Ickes put his personal assistant, Harry Slattery, in charge of cement policy for both the Interior Department and the PWA, but Slattery soon recognized that the problem went beyond the bounds of even these two large agencies. In October, he suggested to his boss that a government-wide investigating committee be established regarding the cost of cement, and that it be composed of experts from the National Recovery Administration, the Bureau of Mines, and the Federal Trade Commission. Ickes thought well of the idea, but his deputy administrator for public works, Col. Henry M. Waite, thought otherwise. He argued that creating such a committee at the outset of the recovery program was premature and also that it would send the wrong message to the industry. It was decided to hold off on Slattery's idea for a committee.

The price-fixing continued. In March of 1934 Ickes received a memo from his exasperated assistant secretary, Oscar Chapman, which read, "Last month I turned down seven bids for cement because they were identical in price and ordered re-advertisement of bids. Today I received nine bids for this cement, all alike. I would like to confer with you about this before I pass on it." [4]

By now it was clear that the battle with the cement monopoly was not going to be won in isolation, so Administrator/Secretary Ickes took it to the president. At the end of April 1934, Roosevelt sent memos to Ickes and to Secretary of War Dern, asking each to appoint an engineer to work with Arthur Morgan, chairman of the Tennessee Valley Authority, to come up with a uniform government policy on cement purchases. But even presidential directives did not resolve the issue; finally, in 1937, the Federal Trade Commission charged the Cement Institute with violating the FTC and Clayton acts. But by then the New Deal's construction program was far underway. For several years Ickes and other administrators had to content themselves with piecemeal victories over the cement trust, such as calling public attention to its corrupt practices and refusing when possible to accept its identical bids.

Cracking the cement trust occupied only a fraction of Harold Ickes's time during the critical summer of 1933 and beyond, but his behavior on that issue hinted at how he would run the PWA generally. It also served to sharpen his personality in the minds of the American public, as he gradually earned the nickname "Honest Harold" for the manner in which he ran his organizations.

AS NOXIOUS AS price-fixing was, or as overdue as departmental reform was, Roosevelt and his administration had a dire emergency to address, and so their primary energies were directed at fashioning a recovery plan that covered virtually the entire economy. By the time of FDR's inauguration, 25 percent of the workforce was unemployed and hungry. Farmers were slaughtering their livestock rather than pay for their transport to market with money they didn't have. Auto workers in Detroit were earning ten cents an hour, and oil in some East Texas fields was selling on the black market for four cents a barrel.[5] The immediate needs were to get Americans back to work and to stabilize critical industries such as oil, coal, agriculture, and automobile manufacturing. Thus the major topic of discussion at the White House and at cabinet meetings through the spring of 1933 was about fashioning the New Deal.

On April 26 Ickes received a phone call from the president's assistant, Col. Marvin McIntyre, asking him to chair a cabinet committee to consider a public works program. It was Ickes's first hint that FDR was considering giving him a major role to play in the recovery program. The next afternoon the secretary met with his colleagues from the departments of Agriculture, Labor, and War. "[We] went carefully over a draft of a bill presented by Miss Perkins," Ickes wrote. "A number of changes and amendments were suggested, and we left it to our solicitors to prepare a draft over night in the hope that we may be in a position to present it at the Cabinet meeting tomorrow."[6]

It took an extra day to get the proposal in shape to present to the president, and on Saturday, the twenty-ninth, the committee went into a long session at the White House in which it presented the draft of a bill that called for an appropriation of some $5 billion, a sum that took the president aback. His first question, Ickes recalled, had to do with "what public works were there that would call for the expenditure of such a large sum?" Labor Secretary Frances Perkins gave him a list prepared by an association of contractors and architects covering the entire country. "The President at once turned to the proposals for the State of New York," Ickes related.

> I had never before seen the President critical in perhaps a captious way, but he proceeded to rip that list to pieces and Miss Perkins was, in effect, put on trial, although she was not responsible for the list but simply presented it as a suggestion. . . . The President was perfectly nice about it all, but I got the impression that he had begun to feel the nervous strain resulting from the extra pressure he has been under as the result of the foreign representatives being here. . . . There was no opportunity to go to Miss Perkins' rescue, much as I wanted to . . . , not that she needed it, as she was perfectly able to handle it herself, but once or twice I did feel a bit sorry for her. . . . In the end we got around to a discussion of the subject matter of the bill and made considerable progress. It is hoped to have the bill perfected and introduced in Congress within ten days.[7]

Out of the work of several executive branch and congressional committees came the legislation that, in June and again in August, gave Harold Ickes two new titles and two tremendously complicated responsibilities. The umbrella-like National Industrial Recovery Act authorized the president to create programs that would expend some $3.3 billion that first year on economic recovery, and he proceeded to divide up responsibilities among those he felt could best deliver immediate action. FDR gave Ickes the title of public works administrator and told him to create an organization where there was none. In August he added a third full-time job to Ickes's repertoire, that of oil administrator under the NIRA. Harry Hopkins's Federal Emergency Relief Administration, created in May, was more or less transferred to the NIRA, and he was told to continue putting the unemployed on work relief payrolls. For his third principal administrator of the NIRA, FDR selected Gen. Hugh "Ironpants" Johnson to implement the industrial codes section of the legislation, otherwise known as the Blue Eagle. The craggy-faced World War I military leader had a reputation for decisive action, and it fell to him to wrest cooperation among the major industries with regard to wages and hours and fair labor practices generally. In addition to his other talents, those at his alma mater, West Point, "remembered Johnson as the most talented hazer and the possessor of the biggest nose in the history of the school," the historian Eric Goldman wrote.[8]

Having worked with Roosevelt for only a matter of months, Harold Ickes was immensely pleased with the fact that his chief had enough confidence in his abilities to give him the PWA. Like most of those around Roosevelt, however, he was less than pleased with the organizational set-up. Through the spring, as the bill was being drafted, Ickes made two suggestions to FDR: First, that the conservation of natural resources be included among the overall objectives of the legislation, and second, that overall administrative responsibility be assigned to a single member of the cabinet. Roosevelt agreed on the former but not on the latter. As is well known, FDR's administrative style could only charitably be called "complex"; he cared little about neat and orderly organization charts, preferring instead to give individuals around him shared authority and overlapping responsibilities. That is precisely what he did with the sweeping recovery legislation passed in June by Congress. Other New Deal legislation, it must be noted, like the acts creating the Civilian Conservation Corps and the Tennessee Valley Authority also were folded in somehow to the NIRA, adding still more administrative confusion to the recovery program.

Roosevelt's loose style was a constant source of torment for individuals with compulsive tendencies, such as Harold Ickes, who continually prodded the president in the direction of orderliness. For example, at a cabinet meeting in early June much of the discussion focused on working out an organization for General Johnson's industries control section of the NIRA. Once asked to serve, the general wasted no time in rounding up personnel for his organization-to-be. Roosevelt and a few cabinet members, however, weren't altogether pleased with some of the choices and particularly with not having been consulted about them. Secretary Ickes then suggested that the problem could be solved if Johnson and his organization were housed under the secretary of commerce.

> I pointed out that this would give him a Cabinet officer to represent him at the Cabinet table; that he would have someone to whom he could go when he had decisions to make; that it would make for better cooperation and administration all along the line; and that when the emergency work entrusted to him began to peter out, the Department . . . could be there to take it over and liquidate it.

Labor Secretary Perkins replied that she doubted whether General Johnson, "with his temperament, would be able to work under a Secretary, and I asked how he could work for four secretaries if he could not work with one."[9]

It turned out that General Johnson was no more pleased with having to work with Harold Ickes than was Ickes delighted at the prospect of sharing authority with Johnson (and Harry Hopkins). The two snapping turtles, as Ickes once referred to himself and Johnson, constantly got in each other's way and competed strenuously for control of the recovery program. When Johnson learned that FDR had given Ickes the public works program, he was determined to hand in his resignation, and only an impassioned plea from Frances Perkins dissuaded him from quitting.[10]

HAROLD ICKES'S PRIMARY TASK during the summer of 1933 was to build an organization whose purpose was to build on a scale that would "rival Cheops."[11] A truly formidable undertaking—far more difficult than taking over an ongoing agency, such as Interior—and Ickes had no professional credentials to fall back on. He was not an architect, engineer, or contractor, but rather a practicing attorney whose avocations had included politics, stamp collecting, and horticulture. He was proud to point out that he had patented the "Anna Ickes Dahlia" while he lived in Winnetka.

Beneath the surface features of his personality, however, there resided talents and characteristics that came to the fore as he set about doing what FDR had asked him to do. "I did have [as a young boy] a vagrant ambition to be a carpenter," Ickes casually wrote at the outset of his autobiography. And although he discovered in high school and at the University of Chicago that his most pronounced—and most marketable—talent resided in his verbal abilities, his childhood ambition surfaced at various times in his life. Shortly after he and Anna married in 1911, for example, the couple decided to build a magnificent home on seven acres of heavily wooded land in an area north of Chicago known as Hubbard Woods. The house was built over the space of several years, and both Anna and Harold—but especially Harold—became deeply involved in all aspects of the enterprise. As the costs mounted, from an initial investment of $25,000 to triple that amount, so too did Ickes's scrutiny of every detail. By 1916 the construction of the palatial Hubbard Woods estate had become virtually an obsession. Ickes succeeded in driving the architects and contractors crazy with his insistence on perfection and getting his money's worth.

But the house had become a labor of love, an expression of his youthful desires, ambitions, and even his disappointments. Ickes wrote as much in his unpublished memoirs: "This house was part of me and I put everything into it that I had, not only carefully but lovingly." [12] Constructed to endure, the imposing Ickes mansion still stands in the middle of Winnetka, just off Lake Michigan, although the seven acres surrounding it have been subdivided and the interior completely renovated. (It is no longer owned by the family.)

Ickes enjoyed building in less tangible ways as well. As a young man in the 1890s he was drawn into politics and discovered he had a talent for organization. Working first in John Harlan's campaigns for mayor of Chicago, he went on to run Charles Merriam's near-victory in 1911, and, as we know, helped form Theodore Roosevelt's Progressive Party in 1912. All during his Chicago "apprenticeship" years, Ickes threw himself into the task of helping to organize and/or to run numerous reform causes.

Ickes and Roosevelt had these aspects of personality in common. They were eminently practical men, and James MacGregor Burns's assessment of FDR could easily describe Ickes as well:

> He was a creative thinker in a "gadget" sense: immediate steps to solve specific day-to-day problems. He had ideas such as the tree shelter belt in the drought areas; transcontinental through-highways with networks of feeder roads; huge dams and irrigation systems; resettlement projects for tenant farmers; civilian conservation work in the woods; a chain of small hospitals across the country; rural electrification; regional development; bridges and houses and parks. Not surprisingly, virtually all these ideas involved building tangible things. What excited Roosevelt was not grand economic or political theory but concrete achievements that people could touch and see and use.[13]

HAROLD ICKES'S FIRST action as public works administrator was to
select a deputy administrator. In July FDR gave him approval to hire
the 64-year-old retired Army engineer and government consultant
Col. Henry M. Waite to be his right-hand man. The two men then
began to build what a few months later Colonel Waite described as
"probably . . . the most unique organization that has ever been drawn
up in the United States or anywhere in the world. Never before has
an organization been started that had to be 100 per cent when it
started." [14]

Staffing and questions about organizational structure had to be accomplished almost overnight. With help from the Interior Department staff, Ickes and Waite began combing the country for engineers,
accountants, lawyers, and business executives to run the PWA. Ickes
wrote several letters to his close friend, public administration expert
Charles Merriam, asking for advice, and he met with another special-
ist, Louis Brownlow, on August 5, just as tempers reached a boiling
point among the staff.

After a tense meeting among Ickes, Assistant Secretary Burlew, and
Deputy Administrator Waite at which Ickes and Burlew thought that
Waite's proposal for elaborate organizations in each state would cost
too much—Burlew estimated that the overhead for the state organizations alone would cost some $2.5 million—"Colonel Waite went
down the hall exclaiming loudly that the trouble with the God-
damned proposition was that there wasn't anyone around the place
who knows a damn thing about what it was all about." Ickes hurriedly
put in a call for help to Louis Brownlow who happened to be in Washington and who came right over.

> We reviewed the whole situation, and it is his opinion that it is necessary
> to set up some such organization as . . . Waite proposes. I am fearful of the
> political pressure that will be brought to bear when it is discovered that
> there is some patronage that can be distributed in the states, but if we have
> to go ahead along this line to get the . . . speediest results, we will have to
> go ahead and I will do what I can to resist political pressure.[15]

Although Ickes recognized that he had to set up a considerably decentralized PWA—more decentralized than he would have preferred—he stood firm on centralizing one primary function of the
organization. After thrashing out the issue with Waite, Burlew, and
Brownlow, Ickes wrote,

I decided that instead of selecting lawyers in the states, we would select lawyers for our staff here and let all the legal work come here. . . . I decided on this policy . . . because the selection of lawyers would be the weakest link in the chain. There are always a lot of incompetent or crooked lawyers with strong political backing, and we can handle that situation better by building up our staff here than by finding a lawyer in each state.

He added that "we ought to be able to find engineers, accountants and that sort of employee who are relatively free from political influence."

To get the kind of legal talent for the PWA that he wanted, Ickes prevailed on two of Felix Frankfurter's most celebrated protégés in Washington during the early New Deal years: Tom Corcoran and Ben Cohen. Corcoran politely declined Ickes's offer of a high position within the new organization, but Ben Cohen, despite reservations, accepted. Cohen worked for about a year as assistant general counsel to the PWA, but he confessed to his mentor, Harvard professor Frankfurter, that "not being an administrator, it is quite a nervous strain and sometimes I fear I may break under it." [16] In 1934 Ickes, who developed a deep affection for the sensitive, brilliant Cohen (an affection reciprocated by the young man), moved him out of the PWA and appointed him general counsel to his National Power Policy Committee. This was a position more congenial to both Cohen's legal abilities and his emotional sensibilities, and in this capacity he and Tom Corcoran made history. They helped draft several of the most famous bills of the New Deal, including the Securities and Exchange Commission Act and the bitterly contested Public Utilities Holding Company Act.

Ickes and his embryonic staff continued resolving structural issues and looking for people to employ, even as they began pumping money into the economy. It was essential to do this right away, and the PWA staff discovered that the quickest route to spending the NIRA appropriation was through existing federal agencies and departments. From the outset, then, and due largely to the emergency situation, the PWA was divided into federal and nonfederal programs: On the federal side of the ledger, substantial sums of money were allocated to begin or to complete construction projects, such as Hoover Dam. As of August 17, 1933, a PWA document showed that out of an initial $100 million allocation authorized by FDR, a little over $76 million was already allotted and transferred. It was no coincidence that the Bureau of Reclamation in Ickes's Interior Department was given the lion's share, an awesome $63 million, whereas the U.S. Army Corps of Engineers received about $6 million, and the Department of Commerce something over $7 million. Another $61 million was allocated, but not yet transferred, to agencies in the Agriculture and War departments, among others.[17]

On the nonfederal side, spending couldn't be accomplished overnight. It took time for states and municipalities to appoint advisory boards, select projects, and pass legislation in order to conform to the requirements of the Public Works Administration, requirements that themselves were in the process of being devised. In an address given before the Conference of Mayors in September of 1933, Administrator Ickes sketched out the basic terms of the nonfederal program: State and municipal governments could apply for an outright grant covering 30 percent of the cost of the project; they could also apply for a federal loan for the other 70 percent, at an interest rate of 4 percent over thirty years, providing they came up with the necessary collateral. "The Public Works Program . . . offers the greatest opportunity for municipal improvements in the history of any country," Ickes told the mayors and the millions of Americans who had tuned in to listen to the speech. He added that he considered the federal government's terms to be very generous, but that he intended to run a tight ship under the new partnership. We cannot solve our economic and social problems "under a doctrine of 'rugged individualism,' " Ickes said, "which to me means precisely the same as 'the devil take the hindmost.' "[18]

Initially, Ickes's PWA was enthusiastically received throughout the country; even Col. Robert McCormick's conservative *Chicago Tribune* had complimentary things to say about it. An editorial run in July commented:

> Secretary Ickes as a resident of Chicago knows how this city has been bled so white by federal taxes for worthless projects at Boulder Dam and elsewhere that it cannot pay its own employees. He has also seen corruption at work at the Boulevard bridge and other Thompson projects. He is therefore well equipped to turn down the pork spoilsmen on the one hand and the contractor spoilsmen on the other.[19]

But with the compliments came the criticism. Ickes's high professional standards for the PWA, which were precisely the old Progressive values of honesty, efficiency, and economy in government, collided with the desperation that shrouded the nation in 1933: He was simply not spending money fast enough. An editorial published in an August edition of *Business Week,* of all places, summed up the criticism that surfaced at the outset of the PWA and that would dog Ickes for the next six years: "Mr. Ickes is running a fire department on the principles of a good, sound bond house," the editor lamented.[20]

Ickes recognized the need for dispatch as well as anyone did, and he did a lot to try to get things going as rapidly as possible—including working twelve-hour days, six days a week, and attempting to abolish the Board of Public Works, which he felt caused unnecessary delays. "It takes four or five hours of valuable time every week doing something that the engineer, the attorney for the Board, and myself could dispose of in half an hour," Ickes wrote at the end of July.[21] Nevertheless, he also understood that he was confronted with a dilemma that probably never would be resolved to everyone's satisfaction. He recognized that the PWA had the potential to be nothing more than a bottomless pork barrel that could ruin the entire Roosevelt presidency. He was utterly determined not to let that happen, either to himself or to the president, and so the price he paid for earning the nickname "Honest Harold" was a barrage of criticism for being too cautious an administrator. It was a trade-off he grudgingly made, and during the six years he ran Public Works he stuck by his guns, though often leveling them, as he loved to do, at his critics.

The delays in the public works program, which were especially evident through the summer and fall of 1933, can be attributed only in part to Harold Ickes's temperament. Scholars of the New Deal tend to exaggerate the importance of Ickes's personality on this point while ignoring other reasons for the start-up delays. Joseph Lash went furthest with his criticism when he wrote, "One will never know what [Gen. Hugh] Johnson might have done with the Public Works title, but giving it to Ickes proved a mistake. The secretary was so determined to keep the program free of graft and corruption that few projects were authorized."[22]

Ickes did indeed hold the public works hoop high, not only with respect to graft, but on aesthetic and equal opportunity employment requirements as well. But the fact that there were delays in spending, especially in the nonfederal portion of the program, had less to do with personal idiosyncrasies and more to do with organizational and institutional politics. It cannot be forgotten that the public works program of 1933 represented a radical departure from the past; it involved a fundamental restructuring of the relationship among federal, state, and local entities—not to mention the fact that the emergency situation mandated the creation, in record time, of a federal organization to embody the new relationship. Harold Ickes and the other New Deal administrators were breaking new political ground.

The frenetic pace of activity in those first months in office allowed Harold Ickes little time for reflection, and so he only dimly discerned this fact. Nevertheless, as early as May, Ickes was acting on the proposition that the new public works program would entail some basic restructuring. On May 20, Ickes wrote a letter to one of his political allies in Chicago, James Denvir, who worked in the bailiff's office, to tell him of the pending NIRA bill. Ickes, who had not yet been named administrator and didn't know for certain that he would be, nevertheless suggested that Denvir get busy so that their hometown of Chicago wouldn't be left out. He wrote:

> I don't know whether you need any additional legislation to enable [the city of] Chicago to apply for a share of these Federal funds. If you do need additional legislation, you ought to have a bill drafted at once so as to put you in the most favorable possible position. There are many things in the way of improvements that Chicago not only could well use but actually needs.[23]

FEDERAL DOLLARS GOING *directly* to municipalities and to private corporations for the construction of bridges, sewage treatment plants, mass transit, public housing, schools, museums, and on and on—this constituted one of the many innovations of Roosevelt's New Deal. While Harry Hopkins was busy putting thousands of unemployed men and women on the dole, and Gen. Hugh Johnson was "strong-arming" key industries into accepting government-initiated codes, Harold Ickes was occupied with restructuring intergovernmental relationships through the PWA.

Not everyone was pleased with the new arrangement. The Democratic governor of Massachusetts, Joseph B. Ely, saw clearly the radical nature of what was happening and proceeded to call it to Ickes's attention. On August 2 Governor Ely telephoned Ickes to discuss the new arrangements. Ickes related in his diary that Ely told him that "there was some administrative body in his state which had some sort of control over municipal finances, and he wanted me to say that no public works would be given to any municipality in Massachusetts without first being submitted to this board and getting its approval." Ickes responded that the PWA policy was already announced, which was to "consider every proposition on its merits," regardless of whether the proposal had come from local or state government. The conversation then became heated and Ickes hung up on the governor after he started to "lay down the law" to him.

But Governor Ely persisted, and the same day as they exchanged views over the telephone he wrote Administrator Ickes a letter, further spelling out his objections to the new policy:

> It has been a very laborious undertaking for Massachusetts to rehabilitate the credit of our municipalities. . . . If you are interested at all in the fundamental theory upon which the federal government was created, and by which the municipalities are created, . . . it would be plain that direct contact between the federal government and the municipalities is an affront to the sovereignty of this Commonwealth.[24]

Two days later Ickes replied to the telephone conversation and follow-up letter. He ignored the constitutional issues raised by the governor, and intimated that the governor's State Emergency Board wanted a veto for "partisan political purposes."

When word of the row between the federal administrator and the governor leaked out, it could have meant trouble for Ickes; instead, Roosevelt was amused. Ickes was among several guests at a Sunday luncheon at the White House on August 13, which he described as "delightful," and where the conversation flowed back and forth "with all the freedom of a family circle." Roosevelt made no mention about the substance of Governor Ely's objections to the PWA program but instead complimented Ickes on how he handled Ely. "At the luncheon the President said that the best story that had come out of Washington since March 4 was the conversation I had over the telephone with Governor Ely. . . . He said it was grand." [25]

Several months later Governor Ely came to Washington and met with Ickes. By then it appeared that Ely had accepted the new institutional arrangements. "It was with him that I had a passage of arms . . . some time ago," Ickes wrote. "He seems like a pretty high-class man and we got along very well." But while the governor lost this early battle over states' rights, the Supreme Court would soon take up the whole issue of the constitutionality of the NIRA and how the

Roosevelt administration had implemented it. Ickes's authority would be questioned again.

ALTHOUGH THERE WERE a number of very good reasons why Ickes's PWA wasn't able to spend money as fast as many people would have liked, Ickes was nevertheless the head of the organization, and so he continued to be held personally accountable. Through the summer and fall of 1933, as applications from state and local governments poured into the agency's mailroom, so did complaints about delays. Not only was Ickes receiving them, but so was FDR. On August 19, the president sent Ickes a short memo, asking him whether he couldn't speed up funds going to the State of Texas, and in early November one of South Carolina's congressmen telegrammed the president to complain about delays in the PWA program. Representative McSwain told the president that only 60 out of 942 federal buildings "contemplated by Congress have been approved." Moreover, there appeared to be gross inequities among the states; McSwain pointed out that one-third of all the buildings approved to date were in New York, Massachusetts, and California.[26]

Concerned about the delays and his friend's career, Charles Merriam wrote Ickes early in October offering more advice about how to run the PWA: He reiterated his earlier observation that Ickes simply had to delegate more responsibility and that he must find a means to accelerate the authorization process. Ickes immediately wrote back, thanking him for his advice, but pointing out that the bottlenecks weren't where Merriam, and many others, thought they were:

> Our real difficulty is not in passing the projects, although there is some delay there, but in getting the work started after we make the allocations. If some way can be devised to speed up the government departments and the State and municipal authorities to which money has been allocated, I would be delighted.
>
> You have one wrong notion about which I would like to set you right. I am not trying to supervise every detail myself. I am giving the widest possible authority to Colonel Waite and his staff. Believe it or not, but I actually sign important contracts involving millions of dollars without even pausing to read them cursorily. I am not sure but that I haven't paid enough attention to details in public works.[27]

The same day as Ickes wrote Merriam, he and Colonel Waite held a meeting of the professional staff of the PWA in order to, as Ickes told the crowd assembled in the Interior Department auditorium, "get better acquainted and see whether it is not possible to cooperate more effectively than we have been cooperating."[28] In his lengthy remarks Ickes highlighted the problem areas within the PWA, but he was also careful not to be too critical; it was essentially a pep talk that he delivered on October 3. The major reason for the delays, Ickes told his staff, resided in the legal division. The engineering, administrative, and financial divisions were operating quite effectively, but the legal staff needed to reorganize. The PWA also needed more lawyers, Ickes observed: "We are willing to employ lawyers. We want to employ lawyers. If anyone here knows of any likely lawyer, we will see that the word gets into the proper channels for consideration. I want a day and night force put on here, if necessary."

Ickes also stressed to the crowd the importance of responsiveness in their dealings with the public. This was something about which he felt very strongly, and during the thirteen years that he held office, communicating with the public—through a variety of channels—became a distinguishing characteristic of his administration. In October Ickes told the PWA about his public philosophy:

> On the question of handling correspondence, I think probably the most important duty we have is to answer all communications promptly. I have always conceived that it was the duty of every public official to welcome communications. It is hard sometimes. If you get some that I do, you will agree with me, but, after all, every citizen has a right to address his government. The mail is the only means of communication for hundreds of thousands of them, and he forms his opinion of the government, whether it is a good government or whether it is not a good government by the promptness of the reply that he receives and by the sympathetic nature of the reply that he receives.[29]

Ickes then proceeded to tell his staff that they had been ignoring his executive order on the subject of mail, that he had ordered Louis Glavis and his Investigations Division to look into the matter, and that they had discovered many irregularities—especially in the Legal Division—about handling mail. Some letters going back nearly sixty days "still remain unanswered," Glavis's report noted. "Unacceptable," Ickes told the PWA staff.

Ickes's insistence at the outset of his tenure about correct procedures for mail handling, among other things, helped form his image as a tough administrator. As one of the Interior Department's solicitors remarked, his success as an executive was due in part to his "generally wholesome talents for terror."[30]

"I AM VERY TIRED this week, more so than usual, but I am trying to hang on," the super cabinet officer who was holding down three full-time job confided to his diary at the beginning of October. He added, though, that "I have one satisfaction and that is that at least I have outlasted General Johnson. He went to the hospital several days ago for a minor operation but . . . he was so run down that he hasn't strength to recuperate as fast as he ought to. While he was going, General Johnson undoubtedly put in longer hours than I did, but when it is considered that I have been working as I have since March 5, I have him beaten by several miles."[31]

Pride goeth before a fall, and Ickes's fall occurred on Monday, December 11. As he was hurrying down the steps of his home on his way to work, he slipped on the early morning ice and landed hard on the ground. He managed to get up and make his way to the car where his chauffeur was waiting. Despite being in great pain, Ickes headed down the road to the office. A few hours later he was lying in bed at the naval hospital: "An X ray at the hospital showed that one rib had been broken and almost broken loose as well from the spinal column. Fortunately, the spinal column . . . was not injured. . . . Accordingly, I was taped and . . . put to bed, where I have been all week with several more days of the same sort of thing in prospect."

Although his forced confinement gave Ickes a much needed rest, he nevertheless found himself in agony during the two weeks he was laid up. But the pain from the broken rib was minor compared with the agony that he experienced when rumors reached him that Roosevelt, in response to the numerous criticisms he'd received that fall, was considering a major reorganization of the recovery program. On December 14 Ickes wrote FDR a note requesting that he not take some $80 million from the PWA and give it to Harry Hopkins's organization. Ickes told the president, "We are making a heroic effort for a better showing in those States that ought to have more allotments."[32]

A few days later Ickes wrote the president another letter. Information reached him that, far worse than merely raiding the PWA allocation, Roosevelt was now considering abolishing the PWA. Ickes pleaded with the president from his hospital bed not to do it. Roosevelt responded with a nice informal note telling Harold not to worry and to take care of himself. At the same time he sent Ickes's letter to Harry Hopkins with a handwritten note, asking, "What do you think of this?" Hopkins returned the letter to FDR with the following handwritten note: "Mr. President: I agree [with Ickes]." [33]

It was a close call. Harold Ickes and Harry Hopkins found themselves competing vigorously in many arenas over the next decade. At times they showed themselves to be intimate friends, and at other times they were spiteful adversaries. More than a few people observed that the two men behaved like siblings. It was ironic that, unknown to Ickes, one of his major rivals turned out to be instrumental in saving his PWA from an early death through reorganization, thus allowing Ickes to accomplish some extraordinary programs under that title.

CHAPTER 5

OVER A BARREL

ICKES'S OIL ADMINISTRATION

EARLY IN SEPTEMBER 1933, about 2,000 railroad cars filled with East Texas oil stood motionless on sidings in Chicago's trainyards. The oil was rushed to market in anticipation of the federal government's crackdown on the interstate transport of oil produced in excess of state quotas. The East Texas producers, along with certain Southern California companies, were notorious for breaking the rules, but they were not the only guilty parties in bringing the oil industry, then the third most important in the country, to virtual anarchy. Upon learning of the situation in Chicago, Petroleum Administrator Ickes sent an urgent memo to Louis Glavis, his director of investigations, to make sure that their new regulations were enforced.[1] But for every successful intervention by the federal government, there were numerous instances of "hot oil" reaching its illegal destination. Regulating the oil industry proved to be Ickes's most difficult assignment during those first two years of the New Deal, and it was one that he reluctantly assumed when FDR gave him his third full-time job on August 29, 1933.

Actually Ickes began wrestling with the oil problem the very first day he took office. His responsibilities as head of the Interior Department nominally covered the entire array of the country's natural resources, including valuable minerals such as coal, oil, copper, silver, and gold. The U.S. Geological Survey and the Bureau of Mines, units within Interior, functioned as data-gathering organizations that provided estimates on the nation's mineral wealth. In addition the secretary of the interior chaired the Federal Oil Conservation Board, a coordinating committee created by a previous Republican administration. The four-member board consisted of the heads of the executive departments with a primary interest in oil—Interior, Navy, War, and Commerce.

Until 1933, however, the Interior secretary's role in oil matters was marginal, except for the occasional headline-making scandal over government collusion with the industry, the most recent of which had been Secretary Albert Fall's Teapot Dome debacle. After a congressional investigation led by Sen. Thomas Walsh (Mont.) uncovered possible illegalities, Fall was convicted in 1923 of accepting bribes from two oil men. Oil and, to a lesser extent, coal were two issues secretaries of the interior knew they had to approach with the utmost care. Harold Ickes knew this as well as anyone. If anything could get him in trouble, it was oil. Indeed, an oil-related issue finally forced his resignation in February 1946, but for thirteen years Ickes managed to steer his way through its treacherous political cross-currents. It was not an insignificant accomplishment.

When the Roosevelt administration took over in March 1933 it could not ignore the fact that the oil industry was out of control. State authority had not been equal to the task of regulating the powerful but fragmented industry, and a number of the governors of the seventeen oil-producing states, including Alf Landon of Kansas and Gifford Pinchot of Pennsylvania, appealed to President Roosevelt to stabilize the industry.

The major problem was overproduction. The nation's 340,000 wells were pumping oil that far exceeded demand, and much of it was being sold on the black market for ridiculously low prices. Ten cents a barrel—and even four cents, less than what a bottle of newly legalized beer cost—was not uncommon. Finding a means of controlling the production of "hot oil," so named because it was produced in excess of what state governments allowed, thus became a major priority for the Roosevelt administration during the early months of the New Deal.

Solving the overproduction problem meant coming to terms with a deeply divided industry. During the 1930s, the principal fault line ran between the "majors" and the "independents," but within the ranks of the independents there was a further split between independents who favored federal controls imposed by a liberally inclined administration and a small group of independents opposed to both state and federal controls. The majors were just that: A group of twenty vertically integrated firms whose names—Standard Oil of New Jersey, Gulf Oil, Texaco, and Standard Oil of California—were familiar to most Americans. The interests of the majors were represented, for the most part, by the American Petroleum Institute (API). The API was a trade association whose influence over government policy grew rapidly during the first three decades of the twentieth century as Americans developed their long-lasting love affair with the gas-guzzling automobile. The hundreds of independent producers—generally much smaller companies that operated with far less capital than the majors— were organized into two groups: the Independent Producers' Association (IPA) and the Independent Producers Association Opposed to Monopoly. While the majors were a powerful group in the 1930s, so were the independents; it was estimated that they controlled over 50 percent of the market in oil production and 40 percent of the retail gasoline market at the outset of the New Deal.[2]

Neither Roosevelt nor his Interior secretary came to the task of regulating oil with any previous experience. In a meeting with a group of independents in April, the president was distressingly candid in telling them that he knew little about the issue. One of the oil men recalled that FDR "was almost boyish as he asked us to reverse in our minds the ordinary conception that 'one teacher usually teaches many pupils.' Today, he laughingly declared, he was the pupil—we were the teachers."[3] Harold Ickes was no expert on oil matters either, but unlike Roosevelt he wasn't about to let that be known. After a month in office he wrote, "Some of the big old oil moguls have the habit of writing to me saying that if I want to see them, they will be glad to call. . . . I tell them very politely that I have no desire to see them, but if they want to see me they may come in."[4]

While Ickes was no expert on oil, he refused to be intimidated by anyone, perhaps especially by the big, old oil moguls whom he distrusted. Moreover, he was not without intellectual resources, including being a very fast learner. When the oil industry was thrown into his lap, Ickes drew upon some strongly held convictions that could be traced back to the Progressivism of his youth and young adulthood. First of all, Ickes believed wholeheartedly in the turn-of-the-century doctrine of the wise use of natural resources, of the necessity of conserving, for future use, the nation's material wealth. Waste bothered him enormously. Lean conditions during his childhood and his mother's tireless efforts to make ends meet left their imprint; throughout most of his life Ickes was a careful, fastidious, even penurious person. These qualities showed up in both the private and public dimensions of his life. Second, he believed strongly in the evils of monopoly capitalism, in the necessity of government to serve as a countervailing power to the private concentrations of wealth and economic power. As did his earliest political heroes, John Harlan, John Altgeld, Louis Brandeis, and especially Theodore Roosevelt, Ickes felt that government should help not just the rich and powerful but the ordinary citizen as well. He thus approached the oil issue with the firm belief that conservation of this irreplaceable natural resource was a necessity, and that the small-fry, the independents, should not be squeezed out of business by government policies.

He was to discover, however, that when it came to oil these two cherished principles were at war with one another. As some of the independents charged all along, conservation was a fine-sounding principle but it was the tool, they said, the majors were using during the Great Depression to drive them out of business. "It would have taken a Solon to resolve that particular dilemma," Ickes's son, Raymond, commented some fifty-five years later about his father's role in regulating oil.[5]

To deal with the overproduction problem, Secretary Ickes began where most efforts at problem-solving begin, with a fact-finding conference. Just days after taking office, he asked the secretary to the Federal Oil Conservation Board, E. S. Rochester, to plan the meeting. Rochester scheduled a three-day conference to begin on March 27 and invited the governors of the oil-producing states and representatives from all factions of the industry. The governors or their representatives (only one governor, Republican Alf Landon of Kansas, showed up in person) were to meet separately from the industry representatives, and from there a joint government-industry committee would be formed to get down to the serious business of drafting federal legislation to address the emergency.

As the oil men and the state officials flocked to Washington and secured rooms at the downtown hotels, Rochester sent Ickes two memos.[6] The first one read, "The Governors' conference is in good shape." The second memo, however, foreshadowed events to come:

> The INDUSTRY conference is NOT in good shape.
> More than 200 industry leaders have arrived in Washington expecting you to accord them a hearing. The American Petroleum Institute directors are here in a body. These are the heads of the giant corporations. Independent Petroleum Association leaders are here in a mass. All day Sunday these organized groups held separate meetings in the big hotels. Congressional leaders were present. . . . Both groups expect you to sit with them and hear their story.

For three days that is what Secretary Ickes did. He officially launched the conference by addressing the whole group in the Interior Department auditorium on Monday the twenty-seventh, and then spent much of Tuesday and Wednesday hearing each group's respective story. The government officials of the oil-producing states posed few problems; they were nearly unanimous in feeling that strong federal intervention was absolutely necessary, and some even went so far as to suggest that an "oil czar" be appointed for a two-year duration. Most of the industry representatives in attendance didn't feel it was necessary to go that far, but they did acknowledge the need for some federal emergency regulation. Governor Landon of Kansas chaired a committee of fifteen, composed of state officials, representatives from the majors, and spokesmen for the independents. On Tuesday they met with Ickes and went over a draft proposal "which on its face looked pretty fair," the secretary commented, "and at least gave us a working basis." [7]

However, a group of independents, mainly from the Southern California oil fields, posed serious problems to an early agreement and also gave Ickes his first appreciation of how byzantine the oil industry was. The group's spokesman was oil executive John B. Elliott, who also was a power in the Democratic Party, having helped elect Woodrow Wilson to two terms as president and Franklin Roosevelt as well. He was also very close to California's Sen. William McAdoo.

Elliott and his delegation came to see Ickes on Tuesday morning and again on Wednesday. At their first meeting, Ickes wrote, "They did a lot of haranguing and speech making. They really had a chip on their shoulders. In the end, I managed to find out that they don't want anything at all done to curtail oil production, but they do want action to break up the big oil combinations, on the theory that they are in restraint of trade." [8] At 8:30 the next morning Elliott and his group were in again. This time they were calmer and more sensible, Ickes observed, but he learned that "the only concrete suggestion they had to make to meet the present emergency was that nothing at all be done [to curb production]."

When the secretary sat in on a meeting of Governor Landon's group of fifteen on Tuesday, he noted that several powerful men were present, including Walter Teagle of Standard of New Jersey, Ralph Holmes of Texaco, and Kenneth Kingsbury, president of Standard of California. Five men representing the independents were on the committee as well, but "how independent the independents are, God alone knows," Ickes wrote. He was learning fast about the divisive state of the industry; that morning "Elliott and his crowd insist[ed] that they [the IPA] are not independent at all, but really are under inescapable obligations to the big fellows." The only real independents were in his group, Elliott alleged.

The substantive results of the three-day conference were meager, although it did provide an important learning opportunity for Ickes and even for the president, who also had heard from oil men while they were in Washington. Some hoped for, but few really expected, a repeat of FDR's New Deal magic that stopped the panicked run on the nation's banks earlier that month. But a resolution to the problems besetting the oil industry could be found only in bridging the deep divisions within the industry itself, and not, unfortunately, in inspired appeals by FDR to millions of Americans to put aside their fears about the solvency of the nation's banks.

Nevertheless, some ideas for federal legislation came out of the conference, and on April 3 the president gave out a press release outlining the problem for the public and clearly demarcating the federal government's role in the oil morass. He rejected the call for a federally imposed moratorium on oil production, throwing it back in the laps of the industry and the state governments. However, the president did commit himself to asking Congress for legislation prohibiting the interstate transport of oil produced in violation of state laws, and he also looked sympathetically on a suggestion emanating from John Elliott's group, the Independent Producers Association Opposed to Monopoly. This was the call for a classic piece of antitrust legislation that would divorce the ownership of interstate oil pipelines "from other branches of the oil industry."[9]

On April 5 the president sent a short memo to Attorney General Cummings and Interior Secretary Ickes asking the two gentlemen to get together

> and study existing pipeline legislation, with the object of giving the Interstate Commerce Commission complete authority over them. The point is that the pipe lines should be divorced in ownership from the producing and refining companies. If we can get a short and simple bill providing for this and for complete Federal control of pipe lines, I think I can get it through Congress.[10]

Ickes supported both the president's views on pipelines and his cautious approach to the overproduction problem. Writing to Sen. Peter Norbeck on April 4, he said, "I do believe that the President is proceeding wisely and sanely. He has taken the position that he is willing to help the States and the industry help themselves, but, after all, the major problem is one for the industry and for the States to solve."[11]

The secretary, however, was not supportive of the behavior of his assistant on oil, E. S. Rochester. Ickes learned that Rochester was bragging about how important he was in the new administration and telling tall tales about writing speeches for cabinet officers and even for senators. Over dinner with Hiram Johnson and his wife on March 31—in his first few months in Washington Ickes dined with them two or three times a week—he listened while the senator read aloud a confidential letter Rochester had written to a close friend. Somehow, the letter found its way into the hands of one of the independent oil men from Southern California, and from there to the senior senator from California, Hiram Johnson, before it was finally relayed to Ickes. The "arrogantly boastful" tone of the letter revealed that Rochester was too much of a wheeler-dealer, Ickes said, adding that "apparently he doesn't realize that he has the great fault of saying too much on paper."[12] On April 1, first thing in the morning, Ickes fired him.

Rochester angrily wrote Ickes the same day, suggesting that he had been set up by some members of the industry:

I am really grateful to you for your brief memorandum telling me I could quit today. . . . It may interest you to know that on two occasions I tendered my resignation, but it was not accepted. I remained as an accommodation to Cabinet officers who seemingly felt that one who had . . . received the personal commendation of the last Democratic President and every single member of his Cabinet . . . might be worthy and of decent caliber.

I might add further . . . that I am not now and never have been under any obligation, directly or indirectly, in any manner, shape, or form, to any living member of the American Petroleum Institute, representing the major interests, or to the great independent units, nor to State representatives.

You have my sympathy in your role as arbiter among the great and near-great of the oil industry.[13]

WHILE SOME SEGMENTS of the economy showed faint signs of recovery through the spring, oil did not. The situation worsened through April and May as the president, his advisors, and members of Congress deliberated about what to do. Miriam A. Ferguson, governor of the nation's largest oil-producing state, wired both FDR and Ickes in early May that the situation in Texas was desperate: The illegal production of oil approximated its legal production, and cutthroat competition had driven the price of a barrel of oil down to the ruinous rate of ten cents. Even a declaration of martial law hadn't helped. The governor likened the oil industry to the state that the banking industry was in on March 4, when Roosevelt took decisive action.[14] She pleaded for the appointment of a federal czar, who would be given emergency powers of at least two years' duration.

At about the same time as the Texas governor wired Washington for help, Ickes wrote the president about the oil mess. He described the legislation that many governors, and the majors, wanted to see enacted during the present session of Congress. He also reiterated the need for action, but stated bluntly that he wasn't sure what was needed:

It is obvious that the Government is without accurate knowledge of the facts involved in this situation. We have listened to charges and counter-charges and we are in no position to say that both charges and counter-charges may not be justified. But . . . we do know that this situation can not continue much longer without disastrous results to the oil industry and to the country. Whether the extraordinary powers provided for in the bill referred to, or some modified powers, should be granted to any present officer of the Government or to a new officer to be selected, is a matter of policy which only you can decide.[15]

A week later, and with no apparent action forthcoming from the White House, Ickes confided to his intimate friend Hiram Johnson that certain political divisions on oil appeared to be stalling action: On the one hand the governor of Texas, along with the governors of Kansas, Oklahoma, and Pennsylvania, were lobbying hard in Washington for federal control. "On the other hand, the Texas State Senate has adopted a resolution protesting against Federal control. . . . This is a most difficult situation. I doubt if any Federal official wants the responsibility that the proposed bill would place upon the Secretary of the Interior. I know I do not want to assume such a burden." When Ickes again brought up the oil situation with FDR, he found him still straddling the fence. "Whether or not the President is going to take any action . . . , I can't quite make up my mind. For my part," he added, "I think drastic action is vitally necessary and that we are running a great risk in postponing action further."[16]

Through the critical month of May Ickes's views solidified but so did the opposition's. He pressed the president for a separate bill on oil, giving the chief executive extensive powers to regulate the industry. FDR, however, along with some powerful congressmen, leaned toward incorporating oil in the NIRA bill. By mid-May Ickes noticed that many of the major oil companies were no longer in favor of stringent federal legislation, as they previously had been, which served only to increase his anxiety about the whole issue. "My apprehension over this oil situation has not abated one particle," he wrote on May 18.[17]

By the end of the month any prospect for a separate bill dealing with oil was dead. The most that Ickes, and other proponents of federal control such as senators Harrison and Thomas, and some of the oil-state governors, could hope for was that the provisions regulating the oil industry would be included in the emergency recovery bill (NIRA). But even that legislation was in trouble on the Hill, as the Senate, through April and May, harassed Roosevelt over the emergency plan. New Deal historian Frank Freidel wrote:

> The Finance Committee seriously battered the measure, adopting by a vote of 12 to 7 McAdoo's proposal to strip it of its enforcement power, the licensing clause. It also voted an amendment running counter to the president's preparation for the London Economic Conference, an embargo on

all imports that would interfere with operation of the recovery program. Further, it had failed only by a narrow margin of 8 to 10 to adopt Senator Bennett Champ Clark's amendment to strike out the entire bill except for the public works provisions. Ominously, seven Democrats had joined Republicans in opposing the Administration.[18]

Senator McAdoo of California was one of them.

By early June the president had garnered enough votes to pass the emergency recovery bill but the question remained whether or not it would include federal oil regulation. On June 7 Secretary Ickes spent most of the day on Capitol Hill, first testifying on behalf of the grazing reform bill in the House and then rushing over to the offices of senators Harrison and Thomas. Earlier that day Roosevelt told Thomas that "while he wanted the power conferred by the [Thomas] amendment, he didn't want the amendment pressed unduly if it meant deferring a final vote on the Industries Control Bill."[19] Ickes and the senators agreed that that would be the strategy they would follow— they would press for oil regulation but not too strenuously. "The situation on the Hill is really dangerous," Ickes noted, "although so far he [FDR] has kept Congress within reasonable bounds."

Tom Connally of Texas and William Gibbs McAdoo of California constituted two big roadblocks in Congress to the administration's plans for economic recovery, including the regulation of oil. Connally happened to see Secretary Ickes literally closeted in the Senate cloakroom with Harrison and Thomas on the seventh, so he rushed over to McAdoo's office, and together they collared Ickes. "The two of them went at me pretty hard," Ickes wrote, threatening to strike out the entire oil amendment if the Connally version wasn't accepted by the administration. McAdoo and Ickes proceeded to cross swords; the senator became dictatorial and condescending—attitudes that were like a red flag to the scrappy Ickes—and while Ickes managed to hold his temper, he bluntly told McAdoo that "he and I just differed fundamentally on the oil question; that I did not believe that any man or set of men had a right, for their own purposes, to exploit an irreplaceable national resource; that the interests of the nation were paramount."

The Thomas amendment, which Ickes favored, was defeated and Henry Doherty, a retired oil man, wrote the president to tell him why, if he didn't know already: "The owners of flush fields in Texas and

California have boasted right along that their representatives in the Senate and the House had the power and would ditch the whole legislative program rather than submit to any restrictions of production in either state." [20]

"We failed to get the oil legislation that we wanted," Ickes wrote to a friend in Kansas City on the day that Congress passed the famous National Industrial Recovery Act.[21] While the provisions contained in Section 9 of the NIRA weren't all that Ickes felt was needed, it did provide for federal intervention in the industry, and provided the basis for the establishment, in August, of a Petroleum Administration. On June 14 President Roosevelt put Gen. Hugh Johnson in charge of what might well have been the most critical task of the New Deal that summer: to negotiate NRA codes with each of the nation's ten major industries, including the oil industry.

Johnson went about his task as befitted a military officer. The president had the entire cabinet in stitches in late July as he described "how Johnson rushed into [my] office two . . . days ago with his coat tails standing out behind him . . . and laid three industrial codes on [my] desk for signature. He said in a hurried voice that they must all be signed at once in order to be taken back and promulgated. As [I] was signing the last one, General Johnson looked at his watch and said he had just five minutes to catch an airplane, and dashed out as rapidly as he had dashed in. . . . He took an airplane with the codes in his pocket and he hasn't been seen since," FDR merrily remarked.

Once Johnson was finished with the oil industry (and vice-versa), it was Ickes's turn. On August 29 the president signed an executive order giving Harold Ickes his third full-time assignment in the New Deal. A thankless task if ever there was one, it was nonetheless an important one, for it marked the first federal attempt at regulating the huge, powerful, and fragmented oil industry, which included not only production but refining, transportation, and the retailing of gasoline and other petroleum products. Though privately he dreaded the assignment, he wrote Roosevelt the following day about policy matters and concluded by saying, "May I take this occasion to thank you most sincerely for giving me this further administrative responsibility? I am conscious of only one desire and that is to do whatever I can to help you work out the policies of your administration." [22]

THE OIL CODE that was hammered out between General Johnson and the industry provided for three measures to achieve a modicum of order: The establishment of federally mandated production quotas for each oil-producing state, import limitations on oil produced overseas, and minimum prices.[23] Harold Ickes's Petroleum Administration encountered problems in implementing all three measures, but price fixing was, understandably, the most problematic. Some groups, both within government and outside of it, wanted no price regulation at all, some wanted only the regulation of crude oil prices, while still others argued for price control down to the gasoline pump.

Roosevelt initially appeared to favor price regulation from producer to consumer. A memo given to him after the passage of the NIRA argued that this was the only way to avoid "the vicious circle in which we now live—successively lower gasoline prices, followed by crude price recessions." The unnamed author explained why:

> It should be remembered that we have two distinctly different kinds of price cutters in the marketing of oil products: First, the small fellow who thinks that the only way he can get business is to undersell. Second, some of the large units who are apparently waging a war of extermination by holding margins and prices at such low levels that only the strongest can long survive. Some of the latter class have plainly stated that it is their purpose to cure the ills of the industry by killing off a large percentage of those engaged in it.[24]

Impressed with the argument, FDR sent it to his new petroleum administrator with a handwritten note telling him to discuss the issue with Governor Pinchot and Michael L. Benedum, a Pennsylvania oil man supportive of the New Deal who helped draft the NRA legislation, and then report back to him.

While the president considered how far to go in regulating oil, Harold Ickes in September occupied himself with setting up yet another organizational unit that would be directed from his office in the Interior Department. He now had three titles over his door, that of Interior secretary, public works administrator, and oil administrator. He barely had time to get acquainted with the Interior Department and its functions before Roosevelt asked him to set up a Public Works Administration. He was in the process of doing that when the president handed him the NRA oil code to administer.

Fortunately, Harold Ickes had a talent for organization, which had not gone unnoticed by FDR, so he put together a preliminary structure in less than a month. Oil executives across the country were asked to form an advisory committee in which "representation [would] be given to all the various groups and factions within the industry." [25] By September 10, a fifty-member Planning and Coordination Committee (P&CC), divided into nine subcommittees, was in place, and a Petroleum Administration Board (PAB), drawn largely from his pool of existing personnel, was created. When Harold Ickes was asked by the president to put in double and triple duty, the secretary had no choice other than to extend that policy to his staff. This was especially the case inasmuch as FDR was insisting on economy in government at the same time as the administration was taking on sweeping new responsibilities. Ickes was fond of pointing out to critics of the New Deal that he held down three full-time jobs but got paid for only one.

A Petroleum Administration thus was formed by overlapping responsibilities and functions. Personnel from the Department's Geological Survey, the Bureau of Mines, the solicitor's office, and the Division of Investigations were assigned to help implement the oil code. The new solicitor for the Interior Department, Nathan Margold, became chairman of the PAB, and Charles Fahy, an attorney hired by Ickes in March, spent much of his time in 1933 and 1934 working on oil issues. Louis Glavis, director of the Investigations Division, also found himself immersed in oil, and frequently bickered with Margold over policy. A memo Glavis sent to Ickes in February 1934 revealed the extent of the overlap among Interior, PWA, and the Oil Administration: Glavis asked for an additional $200,000 for oil enforcement. Two days later Ickes responded by telling him to be patient. "We are hoping that Congress will levy a tax per barrel on crude oil to finance the Oil Administration. I don't want to draw on Public Works funds for . . . this sort of thing [more] than is absolutely necessary." [26]

There was no dearth of advice on whom to select for committees and how to implement the oil code, Ickes discovered. Some of it he welcomed, while other solicitations irritated him no end. An old friend from his Chicago days, Col. Frank Knox, who was publisher of the *Chicago Daily News,* prevailed upon Ickes to have a friend of his appointed to the planning committee. Ickes was quick to comply. On August 31 he wrote Knox: "When I conferred with the President last Monday . . . on the makeup of the oil committee, I suggested that Henry M. Dawes be substituted for one man already on the list and he was kind enough to accept my suggestion. So your friend Dawes is on and he can thank you for it." [27] Ickes also appreciated advice on oil matters from his friend Hiram Johnson.

On the other end of the spectrum were Assistant Secretary of War Harry Woodring, the imposing senator from Nevada, Key Pittman, and Sen. William Gibbs McAdoo. That Harold Ickes was temperamental and had a fairly short fuse is a matter of record. Nevertheless, his responses to individuals had a lot to do with how he was approached, which is not an uncommon trait. At a time when his nerves were frayed to the breaking point by having three jobs at once, Ickes began snapping back. On October 3 he wrote, "A few days ago I received from Assistant Secretary of War Woodring a most astonishing letter in which he expressed strong disapproval of certain acts of mine relating to personnel matters . . . in the Public Works and in the Oil Administration. His letter was not even courteous and he lectured me as if I were a school boy." Ickes replied in kind telling Woodring that "it was absolutely no concern of his how I ran my Department and that I didn't propose to be dictated to by him or anyone else." [28]

At the same time Key Pittman of Nevada wrote what Ickes felt was a critical and discourteous letter. "I shall write him a strong letter also on the theory that if I permit some of these politicians to get the idea that they can shove me around, they will not only do it but others will join them in the exercise. After all, so long as I am head of this Department I am going to run it subject only to the President's expressed wishes."

It was the junior senator from California, however, for whom Ickes initially took a particularly strong dislike—and vice versa. Their adversarial relationship, begun in the spring over oil policy, extended through the fall and winter of 1933 as Harold Ickes struggled to put together an organization to implement the oil code. The tall, lanky McAdoo differed from the stocky, ordinary-looking secretary in ways more important than simply appearance; McAdoo, who was about as well connected to the powers in the Democratic Party and in the business world as anyone could be, was the kind of politician whom Ickes instinctively distrusted. Born into a wealthy Georgia family in 1863, McAdoo followed in the footsteps of his famous jurist father. He earned a law degree, went from Chattanooga to New York City, became president in the 1890s of the Hudson and Manhattan Railroad, helped elect Woodrow Wilson president in 1912, was named secretary of the treasury in the new administration, married Wilson's daughter, ran twice for the Democratic nomination for president in the 1920s, moved to California where he became friends with William Randolph Hearst, and practiced law. Among his clients was A. P. Giannini, president of the Bank of America. He ran for the U.S. Senate in 1932 at age 69 and won. Among other things, Senator McAdoo was determined to protect the interests of a segment of the Southern California oil industry.

In November 1933 Ickes, on the advice of Hiram Johnson, appointed a young attorney named William Scully to be the federal government's Southern California enforcer of the oil code. He did so without consulting Senator McAdoo. After McAdoo telegrammed him to ask just who this Mr. Scully was, and who recommended him, Petroleum Administrator Ickes shot back with a letter insinuating that the senator was in the pocket of the California oil men. He wrote, "Assuming that you really sent me this telegram, I take pleasure in advising you that William S. Scully is a very well-known and capable lawyer . . . who was highly recommended to me by a man upon whom I place the greatest reliance in such matters." McAdoo was furious. On December 19 he replied, "There is no occasion for your 'assuming' that I 'really' sent you this telegram. Of course I sent it. . . . I am not unconscious of the studied discourtesy of your reply to my polite and proper inquiry. I shall not, however, permit it to deter me from the performance of what I conceive to be my duty as Senator." [29]

McAdoo also took issue with the credentials of the 29-year-old Scully. "He may be a very estimable young man," McAdoo said, but he is too young and inexperienced. "A lawyer of wide knowledge and years of experience at the Bar and some acquaintance with the production, refining and marketing of petroleum and its products is manifestly demanded for this important position." After this exchange, Scully was reassigned to the Washington office of the Oil Administration and a lawyer named Frank P. Doherty headed up the important Los Angeles field office.[30]

Setting up an organization and responding to outside pressures, both solicited and unsolicited, occupied Ickes through the fall of 1933. The overriding concern, however, was getting the huge industry to comply with the oil code. It was a herculean task; Glavis and his investigators were sent to Chicago and other points west of Washington to make sure that "hot oil" wasn't getting to market, while Margold and his attorneys drafted the rules and regulations that made the oil code operational. They also prepared for the inevitable lawsuits that they knew would ensue from what the NRA was attempting to do.

The good news was that since the passage of the NIRA in June

crude oil prices crept up. The industry generally showed signs of recovery. The bad news was that flagrant violations of the code were
occurring and the Petroleum Administration was unable to stop all the
leaks. In addition, there was the unanswered question of whether to
invoke price controls. Ickes considered this a last resort, but when a
number of oil men descended on him at the end of September,
gloomily predicting that the bottom was about to fall out of oil prices,
he wrote that "I do think it necessary to [at least] be ready to fix
prices." He added that this day, September 27, "ranks with the worst
days I have had since I came to Washington. . . . All of these negotiations and pulling and hauling are very tiring." [31] To Ickes's relief the
worst-case scenario didn't materialize and so he was able to hold off on
regulating prices.

Nevertheless, there were serious problems from the outset in implementing the government's oil code. Several suits, including the famous
Panama Refining Co. case, were brought almost immediately against
Ickes's Petroleum Administration. A lesser known case, one brought
by a group of gasoline station operators, illustrates as well as any why
the Supreme Court, in 1935, struck down Section 9 of the NIRA. It
was a case that pitted Harry Victor et al. against the federal government
in the fall of 1933.[32]

Harry Victor, owner of a small gasoline station in Detroit, needed
more customers. He had a family to support and employees to pay.
Even in the automobile capital of the world, times were bad, with Ford
Motor Company workers earning a dime an hour, an oil glut depress-
ing prices, too many service stations, and too few customers with
money to buy gasoline and pay for car repairs. So, along with countless
other retailers, Victor began giving away coupons—redeemable for
pretty sets of cheap china—to customers who purchased his gas and
oil. The scheme worked; sales improved. The only problem was that
the "free" china violated the NRA's Oil Code. It led, the government
claimed, to bitter price wars and to the further demoralization of the
whole industry. But that was not Victor's concern. His concern was
staying in business and the coupons helped to do that. So, rather than
abandon the practice, as demanded by the Petroleum Administration,
he sued the federal government for violating his constitutional rights.

The filling station operators' suit, heard on November 7 in the District of Columbia federal court, was, according to Solicitor Margold,
a case of "paramount importance, not only to the rehabilitation of the

petroleum industry, but [to] the success of the entire recovery program." The Victor case didn't turn out to be the test case on the constitutionality of the NIRA that Margold thought it might be, but it
did illustrate, according to a New Deal scholar, another serious problem: a rift between attorneys in the Justice Department and those in
Ickes's Petroleum Administration over regulation of the oil industry.[33]
The rift widened in 1934 and turned into a major headache for Administrator Ickes and his staff that year.

NOTWITHSTANDING ALL the problems encountered in running
three organizations at once, Harold Ickes was in his element. He was
finally at the center of power and experiencing a sense of efficacy un-
matched in any of his previous 59 years. Reporters flocked to his
weekly press conferences—a practice he initiated, like FDR, at the
outset of his administration—not merely because he was the Interior
secretary but because he was also in charge of public works and oil
regulation. Ickes was getting things done, and at these exchanges,
which he clearly enjoyed, the reporters appreciated his candor and
witticisms. "The Secretary made good copy," remarked William
Warne, one of his young aides and, according to Ickes, one of his best,
during the 1930s.[34]

But probably more important for his state of mind was the fact that
his relationship with Roosevelt was developing in a decidedly positive
direction. In October, Colonel House, who had been Woodrow Wilson's right-hand man, came by to meet Ickes. He related what FDR
had told him about his Interior secretary. "Harold is both able and
strong," the president said, and the colonel proceeded to add a further
compliment by telling Ickes that this was "a rare combination" among
government officers. At about the same time Ickes was describing FDR
in his diaries as a "brave, forthright man" who "frankly faces a situation," and was telling him in person that "there wasn't another man
in the United States who could lead the country at this time along the
path that it ought to tread. Of course," Ickes added, "he demurred to
this, but I profoundly believe it to be true."[35]

With the self-confidence that came from the successful launching of
a new public career and a friendship with the president of the United
States, Harold Ickes that fall decided to take the initiative in his personal life, too. The time had come to put his marriage on a new foundation. He chose, perversely, the evening of Anna's first dinner at the

White House to unleash a bombshell. Anna was still serving as an Illinois state legislator and so she wasn't able to spend a lot of time in Washington with Harold through 1933. Nevertheless, she came down on weekends when she could and the couple socialized with the embassy crowd or with other cabinet members and their spouses. (On one occasion that fall they dined with Agriculture Secretary and Mrs. Wallace, and Ickes observed that Henry, due to the enormous strain he was under, "looked completely fagged out.") But Anna did not attend a White House dinner until the president and Mrs. Roosevelt hosted the official cabinet banquet on Friday, November 17.

The evening was pleasant. The Roosevelts were always gracious hosts in their unassuming way, and Anna returned home with Harold feeling content. As they were getting ready for bed, however, Harold wiped away the rosy afterglow by blurting out that he was in love with another woman and wasn't going to give her up. All the pleasure of the moment drained out of Anna, and Harold confessed that he "really felt sorry for Anna that night. It was a blow right between the eyes." [36]

But Anna was a strong-willed individual and she fought back to retain her position in the household. Over the next six months the customary rocky relationship between them worsened; Anna, Harold said, alternated between vicious, angry outbursts and pathetic attempts to win him back to the marital bed. They frequently called on their son Wilmarth to come down from Chicago to settle disputes. Anna also decided that she would not seek reelection in 1934 in order to spend more time with her husband at their Glenbrook home in Washington. The decision didn't especially please Harold.

Over the winter of 1933 and into the spring of 1934 Harold found himself caught between two women and two conflicting desires. On the one hand, he was determined not to give up Marguerite; it was the first time, he said, that he had known complete sexual fulfillment and he was not about to abandon such passion at its peak. On the other hand, he said he refused his mistress's entreaties to divorce Anna and marry her. Anna was already once divorced—in large part because of him—and he claimed that he would not make her bear the stigma of a second divorce. Undoubtedly there was an additional reason, too: Harold Ickes was no ascetic when it came to the good life. He liked to live in more than comfortable surroundings, he knew his fine wines and liquors, he was something of a gourmet, he enjoyed the luxury of being driven by a chauffeur to work, and he dressed almost always in expensive, if conventional, three-piece suits. It is difficult to imagine that he would willingly give up the considerable wealth and status that the marriage to Anna Wilmarth Thompson accorded him.

With neither partner wanting a divorce, which was what Wilmarth counseled, they fought. Life became total hell, Ickes recalled. "We would go through terrible scenes. Anna would become hysterical to a degree that I had never witnessed," Ickes wrote in his unpublished memoirs. On one occasion, in the presence of a friend named Antoinette Funk, "Anna turned on me like a tigress. . . . She would have killed me at that moment if she could. The look of a wild beast came into her eyes and her expression." [37]

Instead of killing her husband that March day, Anna tried half-heartedly to kill herself. She took an overdose of prescription medicine and then called her doctor. Harold returned home from driving Miss Funk back to her hotel at the same time as the family physician, Dr. Sexton, arrived. The two men discovered that Anna hadn't taken enough of the medicine to kill herself, just enough, Ickes noted with disgust, "to make a first-class scene."

Anna's suicide attempt marked the nadir of their relationship. She spent about two weeks recuperating from "nervous exhaustion" in a hospital, and then returned home. By then she had come to terms, Ickes related, with their changed relationship. Anna didn't speak about his affair after that, and accepted his dominant position in the family. Ickes acknowledged that his methods had been "brutal," but at last he felt he had emerged victorious in their twenty-year power struggle. He had secured his emotional and physical independence from his wife.

ALTHOUGH THE Ickeses' marriage survived this six months of turbulence, gossip about their marital problems lingered for a long time as he gained the reputation in Washington of being a rather elderly Lothario. A number of people used the Ickeses' less-than-idyllic personal life as a reason for getting him removed from office. For instance, someone named "A. L. Ickes" wrote Eleanor Roosevelt an astonishingly catty letter at the same time as Anna was convalescing from her nervous breakdown. The one-page letter, dated April 13, 1934, and written long-hand on stationery from the Georgian Hotel in Evanston, Illinois, was authored by a woman who not only hated the First Lady but who could well have been accused of wanting to undermine Ickes's position at the White House. It read in part:

What this country needs is less "investigating and fixing" by Washington Brainless school teachers, called "Brain Trust," as well as more dignity and less airmail and radio stunts by the mistress of the White House, whom you assume to represent, yet you are really a Circus Rider and Clown, compared to Mrs. Wilson or Mrs. Taft. . . . It must be very humiliating to your weak, invalid husband, whose mind seems also affected, to have such a pugialistic, marathon wife, butting in everywhere and everything. Womans Clubs every-where are poking fun at the long legged, homely Eleanor, who will be "It" and doing high air stunts all the time. . . . The good sensible Democrats like Senator Lewis, Glass and a few others will never vote for Roosevelt again. The whole clan is disgusting and want to run everything when you can't keep your own family together—half of them divorced and living on Uncle Sam, at the White House. You have a job in your own home and back yard, attend to it. . . .

Yours truly,

A.L. Ickes[38]

Whether Eleanor Roosevelt ever saw this poison-pen letter is not known. Mrs. Roosevelt was a controversial First Lady and received a number of letters that her secretary placed in a file labeled "disagreeable." But if she or her husband was aware of the nasty letter sent by someone with the unusual name of "Ickes," it didn't have the intended effect. Harold Ickes and the president continued to get along famously through 1934. And while the Interior secretary's relationship with Mrs. Roosevelt was a more distant and formal one, they nevertheless worked together on a number of liberal fronts through the years. Ickes invariably spoke respectfully of Eleanor Roosevelt, and he particularly admired her courageous stand on minority issues. But he also admitted that he never could feel close to her: She reminded him too much of Anna, he said.

CHAPTER 6

THE JUGGLER

INTERIOR, OIL,

AND PUBLIC WORKS

IT WAS TIME to relax a bit. Roosevelt and his administrators were about to celebrate their first anniversary in office, and even if the emergency was nearly as dire as it was in March of 1933 there was, nevertheless, an easing of tension and a sense of forward movement. Americans no longer felt the cold, nameless fear that FDR promised to rout in his first inaugural, and they could see or read about real improvements that were underway in their towns, cities, and regions. So by the end of January the president began urging his overworked cabinet members to take a vacation. "Yesterday when Henry Wallace and I lunched with him," Ickes wrote in his diaries, "he told us he wanted both of us to go away. . . . He said he didn't want any members of the Cabinet to break down and he especially wanted Henry and me to go away for a week or two. . . . He was quite insistent about it. He told me that it was beginning to worry him just to look at me and that if I didn't go away he would get mad." [1]

That was January 25. A week later Roosevelt gave Ickes another responsibility. On February 2, at the customary Friday cabinet meeting Roosevelt proceeded to name Harold Ickes chairman of a national resources planning committee, with the other members being Agriculture Secretary Henry Wallace, Frances Perkins of Labor, and Secretary of War George Dern. The president, whom Ickes noted was in fine form that day, "his spirits soar[ing] high and . . . full of good humor," announced that it was time for the New Deal to take the long view. He told his cabinet that he was being inundated with pressure from all parts of the country to spend emergency funds on flood control, and rather than revert to the traditional pork-barrel method Roosevelt hoped to introduce comprehensive planning. After meeting with a number of congressmen clamoring for projects in their respective districts, the president convinced them to pass a resolution creating a national resources planning committee. It was this committee which the Interior secretary was asked to chair.

Roosevelt, who was no novice when it came to issues of resource conservation, proceeded to outline his ideas at the February 2 cabinet meeting. First, he told his newly appointed four-member committee to organize a number of subcommittees to study the major river basin drainage areas—one for the Atlantic seaboard, at least one for the Pacific Coast states, one for the Colorado River, and at least two for the mightiest of all rivers in America, the Mississippi. "We are to consider not only flood control, but navigation, soil erosion, irrigation, reclamation, sewage, power, and reforestation," Ickes wrote. Moreover, it was FDR's hope that once the present emergency had passed, which resulted in extraordinary expenditures for "more or less unrelated public works, a considerable sum of money, say $500,000 a year, should be expended for . . . perhaps twenty-five years in carrying out a broad national plan along the lines to be covered at least in part by this study."

HAROLD ICKES'S LATEST responsibility was not so much a completely new job, as was the case when FDR named him public works administrator and oil administrator, as it was a new way of thinking about his three responsibilities. But Ickes hardly needed much urging on that score: He had tried to take the long, integrated view in running the Interior Department, in administering the public works program, and in regulating oil. Chairing what became known as the National Resources Planning Board and, a little later, the National Power Policy Committee simply gave him additional authority to proceed further in the direction he had been taking all along.

One of the many reasons for the delay in getting the Public Works Administration out of the starting gate had to do with the fact that Ickes insisted on running a construction program that stressed permanence and utilitarianism. This was also Roosevelt's philosophy or, more precisely, *part* of Roosevelt's philosophy, for in his view the Great Depression necessitated an all-out attack on different fronts simultaneously. This is one reason the president divided up responsibilities among his assistants; for example, Harry Hopkins, the social worker, was given the title of federal emergency relief administrator because of his concern with the immediacy of the situation in 1933. "People do not eat in the long run," said Hopkins. The phrase became famous in summing up his attitude during the early New Deal years.

While Ickes agreed with his colleague's pithy observation, he also recognized that both Hopkins's organization and Robert Fechner's, the Civilian Conservation Corps, were working 'round the clock to arm the unemployed with rakes, shovels, and pick-axes. Ickes's PWA, therefore, would distinguish itself by emphasizing the long term: Projects successfully passing through PWA review (a process that included both Ickes and Roosevelt) would be socially and economically beneficial, aesthetically pleasing, and built to last. The projects would also be built by a workforce, as Ickes ordered in one of his first directives as administrator, that reflected the racial composition of the United States. It was the first time that a federal officer ordered a quota system in hiring, and although it fell far short of expectations, it set an important precedent.

Some of the first allocations made under the PWA epitomized the comprehensive planning approach. Construction of the greatest multipurpose project ever undertaken by the federal government to that time, Hoover Dam on the Colorado River, was completed two and one-half years ahead of schedule, thanks to generous PWA appropriations. This engineering marvel was dedicated by President Roosevelt on September 30, 1935, with Ickes present and still determined to call it Boulder, not Hoover, Dam. From the outset of his tenure, Ickes pushed for the original dam name and received several complimentary letters; for example, a Los Angeles resident wrote him in May 1933:

Mr. Hoover deserves no credit for the project, as he was allied with the power trust and never aided Senator Johnson nor Representative Swing in their efforts to have this great resource developed for the people. . . . The plan to rename Boulder Dam was hatched by the Hoover-Wilbur-Stanford University gang, and was never popular with the people here, who felt that its sponsors were in sympathy with the Insull-Doherty-Mitchell-Morgan etc. power trust.[2]

Whatever its name, it was a breathtaking accomplishment. "Almost twice as high as the next highest dam, the 726-foot structure dwarfs the pyramids of Egypt and towers above all but a few modern skyscrapers," Ickes wrote in his 1935 book, *Back to Work: The Story of PWA*. But words failed even Ickes in describing this manmade wonder that weighed in at 6.6 million tons, was 660 feet thick at its base, and was built to withstand water pressure of 45,000 pounds per square foot: "It must be seen to be appreciated," he concluded.[3]

Long before Boulder Dam was completed, a number of similar projects were underway that would make this mighty dam look almost ordinary. PWA funds were pouring into the construction of huge multipurpose projects to bring water and cheap electricity to American communities throughout the country, from those great structures in the west, Grand Coulee, Bonneville, Fort Peck, and later Shasta, to the Norris and Wheeler dams in the Tennessee Valley in the east. The New Deal years were the Golden Age of dam-building in the United States, and while contemporary environmentalists look upon them as cement- and earth-filled dinosaurs with ugly power-line arms stretching out in every direction, they were the product of dedicated and sincere conservationists—New Dealers, in other words.

Most Americans loved the new works. "Almost every community in the West felt the beneficent influence of the stepped-up construction programs," William Warne, an aide to Ickes, wrote. In the 1930s, he said, "the nation needed the inspiration of remarkable achievements in order to offset the psychological effects of the Great Depression."[4] Another time, another value system.

The PWA built not just dams, of course. In *Back to Work* Ickes and his staff documented what had been accomplished as of January 1, 1935: More than 19,000 projects completed or underway, spread through 3,040 of the 3,073 counties of the United States, as well as in all of the territories from Hawaii to the Virgin Islands and from the Panama Canal Zone to Alaska. They included the construction of 522 schools, 87 hospitals, almost 600 municipal water systems, 433 sewer lines and sewage disposal plants, and 360 local street and highway improvements.[5]

Ickes held the public works hoop high, keeping it as free of graft as possible, and emphasizing the long-term nature of the infrastructure he was helping to build. He insisted on being an equal opportunity employer as well. In the fall of 1933 the NAACP charged that, in spite of Ickes's new affirmative action hiring policy, Negro workers comprised a grand total of 11 out of a labor force of 4,000 on the Boulder Dam project. Ickes immediately ordered Clark Foreman to look into the matter. Foreman reported back that it was difficult to rectify that particular situation because the contracts were let under the Hoover administration.[6] A rather chagrined Ickes thus found himself having to explain this to the NAACP, but at the same time he redoubled his efforts at including minorities in all phases of federal activity. In November 1934 he sent a memo to his deputy for public works reiterating his commitment: "I want to be very sure that not only the contracts, but the specifications, shall contain this [anti-discriminatory] language. I want to leave nothing undone to show that it is our purpose . . . to avoid race discrimination in our housing projects."[7]

Finally, Harold Ickes wanted the projects built under his administration to be visually pleasing. He took to heart historian Lewis Mumford's admonition in the *New Republic* that "a permanent public works program could be 'irreparably damaged if our first venture results in the dotting of the country from coast to coast with monstrous and ill-planned monuments.'"[8] In early October Ickes asked Roosevelt what he thought about his approach to post office construction, an important segment of the public works agenda that first year. "My theory," Ickes told FDR, "is that instead of erecting monuments in small towns, more appropriate buildings providing necessary space but conforming architecturally to the towns themselves can be built for much less money." Roosevelt, Ickes noted, agreed and told him to proceed along those lines.[9] Ickes was pleased that his boss also agreed with his goal of running a graft-free program. In June 1934, after FDR was apprised by Ickes's Division of Investigations that there appeared to be some irregularities regarding the selection of post office sites by the Treasury Department, he wrote the Treasury secretary that "I think you will want to start an immediate investigation even though it may hit friend and foe alike."[10]

While the administration was pushing ahead with its plans for comprehensive regional development of the country's natural resources, it was also breaking new ground in its urban policies. For the first time in history, the federal government embarked on a commitment to provide decent, affordable housing to the approximately one-third of America that FDR called attention to in his famous second inaugural address in 1937. Of concern to the New Dealers were the neglected third who remained ill-fed, ill-clothed, and ill-housed in the thirties. Many of these Americans were minorities who had migrated to the cities over the past half-century looking for the American Dream. Instead, they lived in squalor, in places like Hell's Kitchen in New York, the Arks of Memphis and New Orleans, the Corrals of San Antonio, the Monkey's Nest of Youngstown, and Philadelphia's Band-boxes.[11]

Having been a city-dweller for all of his adult life, and a friend of urban reformer Jane Addams, Harold Ickes knew first-hand about the appalling living conditions of the poor in the nation's urban centers. Once he became head of the Public Works Administration, he set up what he described as one of the most significant aspects of the entire emergency effort, the housing program. Not only was it significant in terms of what it hoped to accomplish in the long run, which was the eradication of the nation's slums and their replacement with livable, publicly subsidized apartments, but it was novel in its method of attacking the problem. In *Back to Work,* Ickes explained:

> Twice a week . . . , around a table in the Interior Department, a group of men discuss one of the most significant phases of PWA's program. . . . Seated in the room are the branch chiefs of the Housing Division. . . . Rubbing shoulders are architects, demolition experts, real-estate authorities, building contractors, apartment managers and lawyers, all working harmoniously on the really intricate problem of low-cost housing. The uncommonness of the group becomes apparent when it is realized that never before has housing been considered as one complete process from land acquisition to apartment management.[12]

At the outset of 1934 Ickes's enthusiasm for the program was at its peak, as was his enthusiasm for Roosevelt. In late January he gave a speech to the National Conference on Public Housing in which the president received gushing praise for instituting the bold new urban program:

> Hope at last for a definite and notable beginning in the erection of low-cost housing is now running high. This is because we have in the White House a man of greater social vision than any of his predecessors. . . . This

practical idealist has a conviction that the way to promote low-cost housing is to build low-cost housing. Accordingly . . . there has been created a
Federal Housing Corporation, to which the sum of $100,000,000 has been
allotted out of the Public Works fund . . . to be devoted to slum clearance
and . . . low-cost housing. So since the President has embarked on a program of slum clearance you may rest assured that the rest of us are for slum
clearance and will do all we can to bring it about.[13]

Ickes's admiration for the primary architect of the social revolution
then underway was verbalized often that year, but he was especially
prescient in what he said in February before the Cook County League
of Women Voters: "I can envisage the time a generation or more
hence when descendants of the present-day reactionaries will in their
turn attempt to block another necessary and over-due social advance
by misapplying the words of that man with the social vision who sits
in the White House today."[14] Did Ickes predict the appearance of a
president of the 1980s who vowed to be "Roosevelt in reverse," one
wonders? Incidentally, Ickes nearly canceled his speech to the League
because he learned at the last minute that it was charging $1.65 admis-
sion, and he believed that no one should have to pay to hear a public
official speak.

Through 1934 the housing program, along with the entire public
works agenda, moved ahead. Fewer complaints were voiced about the
slowness of Ickes's agency, although there were some. In fact, as late as
1938 Ickes was still being criticized. He seriously considered suing
Freda Kirchwey, editor of the *Nation,* when she wrote that his performance on housing amounted to a "public scandal."[15] But that was
later; through the second year of the New Deal the program made
progress, and by October 1934 the government was about to embark
on its first slum clearance project. For the historic occasion, Ickes took
the train from Washington to Atlanta, arriving at 8:35 A.M. on a crisp
fall Saturday. The administrator and his small entourage proceeded to
the two sites scheduled for demolition, one near Atlanta University,
which he described in his diaries as a "black college," and the other
adjacent to the white college, Georgia Tech. "There," Ickes wrote, "I
made another extemporaneous speech from a temporary platform,
spoke for a couple of minutes before the newsreel machine, and then
blew up another house."[16]

By the end of 1934 it was abundantly evident that Harold Ickes, as
head of Public Works, was in much better standing with Roosevelt

INTERIOR, OIL, AND PUBLIC WORKS 101

than he had been just a year earlier, when FDR considered taking the program from him while he languished (and anguished) in a hospital bed. At the last cabinet meeting of the year, held on December 29, Roosevelt paid Ickes a fine compliment, telling the group:

> When Harold took hold of public works, he had to start cold. He had no program and he had no organization. It was necessary to develop both. A lot of people thought that all he would have to do would be to shovel money out of the window. There have been a good many complaints about the slowness of the works program and Harold's caution. There hasn't been even a minor scandal in public works and that is some record.[17]

IN HIS SOLON-LIKE role as oil administrator, Harold Ickes also tried to take the long view, which meant conserving the nation's finite supplies of oil and natural gas for future use. Strenuous opposition to the policy came from certain segments of the industry, as well as from their supporters in state legislatures and Congress, as both groups argued that the policy was little more than a means used by the majors to kill them off. Opposition from some sectors of the fragmented industry was more or less to be expected, Ickes acknowledged, but he had not expected roadblocks from within the Roosevelt administration itself. Dealing with cabinet colleagues who didn't happen to share Ickes's perspective proved to be as problematic for him in 1934 as regulating the hot oil crowd. In fact, the two problems were related.

Just as the New Deal experiment was heading down the stretch of its first year's loop around the political racetrack, the president received two letters from the assistant attorney general of the Justice Department, Harold M. Stephens. Late in February 1934 Stephens apprised FDR of a problem that had arisen in connection with the Petroleum Administration. Unfortunately, Stephens wrote, some of the federal government's actions pursuant to stabilizing the oil industry had to be viewed as violations of the antitrust laws. He pointed to the gasoline marketing agreement between the government and one of the two most trouble-prone sectors of the industry, the Southern California producers. In the Justice Department's view, the agreement established a cartel in California, and that of course violated antitrust laws. "I respectfully suggest that the issue above set forth presents so important a question of policy for the entire administration that it should receive the consideration of the President," the assistant attorney general wrote.[18]

The president was concerned. Similar objections were being raised to other programs falling under the NIRA, and also to activities of the Federal Trade Commission and the Agriculture Department's administration of the Agricultural Adjustment Act (AAA). Thus a major task of the president and his New Deal administrators through 1934 was to steer a treacherous course between continuing with the economic recovery program, on the one hand, and allowing the attorney general to pursue cases that violated the antitrust laws on the other. It was not easy for any of the participants. The New Dealers' overall approach to implementing the NIRA fell somewhere between cooperation and collusion with the private sector,[19] until the Supreme Court in 1935 forced a major redirection. It was a classic example of muddling through.

No sectors of the oil industry were more resistant to regulation than were the East Texas and Southern California producers. The Oil Administration expended a great deal of effort bringing these groups into line, and in January 1934 Administrator Ickes wrote the attorney general that they were about to take unusual steps to get compliance.

> As you know, we have had all sorts of difficulty in making certain oil interests in California realize that the Oil Code and the Federal regulations thereunder mean anything at all. I think it is absolutely necessary, if we are to make any progress toward the stabilization of the oil industry in California, to proceed not only vigorously but expeditiously.[20]

The resulting agreement, however, brought the Justice Department directly into the fray, so that for the rest of the time that Ickes tried to regulate oil he had to acknowledge the substantial interest that Justice had in his actions. He found the lawyers of the antitrust division constantly peering over his shoulder and he didn't much like it.

Enforcing the oil code was such a complicated enterprise that Ickes found that he, too, had to rely on other government agents—in addition to his own staff and the Division of Investigations—to do the job. Through 1934 he spent some of his time informing other administration officials about violations that fell under their jurisdictions. At about the same time that he wrote the attorney general about the California situation (asking him indirectly not to intervene) he wrote Jesse Jones, chairman of the Reconstruction Finance Corporation, and Gen. Hugh Johnson, chairman of the National Recovery Administration. Jones was informed of a complaint from Oklahoman Bert Aston, president of the Aston Oil Company, about "oppressive practices on the part of certain bankers in the Southwest upon which the small oil companies have to depend for credit in order to do business." General Johnson was also apprised of these questionable banking practices, which Ickes thought might violate the NIRA's banking code: "It may be that some method can be found for handling a situation of this kind," Ickes suggested.[21]

In March, just as Harold Ickes was celebrating his sixtieth birthday and his first year in high political office, the disagreement between the Justice Department and the Oil Administration came to a head. The attorney general brought indictments against the Southern California oil companies that had signed the Petroleum Administration Board's gasoline marketing agreement. A very frustrated Ickes wrote the president on March 24, explaining the agreement and asking him to do something. In his letter to FDR, Ickes pointed out that due to the attorney general's intervention, once again there was overproduction of oil both in the rich California fields and in the other "bad boy" area, East Texas. Ickes appealed to FDR to untie his hands, which had just been tied by the attorney general: "To have this industry that was one of the leaders in the recovery program go into another tailspin cannot have a beneficial effect."[22]

At the same time he fired off an angry letter to Pierson Hall, the U.S. attorney in Los Angeles, objecting to a statement Hall made which gave the impression that Ickes approved of the indictments. In fact, Ickes said, his own staff of lawyers did not believe that the indictments were legally justified.

> The thing that really disturbs me, however, is the terrific blow that these indictments have caused our Oil Administration. I may say . . . that this is the only instance since the Oil Code was adopted and I was appointed Administrator that any action has been taken by any member of the Department of Justice, not only without the approval of the Oil Administrator, but in opposition to his expressed wishes. . . . Least of all do I want men connected with the oil industry to think . . . that I am double-crossing them—assenting in one breath to a cartel and with the next urging . . . that indictments should be brought.[23]

It certainly looked bad for everyone, including the president. On March 27 Ickes and Attorney General Homer Cummings managed to get in a few minutes with Roosevelt to discuss the dilemma. Ickes wrote that the president said "that he thought the Attorney General and I ought to be locked together in a room until we could iron the matter out." Cummings responded that he and Ickes had "agreed to disagree," and FDR casually replied, "You oughtn't to do that." [24] With little help from the president, over the next several months the Petroleum Administration worked grudgingly with the Justice Department and both worked with the California companies on a marketing agreement that wouldn't be in restraint of trade. But at the same time, the Panama Refining Company's lawsuit was winding its way through the federal courts, and the U.S. Congress was considering tougher oil legislation. It was a mess.

Through the spring Ickes and his staff worked on a new oil bill. Again there was no shortage of suggestions, ranging from radical to reactionary, about what the government should do to regulate oil. On April 2 Ickes, joined by Solicitor Nathan Margold and two other staff members, met with a group of oil men who represented "eighty percent of the oil industry, as measured by capital invested." They discussed what should go into the new bill. Ickes noted that this group backed a provision that would give the oil administrator the fullest possible power to regulate the production of crude oil, but that they didn't think that the refining of gasoline should be included, as Ickes and his staff were pushing for. "The oil people say that they can manage that by voluntary agreement, but I am skeptical," Ickes wrote after the meeting.

The next day one of the participants, Walter Teagle, president of Standard Oil of New Jersey, came in alone to see Ickes. He made what the administrator described as a "startling proposition." Teagle argued that the government should make an oil reserve out of the entire East Texas oil field, because that was the only way to control the production of hot oil. The proposal was not only drastic, but it was particularly surprising in that it came from Teagle, whose company was the largest producer in the East Texas field.[25] A clearly perplexed Ickes didn't know what to make of the suggestion, except that it added more fuel to fire his already substantial suspicions about the byzantine oil business.

The suggestion also happened to come at a time when, Ickes told FDR, he believed that there was "a well-conceived conspiracy . . . being carried out to make my position in the Cabinet untenable." The conspiracy may or may not have had anything to do with oil—indeed, it was difficult to prove that it actually existed at all—but at the time Harold Ickes was convinced that certain people were out to get him and that he had to watch his actions very carefully. Of course, his own carryings-on with his mistress in 1933 and 1934 had contributed to the feeling on the part of some people that he ought to be out of office. Fortunately, FDR didn't share that view.

In May the administration's new oil bill was introduced in Congress by two members of the Oklahoma delegation, Sen. Elmer Thomas and Rep. Wesley Disney. The bill gave the oil administrator more power to regulate the output of crude oil, an activity that had been severely compromised by court injunctions over the previous year. "The overwhelming mass of the industry, so far as we can ascertain, is in favor of this bill," Ickes wrote on May 11. "The hot oil people are, of course, opposed to it, just as they have opposed every bit of regulation."

The battle over the Thomas-Disney bill went on for a month, with a number of the independent producers fiercely objecting not only to it but to the petroleum administrator himself. On May 23 the president received a telegram from Southern California oil man John Elliott complaining about Ickes's administration; he said he was supported by a number of agencies in California that had voted unanimously to condemn Ickes's handling of the Oil Code.[26] At the same time the influential congressman from Texas, Sam Rayburn, was stalling the bill in his committee. He believed that the president did not support the bill and so he wasn't about to push it in the face of opposition from some of the oil interests in his state.

Was the president for the bill, or wasn't he? In early June Ickes appealed to FDR to put pressure on Rayburn to get the bill out of committee, but Roosevelt demurred. "Unfortunately, the President is anxious for an early adjournment," Ickes wrote, "and some . . . Congressional leaders have . . . persuaded him that the session would be prolonged by as much as two weeks if he should insist upon the passage of the oil bill, which he in reality strongly favors."[27]

That was the end of the Thomas-Disney bill. Its fate was testimony to the political power wielded by the East Texas and Southern California oil interests and also to Roosevelt's inability to reconcile the competing divisions in the industry. What historian Frank Freidel wrote concerning FDR and oil in 1933 applies equally to his actions not only through 1934 but up until the Supreme Court invalidated the oil code in 1935. Freidel wrote:

The conflicting demands of major and independent oil producers, of importers and their beneficiaries in New England, and those who opposed both importation and restrictive quotas within the United States, created irreconcilable political problems for Roosevelt. He could not take any course of action that would please everyone, and gave the impression that in the end he acted only because the pressure for him to do something was considerably greater than the negative forces.[28]

Despite this defeat, Ickes's Petroleum Administration and certain members of Congress doggedly pursued what more and more appeared to be chimerical: A solution to the overproduction problem. That summer congressmen Martin Dies and William Cole set up an investigating committee to look into all phases of the oil business, and Ickes was hopeful that out of their work, and his Petroleum Administration, a new bill would be forthcoming in Congress's next session.

Through another sticky, oppressively hot summer the Petroleum Administration worked with the Cole subcommittee investigating oil. Something of great importance to the conservation cause actually came out of their work, having to do with the scandalous fact that natural gas was literally being blown to the winds. Late in June Charles B. Ames, chairman of the board of the Texas Company (Texaco), wrote Ickes about this shocking situation in the oil fields of America. Somewhere "between 500 and 600 million feet of [natural] gas are blown into the air every day," Ames wrote Ickes.[29] The utter waste of another natural resource appalled the petroleum administrator, and he immediately passed on this critical information to the subcommittee. Although it took some time to rectify, the government's recognition of natural gas as a valuable energy resource, and not just something to be blown off in order to get at underground oil, was one of the major accomplishments of the early New Deal.

Just when Ickes thought that there would never be a solution to the hot oil problem, the situation started to improve. At the outset of October Ickes was distressed about the East Texas situation. He wrote, "I frankly admit that the Oil Administration has not done a good job in this matter." A significant factor was that his director of investigations, Louis Glavis, was spending far too much time meddling in the Oil Administration in the attempt to find something on his intradepartmental rival, Solicitor Nathan Margold. After a meeting with the president, Ickes laid down the law to Glavis: "I made it distinctly clear to him that the probability was that we would have to admit failure in this Administration and that failure would be chargeable to him. I literally beat his head against the wall," Ickes wrote.[30]

Glavis promised to try to save the situation while Ickes, later in October, went to see the attorney general. "In my desperation," he wrote, "I went to see Cummings to ask him whether we could not start some prosecutions [in East Texas]."

They did. At the end of the troubling month, Charles Fahy, one of Ickes's lawyers who spent most of his time that year working on oil, sent his boss an encouraging Western Union message from the oil fields:

> Federal Tender Board in East Texas continues successful operation all movements of illegal crude or its products at standstill. Justice filed its first injunction suit yesterday based on cases we prepared before I returned and obtained temporary restraining order as we predicted could be done. At present moment control in East Texas as perfect as could be wished. Whether this can be maintained remains to be seen but at long last control actually exists now.[31]

IN HAROLD ICKES's third primary area of responsibility, that of running the Interior Department, he took the long view when he could and championed the conservation cause. If Ickes wasn't able to devote himself entirely to his department in his first two years in office, it was due to the dire national emergency confronting the government and the fact that his other two jobs necessitated immediate action. Ickes characteristically threw himself into whatever task Roosevelt gave him, but one program in particular moved him in the deepest recesses of his heart, and that was the national parks. During 1933 and 1934 he somehow found time to lay the groundwork for his long-range plan to expand and redirect the national park system, gain control of the national forest system from the Agriculture Department, collect the other federal resource-managing agencies from the departments of his cabinet colleagues, and thus transform Interior into a genuine Department of Conservation. It was a grand, idealistic dream that made too much sense.

Henry Wallace and Harold Ickes, both midwestern Progressive Republicans, had been in office a little over a month when they began talking about parks and forests. On April 18, 1933, Ickes related in his diaries, "Secretary Wallace came up to discuss with me the proposition of putting the Forest Service and the National Parks in the same department, but I thought that department was Interior and not Agriculture." Ickes gave Wallace some of his reasons: First, it was time to give Ickes a chance to restore public confidence in the Interior Department, whose reputation was badly damaged by the Pinchot-Ballinger dispute during the Taft administration and by the even more tawdry Teapot Dome scandal that had sent Interior Secretary Albert Fall to jail. Second, he was particularly interested in the national parks, and that "fifty percent" of his interest in the Interior Department would vanish if they were transferred to Agriculture. Third, the national forests had originally been in Interior, before Gifford Pinchot moved them to Agriculture, and that was where they naturally belonged.[32]

Only a day after their friendly exchange of views, however, Ickes said he got wind of "a disturbing rumor" that the Agriculture Department was launching an effort to get the national parks transferred to its domain; "this is a matter of real concern to me and I hope it isn't true," Ickes wrote. But the following day, the dialogue intensified when the secretary received a copy of a letter that his friend Gifford Pinchot wrote to Roosevelt "protesting in the strongest terms against bringing the National Forest Service over here [to Interior]." It had taken exactly forty-eight hours for the first chief of the Forest Service, who believed it was his solemn duty to protect his creation so long as he drew a breath, to enter the fray. Ickes immediately fired back a letter telling Gifford that while he thought that the national forests belonged in Interior he hadn't raised his hand to bring that about. "I shall be content if the National Forests stay in Agriculture and the National parks are permitted to stay here," he claimed. But in reality these initial exchanges between Ickes, Wallace, and Pinchot, while amusing to onlookers, touched off a decade-long argument over where the national forests "properly" belonged.

A few weeks after the Ickes-Pinchot exchange, the secretary was on the stump to deliver speeches in which he first articulated to the public his plans for the nation's fledgling park system. Before the American Civic Association and then the National Parks Association, the Interior secretary made it clear which side he was on in the debate that has engulfed the National Park Service since its creation in 1916, the debate over "public use" versus "preservation." Ickes told his audiences that he intended to keep roads and tourist facilities in and around the national parks to an absolute minimum, because "crowds and parks are incompatible." But he also promised to add more parks to the system. "You cannot have too many national parks so far as I am concerned."[33]

By simultaneously pursuing an aggressive policy of park expansion while promoting wilderness values in some of the national parks, Harold Ickes thus skillfully came down on both sides of the issue. Wilderness advocates benefited from his thirteen-year tenure as Interior secretary and so did the recreationists. Nevertheless, because he was the first Interior secretary since the department was created in 1849 to speak out and act on behalf of wilderness, his contribution to that cause was unique. Most secretaries have opted for the politically more attractive position promoting increased tourism.

Harold Ickes had some powerful allies in his long-range plans to build up the national park system. One of them was Franklin Roosevelt and another was the slight, soft-spoken millionaire, John D. Rockefeller Jr., who, Ickes estimated in 1935, had contributed somewhere between $12 and $15 million to the cause.[34] By the time Ickes entered office Rockefeller already had saved a spectacular grove of sugar pines from the woodsman's axe by purchasing them and giving them to the government as an addition to Yosemite National Park. In 1933, not only was his foundation well on its way to restoring Williamsburg, Virginia, to its original simple, yet inspired, colonial charm, but his Snake River Land Company was buying up Jackson Hole in Wyoming in order to expand Grand Teton National Park.

In May Ickes began cultivating a relationship with the wealthy philanthropist who loved parks and American history. One of Ickes's first excursions outside Washington was to visit the Williamsburg project site. With its gardens blooming and the trees sporting their new foliage, he came away deeply impressed. When he returned to his office he wrote Rockefeller a letter complimenting him on this achievement: "To my way of thinking the restoration of Williamsburg is the most significant physical, artistic and aesthetic expression in America today."[35] Although the two men didn't actually meet until 1935, nevertheless they worked in concert to enlarge the park system from 1933 right up until Ickes left office in 1946.

Adding to the nation's parks was generally a popular policy, and Rockefeller's generosity was widely appreciated not only by Ickes and Roosevelt but throughout society. But there were a few exceptions. Just as negotiations began between the Interior Department and the Snake River Land Company to turn over some 33,000 acres of land in

Wyoming to expand Grand Teton National Park, Ickes received a strong letter in protest. On August 21, 1933, Wyoming's Sen. Robert Carey wrote him charging collusion between the National Park Service, under the directorship of Horace Albright, and the Rockefeller interests. "Briefly," Carey alleged, "the record shows that the Director was responsible in interesting Mr. Rockefeller in the purchase of lands in the Jackson's Hole area and that for a considerable time the people of Wyoming were deceived as to the purpose of these purchases." [36]

Carey's objections didn't dissuade Ickes from proceeding with the land exchange, but certain interests in Wyoming bitterly fought what they claimed was a smelly deal to "lock up" valuable forest and range land in national park status. Through the 1930s Jackson Hole became a *cause célèbre*. The battle continued for nearly twenty years before Pres. Harry Truman, in 1950, signed a compromise law that provided for an expanded Grand Teton National Park encompassing nearly 300,000 acres but with special provisions for tax revenue compensation and for hunting. Setting their sights on FDR's executive proclamation issued in 1943, Congress also prohibited establishing or enlarging national parks thereafter in Wyoming without express congressional authorization. [37]

But for every Jackson Hole there was an Acadia National Park in Maine, a Great Smoky National Park straddling Tennessee and North Carolina, and a Virgin Islands National Park in the Caribbean. These national treasures came into the park system through the Rockefeller family, and generally with far less controversy. Clearly no single family in America did more on behalf of the national parks than did the Rockefellers, and it was the Roosevelt administration's good fortune to have the family's original park enthusiast, John D. Rockefeller Jr., in his prime during the 1930s. Rockefeller was the same age as Harold Ickes, having been born in 1874, and he was eager to help out the national government during the Great Depression. The philanthropist thus spent many millions of his Standard Oil fortune on land and park preservation.

In contrast to his hesitancy on oil policy, President Roosevelt knew exactly what he wanted when it came to national parks and forests. He loved nature in all of its manifestations, but he was especially drawn to the sea, where he frequently went to relax and get away from it all, and to the forests, which were home to an abundance of trees, shrubs, flowers, grasses, animals, and birds. On the family's Hyde Park estate

FDR was the country squire. Even as president he found time to experiment with planting new species of trees on the spacious grounds overlooking the Hudson River. He was a self-educated agronomist and silviculturalist who sometimes listed his occupation as "farmer," and as soon as he was in office, like his cousin Theodore some thirty years earlier, Franklin began building a reputation as one of this century's greatest conservationists.

With help from many people, but especially from two of his cabinet officers, Interior Secretary Ickes and Agriculture Secretary Wallace, the president embarked on a long-range policy of park and forest expansion. "The more the better" summed up the New Deal attitude toward land and resource conservation.

On his last day in office, March 3, 1933, Herbert Hoover signed a bill giving the president the power to reorganize the executive branch of government. On June 10 and July 28 Roosevelt signed executive orders that consolidated all the existing national parks, national monuments, military sites, cemeteries, and monuments in the nation's capital under a single authority, the Interior Department's National Park Service. Over fifty separate areas previously administered by the War and the Agriculture departments—including such famous places as Gettysburg Battlefield in Pennsylvania and Devil's Postpile in California—were incorporated into the national park system during the summer of 1933. This reorganization transformed the agency from a small, western-oriented bureau into a truly national entity whose responsibilities now encompassed the entire country, and not just its unique natural environments but also its historic areas.[38]

Many considered Roosevelt's reorganization as the single most important development in the history of the National Park Service. Needless to say, Harold Ickes was among them. He was delighted to see one of his favorite agencies in the Interior Department so swiftly transformed, and it gave him yet another reason for not wanting to lose it to the Agriculture Department.

At the same time as he was shifting valuable acreage to the National Park Service for administration, however, Roosevelt moved to expand the national forest system, which was administered by the U.S. Forest Service in the Agriculture Department. In 1933, virtually no national forests existed east of the Mississippi River. Whatever was left of the original wooded areas in the East—and Gifford Pinchot at the turn of the century estimated that Americans had cut down 90 percent of their forests by that time—was in the hands of state government or the private sector. FDR decided to change that situation. In July 1933 he sent a memo to Henry Wallace, saying, "It is my thought that our Government policy [of land acquisition] should take us distinctly into the yellow pine belt in Florida, Georgia, Alabama, Mississippi, and Louisiana," and that the government should also look at the coastal plains of North and South Carolina, and southeastern Texas.[39]

It took only the slightest nudging to get Wallace and the Forest Service moving in an easterly direction. Over the next several years the federal government acquired about 22 million acres of valuable forest land primarily in the populated eastern third of the United States. Some of it, like the cut-over lands in Louisiana's Winnfield Parish where Huey Long was born and raised, was bought at bargain basement prices, thanks to the Great Depression. The federal government paid financially strapped owners as little as 50 cents an acre for what became Kisatchie National Forest in the heart of the southern pine belt.[40] With further additions along the mountain ranges and coastal plains of the eastern United States, the forest system, like the park system, developed during the New Deal into a truly national entity.

Ickes, of course, agreed entirely with Roosevelt's expanding the government's land holdings, especially when it came to the "jewels in the crown," the national parks. Once the summer reorganization was effected, the secretary kept watch over the Park Service to make sure that its officials were aggressively pursuing an expansionist policy. Ickes unfortunately lost Horace Albright, the energetic director of the agency through the 1920s, when he decided to retire in 1933. (Albright did, however, stay in touch with Ickes and for years he lobbied on behalf of the Park Service from outside of the government.) Ickes was determined to replace Albright with a career official rather than a political appointee, and so he named a man who had risen through the ranks as the agency's third director. Arno Cammerer served as director from 1933 until 1940, but unfortunately the two men never got along very well. Ickes quickly developed a deep dislike both for Cammerer's demeanor and for his administrative style, finding the director to be ever the cautious bureaucrat. The result was that the secretary spent much more time than he ordinarily would have overseeing his pet agency.

Ickes's close scrutiny of the Park Service was a mixed blessing for agency officials. On the one hand, the secretary could be counted on to fight for the agency in the congressional appropriations process, to protect it from budget cuts from the president's fiscally conservative budget director, and to keep its activities in the limelight. Ickes was one of the best friends that the agency has ever had: During Ickes's tenure forty-seven new park areas were added to the national park system, ranging from Olympic National Park in Washington State to Cape Hatteras National Seashore in North Carolina.[41] (These forty-seven were in addition to the over fifty sites that resulted from the 1933 reorganization.) Ickes saw potential national parks almost everywhere he looked, and in the fall of 1933 he even tried to interest the secretary of state in establishing an international wildlife refuge on the Galapagos Islands in the Pacific. Ickes's unflattering views about Cordell Hull—he once remarked that his typical facial expression was that of a "Christian martyr"—probably had something to do with Hull's cautious response on the Galapagos idea. Hull wrote Ickes that "this whole matter [is] so delicate that I should hesitate very much to take it up even informally with the Ecuadorian authorities."[42]

Although his initiatives at establishing new parks were not always successful, as for instance with the Galapagos Islands, nevertheless the system was much larger, much more diverse, and better managed after Ickes's thirteen years in office. By any measure, it was an impressive record and a boon to the agency.

On the other hand, in part because he didn't like Cammerer and in part because he had a particular interest in the national parks, Ickes involved himself in minutiae that no previous secretary bothered about. He cared deeply about language and how it was used, or misused, in the national parks. He vowed that there never would be a "Mount Ickes" charged to his administration, believing that living persons should not be so canonized. (One was designated in California long after his death.) He also preferred whenever possible to use indigenous names. In June of 1934 he sent a curt memo to the acting director of the agency about the naming of sites in Utah's Bryce Canyon National Park. He told Arthur Demaray, who was filling in for Cammerer:

> I don't fancy the name Peekaboo Canyon.
> Neither do I care overmuch for Queens Garden.
> Least of all do I fancy Shakespeare Point.[43]

Alas, Ickes's opinions weren't always heeded by the agency: There is today a "Peek-A-Boo Trail" in Bryce Canyon National Park. At the time, though, Ickes's close scrutiny often unnerved the staff. A former employee of the Park Service who served in the 1930s as its chief historian claimed that Ickes's overbearing and aggressive style was the reason that Horace Albright chose to retire in 1933, and that the secretary was so hard on Arno Cammerer for so many years that he caused his fatal heart attack in 1941. "Ickes," Verne Chatelain said in 1988, "drove Arno Cammerer to his grave!" Chatelain was also convinced that he was forced out of his position in the Park Service because of a personality conflict with Ickes. Some fifty years later Chatelain continued to take a dim view of his former boss's executive style. The secretary used "terror tactics" to keep his people in line, Chatelain said. When he was asked if he felt that perhaps Ickes's administrative style improved as he went along (Chatelain's unhappy experience with him occurred in 1935), the historian quickly responded, "No, he got worse! That is why Truman fired him!" [44]

PRESIDENT FRANKLIN ROOSEVELT designated 1934 "National Parks Year," the year that Americans ought to get acquainted with the country's scenic splendor. The First Family proceeded to lead the way in visiting some parks that summer. Since January FDR had been after his Interior secretary to take a vacation, and when Ickes didn't comply with his numerous "executive orders" on the subject, the president invited him to join himself and Mrs. Roosevelt and their entourage in an extended excursion out west. This was an invitation he couldn't refuse, so Ickes hopped aboard the *Pennsylvania* at Union Station on Friday, July 20, spent the hottest day he could ever remember in Chicago, and then boarded the train leaving Chicago's Northwestern station for Sacramento the next day. It had been many years, he said, since he crossed the midsection of the continent and he was anxious to see what drought and depression had done.

It was hot all across the country. "Iowa and Nebraska seemed to be burning up," he wrote. "The corn looked dried out and the tassels were a bad color and seemed to lack vitality. I have never seen the country look so dry." [45] Wyoming looked better to him, as the train crossed it on their second day out: "I fell in love all over again with that country," he mused.

Once he arrived in California, where it continued to be unusually hot, one of the secretary's first stops was at John Muir's fabulous legacy to future generations, Yosemite National Park. At Yosemite Ickes combined business with relaxation; he toured the campsites in the valley and concluded that the rangers were doing a fine job at keeping things neat and clean despite the thousands of visitors who camped there every season. Then he drove to Glacier Point and on to Mariposa Grove to view the world's oldest living things, the Sequoia gigantea. Surviving for thirty-six centuries, Ickes thought that they looked "as irresistible as time."

"I have already begun to feel the benefit of my trip," Ickes wrote in Yosemite. "There isn't any doubt that one should get away once in a while as far as possible from human contacts. To contemplate nature, magnificently garbed as it is in this country, is to restore peace to the mind, even if it does make one realize how small and petty and futile the human individual really is."

From Yosemite Ickes headed north to see Crater Lake for the first time and to visit the nearby Klamath Indian reservation where some rehabilitation work was going on. The secretary was more interested in visiting the national parks on this trip than he was in seeing what was happening on Indian reservations, but he went anyway. On July 30 he wrote Hiram Johnson, who was back in California to campaign for reelection, that "after lunch I shall drive down to the Klamath Indian Agency and the Klamath Reclamation Project. The latter is especially a dutiful deed, but I can't escape it very well since Reclamation, as well as Indians, is in my Department. I could overlook it if it weren't right under my nose, and I would if I could." [46]

Ickes was met by Wade Crawford, the Indian Bureau's supervisor on the reservation, and Robert Marshall, the agency's chief forester. The group toured the reservation and Ickes observed that it was situated in the heart of a million-acre forest of valuable yellow pines, thus making the 1,500 members of the Klamath Indian tribe the wealthiest Indians per capita of any tribe in the country. "The lumber companies . . . have made great inroads on these forests and are busy trying to acquire additional rights," Ickes said. But, he added, "It is Crawford's policy, as it is that of the Indian Bureau, to preserve all of these rights for the benefit of the Indians themselves. We hope in time to have timber manufactured in small sawmill units by the Indians themselves." [47]

Then it was on to visit Mount Rainier National Park outside Seattle, and down to Portland on August 3 where Ickes joined the president's party aboard the *Houston*. Roosevelt had taken a different route to the Pacific Northwest, one that allowed him time to relax aboard the presidential yacht before traveling inland to look at national parks and reclamation projects—and to campaign for New Deal candidates in the upcoming midterm elections. Ickes and Secretary of War George Dern were among those who lunched with Roosevelt aboard the ship. "The President looked fine and he was especially cordial in his greeting of me," Ickes related.

Tremendous crowds greeted the president and his companions across the entire Pacific Northwest. Ickes thought that all of Portland turned out to watch the president's motorcade as it toured the city, and that another huge crowd was at the Bonneville Dam site some eighty miles east of Portland. There the president made a brief speech. The Army Corps of Engineers had already begun work on this colossal power and navigation project whose unique conservation feature was to be the fish ladder. In one of their efforts to reconcile nature and economic development, the New Dealers—with FDR personally pushing the idea—spent hundreds of thousands of dollars on planning and constructing the series of jumping pools that the Pacific salmon would use, it was hoped, on their annual migration upstream to spawn.

The residents of the little community of Ephrata in eastern Washington had never seen anything like it. On the morning of August 4, 1934, the president's train was stopped on a siding in their town, and Roosevelt himself was scheduled to deliver a speech later that day at the Grand Coulee damsite. Again, Ickes noted, there were crowds everywhere to greet FDR, "but the greatest surprise of all was when we got to the damsite itself. Here there was a very large concourse of people, some said more than 20,000. It was perfectly astounding to see so many people in a desert country. Some of them," Ickes believed, "must have driven two or three hundred miles to see and hear the President." [48]

Grand Coulee was destined to become Roosevelt's Tennessee Valley Authority for the high desert plains of Idaho, Washington, and Oregon. As ambitious in its objectives as the TVA, which was FDR's first effort to join natural resources planning with economic development, the Grand Coulee (and the other dams that later sprouted up throughout the region bearing colorful names like Chief Joseph and Hungry Horse) embodied Roosevelt's grandiose dream for America. It was nothing less, in its aspiration if not in its eventual effect, than rebuilding an agrarian democracy of the kind that Thomas Jefferson so eloquently championed in the nineteenth century. In little towns like Ephrata and Spokane and Umatilla, Roosevelt believed he saw the future of America: With a million acres of fertile land needing only the low-cost power and water that the Grand Coulee would supply, and with a surplus labor force of many millions in the cities, the New Deal would transform America. Deep in his heart Roosevelt felt that the nation's cities were "hopeless," and that, if only given the opportunity, the people would return to the land.

This was the message the thousands of people who had driven in their jalopies to Grand Coulee wanted to hear. Roosevelt delivered it in a speech on that day, and in just a few years, he delivered it in deed. The Interior Department's Bureau of Reclamation completed the building of the largest manmade structure in the world in order to tame the mighty Columbia River.

The vacation was capped, appropriately enough, by a visit to what was probably Harold Ickes's favorite "jewel," the spectacular Glacier National Park in northwestern Montana. The Roosevelts, along with some of their children, a few cabinet members, senators, and congressmen, and a throng of journalists and photographers, arrived by train at Belton Station, near the western entrance to the park, on Sunday, August 5. "After breakfast we all boarded seven-passenger touring cars . . . [and] started up the west side of the park along the shore of Lake MacDonald," Ickes wrote. Traveling over the newly finished Going-to-the-Sun road, "we saw magnificent scenery—high mountains, glaciers, deep valleys and wooded plateaus, and there were beautiful lakes and waterfalls, and water trickling over sharp precipices. . . . Few in the party had ever before seen Glacier Park and all . . . seemed to be very much impressed."

In the afternoon the president delivered a speech from the chalet built along the shores of Two Medicine Lake on Glacier's east side. It was broadcast across the country, and Roosevelt spoke about the idea of parks and why he designated 1934 as National Park Year. "There is nothing so American as our national parks," he said. "The scenery and the wild life are native and the fundamental idea behind the parks is native. It is, in brief, that the country belongs to the people; that what it is and what it is in the process of making is for the enrichment of the lives of all of us. Thus the parks stand for the outward symbol of this great human principle." [49]

After his speech the president, the First Lady, and Secretary Ickes met with a group of Blackfeet Indians who came to Two Medicine Lake for the occasion. "They were a fine-looking bunch of Indians,"

Ickes wrote, "and they had on ceremonial habiliments. They chanted and some of the children danced and then they proceeded to make the President and Mrs. Roosevelt and myself members of the tribe. . . . They gave the name 'Lone Chief' to the President and the name 'Big Bear' to me. In Blackfeet my Indian name is 'Omuc Ki Yo'. . . . The Blackfeet Indians . . . constitute one of our very best tribes," Ickes observed, and the next day he promised to help them with housing and economic development.[50]

The three-week trip was a great success. Harold Ickes not only got the rest and relaxation he desperately needed after a year and a half of helping to put together the New Deal, but the Roosevelts' appearance generated enthusiasm wherever they went for liberal candidates in the upcoming elections. Roosevelt's popularity in the West was nothing short of astounding, many thought. Hiram Johnson noted in a letter to Ickes in September that "you can be assured, the President has lost none of his popularity [in California]." Johnson added that his own reelection seemed certain; in the primary he received a large Republican vote and "an enormous Democratic vote" that would translate into a November victory. The only Republicans voting against him were the oldest of the old guard who would have voted for the "Ahkoond of Swat" if he had been running against him, Johnson said.[51]

In one other way the summer trip was important for Harold Ickes. He had traveled through some spectacular natural areas in California, Oregon, Washington, Idaho, and Montana, and he had gotten the gleam of aggrandizement in his eyes. The country, he felt, could benefit from many more national parks.

CHAPTER 7

"A DASH FOR THE TIMBER"

AGRICULTURE AND

CONSERVATION

In January 1934 the recently appointed director of the National Park Service, Arno Cammerer, was attending to his job. Sometime during that first month of the new year a Senate pamphlet titled "A Plan for National Conservation" crossed the director's desk in the Interior Department. The average citizen would have found absolutely nothing remarkable about it. Pamphlets and reports of this sort were (and are) published with stupefying regularity in Washington and typically have about the same lifespan as does a moth. But this particular document was a red flag to the director of the Park Service, for it spelled out a national conservation plan that made no mention of the Interior Department. Instead it focused exclusively on the Agriculture Department and its conservation programs. Worse yet, the authors of the pamphlet discussed Agriculture's plans for expansion, which, they claimed, were already on their way to the White House for approval.

Cammerer fired off a memo to Secretary Ickes, calling his attention to this slight,[1] but Ickes was far too busy with the oil and public works programs to respond immediately. However, Cammerer's memo served to deepen Ickes's suspicions regarding what Henry Wallace and the Agriculture Department were up to. In his view, they were trying to lay claim to the title of being the federal government's premier conservation department, and in the process they would be raiding Ickes's domain. As in Frederic Remington's 1889 painting, it wasn't long before Ickes mounted a counteroffensive for the conservation title by making "a dash for the timber." He found out, however, in his gallop toward rounding up the national forests of the country that they were ably protected by Agriculture Secretary Henry Wallace, Chief Forester Ferdinand Silcox, former chief forester Gifford Pinchot, and a host of auxiliary troops—that is, interest groups—lined up behind the officers.

HAROLD ICKES'S FUNDAMENTAL and long-range objectives with respect to the Department of the Interior were, simply, to rebuild and expand it. Public confidence in the agency had been sorely tried during the Teapot Dome scandal. The ten years intervening were not sufficient time to erase in the public's mind the aura of corruption surrounding Interior; so its reform, which included getting hold of one of the most respected agencies of government, the U.S. Forest Service, became a personal crusade, a tenaciously held organizational imperative for the man who prided himself on running an honest administration. On this issue Ickes acted as though he conceived of the Interior Department as if it were a fallen woman, and he would be her savior. In fact, he used words to that effect to describe his goal.

However, Ickes's desire to restore the stature of Interior meant, if not actually stomping on some of his cabinet colleagues' toes, then surreptiously invading their terrain. Toward the end of 1934, when his plans for rebuilding his department began to take definite shape, Ickes found himself getting into rows with both Secretary of the Treasury Henry Morgenthau and Henry Wallace of Agriculture. The disagreement with the president's close friend and fellow upstate New Yorker Henry Morgenthau, who took over Treasury when William Woodin died in the spring of 1934, was over the most literal manifestation of Ickes's goal—the construction of a new and imposing Interior Department building. It was hardly a coincidence that one of the first federal projects approved under the Public Works Administration program was a spacious, air-conditioned, five-winged, six-floored, state-of-the-art building to house Ickes's expanding department.

Early in 1934 Roosevelt approved nearly $13 million for its construction, and Ickes, acting on the advice of the president's uncle, Frederic Delano, selected well-known Washington architect Waddy B. Wood to draw up the plans. Toward the end of June Ickes signed a contract with Wood. Work on the plans, which the secretary scrutinized down to the smallest detail, was about to begin when Morgenthau objected to the contract. He argued that the planning and construction of the new federal building should be done, as was the custom, under the supervision of the Public Buildings Branch of the Treasury Department and not by direct contract between Ickes and Wood.[2]

After several months of wrangling over who was to supervise construction, Ickes lost his temper. He ran into Henry Morgenthau at the White House in early November and when Morgenthau told him he hadn't yet signed the contract with Wood because his general counsel had objected, Ickes wrote,

> I became angry and told him that I was tired of fussing with the thing and that we could just forget about the Interior Building. I proposed that we build an Army or Navy building instead and let the Interior Building go by the boards. I told him further that I did not know who his lawyer was, but if that was the advice he had given him, he was not very much of a lawyer. . . . I regarded the thing as a mean renege on his part and strongly indicated my views on the subject. He began to show the yellow feather.[3]

But with Henry Wallace locking horns wasn't just an occasional incident, it was a pattern. The two department heads battled over conservation policy from their initial conversation in April 1933 about where the Forest Service belonged until Wallace left Agriculture to become vice-president during FDR's unprecedented third term in office. (After Wallace left, Ickes carried on the battle with his successor, Claude Wickard.)

The natural rivalry between Interior and Agriculture was exacerbated not only by the personalities of Ickes and Wallace but by the administration's speedy response to the Great Depression. Federal agencies sprouted up in Washington's fertile soil like mushrooms after a rain, and by the fall of 1934 it was acknowledged, from the president on down the line, that some reorganization of governmental functions was needed. Nowhere did there exist more overlap than between the Agriculture and Interior programs. For instance Ickes, in 1933, created a soil erosion unit using public works funds and hired the government's foremost expert, Hugh Hammond Bennett, to head the new program.

Bennett, the author of a widely read report that circulated in the 1920s called "Soil Erosion: A Natural Menace," happened to have been hired by Ickes out from under Henry Wallace. The Agriculture secretary was none too happy with Ickes's move. And so it went. Both Ickes and Wallace saw opportunities to extend their respective domains via the president's desire to bring a little order out of the New Deal chaos, and they often used their programs and agencies as chessmen. So did FDR.

In December 1934 Harold Ickes thought that he had arrived at a satisfactory arrangement with Henry Wallace over which agencies belonged where. But not long after his run-in with Henry Morgenthau he learned that Wallace apparently had changed his mind about the reorganization. On December 22 Ickes wrote in his diary:

> Another matter that has disappointed me is the change in the attitude of Henry Wallace with respect to a certain reorganization as between our Departments which would bring over here Forestry, the Bureau of Roads and Biological Survey, and take from here to Agriculture, Reclamation, Lands, Subsistence Homesteads, and Erosion Control. I am firmly of the opinion that, in the interest of a broad policy of conservation, all of the conservation activities ought to be grouped in the Interior Department, which now has the major portion of them, and which is the natural home for such activities. . . . With the approval of the President, I have asked for the setting up of an Under Secretaryship and my hope has been that I can persuade Rex Tugwell to come over from Agriculture as Under Secretary to have jurisdiction over all the conservation bureaus.[4]

The new year, 1935, didn't bring a satisfactory arrangement among Ickes, Wallace, and the president over how to divide up responsibilities. In fact, in Ickes's opinion, it brought him a stab in the back. Worse yet, it was administered by the person whom he had idolized until that time, Franklin Roosevelt. When the secretary, along with Anna, their son Raymond, and Indian Bureau Director John Collier, left Washington on March 17 to pay an official visit to Florida's Seminole Indian tribe, Roosevelt made his move. During the week in which Secretary Ickes was touring the Everglades, thinking about the creation of a new national park to preserve what was left of the original swamps, and considering the acquisition of more land for the 600 or so remaining Seminoles of Florida, the president transferred Hugh Bennett and the soil erosion service to the Agriculture Department.

Ickes was more than furious over the transfer; he was shocked to see a side of the president that he hadn't seen before. Right after returning to Washington, and just hours after the transfer was effected, Ickes wrote, "I am not at all pleased with this situation. . . . The President owed it to me to give me a hearing, and . . . there was no reason to call a meeting of the board [to approve the transfer] at four o'clock yesterday afternoon when I was to be back in Washington this morning." Ickes considered what he ought to do about it:

> I have no disposition to submit to many incidents of this sort. At the very least I shall feel obliged to speak quite frankly to the President. He had no right to go over my head in my absence. It looks like disciplinary action. Neither do I think he has the right to do what he does so frequently, namely, calling in members of my staff for consultation on Department matters, without consulting me or advising with me.

The loss of an agency to Agriculture was bad enough, but even worse for Ickes was feeling betrayed by the man to whom he'd been utterly devoted up to that time and whom he perceived as being absolutely faultless. But Roosevelt—who, one aide quipped, was so free of self-pity and other common frailties that he must have been psychoanalyzed by God—was human after all. The president had his faults, of course; and in 1935 Ickes was seeing one of them for the first time when the president was "reminded that Ickes was away" and seized the opportunity to do something he felt needed to be done.

The character trait that nearly everyone around FDR saw was his inability to be firm at close quarters. Roosevelt had a lot of trouble saying "no" to people he liked, he had great difficulty firing subordinates, even when they were incompetent or an embarrassment to the administration, and he could not very often bring himself to give anyone bad news directly. Ickes did not share these personality characteristics and so didn't understand why FDR resorted sometimes to devious, circuitous, and indirect methods.

Immediately upon his return from Florida, and smarting over the loss of the soil erosion program, Ickes launched his counteroffensive against the Agriculture Department. On April 10 he met with the president to discuss the proposed new public works setup and also his plans for the Interior Department. "I found him looking well and in good spirits. His manner to me was most friendly," Ickes wrote in the diaries. After FDR broke the ice by telling Ickes some amusing stories about his recent fishing trip, the two got down to business. Ickes asked Roosevelt whether he was trying to discipline him in transferring the soil erosion program to Agriculture. The president replied, "Certainly not," and asked Ickes why he felt that way. Ickes told him why:

> I told him that he had promised me a hearing and that the transfer was made late . . . Friday . . . and I was due back in Washington the following morning. He said that he had found a bad legislative situation and had to take quick action. I told him I knew all about the legislative situation and that if it had been let alone, Congress would have passed a bill making Soil Erosion a permanent function of this Department. The President said that he thought it belonged in Agriculture and I told him that . . . I believed that it was a matter of conservation.

But, Roosevelt proceeded to argue, a great deal of soil erosion work is done in connection with the national forests and they are in Agriculture. Ickes replied, "They are but they belong in Interior." He then asked Roosevelt whether he could go ahead with his "Conservation Department Bill" and FDR replied, "All right, go ahead." Finally, Ickes pressed the matter by asking him whether he would make it an administration measure. "He hesitated and then said that perhaps he might. I told him that I was having the bill drafted."

Soon after this talk, Ickes's staff prepared a chart that drew comparisons between the Interior and Agriculture departments, showing the latter to be much larger (read: unwieldy) than the former (see Table 1). At the same time as these invidious comparisons were being made, Ickes's legal staff drafted a bill to "simply" change the name of the Interior Department to the Department of Conservation and Works. However, the fine print in the legislation gave the president the authority to reorganize certain functions in the executive branch for up to two years without congressional approval. The bill was introduced by two of Ickes's allies, Sen. J. Hamilton Lewis of Illinois and Congressman John Cochran of neighboring St. Louis, Missouri.[5]

Immediately the controversy widened. Reorganization always has been a sensitive topic with Congress, and it became especially so in this

Table 1. Comparison of Departments of Agriculture and Interior

	Employees	Office space in D.C. (sq. ft.)	Bureaus
Interior	46,392	813,700	7
Agriculture	107,771	1,664,900	23[a]

[a] Includes bureaus and offices.

Source: Ickes, organization chart, c. May 1935, Conservation File, LC-HLIP.

case because of the well-known disagreements between the two department heads. No longer confined to more or less polite debates among the president, Wallace, and Ickes over where the Forest Service belonged, Senate Bill 2665 brought lobbying groups from all over the country into the fray.

Naturally the old Bull Mooser Gifford Pinchot, operating from the family's formidable-looking Pennsylvania estate, Grey Towers, led the charge. Since Pinchot was no longer occupied with the duties of governor, he had time to mobilize one of the strongest lobbies Washington has ever seen, the forestry lobby, to oppose Ickes's bill. (Pinchot, incidentally, was not only a principal force behind the creation of the Forest Service in 1905, but he also helped organize during the Roosevelt, Taft, and Wilson years the private network of interest groups that have insulated and protected the agency from that day to the present.) Pinchot and the president of the Society of American Foresters, Prof. H. H. Chapman of Yale, were the first of many to speak out against the Department of Conservation and Works.

On June 24, 1935, the opening salvo was issued in the form of a press release from the foresters' society. It pulled no punches:

> The Society of American Foresters holds that such proposed concentration and transfer of conservation of forests, grazing, and wild life from Agriculture to Interior, would be against the public interest and would tend to destroy the efficiency of existing agencies now operating successfully in . . . Agriculture. The purpose of these repeated efforts of the officials of the Department of the Interior to extend its functions to include the work of the Biological Survey, the control of all public grazing, and the U.S. Forest Service, is to replace in this manner losses suffered by the decline of its principal activity, namely, the dissipation of the vast areas of public lands by grants to private owners. This policy, pursued unremittingly until all lands worth taking, and which had not been saved to the public by other agencies, were gone, has been the chief cause of the unparalleled waste of natural resources for which the nation is now suffering the consequences.[6]

Through the early summer Ickes and Chapman engaged in a candid exchange of views, in which Chapman pointed out the secretary's political naivete in thinking that "this little bill could be slipped through a committee without attracting attention."[7] The secretary rebutted with a charge of impropriety on the part of the Forest Service. He learned from one of his investigators that "a member of the Forest Service had sent letters to the various Chambers of Commerce and to others in his state, urging them to write letters of protest against this bill."[8]

Pinchot's open letter of July 9, sent to friends of the Forest Service, was even more blunt. He, too, pointed out the disingenuous nature of the bill, which did not specifically mention the transfer of the Forest Service, "but [which] is planned for later on." The agency, he wrote, has prospered in the Agriculture Department, "where the forests are safe and the work well done," and he cautioned against moving them to that other department. "The record of the Interior Department is far and away the worst in Washington," Pinchot announced. "Every natural resource . . . that has been held for disposal by the Interior Department—public lands, Indian lands, coal, oil, water power, and timber—has been wasted and squandered at one time or another. It is one long story of fraud in public lands, theft in Indian lands, and throwing the people's property away."[9]

Ickes was very much stung by his old friend's aspersions on, if not him personally, then his department. He wrote Gifford a sarcastic letter a week later. Pinchot responded by saying that the two of them should agree to disagree on this issue. But the estrangement between these two stubborn and self-righteous Progressives deepened over the next several years, as both men became more firmly convinced that they were right in knowing what conservation "really" meant, and where the Forest Service naturally belonged. Ickes and Pinchot were both cast too much in the Theodore Roosevelt mold to concede any ground in this battle; and both adopted for the fight what Arthur Schlesinger Jr. called "the Bull Moose rhetorical convention of picturesque exaggeration by which nothing seemed worth saying if not said at the top of one's voice."[10] It made for comic opera at times, providing some amusement and distraction from a number of more serious issues facing the country in the 1930s.

The Pinchot-Ickes dispute that publicly erupted in 1935 actually had been in the making since the previous year. It had a political dimension in addition to the substantive, even philosophical, question over the true nature of the forestry enterprise: Was it tree farming, as Pinchot and others argued, or was it preservation, as Ickes was inclined to believe? Pinchot not only differed with Ickes on that question but he had been disappointed with both Harold and his superior, Franklin, when they didn't support his idea that he run as an independent in the 1934 Senate election. Initially, Ickes had wanted to campaign for his old friend, but Roosevelt was being careful about whom the adminis-tration would support in the midterm congressional races. The Senate race in Pennsylvania was one where the president treaded lightly. The Democratic nominee was the party stalwart, Joseph Guffey, and he was pitted against the "reactionary" Republican incumbent, David Reed, who had won his party's primary against some stiff competition. Pin-chot then conceived of the idea, Ickes said, "of the setting up of a new ticket, which would be a combination of his followers and the Demo-crats in the state and on which ticket, Earle, the Democratic candidate for Governor, would be the candidate, and he, Pinchot, the candidate for Senator." [11]

Both the governor and Mrs. Pinchot spoke with the president and Ickes about the proposal but got nowhere: Roosevelt publicly steered clear of the Pennsylvania races, while he quietly favored Guffey who, Ickes observed, "would go along [with the New Deal] like a led lamb." [12] When a White House aide asked Pinchot to support Guffey for senator and Earle for governor in the November elections, he wrote Roosevelt a long and personal letter telling him that he couldn't stand either man, and that he especially disliked Guffey. Therefore he would not compromise his principles for the sake of the New Deal. "If in your opinion that means war with you, war it will have to be," Pinchot wrote on October 29, 1934. "In my judgment it should not mean war. But the last word is yours," he declared ominously. By October, Ickes noted in his diaries, "the President was off of the Pinchots." [13]

On the forestry issue that served to widen the rift between Ickes and Pinchot in 1935, Roosevelt found himself caught in the middle, al-though he inclined toward the more utilitarian view. The president knew a great deal about conservation in general and forestry in par-ticular, but unlike Ickes, Wallace, and Pinchot he never felt strongly about the organizational issue of where the Forest Service properly belonged. Through the years he sometimes sided with his secretary of the interior, and at other times with the Agriculture secretary. He tried his best to placate both men, although some thought that FDR took perverse pleasure in dangling Forestry before Ickes's eyes but never delivering it. The debate both amused and, at times, exasperated FDR—as when he said that instead of Interior and Agriculture they should be called the "Department of the North" and the "Department of the South" with their respective responsibilities divided by the Mason-Dixon line.

During this first skirmish, in the summer of 1935, the president was noncommittal. Although Ickes tried his best to get him to take a stand, Roosevelt managed to slip past the secretary's entreaties. In June Ickes wrote:

> Last Saturday morning I had a session with the President in his study at the White House. When I told him that there had been another hearing before the House Committee on Expenditures . . . on my Department Bill at which Henry Wallace had appeared, he said, "Why, I told him not to do that." [14]

BY THE MIDDLE of another sticky, humid summer in Washington it was clear that Ickes was losing the first round in this battle. Congress was winding down from one of the most impressive sessions in all of its history, having passed, to name just a few measures, a new oil bill, the Public Utilities Holding Company Act, social security legislation, an enlarged emergency relief bill, and moderately progressive tax legislation. But it did not pass Ickes's bill. On August 13 the members of the House Committee on Expenditures—selected over the Public Lands Committee to hold hearings because of its presumed support—defeated Interior's bill by a 10 to 5 vote. "This was not only a disappointment to me, it was a shock," Ickes confided in his diary.

Many people would have given up at this point. Not Ickes, however, whose Scotch-German heritage undoubtedly contributed to his stubbornness. Genes aside, Ickes decided not to give up for two reasons: He'd become convinced that he was correct about the need for a conservation department that included forestry (and, ideally, the other resource agencies of government), and he genuinely loved political combat. As his early years as a Chicago campaigner attest, he relished battling when the odds were very much against him. So instead of admitting defeat he decided to pull back, regroup, and reintroduce a new bill early in 1936. Perhaps Congress's agenda would not be so crowded then. Perhaps he even could convince the president to get into this fight as well.

It was a difficult summer all around. Not only did his conservation department never get out of committee, but his actions in connection with one of the Interior Department's bureaus, the Division of Islands and Territories, were being investigated by a Senate committee. Altogether, he was under enormous stress that summer. He wrote on July 22 that "I had an exceptionally bad night last night. I hardly slept at all, in spite of liberal libations of whisky, which usually puts me to sleep. I suppose I was overtired but undoubtedly the Virgin Islands situation was working on my subconsciousness." [15]

Certain personnel changes that Secretary Ickes made in the Virgin Islands—positions that for obvious reasons were often used as political rewards—displeased certain senators, and back in February Ickes went to the Capitol to see one of them in the hopes of coming to an agreement about the reassignment of Federal Judge Thomas Webber Wilson. He went to talk to Sen. Pat Harrison of Mississippi, who in 1933 had recommended his fellow Mississippian and former congressman to that post in the Virgin Islands. "I can usually sit down with a man, even if he feels pretty bitter about me, and arrive at some sort of an understanding, but I couldn't get anywhere with whiny Pat," Ickes wrote after their meeting. "He doesn't fight things man-fashion. He was like an old, complaining woman, and, also like a woman, he keeps running around in circles and coming back to the point of departure." When Harrison complained of getting no consideration from the Interior Department the secretary pointed out that he had been given over sixty jobs in the agency, and that "if he had that many from the other departments, that would make a total of over six hundred, without counting appointments from the independent agencies and emergency organizations."

Notwithstanding such enormous patronage, the senator remained angry over Ickes's outspoken objections to Judge Wilson, and in March Vice-President Garner told Ickes that the Senate just passed a resolution to appoint an investigative committee to look into the Virgin Islands situation. Millard Tydings of Maryland was to chair the committee, Garner said, and it "would be a fair one. Senator Tydings' idea . . . is to send a first-class investigator to the Virgin Islands. If he brings back a report that there is nothing to all the hullabaloo down there, then the investigation would be dropped." Ickes then said that he told the vice-president that "I was ready to go on the stand any day and that I had my statement all prepared."

Secretary Ickes was among the first witnesses to be called when the Tydings committee began its investigation on July 2, 1935. The hearings continued for about three weeks as Ickes, Gov. Paul Pearson of the Virgin Islands (who was the father of influential Washington correspondent Drew Pearson), Judge Wilson, a former aide of Pearson's named Paul Yates, and many others were called to testify. One of the high points of the nasty affair occurred on the first day when Robert Allen (who was Drew Pearson's collaborator on the popular "Washington Merry-Go-Round" column) and Paul Yates encountered one another in the Senate Office building. They got into a fistfight. "Allen called Yates a double-crosser and Yates called Allen a son of a bitch, whereupon Allen, who is a little fellow but husky, proceeded to beat Yates up. He knocked him down once or twice, closing one eye and cutting his lip. . . . Yates had to be carted off to a hospital . . . and [so] wasn't available to go on as the first witness," Ickes noted dryly.

The investigation was fought on a number of fronts—the Senate hearing room, the corridor outside the hearing room, the White House, the secretary's office, in the newspapers, and in the Virgin Islands itself. It had a peculiar aspect, in that most of the people involved were connected in one way or another to the newspaper business. There thus appeared to be ulterior motives involved. In his diaries Ickes said that he hadn't the "slightest doubt" that senators Tydings and Harrison were not interested in an impartial investigation of the Virgin Islands administration but rather were out to get Governor Pearson fired. Paul Pearson's ties to the newspaper business obviously included his son, Drew, and Drew's collaborator, Robert Allen. And testifying against Pearson and Ickes were the former newspaperman Paul Yates and a shadowy young man named John Hinshaw, whom Ickes described as having been employed at about this time as "a leg man for Drew Pearson." [16]

Moreover, Ickes himself was on good terms with both Drew Pearson and Robert Allen. He occasionally supplied them with inside information for their column. When Senator Tydings denied the secretary's request to cross-examine the witnesses, Ickes turned to the press to get his side across. The second week into the hearings he wrote, "My theory is that since we are denied the right of cross-examination and since Tydings seems bent on smearing us all he can, we ought to fight back day by day through the newspapers, which is the only means available to us to meet the vague charges that are being produced before the . . . committee." [17] The next day Ickes put his "theory" into action and made public a letter he'd written to Tydings, accusing him of "gross partiality" and of "whitewashing Judge Wilson." Tydings, Ickes said, "became berserk." He scolded Ickes "like a fish wife" and then proceeded to give out a copy of his letter to Ickes to the press. In many different ways the press was tangled up in the Tydings investigation.

At the same time that Ickes went public, Tydings and a few other senators appealed to FDR to rein in the Interior secretary. At 9 A.M. on Thursday, July 11, Ickes met with FDR who was still in his bedroom. "The reason he wanted to see me so early was that he had a later appointment with Senators Tydings, Robinson, and Harrison," Ickes related.[18] Ickes gave Roosevelt his side of the story, which included his grievances against Tydings and why he felt his only recourse "was to carry the thing to the newspapers." Ickes then told the president that "I had done that deliberately and that I was able to lick Tydings' pants off him in that kind of a battle because I had the facts." Roosevelt, who appeared quite cordial to Ickes throughout their 45-minute discussion, responded by saying, "I know you can."

The fallout was predictable. After Roosevelt listened to Ickes's and to Tydings' respective grievances, he decided to do some housecleaning. On July 23, he wrote Governor Pearson that "though it is a source of satisfaction to know that the current investigation of the Virgin Islands has developed no facts that reflect upon your honesty, or integrity, yet you may wish to transfer to another field of service."[19] Pearson subsequently was given a position in the housing division within Ickes's PWA. FDR did likewise with the congressionally backed Judge Wilson: He was reassigned to the Federal Parole Board.

The president's even-handed actions on July 23 quite possibly were taken to spare his valuable assistant, Harold Ickes, from some real mudslinging. Senator Tydings received a two-page letter dated July 22, 1935, in which the unnamed author charged the secretary with a number of serious improprieties, including keeping his mistress, Marguerite Brumbaugh, on the PWA payroll for about a year, using his office for their trysts, and even having his assistant, Ebert Burlew, pay her $5,000 to keep her quiet. The letter further quoted Burlew as saying, when he was told that Secretary Ickes wanted him to see a certain young woman regarding a promotion, "Is this to be another Brumbaugh case?" Burlew then went off on a diatribe, according to the author of the letter (whose identity can be surmised), about having to "bear the burden of suppressing the scandal."[20]

Although these were only allegations, there was sufficient truth in some of them to have made Ickes's position untenable had they become public. Instead, the president brought to a close the Tydings investigation by reassigning both Pearson and Wilson. Some of FDR's aides didn't agree with his solution. They thought that the well-publicized row between Ickes and Tydings, not to mention what didn't get publicized, was adversely affecting the president's legislative program. They argued that he should rebuke his feisty secretary. (Marvin McIntyre, one of the president's secretaries, was absolutely frigid toward him at this time, Ickes observed.)

Instead of calling Ickes on the carpet or even firing him, FDR paid him some compliments. In early August their mutual friend, Felix Frankfurter, met with Ickes and told him that he'd been with FDR when the storm broke over the Tydings-Ickes exchange. "He was with him that night . . . and the following morning," Ickes related. Frankfurter said that "this was a real political crisis, a matter of major concern, and yet the president never by word, expression, or tone indicated impatience or displeasure with me [Ickes] for having stirred up the hornet's nest." Rather, FDR told his dinner guests that "Ickes would be a tower of strength in any Administration." [21]

BY THIS TIME the president knew whereof he spoke. Harold Ickes's ability to withstand pressure—which came from both his public and private life—was nothing short of extraordinary. For over two years Ickes's endurance had been tested, and he had, as Roosevelt observed, come through. But at the end of a very trying summer Ickes's strength was tested again. On August 31 Anna Ickes was killed in an automobile accident.

The Ickeses' marriage had taken on a veneer of normalcy after the climactic events of 1933 and 1934, when Ickes told Anna of his love for another woman and when she, a few months later, took an overdose of medicine and called the doctor. After that crisis, Anna became reconciled to the change in their relationship. She didn't run for re-election to the Illinois legislature, and instead came down to Washington to live with her husband on Glenbrook Road in northwest Washington. In this milieu she enjoyed the status of being the wife of a cabinet officer. Although she knew that her husband was still seeing his mistress, Ickes observed that she never taunted him about it. Nor did she insist on a physical dimension to their marriage of twenty-five years' duration. Like many a middle-aged couple—both were entering their sixties by 1934—the union was allowed to slip into a comfortable accommodation. In this respect it was not unlike the marriage of Franklin and Eleanor.

Ickes claimed that he and Anna had resolved "quite satisfactorily" their differences by 1935.[22] They entertained, attended social functions together, and enjoyed having their children, especially 22-year-old Raymond, visit them on holidays. Anna continued with her interest in Native Americans, and she and Raymond accompanied Harold when he went to Florida at the invitation of the Seminole Indian tribe in March of 1935.

She also continued to spend part of her summers at their home near Gallup, New Mexico. While she was out in her favorite part of the country she wrote frequently to her husband about what she witnessed first-hand concerning Interior Department programs. Anna's feelings were well defined and she was never reluctant to make strong suggestions about what to do about those issues she cared about. In the summer of 1933, for example, she wired her husband from the Grand Canyon, telling him that she was much alarmed over who was to be named superintendent of Mesa Verde National Monument in Colorado. She told the secretary to consult Park Service Director Horace Albright about the appointment and then to wire her, the next day, at Coolidge, Arizona, where she was visiting the Casa Grande National Monument.[23]

Anna's interest in the department her husband ran continued when she moved to Washington. Although some significant alterations had occurred in their personal affairs, Anna remained Anna. In a word, she could be very overbearing, a trait she shared with her husband, who ordinarily found it, in her, annoying. For example, early in January 1935, Anna contacted the staff of the National Park Service to make some renovations on their home on Glenbrook Road. On January 11, Associate Director Arthur Demaray of the Park Service sent a memo to Ebert Burlew, Ickes's budget officer for the department, spelling out the problem:

> Engineers Peters and Gillen went to the Secretary's home and talked with Mrs. Ickes about glassing in the porch. I understand Mrs. Ickes desired our engineers to urge the Secretary to have this work done. She also wanted the work completed by January 23 and there is just about time enough to do so if authority is given to go ahead early Monday morning. Three estimates of cost were prepared and they range from $1,000 to $1,500. . . . The work which will be most difficult to get done satisfactorily and on time is

the millwork. It will be necessary to have one of our architects detail the millwork so as much stock can be used as possible. We can handle the specifications and advertising and can probably get representatives of mills from Baltimore and Washington to bid on the job. We would like your authority to use one or two of our men in doing this work.[24]

The secretary initialed the memo, indicating that he had seen it, but he didn't indicate whether or not he approved the use of the Park Service to glass in their porch in time for Anna's sixty-second birthday. For an individual who prided himself on his incorruptibility, however, Anna's request must have caused him consternation.

On Thursday, August 1, 1935, Anna said goodbye to Harold and left Washington by train for Chicago. That was the last time he saw her alive. She spent a few hours in Chicago on Friday, and then took an airplane bound for Albuquerque. With a friend, Genevieve Forbes Herrick, Anna spent the next month at her vacation home outside of Gallup. She and her friends did the things they loved doing—motoring over the dusty roads of northwestern New Mexico to visit the peoples of the Taos and Navajo tribes and to visit the ruins of earlier civilizations. On August 31 Anna and Genevieve, along with Ibrahim Seyfullah from the Turkish Embassy, were driven by Anna's chauffeur, Frank Allen, to the Taos Pueblo north of Santa Fe.

After spending the day in Taos the group headed south, toward Espanola and Santa Fe. Allen was driving on the road that follows the Rio Grande River as it meanders through New Mexico and that hugs the western edge of the Sangre de Cristo Mountains. In the late afternoon light the mountain range is usually very beautiful. Near the little village of Alcalde, the driver lost control of the car, it skidded off the pavement, rolled a few times, and came to rest upright in a dry wash. Anna Ickes died almost instantly, as did Frank Allen. Both of them had broken through the top of the automobile with their heads.[25]

Harold Ickes was working in his office when about 8:45 on Saturday night his private secretary, Fred Marx, came to the door with the news that Anna had been in a serious automobile accident. "I called Santa Fe by long distance at once and got the hospital that Fred told me Anna had been taken to," Ickes wrote in his diary. "It was St. Vincent's. I asked the sister . . . whether they had an accident case there and she said to wait a minute, that the ambulance was just coming in. Then the driver of the ambulance took the telephone and told me that Anna had been killed." Fortunately, Ickes said, death was probably instantaneous for both Anna and Allen.

He stayed in the office late that night contacting the children and making funeral arrangements in Winnetka. The president called him to express his sympathy, and told him that he'd cancel his Hyde Park trip if he could be of any assistance. He also sent over Tom Corcoran and Felix Frankfurter, who were at the White House, to help Ickes through the long evening.

"On Sunday I perfected the plans and took the 4:30 train to Chicago," Ickes wrote.[26] On Monday he and Anna's first-born son, Wilmarth, selected a plot at Memorial Park Cemetery, although Anna's family, the Wilmarths, already had a plot for her at Graceland, another cemetery in the area. "But it is pretty well filled and, besides, I wanted my own," Ickes said.

The funeral was held the next day, on Tuesday, September 3. "It was the coldest funeral that I have ever attended," Ickes wrote.[27] Certainly Harold made no pretense of being saddened by the death of his wife of nearly 25 years, and neither did all but one of the children, he claimed. Anna was a formal and "austere" woman, her son, Raymond explained.[28] She didn't often express affection and so not much was expressed when she died. Ironically, it was Robert, the little boy whom Anna and Harold took in as a playmate for Raymond in 1915, and whom they never got around to legally adopting, who shed tears over his mother's unexpected death.

The mechanics of the funeral kept Harold occupied during the several days he spent in Winnetka. Although it was a pretty emotionless affair, it nevertheless was executed in a dignified yet simple manner, which was how he wanted it. People and organizations "from everywhere" sent over 200 floral pieces, "and they made a wonderful showing against the paneled walls of the living room and the stone walls of the hall." Anna's closed coffin was draped with a simple blanket of asparagus fern, which her husband selected, and with the wreath of white asters and white gladioli that the president and Mrs. Roosevelt sent.

The beautiful house at Hubbard Woods which Harold and Anna had built painstakingly 20 years earlier was filled that Tuesday afternoon with Anna's family, her friends, and the nation's leaders. Mrs. Eleanor Roosevelt came to pay her respects; so did Secretary of War and Mrs. George Dern; Postmaster General James Farley; Secretary of Commerce and Mrs. Roper; Mrs. Henry Wallace; Works Progress Administrator Harry Hopkins; Illinois's Gov. Henry Horner; Sen. William Dieterich; and Chicago's Mayor Edward Kelly. They and others of lesser stature came to offer their last respects to Mrs. Anna Wilmarth Ickes.

If Anna's death did not engender strong emotions, the disclosure that week of the contents of her will did. To the astonishment of all of her children, except perhaps Raymond, Anna's will left virtually all of her sizable estate to her husband. Wilmarth in particular was not only angry, he was incredulous, for he knew that his mother had written a codicil to her will in 1933, after she had learned about her husband's affair. Sometime that week Wilmarth went to see his mother's attorney, Charles Thomson, to ask about the codicil. Thomson gave Wilmarth the bad news that while there had been one written up— one that left most of her fortune to her four children—Anna Ickes subsequently instructed him to destroy it. Wilmarth, who desperately needed the money to pay gambling debts and other bills, returned to the family home at Hubbard Woods, stormed in, and told Robert, in the presence of Raymond, "Well, you and I are sunk; the old man gets everything." [29]

Wilmarth and Robert could hardly believe that their mother had reversed the codicil. Indeed, as Harold Ickes himself related the event in his unpublished memoirs, the reversal was done in a highly unusual way. At the time of Anna's funeral Harold, too, spoke to Charles Thomson about the will and whether there was a codicil. The attorney, Ickes wrote, told him that he had met Anna on Michigan Avenue in downtown Chicago in early August. Anna was in the city for just a few hours before she flew to New Mexico, and it was at this chance meeting on the street that Anna told Thomson that she had changed her mind about the codicil. She wanted him to destroy it. Thomson, Ickes related, urged Anna to return to his nearby office and take care of it in person. "No, I haven't time," the attorney recalled her saying. "You do it for me."

But when Harold called upon Thomson after his wife's death, the attorney had not yet destroyed the codicil. Thomson, Ickes wrote, was in a quandary as to what to do. Ickes claimed to have told him that he should do what he thought right. Charles Thomson then destroyed the codicil. [30]

Thus in a matter of days, Harold Ickes was released from twenty-five years of marital turbulence and became the sole beneficiary of Anna's estate. While that estate was not so big as to make him fabulously wealthy, it did give him, among other assets, their palatial Hubbard Woods property, the house in which Wilmarth, Betty, and their children lived, and some high-rent property on State Street in the Loop. It was enough to make him a reasonably wealthy man for the rest of his life. It also earned him Wilmarth's enmity.

NOTHING KEPT HAROLD ICKES from his work for very long. He was back at work in Washington and dictating his memoirs on Friday, September 6, just four days after his wife's funeral. Before he discussed Anna's sudden death and her funeral, the secretary carefully picked up where he had left off dictating on Saturday night, August 31. At least he was living up to his reputation for honesty when he made no show at being much affected by his wife's death. "Life settled down very pleasantly for me after Anna's death," he wrote in the memoirs.[31]

Resuming the diaries on the sixth, Ickes wrote, "Morgenthau and Hopkins are, of course, fighting me on different fronts."[32] While his principal objectives that fall were to make sure that Harry Hopkins didn't get control of his Public Works Administration, and to counter Henry Morgenthau's power grab, Ickes also found time to make sure that his row with Henry Wallace over the Forest Service wasn't completely neglected. On September 30 Ickes and FDR were on the Arizona-Nevada border for the dedication of Hoover Dam. While he was there, the secretary sent his assistant, Harry Slattery, a memo, telling him to make a thorough investigation of the Forest Service in connection with lobbying activities against their Department of Conservation bill. "I want to be able . . . to make out such a complete case against the Forest Service that we can put it on the defensive," he wired Slattery.[33]

Ickes intended to make another dash for the timber early in 1936, and this time he wanted to be better prepared. After the defeat in August, at least he knew how strongly defended they were, and what it might take to get control of the nation's trees.

CHAPTER 8

"I AM NOT A BOONDOGGLER"

IN THE RING WITH

HARRY HOPKINS

THREE WEEKS AFTER Anna's death, and a few days before
he left on another vacation with FDR, Harold Ickes wrote
Hiram Johnson a chatty, six-page letter designed to fill in his
ailing friend on what was going on in the administration. The
senator was convalescing in his suite at the Mark Hopkins Hotel in San Francisco, and one reason for the letter was to urge
Johnson to attend the dedication of Boulder Dam at the end
of September. As Ickes reminded him, "You, more than any
other man in the country, are the one who ought to be there
on that occasion because without you there wouldn't be any
Boulder Dam to dedicate." [1]

Most of the six pages concerned the nearly $5-billion work
relief program Congress had authorized earlier in 1935, and
how little of it was going to be spent by Ickes's Public Works
Administration. In Ickes's mind, there was no doubt that the
paltry sum the president had just allocated to him was the direct result of scheming on the part of Harry Hopkins:

In my judgment, the administrative setup for the works-relief program was bad from the beginning. There should have been one man charged with responsibility, and that man should not have been the President. The President has tried to reconcile two widely divergent points of view but without . . . success. Moreover, there has been overlapping, bidding against each other, and administrative friction. Hopkins from the beginning has tried to hog the whole program, both his and mine. Even if I had been disposed to occupy the whole field, I couldn't have done so because I am not a boondoggler, and besides the programs were such that I couldn't encroach on Hopkins while he could very well encroach on me. This he has attempted to do at every stage. At intervals the situation would become so bad that I would go to the President. Then he would redefine Hopkins' sphere and the next day Hopkins would be over my back fence again. He even arrogated to himself the right to veto public works projects on one flimsy excuse after another, until a point was reached where it was apparent that there wouldn't be any public works program at all unless a radical change was made.[2]

Ickes's one-sided analysis of the situation wouldn't have fooled his old friend. The two men had fought together for liberal causes for some twenty years, and while Johnson sincerely believed Ickes to be a first-rate administrator, he also knew that Ickes not only politicked on behalf of his programs as fiercely as anyone in Washington in the 1930s, but that he was anybody's equal when it came to reaching out for more power.

In fact, as most Washington insiders knew, the competition between Hopkins and Ickes for control of the work-relief program was intense through most of 1935. Their power struggle continued until the 1939 overhaul of the New Deal programs. While the two men managed to work together in the spring of 1935 on drawing up a comprehensive recovery plan to give to FDR for submission to Congress, behind the scenes it was a bitter struggle not only for control of the work relief program but for the president's attention and affection. Newspaper cartoonists had a field day caricaturing Roosevelt's two bickering boys.

While Harold Ickes and Harry Hopkins had a great deal in common, temperamentally they were very different. Neither trusted the other. If Ickes complained to friends like Hiram Johnson about Hopkins, Hopkins in turn did the same. In May, when the two were working on the new relief plan, Hopkins confided to his diary, "All day planning the work program, which would be a great deal easier if Ickes would play ball—but he is stubborn and righteous which is a hard combination. He is also the 'great resigner.' . . . He bores me." [3] At about the same time Ickes wrote in his diary,

> I am becoming more and more sick of this whole setup and wish that I could find a way to get out of it. The thing is clumsy and cumbersome. It takes altogether too much time conferring with Hopkins and [Frank] Walker and then with the President and then presiding over this town meeting that we call an Advisory Allotment Board. What this organization needs is an Administrator and I wish the President would see that. [4]

Hopkins and Ickes got where they did in 1935—at the center of power in Washington, and among the president's closest associates— by traveling roughly similar paths in life. Although Hopkins was some sixteen years Ickes's junior (born on August 17, 1890, in Sioux City, Iowa), the two men nevertheless came of age politically during the intensely optimistic and colorful Progressive Era, when the larger-than-life Theodore Roosevelt captured the public's attention as no president had done for generations. It was during the 1912 presidential contest that both Hopkins and Ickes saw their Progressive hero in the flesh and were duly impressed: Ickes met him on a westbound train headed to Chicago for the convention, and Hopkins, who had just graduated from Grinnell College, got his first glimpse of the Bull Moose when he got off the train in Chicago to watch the Republican National Convention. The 22-year-old Hopkins was on his way to take his first job as a social worker in New York City's slums when "he heard Theodore Roosevelt shout that thieves were running the Republican Party—that the renomination of . . . Taft was 'naked theft.' " [5] He then stopped off in Baltimore where the Democrats were meeting. There he watched William Jennings Bryan's historic struggle to get the Democratic nomination for the relatively unknown Princeton University president and New Jersey governor Woodrow Wilson. After watching these dramatic spectacles, with political giants like Roosevelt and Bryan in starring roles, Hopkins decided that he would be in on the action someday. Harold Ickes had similar aspirations.

During the 'teens, when Woodrow Wilson was in the bully pulpit preaching reform in Washington, Harry Hopkins did in New York many of the things that Ickes did in Chicago. Both men spent a good deal of time in the urban reform movement aimed at eradicating slums, poverty, and corruption in city halls. Ickes came at the problems as a liberal Republican who enlisted in Roosevelt's Progressive Party for as long as it lasted (which wasn't long), and Hopkins approached them as a liberal Democrat. It was a movement that spanned both parties.

When the United States entered the First World War in 1917 both men sought out opportunities to be in on the war effort. Hopkins tried to enlist in the armed services but wasn't taken because of a detached retina. He then joined the Red Cross and was sent to New Orleans to direct the Gulf Division. Ickes, who by then was in his forties, had to content himself with a position in France working with the YMCA. Both men also left behind their wives and young children to participate in the "war to end all wars." During the Second World War, Hopkins's three sons from his first marriage to Ethel Gross all saw combat. Their youngest son, Stephen, was killed in action when the Marines attacked Kwajalein Atoll in February 1944. He was only 18 years old. Harold's and Anna's 30-year-old son, Raymond, also served in the Marine Corps. He was seriously wounded during the storming of Iwo Jima in February of 1945.

During the roaring, Republican-dominated twenties, Ickes and Hopkins stayed the liberal course, even though their numbers dwindled to a "corporal's guard" because few Americans wished to be reminded that the nation still had social and economic problems to address. Hopkins, however, met a moderately liberal and very personable candidate for governor of New York in the 1928 race. His association with Franklin Roosevelt dated from the time he enlisted in FDR's critical comeback campaign, during which Roosevelt first displayed to the public his remarkable resiliency: After contracting polio in 1921, the man was crippled for the rest of his life. It of course took unusual courage and stamina to campaign with that handicap, even allowing for the fact that the press was far more considerate of public figures than it is today.

The emerging friendship between Roosevelt and Hopkins was based on many things, not least of which were similar qualities of character. Robert Sherwood, one of FDR's speechwriters and a close friend of Harry Hopkins, wrote that "despite all their differences . . . Roosevelt and Hopkins were alike in one important way: they were thoroughly and gloriously unpompous. The predominant qualities in both were unconquerable confidence, courage and good humor." [6]

Similar political convictions initially brought Ickes, FDR, and Hopkins together, but friendships among and between them developed as a result of their shared liberalism and pragmatism. All three men loved their work. While Ickes and Roosevelt never became as close as did Hopkins and Roosevelt, a deep current of affection traveled between the president and the old curmudgeon. As for Hopkins and Ickes, although their rivalry usually obscured the more positive aspects of their relationship, there were occasions during the thirteen years they worked together when expressions of genuine affection for each other burst forth to put the power struggle on hold. They weren't frequent, but they were there, like a leitmotif.

ROOSEVELT'S LEGENDARY administrative style, of course, served to exacerbate the personal rivalries among his aides, which blossomed like flowers in an English garden. Through much of 1935 the president contributed to the Hopkins-Ickes rivalry by not deciding who was to administer the $4- to $5-billion works program that would carry the administration through 1936 and into the presidential election. In January 1935 Ickes wrote, "I am still in utter ignorance as to what the new PWA setup is to be," and speculated that FDR might give the entire program to Harry Hopkins. A few weeks later, Ickes and FDR discussed the same topic, and Ickes noted, "Apparently he has in mind to set up quite a large works Board along the English plan," a plan that Ickes dismissed as "unworkable." [7]

The suspense continued through the summer of 1935, and the president, perhaps unwittingly, added further stress for Ickes when he kept him guessing as to who would administer the multibillion-dollar relief program. Ickes's nerves finally gave way on August 22 when he received a letter about the PWA from FDR and later that day read the headline in the *Washington Star,* "Ickes Is Shorn of PWA Power." The headline was based on Roosevelt's letter, which opened with the following:

> I am writing to inform you that, with respect to public works funds available for carrying out the purposes of the National Industrial Recovery Act, as amended, I desire that all future applications for allocations and all cancellations, rescissions, and modifications of previous allocations be submitted to the Advisory Committee on Allotments, to be acted upon in the same manner and to the same extent as that committee acts with respect to allocations made under the Emergency Relief Appropriations Act of 1935.

Ickes deciphered this to mean that he was being cut out. "I went right up into the air," he said, and after calling Hiram Johnson to complain loudly about the president's cavalier manner of handling him and his PWA, he called Roosevelt himself. It was almost 9 o'clock in the evening when Ickes asked if he could come over to the White House. "What is this all about?" Roosevelt asked. Ickes proceeded to tell him.

> I was pretty angry and I showed it. I never thought I would talk to a President of the United States the way I talked to President Roosevelt. . . . I think I made it pretty clear that I wasn't going to stand for much more of the same kind of medicine. I reminded him that I had had occasion to complain before that Executive Orders affecting my Department had been issued without my being advised of them, and that more than once the first information of important news affecting myself I had gotten from the newspapers.

Roosevelt told Ickes that the story in the *Star* was not justified, and that he had no intention of changing his status as PWA administrator. "Don't be childish, Harold," the president said. "The newspapers are cockeyed." Finally, Roosevelt told his seething secretary that he would have his press secretary, Steve Early, give a statement the next day saying that Roosevelt's letter was misinterpreted by the press. Steve Early called Ickes back later that evening and read FDR's announcement to him. "The statement was as good as was possible in the circumstances," Ickes admitted. "It did categorically deny that there was any intention to change my status as Administrator of Public Works. The statement sounded fishy to me, but I couldn't suggest any improvement," he added.

Worried that the PWA was about to slip from his grasp, Ickes proceeded to mount a lobbying campaign designed to forestall that move on FDR's part. Through the end of August and into September—during the time that he dealt with his wife's death—Ickes and his PWA staff called on their allies to pressure the White House to keep him in charge of public works. A confidential memo from Steve Early to Marvin McIntyre revealed that in September they learned of some of Ickes's machinations. In the memo Early told McIntyre to apprise FDR of the situation:

> Have reasons to suspect that Dickinson's telegram was inspired by Ickes as part of his propaganda against Hopkins. Still very confidentially Tugwell just telephoned to tell me that he has heard Ickes is asking A F of L officials to get behind Public Works program if it is to be saved. Have also heard that he has asked State Directors of Public Works to get busy.[8]

Newspaper columnists and administration officials also jumped into the fray. Raymond Clapper, a *Washington Post* columnist sympathetic to Ickes, wrote in his column that "Ickes' Fault Was Lingering Too Long at the Altar of Public Honesty." It was becoming clear, Clapper wrote, that FDR was about to choose Harry Hopkins and Rexford Tugwell to run the works relief show—"the jocund pair after whom Mr. Roosevelt has named a span of mules on his Warm Springs farm." [9]

Tom Corcoran and Ben Cohen also sided with their friend, the public works administrator, and spoke with their White House contacts on Ickes's behalf. They believed, along with Ickes, that Hopkins was deliberately trying to discredit the PWA,[10] just as Ickes was trying to discredit Hopkins and his leaf-raking program.

By the middle of September the president decided that it was time to end the waiting game over the relief program. All the principal contenders were invited to a conference at Hyde Park, presided over by FDR. The setting was lovely, with the trees turning various shades of gold and red, and the Hudson River reflecting the thinning autumn light. Characteristically, Roosevelt tried to placate all of his loyal aides by dividing up responsibilities, just what Ickes had feared he would do all along. This time he formed a triumvirate to administer the $4.5-billion emergency relief program, which consisted of Harry Hopkins, Harold Ickes, and the very genial Frank Walker, who, the president hoped, would act as a Hopkins-Ickes go-between. Others, like Tugwell of the Agriculture Department, were also given portions of the program to administer.

If the president thought that the soothing fall atmosphere at his estate would contribute to a spirit of acceptance, he was wrong. To Ickes, as well as to some others, it looked like a rout. In his September 21 letter to Hiram Johnson, he said:

> The settlement at Hyde Park was a mere compromise, and not a satisfactory one at that . . . from the President's own point of view. Too much money was given to Tugwell to play around with on schemes that the country is really not interested in. Low-cost housing was cut from $249,000,000 to $100,000,000, although, in my judgment, this is one of the best things we are doing. He shaved $20,000,000 from reclamation, pared a little here and . . . there, with the result that he told me that I could count on $200,000,000 out of the new funds, in addition to the $127,000,000 that had already been allocated for public works out of those funds. . . .

My own feeling is that if the President is defeated next year, and . . . I am not at all sure that he will be reelected, the major factor in that defeat will be his insistence on the Hopkins program.[11]

ALTHOUGH ICKES WAS quick to conclude that FDR no longer supported his PWA and that Harry Hopkins came out the clear victor in the emergency relief ring, the president himself didn't share those views. Rather, Roosevelt's Hyde Park Accord of September 1935 reflected more than anything else his administrative style and the huge sums of money he was allocating. These amounts were unprecedented during peacetime. By carving up the massive multibillion-dollar program, and giving different parts of it to individuals with different temperaments and different objectives, FDR believed he could get the most out of his men—and the program. Roosevelt, as usual, retained ultimate control.

The major complaint against Ickes's administration of public works was that he was too slow in expending funds. So FDR had Harry Hopkins, the freewheeling spender who in his spare time played the horses, there to counterbalance Ickes's careful and high-minded approach. Hopkins, ironically, was criticized for spending money too fast and with too little accountability. FDR recognized that it was impossible to please everyone with a single emergency effort, and thus he divided it up, playing to each man's strength.

On several occasions, moreover, Roosevelt complimented Ickes's cautious handling of the PWA, and the fact that the president retained him in that capacity through most of his troubled second term was testimony to his confidence in him as an administrator. Harold Ickes served in that position from 1933 to 1939, longer than most people serve in any governmental office. And although Ickes never felt very secure in his position—he once joked that he slept with his hat on the bedpost—much of his insecurity was internally generated. It was not an accurate assessment of his boss's estimation.

Roosevelt appreciated not only Ickes's administrative skills but also the fact that his PWA administrator had taken the heat for him in two very controversial situations that came to a head in 1935. At a cabinet meeting in early February of that year, Ickes noted in his diary that Roosevelt said "that everyone had to have a whipping post and that I had been his since Hugh Johnson resigned."[12] The president was referring to the beating that the public works administrator was taking from the press over the "Moses affair." As Ickes explained it,

> I am being subjected to very heavy fire by every newspaper in New York, so far as I know, except one. The occasion of these attacks grew out of my effort to terminate the services of Robert Moses, who was appointed by Mayor LaGuardia as a member of the Triborough Bridge Authority. I have done this at the President's specific request.

Franklin Roosevelt actively hated few people, but the celebrated architect of New York City, Robert Moses, was one of those select few. The feud between the two New Yorkers went back many years and contained both political and personal dimensions. When he became president, FDR did not forget Moses's insinuations about him, his family, and close associates like Louis Howe. So when New York City's mayor, Fiorello LaGuardia, unwittingly appointed Moses to be a member of the Triborough Bridge Authority in 1934, the president insisted that his old foe have nothing to do with the construction, out of PWA funds, of the largest and most expensive construction project in the East. Acting through Harold Ickes, FDR got the word to LaGuardia that he had to dismiss Moses if he wanted federal funds for the project.

On February 21, 1934, the mayor came down to Washington by train, quietly met with Ickes, and was given the ultimatum. The next day, back in New York, the mayor called upon one of the city's attorneys, Paul Windels, who gave a colorful account of LaGuardia's reaction to being put in this political bind. No sooner did Windels sit down in the car with the mayor than LaGuardia burst forth with curses and howls: "Jesus Christ, of all the people in the City of New York I had to pick the one man who Roosevelt won't stand for and he won't give me any more money unless I get rid of him. Jesus Christ, I had to pick the one that he hated. Jesus Christ!" According to Windels, he was shaking his fists in the air and shouting "Jesus Christ! Jesus Christ! Seven million people in the city and I had to pick the one Roosevelt can't stand!" [13]

The standoff lasted nearly a year. The powerful, acid-tongued Robert Moses refused to resign and go quietly when the mayor requested him to do so, and the president was equally stubborn. It was testimony to the depth of his animosity for Moses that he would put both Ickes and Mayor LaGuardia, two men whom he liked very much, in such a politically disastrous situation. After months of stalling in the mayor's office, and with requisition orders for the bridge left unsigned on Ickes's desk, the stalemate was broken late in December when Public Works Administrator Ickes issued the infamous Order 129, which fired Robert Moses from his position on the Triborough Bridge Authority. Through all of 1934 the drama had been enacted behind closed doors in Washington and New York, but when Moses leaked the order to the press around Christmas, all hell broke loose. Newspapers across the country cited it as an example of the Public Works Administration being used for political purposes, which, in this instance, it was.

It was "Honest Harold" who came in for most of the criticism, though the real battle was between FDR and Moses. Ickes suffered the political heat until the end of the affair, which came in February 1935. The president finally realized that public outcry was so intense that he had to back down. Roosevelt told Ickes in effect to rescind Order 129, an administrative sleight-of-hand that everybody saw through. Robert Moses came out the winner: He stayed on the Triborough Bridge Authority and was on hand for the dedication ceremony of the famous bridge in 1936—along with the rest of the principals.

Although the president's reputation came through the sordid affair hardly tarnished, years later Harold Ickes wrote that the Moses uproar did him more damage than any other single event in his twelve years with FDR. It was natural, then, that FDR was grateful to Ickes for serving as his frontman in this affair.

While Ickes found being the whipping post for Roosevelt extremely uncomfortable in the Moses case, he had no such discomfort when it came to giving another foe of the administration, Sen. Huey P. Long of Louisiana, similar treatment. In fact, Ickes jumped into this mud-slinging fray with both arms swinging. Just after he took it on the chin over Moses (a letter to the editor of the *Brooklyn Eagle* asked whether the city's citizens were going to let "a political mongrel from the Midwest instruct us as to who should build our bridges?"),[14] Ickes went public with his dislike for the vociferous, increasingly popular Populist from Louisiana. In March 1935, Harold Ickes amused the correspondents at his weekly press conference when he remarked in an offhand way that Senator Long had "halitosis of the intellect. That's presuming Emperor Long has an intellect."[15] Any man's match for colorful phrases, Huey Long began referring to Ickes as "the Chinchbug of Chicago," and Roosevelt became "Prince Franklin, Knight of the Nourmahal" (in reference to the presidential yacht).[16]

Naturally the name-calling between Ickes and Long signified more than simply a desire to indulge their penchant for colorful and highly charged public utterances; it emanated from a rift that had opened, and deepened, between President Roosevelt and Senator Long from the inception of the New Deal. Although Huey Long had been an enthusiastic supporter of FDR's candidacy in 1932, once the two men assumed their respective offices and began working on a national recovery program, Long's enthusiasm waned. FDR was being much too conservative, the senator felt. As early as the spring of 1933, "Roosevelt decided to write Long off—a decision expressed in a determination to deny him patronage. . . . He would not let federal patronage or presidential favor strengthen the Louisiana despotism further." [17]

But in June the president decided to meet with Long to see whether something could be salvaged from the association. Postmaster General James Farley, who also served as the primary dispenser of federal patronage, brought the boyish-looking, slightly paunchy senator over to the White House. Long looked like he stepped out of the pages of a Faulkner novel; he was dressed in a light summer suit, his tie ending a little too far above his belt, and he sported a straw hat with a colored band. As the three men sat in the president's office and engaged in polite conversation, Senator Long's hat became the focal point of the meeting: He kept it on, except for a few occasions when he took it off to underscore a point or to use it to poke the president on the knee or elbow. Farley squirmed at the senator's studied discourtesy but FDR kept his equanimity. When Huey Long walked out of the White House he told the press assembled on the steps that everything worked out just fine between him and FDR. But, he grumbled beneath his breath, "I'm never goin' over there again."

Ickes supported the president's decision to use the federal works program to weaken Huey Long, whom he considered to be an irresponsible and politically dangerous demagogue, albeit a very bright one who shared many of his own liberal views. The Roosevelt administration did this by withholding public works funds for projects endorsed by the senator and his backers, and in turn giving funds to his opposition. In the fall of 1933 the administration teamed up with the mayor of New Orleans, who was then up for reelection and who opposed the Kingfish, by granting unusually liberal terms on the PWA's New Orleans bridge project. An unsigned memo in the president's official files, dated September 14, 1933, was sent to Jesse Jones, head of the Reconstruction Finance Corporation, and to PWA head Harold Ickes. It read: "To get together on the New Orleans bridge; reduce rate of interest from 5 to 4, or waive all interest during construction." The mayor was subsequently reelected early in 1934 "over Long's envenomed opposition."[18]

As late as July 15, 1935, Administrator Ickes still was vetoing projects for Louisiana. Ickes wrote,

> Three representatives of Senator Huey Long came in to see me yesterday about Louisiana projects. They told me how badly the projects were needed and that the people needed work as well. . . . President Smith [of Louisiana State College] then asked me why there had been so much delay in passing upon applications for projects from State College. I told him that some people believed that this wasn't so much an educational institution as it was a political institution. He announced that he took great exception to that statement and I told him that was his privilege.[19]

By 1935 Huey Long had become more than just a nuisance or an embarrassment to the Democratic Party. He was beginning to campaign for the presidency, and while he knew he had no chance of winning the 1936 election, he could conceivably be a "spoiler." By drawing enough votes away from FDR in a three-way race, the Republican contender would win, thus opening the way for a true Populist president, Huey Pierce Long, in 1940. The fight with the Roosevelt administration thus became more public and more pitched in the year preceding the 1936 contest.

Angry with the administration's treatment of him and his needy state, Senator Long spoke before a crowded Senate chamber on March 6, 1935. The primary object of this attack was the "Big Bag Man," Jim Farley. Long alleged that Farley's New York-based General Builders Supply Corporation was benefiting quite handsomely from the New Deal.[20] To prove the charge, the Louisiana senator was prepared to call for the testimony of Commissioner Robert Moses of New York, "and the data which he has assembled" against Farley and FDR. Strange bedfellows they certainly made: The aristocratic, Yale-educated man of Jewish heritage teamed up with the red-earth, farm-bred, self-taught populist who liked quoting the King James Version of the Bible. But what they had in common, a wellspring of bitterness for the Roosevelt administration, transcended in 1935 their cultural differences.

Only a few days prior to Senator Long's salvo in the Senate, Roosevelt decided to rescind the punitive Order 129 against Robert Moses. This was a wise political move (and probably a necessary one given the public outcry) for it reduced the chances that Moses and Long would forge a political alliance based on charges of misuse of PWA funds and abuse of power. But if FDR backed off on Moses there was no such reaction to Huey Long through 1935. Polls by the administration showed his popularity was on the rise, and so the New Dealers continued to withhold funds requested by the Louisiana "Longislature." Huey Long continued to launch his presidential bid over the airwaves of the nation and from the floor of the Senate chamber.

Long spoke there for the last time on Saturday evening, August 24, 1935. After working late in his office, Ickes had dinner and then decided to drop in for the closing session of the Senate. Huey Long, Ickes observed from his seat above the Senate floor, delivered one of his typical speeches:

> I had never really seen him at his best, and he was at his best Saturday night. He waved his arms, he contorted, he swayed, and at all times he talked in a very loud voice. I must admit, however, that he was clever. Any Senator who ventured to cross swords with him was usually discomfited. He has a sharp, quick wit, even though he is a blatant and unconscionable demagogue.[21]

Huey Pierce Long made his last trip between Washington and Louisiana at the end of August. On Sunday, September 8, at about 9:30 at night, Long was coming out of the Capitol building in Baton Rouge when several bullets were fired into him. Long's bodyguards immediately opened fire on the assassin, a young medical doctor named Carl Weiss. Weiss died instantly from the barrage, but the senator was still alive and taken immediately to Our Lady of the Lake Hospital. Long lingered for two days, wondering why the young medical doctor had shot him. He died on September 10 without learning why; but if he had he would have discovered that Carl Weiss's motives were intensely personal and far removed from the political battles that had been going on at the highest levels of government for the preceding two years.[22]

SEPTEMBER WAS A history-making month. Not only was Harold Ickes's personal life changed forever but perhaps the nation's history was as well. The autumn abounded in finality. If Ickes had had either the time or inclination for reflection, he could have appreciated why poets, philosophers, artists, and writers love the symbolism of the fall season—or why Robert Penn Warren concluded his great novel about Jack Burden and Willie Stark with the observation that "all knowledge that is worth anything is maybe paid for by blood."

Anna Ickes's funeral was held on September 3, and with her accidental death a long chapter in her husband's life was closed. It was an end and a beginning. The other women in his life suddenly became more accessible. The affair with Marguerite continued, although by this time she was remarried and the initial passion he had for her had run its course. A casual friendship with the wealthy Washingtonian, Eleanor "Cissy" Patterson, took on a decidedly more intimate aspect after Anna's death.[23] Although Harold claimed he never saw their relationship in such terms, Cissy at any rate seemed to have marital aspirations. But Harold's real romantic interest emerged shortly after his wife's death in the form of an attractive, 22-year-old woman named Jane Dahlman. Jane was the youngest sister of Wilmarth's wife Betty. When she arrived in Washington that fall, Harold claimed that it was love at first sight. He courted her for two years while she agonized over the decision to marry a man forty years her senior, and while Harold agonized over her indecision.

On September 8, less than a week after Anna's funeral, Huey Pierce Long was assassinated. With his death the Populist critics of the New Deal lost their true voice, thus virtually insuring a Roosevelt victory in 1936. No one in American politics could replace the brilliant orator who sprang out of the backwoods of Louisiana and who spoke for millions of Americans during the depths of the Great Depression. With Huey Long out of the picture, the administration ended their quarantine and moved forward with much needed works projects in Louisiana. It was another end and a beginning.

At the meeting at Hyde Park in mid-September Harold Ickes was given a continuing role to play in the emergency relief program, but it was not enough to assuage the sense of loss he felt. In his view he had been beaten badly by Harry Hopkins and was being eased out of a post he cherished. Nevertheless, he resigned himself to the president's decision, and he and Hopkins managed to bicker over the boundaries dividing the PWA and the WPA for several more years. Some things didn't change.

IF THERE WAS too much brooding over death and politics that fall, Roosevelt decided to break the melancholy mood. He declared that it was time for a long vacation, and he invited Harold Ickes, Harry Hopkins, and a few other friends to join him on a train trip across the country and then on a cruise from San Diego, down the coast of Baja California, through the Panama Canal, across the Gulf of Mexico, and back up the Atlantic seaboard. Ickes, who was given to seasickness, wasn't overjoyed by the invitation to spend three weeks aboard the presidential yacht. He confided to his diary that "I really don't feel like going on that trip with the President. I am desperately tired and my morale is not any too good these days." [24] Roosevelt insisted, however, and so he went—and enjoyed himself immensely.

With his son Raymond, who in June had earned his bachelor's degree from the University of Chicago, accompanying him, Ickes joined the president, Mrs. Roosevelt, and their entourage at Union Station on September 26. "On the whole, the trip has been pretty good," Ickes admitted four days later. "Raymond and I have been quite comfortable in a drawing room in the car next to the President's private car." They played a little poker, watched the scenery, dined twice with the president, and worked on the speeches which the secretary of the interior and the president were to deliver at the dedication ceremony of Boulder Dam on Monday, the thirtieth. Ickes whipped his into final shape on Sunday, he said, and then helped Roosevelt, who was having "a great deal of trouble in getting out a satisfactory speech," that night. Working with Steve Early and Marriner Eccles, Ickes went over the president's draft and completed it just hours before the morning ceremony.

They arrived at the dam around 9:30 A.M., an hour or so before the dedication. "It certainly was a sight well worth seeing," Ickes noted. "It is a marvel of engineering skill in its picturesque and rugged beauty of setting. Over four hundred feet of water . . . have already been impounded just above the dam and the beautiful lake in process of formation already extends some eighty miles upstream." Ickes was the first to speak and his twelve-minute address, which was broadcast nationwide, seemed to go over well. "One thing I did in my speech was to try to nail down for good and all the name Boulder Dam," he wrote.

From Boulder City the train pulled out for Los Angeles, where Roosevelt was greeted by nearly a million cheering people. He spoke to a huge audience at the Coliseum on October 1, and the streets where his motorcade traveled were lined with hundreds of thousands of supporters. "It was a great demonstration and proof of the President's personal popularity," Ickes observed.

With business finished, the fun began on October 2. Ickes said goodbye to Raymond, who was returning by train to Chicago, and just managed to get aboard the *Houston* before it sailed out of San Diego. "I pushed my way through the crowd and was part way over the gangplank when I heard a voice call out 'good-bye' and, looking around, I saw Mrs. Roosevelt," Ickes related. "I stepped back to shake hands with her and then went aboard. . . . We sailed with due ceremony as soon as I got aboard."

It was a delightful trip in every respect. Ickes had comfortable private quarters, the food was excellent (except for the coffee), and he thoroughly enjoyed the company of the president and the other guests, which included Harry Hopkins, the president's physician, Dr. Ross McIntire, Col. Edwin "Pa" Watson, Roosevelt's military aide, and Capt. Wilson Brown, his naval aide. Pa Watson turned into the life of the party, and Ickes couldn't say enough good things about him. On October 4 they were fishing in Magdalena Bay, off Baja, and Ickes said, "It was worth the trip to be Watson's fishing companion. He is one of the best fellows I have ever known, bubbling over with genuine good humor and full of spontaneous fun. The way he talks to a fish after he has hooked it and is trying to land it beats the soliloquy of any intense crap player in the world."

They fished all the way down the coast and anchored at Cocos Island, off the coast of Costa Rica, on the ninth. They fished some more, and Roosevelt, Ickes was pleased to note, caught a 109-pound sailfish. "This was the first sailfish he had ever caught," he said, and "it was fine to see the way the President handled that fish. . . . On this whole trip I marveled again and again at his high cheer and at his disposition."

Everybody was in good humor as they toured tropical rainforests in Central America, met the San Blas Indians, fished, played poker, gossiped, and kidded one another. On the trip Ickes learned, for instance, that "FDR hates [Lewis] Douglas," and that he was still on the outs with the Pinchots.[25] Even Harry and Harold got along famously, which was obviously Roosevelt's ulterior motive for inviting them both on the trip. Everybody came in for some good-natured kidding, and the Hopkins-Ickes feud of 1935 was caricatured by FDR in a little piece he wrote for the ship's paper. He titled it "Buried at Sea" and went on to describe his two assistants:

> Hopkins, as usual, was dressed in his immaculate blues, browns and whites, his fine figure making a pretty sight with the moon-drifted sea in the foreground.
> Ickes wore his conventional faded grays, Mona Lisa smile and carried his stamp collection.[26]

The October vacation was the perfect tonic for Harold Ickes. After docking at Charleston he wrote, "I am glad I took this trip. I did not want to go and finally did go only under pressure from the President. . . . I had a complete change and rest and there is no doubt at all that I badly needed them. . . . We had a congenial crowd and everything went off beautifully." He then returned to describing Pa Watson, who "is one of the best fellows I have ever known. He simply bubbles with good humor and one cannot feel grouchy or dispirited when he is about . . . He was really the life of the party without being in any sense a sparkling wit. I have never known anyone . . . like him."

Everyone, however, was fun to be with. "Captain Brown . . . has a quiet humor and a capacity for good fellowship. Captain McIntire, the president's personal physician, was pleasant, and Harry Hopkins fitted in well with his easy manners and keen wit. The president is always a delightful host, ready to laugh at a joke or tell a good story."

Ickes's good mood remained intact once he returned to his office. He was pleasantly surprised to find that it was in good shape, that no catastrophes had occurred in his absence, and that Louis Glavis had carried out his orders to suspend two members of the Oil Administration when it was learned that they had acquired interests in an oil well while they were on the federal payroll.[27] Then, it was back to work as usual, and the start of his new life without Anna.

CHAPTER 9

"BACK TO WORK"

PLANNING, POLITICS,

AND THE PWA

FRANKLIN ROOSEVELT savored the autumn of 1935. He turned it into a breathing spell from the frenetic, precedent-breaking New Deal activity that marked the previous nine months of his third year in office.[1] The Hyde Park settlement laid to rest, he hoped, the quarrel over control of the multi-billion-dollar relief program. Through the Hopkins-Ickes-Walker triumvirate, the president saw it continuing to oper-ate smoothly through the election year. The threat from the political Left to his re-election was gone; Carl Weiss put an end to Huey Long's short but significant life. Moreover, the economy showed signs of increased vigor in that delightful Indian summer. It was time for a good, long vacation—the trip to the West Coast and the cruise on the *Houston* back to Charleston, South Carolina—before tackling the issues that would dominate 1936: The presidential election and the Su-preme Court's conservatism. Roosevelt was characteristically optimistic about the election. Ickes noted in a diary entry in

November 1935 that Roosevelt predicted, "We will win easily next year but we are going to make it a crusade."[2]

Ickes did not share the president's rosy forecast, however; he was much more of an alarmist than was his boss. In addition, the ongoing fight with Harry Hopkins colored his judgment. Ickes was convinced that Hopkins's rival WPA program would become a major election issue. Unlike his own PWA, Ickes felt that Hopkins's program was badly administered, and that neither Harry Hopkins nor his program was very popular on the Hill. In December he wrote that "the President is likely to find himself short of money just at the critical time before the election, with the result of throwing men out of jobs and even of denying them relief, which may be serious enough to return the Republicans to power. I have no confidence in the situation and I hate to see more money go down the Hopkins rat hole."[3]

A few weeks later, Ickes learned that FDR was on top of that eventuality. The president planned to ask Congress in 1936 for somewhere between $1 and $2 billion for a continuation of Hopkins's work-relief program to carry it through the next fiscal year. "I suspect that there will be some explosive language on the Hill when he sends up such a program," Ickes dourly wrote.

Although on one level Hopkins and Ickes were engaged in the same endeavor—namely, a frontal attack on the Great Depression—at another, the operating level, there existed real philosophical and administrative differences between their programs. But these differences became more blurred, Ickes believed, by Hopkins's decision sometime in 1935 to rename his Federal Emergency Relief Administration the Works Progress Administration. The acronyms, PWA and WPA, naturally added to the confusion existing in the public's mind over the New Deal relief agencies, and Ickes was convinced that his program suffered as a consequence.

Differences in temperament were at the base of the approach each man took toward spending the taxpayers' money on economic recovery. Harold Ickes's approach was, to use Robert Sherwood's insight, that "of a hardheaded businessman as well as a conscientious public servant. Ickes was concerned about the return on the taxpayers' investment." In contrast, "Hopkins did not give a damn about the return; his approach was that of a social worker . . . interested only in getting relief to the miserable and getting it there quickly."[4]

At the outset of the New Deal, Harry Hopkins proceeded to set himself up in an empty office in the Commerce Department building and, keeping himself going on a bottomless cup of black coffee and a chain of cigarettes whose ashes were spilled carelessly onto his rumpled suit, managed to spend millions of dollars on putting men back to work in a few weeks' time. Later, of course, Hopkins moved into a more comfortable setting (and much later into the White House, where he lived for a few years), but he continued to believe in the kind of economy that he practiced in his first year working for Roosevelt. He had a small, hardworking, and frugal-minded staff that at the end of its first year in operation had put about 17 million Americans to work and had spent $1.5 billion on relief. Hopkins's organization in 1933, however, consisted of only 120 people and its payroll amounted to $21,000 per month.[5] Congress begrudged Hopkins even his modest annual salary of $12,000. In 1937, in the midst of the bitterly contested Supreme Court battle, the House voted to cut it by $2,000.

Harold Ickes was as firmly committed as was Hopkins to economy in his programs, and employees' complaints about being underpaid and overworked were frequent during his tenure. Also, he set the standard for his department by holding down as many as three full-time jobs, while being paid for only one. Ickes considered making some invidious comparisons between salaries in his Oil Administration and those in the private sector for his 1935 *Saturday Evening Post* article, "After the Oil Deluge, What Price Gasoline?" A memo to Ickes dated December 22, 1934, included these data: "Salaries of the presidents of some of these [oil] companies ranged from $48,000 a year to $136,000. The Oil Administrator [Ickes] works for nothing."[6] The interesting comparisons, however, didn't appear in the February 16, 1935, article.

Although both Hopkins and Ickes were committed to Roosevelt's overall objective of economy in government, nevertheless Ickes's program proved to be the more cumbersome and expensive of the two. Because he was convinced that the nation needed a recovery program that spent money on durable, long-term projects of a socially useful nature, a larger and more complicated organization than Hopkins's shop was necessary. He also insisted on a graft-free program, as far as that was humanly possible, so the result was a public works organization, operating within Interior, that carefully reviewed each of the many thousands of applications that came into it.

Each application passed through the three main divisions within the PWA: An engineering division, staffed by civil engineers who reviewed the technical and design aspects of the project; a financial division, where accountants inspected the costs of the project; and a legal division, where, Ickes often complained, ever-too-cautious lawyers determined whether the project conformed to existing state and federal laws. If it didn't, which happened often in the public housing component of PWA, the legal staff had to consider whether and how to amend the laws.

Once a project passed through this three-stage review, it went before what Administrator Ickes called "this town hall meeting that we call a Board." To Ickes, a man who had a visceral abhorrence of wasting time, the board's review was irritatingly slow; he claimed he could have completed the reviews in far less time working by himself. After the review board finished its job, Ickes took the list of projects accepted and rejected over to 1600 Pennsylvania Avenue. Especially at first, Roosevelt displayed acute interest in the public works program, and he carefully reviewed the lists that Ickes brought to him. Once that was done, the list of projects approved by the president was given to the press, which invariably was anxious to get this important news item in a town that thrived on the latest New Deal news.

One reason Harold Ickes fought tooth and nail, over the years, with competitors like Hugh Johnson and Harry Hopkins for control of public works was obvious: It conferred great power on him. Ickes loved power as much as Roosevelt did. But he was objective enough to realize (most of the time) that he lacked the political skills with which his boss was so abundantly endowed, and thus would never be a viable candidate for office. "I never have been popular," Ickes once confided to his diary.[7] But being in charge of a vast, new federal spending program—a program that eventually had a visible, enduring impact in virtually every town and city of the nation—gave Ickes near-celebrity status, and he reveled in it. The title, public works administrator, was, in the 1930s, far more important than the relatively obscure, faintly parochial position of secretary of the interior.

"The news capital of the world had shifted suddenly from New York to Washington, D.C., and the Public Works Administration was bursting on the consciousness of the public like a bombshell," one of Ickes's assistants remembered some fifty years later.[8] In 1933 William Warne (pronounced "Warren") had just graduated from the University of California at Berkeley and was beginning his career as a staff writer for the Associated Press in Washington. Because of his western background he was assigned the Interior Department and the newly formed Public Works Administration.

The first time he saw Harold Ickes was at one of the secretary's weekly press conferences in September 1933. "About 50 newspapers were represented at these conferences," Warne recalled, and they were usually pretty "lively." With the crowd of reporters in attendance, Secretary Ickes would come into a big room in the old Interior Department (now the GSA building), sit down at his desk, and "take all questions." With him was Michael Straus, his public information officer for the PWA. "Ickes was very aggressive," Warne said, and reporters liked his direct style. Harold Ickes proved to be, over the years, very popular with the press. "Hugh 'Ironpants' Johnson was about the only rival of Ickes' for the chief news source in the city, outside of the White House itself," Warne claimed. "He knew how to give the press a good line."

Almost immediately Ickes grasped the strategic importance of having Public Works under his control. At a time when FDR was insisting on cutbacks in ongoing governmental programs Ickes realized that he could use the PWA as a conduit for augmenting the Interior Department's relatively small staff. By hiring bright young men and women he could also add a little leaven to the population of ageless bureaucrats in Interior. Right away he lured Mike Straus away from his position as Washington bureau chief for the Universal News Service and put him in charge of the public information office for the PWA. Ickes already had a public information officer for the Interior Department, but, Warne noted, "he didn't do anything but play pinochle," so Straus was hired to run the entire show.

In 1935 Ickes succeeded in hiring William Warne from the AP, and he became "one of the two best men I have in Interior," Ickes noted in his diaries. The two men worked together for eleven years. On June 1 Warne joined the staff of the Bureau of Reclamation within the department and was given the title of editor. But, he said, he was on the PWA payroll for two years before he became covered by the civil service and therefore paid directly out of bureau funds. "That's the way he elaborated the staffs of several agencies," Warne said, "not only in the information line . . . but in some of the other lines where they were short of people who could handle these new and more elaborate programs that he was propounding."

Working through the PWA, from 1933 to 1939, Ickes thus was able to make significant progress in achieving one of his long-range objectives, that of rebuilding Interior. He did this not only through adding staff via the PWA but by making sure that the several bureaus within the Interior Department got their share of work to do through the federal portion of the PWA program. There was nothing illegal or even suspect about doing this. Rather, it was a happy coincidence for the Interior Department that its secretary also had the title of public works administrator, and was not reluctant to help his own executive department get into the mainstream of activity during the economic crisis.

The PWA was designed to fund construction projects in two ways: It worked through the existing federal bureaucracy, and thus allotted moneys to, for example, the Treasury Department to construct post offices throughout the country. But it also worked through the states and the municipalities by funding a fraction of the applications for projects that streamed into Washington for some seven years. Each state was thus given a "federal" and "nonfederal" allotment by the PWA, determined largely by population figures and unemployment statistics. A PWA chart prepared on July 14, 1934, listed all of the states and how much of their allotment they had by then received. It noted that the states' quotas were based on "75% population and 25% unemployment." [9]

Initially, money was pumped into the depressed economy through existing federal agencies; $100 million of the first appropriation passed in 1933 went to the Agriculture, Commerce, War, and Interior departments, and the Federal Power Commission. As the massive spending program evolved, other federal agencies became substantial beneficiaries, as did the states and cities. Looking at the budget books in 1938, for instance, Gen. George Marshall discovered that the War Department received about $250 million from the emergency programs which it spent on ships, planes, tanks, and artillery.[10] This was in addition to its annual appropriations. Much of the country's military preparedness in 1940, such as it was, can be traced to PWA, FERA, and WPA spending. Rebuilding the military, especially the Navy, was one of Roosevelt's long-range objectives in the 1930s. It was not popular with the isolationists in Congress.

Within Ickes's domain of Interior, several agencies benefited from the PWA coffers. The National Park Service, one of Ickes's favorite agencies, was able to do important rehabilitative work within the park system with PWA allotments: A $32,000 grant in 1937 allowed park personnel to restore the worn, yet charming buildings of one of the earliest mission churches in the Southwest, that of Tumacacori near the Arizona-Mexico border.[11] Emergency funds also allowed the Park Service to expand its mission in a direction that the president pushed enthusiastically: The Blue Ridge, Skyline Drive, and Natchez Trace scenic parkways were planned and constructed, as was the impressive Jefferson Memorial near the Mall. The national park system expanded dramatically and visibly while Secretary Ickes was public works administrator, and the 1930s became one of the few periods in the agency's seventy-five-year history when it had money to spend on something other than the absolute necessities, such as operations and maintenance.

Under John Collier's and Ickes's leadership, in 1933 the Indian Service launched what quickly evolved into a nationwide program covering many of the country's farmers, that of soil conservation. Using PWA funds and the vast Navajo Indian Reservation in Arizona and New Mexico as their experiment station, Collier, soil scientist Hugh Bennett, and others began attacking the catastrophe of soil erosion.[12] But for the Navajos, who were then totally dependent on their sheep herds for survival, the soil conservation program itself was an economic disaster. The tribe bitterly resented the government's imposition of significant stock reductions during the 1930s. "It left a scar on the Navajos' psyche, from which they have not yet recovered," a Native American scholar said recently.[13]

Ickes found that he had to keep close watch over the Indian Service to get the results he wanted. It was especially prone to delay, thus compounding his problem with spending money as quickly as possible. Although he personally wrote Budget Director Lewis Douglas in January 1934 asking for more funds for medical services for the Indians, he was very upset to learn a year later that the bureau hadn't even expended its entire 1933 appropriation. In February 1935, Ickes wrote Assistant Director Zimmerman: "I am frank to say that I am keenly disappointed that your Bureau has failed to take advantage of the opportunity that . . . these funds gave to do something substantial for the Indians with these two million five hundred thousand dollars that now are impounded."[14]

No agency within the Interior Department benefited more than did the Bureau of Reclamation from the happy circumstance of having

Ickes wear two administrative hats. William Warne, who became its assistant commissioner during the 1940s, called the decade the "Golden Years of Reclamation." All in all, PWA allotments to the Bureau of Reclamation totaled $192 million during the five-year period 1933–38, when the PWA was in operation.[15] Its most awesome engineering feats were accomplished, probably not coincidentally, when enthusiasm for public works was at its height.

But the entire Interior Department profited from the construction of a grand new building to house the growing agency. In 1934 Roosevelt had authorized $13 million of PWA funds to construct the new office building that would occupy two city blocks just off Constitution Avenue and the Mall. As Ickes had done some twenty years earlier with the construction of his luxurious home at Hubbard Woods, he scrutinized the plans and dictated many of the finest details for the new building. From the basic floor plan of a wide central corridor with six wings spreading out to the east and the west—designed to give every office at least one window—to the specially handcrafted buffalo-emblazoned doorknobs in the executive suite, and the twenty-seven striking murals adorning the corridors, Harold Ickes's personality was stamped forever on the new Interior Department building. Construction, which had begun in April 1935, was finished in record time. President Roosevelt dedicated the building a year later, and the final touches were completed in December 1936. Ickes and his staff thus began the new year, and their second term in office, by moving into the air-conditioned, marble-floored, spacious, muraled building that was and is one of the most attractive government buildings in the capital. It surely was a morale-builder for the employees of one of the less prestigious departments of government.

Although Harold Ickes managed to get into a few conflicts with his fellow cabinet officers over how he ran the PWA, nevertheless he and his staff generally had a much easier time administering the federal portion of the PWA than the nonfederal. The reasons were clear: First, they were dealing with many more applicants in the nonfederal sector. The forty-eight state governments, as well as thousands of municipalities, and the nation's territorial possessions, all were eligible to apply. Apply they did. However, only a fraction of all proposals could be funded. Second, the PWA was obliged to demonstrate that each state was being treated equitably in the distribution of money for projects. Invidious comparisons were endemic in the nature of the program, as were charges that politics entered the selection process. And third, the opportunities for all manner of graft were great, given the far-flung, geographically dispersed program. The PWA administrators were, after all, dealing primarily with construction projects, and many of the construction industries were notorious in the 1930s for their disregard of the law.

Virtually all of the problems that Ickes encountered in his capacity as administrator derived from one of these three conditions, or a combination of them. That he emerged in the 1930s as "the old curmudgeon—the terrible-tempered but honest figure so beloved in American folklore" [16] is testimony to the effort he put into managing this complex program.

But, Ickes acknowledged, it was a continual battle to maintain the high standards he set for the PWA. Although his overall record was exemplary, and has been matched by only a few federal officers in the nation's history, inevitably there was some backsliding. In a 1939 letter to his close friend, Frank Knox, the publisher of the *Chicago Daily News,* he said:

> As letters come in from my executives from all parts of the country, as members of my staff have come in to see me, without exception, they have all commented upon the high standards that we have set and the fact that, so far as was humanly possible, there has been no graft or corruption in PWA. Of course there has been some. That was inevitable but I have never let up in my determination that there should be none that was preventable. I had hardly taken PWA over before I brought about the indictment of the Democratic Lieutenant-Governor (later the Governor) of Iowa. And I concluded my service by rapping the prehensile fingers of "Chip" Robert, Secretary of the Democratic National Committee.[17]

From the outset, the PWA had to contend with charges of favoritism, that some states and regions were getting more than their fair share of public works funds. On December 28, 1933, a member of the Public Works Board, Turner Battle, wrote a confidential memo to FDR's assistant, Marvin McIntyre, bitterly complaining about the large allotments voted through for California on that very day. Ickes was convalescing in Bethesda Naval Hospital at the time. The meeting of the board was held irrespective of the secretary's wish that there be no more meetings until after the first of the year. Battle wrote:

> I do not wish Mr. Ickes to know that I am giving you this information, and am leaving it to you as to whether you think this matter should be brought to the attention of the President, but all of these projects which have been

held up and turned down by the Board, were railroaded through today in the absence of Judge Biggs, Chip Robert, Rex Tugwell, who had left the meeting, Secretary Roper, and the representative of the Director of the Budget. I asked to be recorded as voting "no," and inasmuch as today marked the completion of the allocation of the entire $3,300,000,000, while many worthy projects in areas where there is excessive unemployment as compared to California, I know that there is going to be bitter criticism of the enormous amount allocated to California.[18]

Although Battle's memo was confidential, his complaint was becoming common. Ickes and others were quite aware of the fact that the westernmost states, and especially California, were receiving great sums of money from the PWA.[19] The senior senator from California, Hiram Johnson, proved to be a very effective lobbyist for his state. He wasted no time in presenting his requests before the administration: Ickes received a letter from Johnson in May 1933, and the correspondence continued over the next five years. The first missive from the senator to Ickes was a letter of introduction for the California congressman Phil Swing, "who comes to Washington to talk to you about the contemplated construction of the All-American Canal."[20] This project, funded initially out of the PWA allotment, evolved over the years into the colossal Central Valley Project (CVP), which transformed California's arid interior into the nation's breadbasket and center of agribusiness that it has been since the New Deal.

A few months later, on October 17, the senator wrote the secretary a long letter discussing, among other things, a heated exchange that took place between Ickes and Nevada's Sen. Key Pittman over the PWA. He assured his friend that he got the best of it, but that he had better be on his guard, for "you are standing between greed and graft and the Government." Johnson, however, unwittingly underscored his observation when he added a three-page postscript complaining about the growing "misperception" that California was being treated too well by the PWA. If it was, there were good reasons for it, Johnson said.

I have been growing more and more incensed at the growing prejudice in Washington concerning projects from our State. . . . It happens we are a new commonwealth with innumerable projects. With a rapid increase in population, greater proportionately than that of any other State in the union, with a peculiar situation which brings to us the sick, the lame and the halt, and the unemployed of all other States, so that the proportion of unemployed in Southern California for instance is greater than that of any other locality . . . , we are feeding today not only our own but those who have come to us from all the other States, and they constitute a proportion of the needy such as is not encountered in any other State.[21]

The ink had hardly dried on this communiqué when Senator Johnson wrote Ickes again, lobbying for new school buildings in Southern California and for Los Angeles's Metropolitan Water District project. Two days later, on November 9, 1933, Ickes wrote a "Dear Hiram" letter to his fellow Progressive:

Frankly it has gotten down to a question of how far we can make the balance of our money go. . . . We still must make some sort of a showing in a number of the populous States east of the Mississippi River which are now far below any reasonable quota. There is a terrible lag in . . . Pennsylvania, Indiana, Iowa, Kansas, Kentucky, Maryland, Massachusetts, Michigan, Minnesota, Missouri, Wisconsin, New York, Ohio and Pennsylvania, to say nothing of some of the southern States. On the other hand, all of the Pacific Coast States are way over their quotas. The representatives of some of these States that have not yet had anywhere near an equitable share in public works funds are raising particular hell.[22]

Johnson's interest in the PWA continued into 1934. In the fall of that year he and Ickes locked horns over the Sausalito Harbor Project, an application sponsored by the city of Sausalito and Hiram Johnson's son. The project was winding its way through the review process when Ickes wrote the senator on November 9 a candid letter, expressing his view that it was not a very good project—that of building a yacht harbor for the privileged residents of this Marin County community—and that the only reason it was still alive was because of their long-standing and intimate friendship. Hiram Johnson, who was Ickes's match when it came to self-righteous indignation, wrote an angry reply a few days later protesting any personal interest in the project merely because his son was the attorney for it. He intervened, he said, "because of the interminable and innumerable delays" and because "I suspected what I deemed a legitimate project of constituents of mine was being hamstrung and sabotaged because my son's name appeared as attorney." Johnson closed with this salvo: "If I did not make myself plain in the days gone by, let me now make it so plain that there can be no misunderstanding: I ask no personal favors from you or any man and I want none."[23]

A certain coolness entered into the relationship at this time, although Ickes redoubled his efforts at finding ways to fund this and another California yacht harbor project, the Hueneme in Southern California. On July 20, 1935, Ickes sent Johnson the good news that the Sausalito Project was about to clear its last administrative hurdle. If Ickes thought that that was the end of the troublesome project, he was wrong. Hiram Johnson Jr. turned around and asked the PWA for an additional $40,000 loan on top of the $360,000 allotment! Through the end of 1935 the review process was still dragging on, as many PWA officials objected to yet another annoying request from the younger Johnson.[24]

The senior senator from California, the man who in temperament and physical appearance closely resembled Harold Ickes, was one of the most effective lobbyists for PWA funds. But many others felt just as strongly that their state or community deserved special consideration. Although Ickes and Roosevelt, who was the ultimate authority, didn't often play politics with Public Works, there were a few instances where political considerations sneaked into the selection process. It happened in Huey Long's Louisiana, it occurred in California where Hiram Johnson pointed out the state's unusual circumstances (subsequently made famous by John Steinbeck's *Grapes of Wrath*), and it occurred also with another man who coincidentally had the same last name as the senior senator from the Golden State—the young man from the Lone Star State who had boundless enthusiasm for FDR and the New Deal, Lyndon Baines Johnson.

Roosevelt first met Lyndon Johnson on a trip to Texas during his 1936 reelection campaign. The president was immediately taken with the tall, lanky, handsome young man who radiated energy. FDR told several of his assistants, including Ickes, Hopkins, and Tom Corcoran, that he "liked this boy." They should, he said, help him any way they could. He even predicted that Lyndon Johnson "could well be the first Southern President"[25] since Reconstruction. The next year Roosevelt was back in the White House and Johnson was in Congress. The young man was chosen to fill the seat vacated when Rep. James Buchanan died of a heart attack.

Once in office, Johnson discovered that he needed to deliver on the Marshall Ford Dam, a project of questionable benefit which nevertheless FDR had promised to Buchanan. It had been pushed through the PWA in 1936, over both Ickes's and Louis Glavis's protests. What

they particularly objected to was the money wealthy Texas businessman Ralph Morrison was raking off from the Lower Colorado River
Project. Ickes noted in May 1936 that Morrison had already drawn
$800,000 in commissions, that he might end up making as much as
$1.5 million, and that his friend Vice-President Garner was pushing
for his appointment to the Federal Reserve Board.[26] Ickes thought
he'd like to look at Morrison's tax returns.

When LBJ came to FDR in 1937 asking for money to complete the
project, Tom Corcoran recalled the president saying, "Give the kid the
dam." Ickes, however, achieved a small victory over the dam he didn't
care for: The additional $5 million this time came from Hopkins's and
not Ickes's coffers, although Hopkins too had objections to the project.[27] All were overruled by the president. According to one of Johnson's biographers, Robert Caro, the completion of the Marshall Ford
Dam (which was later renamed the Buchanan Dam) secured Johnson's
political career.

Pressure came from everywhere. Even Eleanor Roosevelt kept her
eye on the PWA and tried to move it in directions that would help
those groups and individuals most in need. She frequently prevailed
upon Ickes to cut through red tape for projects with benefits going to
the most disadvantaged groups in American society. Ickes usually was
anxious to comply with her requests, not only because she was Mrs.
Roosevelt but because he shared her concerns and felt that they were
a legitimate and proper objective of the PWA. However, there were
occasions when he objected to her "meddling." One of those times
occurred shortly after Anna's death, and when he was worried sick that
the president was about to take the PWA from him. He wrote, "This
episode [with Mrs. Roosevelt] is typical of some of the things that have
happened right along under this administration. Soon I will expect
Sistie and Buzzy [the Roosevelts' grandchildren] to be issuing orders
to members of my staff. Fortunately they can't write yet."[28]

But the First Lady also was aware of how much effort it took to get
anything accomplished administratively. She received a memo attached to a newspaper clipping on April 7, 1937, regarding the Detroit
Slum Clearance Project. The brief memo from one of her assistants
read, "This is what happens when you withdraw your valuable interest—just nothing." Two days later Mrs. Roosevelt wrote Ickes a polite
note asking him to inform her about the current status of the Detroit
project.[29] Her interest pushed forward many New Deal projects that

undoubtedly would have gotten lost in the bureaucratic shuffle and mad scramble for money, and the black community loved her for it.

NATURALLY THE PRESS—especially the conservative newspapers owned and operated by William Randolph Hearst, Col. Robert Mc-Cormick, and siblings Joseph and Eleanor "Cissy" Patterson—quickly pounced on the least suggestion of favoritism within the PWA. One of Ickes's most famous feuds, the one with McCormick, was fueled by such charges. Ironically, the publisher of the *Chicago Tribune* began by praising the selection of Harold Ickes as public works administrator. An editorial in July 1933 commented upon Ickes's reputation for honesty and fairness. Ickes immediately wrote a thank-you note to the colonel, and McCormick replied with a brief note saying, "There is surely nothing to thank me for. You have made your reputation what it is, not I." [30]

The era of goodwill between these two Chicagoans—the scrappy liberal reformer and the imperious, haughty veteran of World War I— didn't last long. By August of 1934 the *Tribune* was on the attack; it ran an article claiming that Ickes was making some inside trades through the Chicago firm of Bartlett Frazier. Both Ickes and the vice-president of the firm, J. W. McCulloh, denied the allegation. Two weeks later, the paper's editorial was titled, "Who's Getting the Big Money in PWA?" The editor criticized a number of recently approved projects—Maine's Passamaquoddy project, Arizona's Rio Verde, Nebraska's Loup, and Wyoming's Casper-Alcova. All of them, incidentally, were traditional pork-barrel projects of the Corps of Engineers and the Bureau of Reclamation. There was nothing unusual in the New Deal's funding of these water development projects, although Ickes himself privately criticized some of them.

Those were the first shots, and they were aimed primarily at Ickes's PWA. By the fall of 1934, however, McCormick's *Tribune* broadened its investigation of Ickes, and although it didn't print the gossip about his extramarital affair, reporters began looking into other aspects of his personal life and business dealings. Ickes wrote on October 11, 1934, that the *Tribune*'s John Boettiger had asked him a lot of embarrassing questions, such as whether the Democratic National Committee paid Ickes's $90,000 overdue account with the Slaughter, Anderson and Fox brokerage firm. Ickes wrote that what Boettiger alleged "was ninety-nine percent lie." [31]

Somehow, though, Boettiger had learned of a high-level meeting

that took place the previous November—when Judge Malmin was after Ickes, when the anonymous letters about his affair were appearing
everywhere, and when there was a possibility of a lawsuit against him
regarding an overdue account. It was a meeting at which the president, Ickes, and Roosevelt's secretary, Marvin McIntyre, engaged in a
lengthy discussion about Ickes's financial woes. The president, Ickes
related, said, "Well, Harold, I see they are after you now. . . . All of us
have been in trouble some time or other." FDR then told Ickes to try
to make a reasonable settlement of this account, "and if I couldn't
make the grade myself he would call in some friends of the administration and see whether enough couldn't be raised to handle the matter."
Ickes replied that he "naturally demurred strongly at such a suggestion
as this but he [FDR] said it was nonsense; that it wasn't a personal
matter at all but a public matter." [32]

Several months after Boettiger's interview with Ickes, Colonel Mc-
Cormick ran an insulting editorial that cast aspersions on Ickes's character. The editorial of February 2, 1935, was titled, "Honest Harold,
The No-Sayer." It ridiculed Ickes's claims to honesty and ticked off a
number of instances where, in the opinion of the editor, the PWA was
being used for blatant political ends. They again included Arthur Mullen's Loup and Platte River developments in Nebraska, the Buchanan
Dam in Texas, pushed forward by utility magnate Ralph Morrison,
and the "outrageous Rio Verde irrigation scheme in Arizona," designed to benefit primarily Indians. The editorial also criticized
Ickes's firing of Robert Moses, who happened to be "one of the few
figures in municipal politics in New York who is above suspicion of
dishonesty."

This was war. Harold Ickes began his counterattack on the colonel
by looking into the *Tribune* building's 10,000,000-gallon-per-day water habit. On June 7, 1935, Administrator Ickes wrote the president of
the Chicago Sanitary District, Ross A. Woodhull, asking him for information on whether the *Tribune* building, then being refurbished
for air conditioning, would "return this [city] water to the river by a
private outlet or whether it is the intention to turn it into the sewage system." He further reminded Woodhull that "in discussing the
proposition made by the Sanitary District of Chicago to PWA for a
loan and grant, I took the position that those who cast an exceptional
burden upon the sewage system should be required to pay in proportion to the benefits received." [33]

Woodhull kept Ickes informed. He told him that a bill coming out of the state legislature would take care of the problem. Nevertheless, Ickes sent to Chicago the director of the Inspection Division for the PWA to investigate the matter and to make sure the colonel paid his full water bill.

From there the attacks and counterattacks between the curmudgeon and the colonel branched out in several directions. Ickes was criticized in 1935 for wasting the taxpayers' money with the publication of his book on the PWA, *Back to Work*. The press intimated that it was not only ghostwritten but done on company time. Ickes coolly replied that in the writing of the book he availed himself of the same informational services from the Interior Department that were provided to any citizen in the country. Also at about this time, the secretary was apprised of a lawsuit that Chicago attorney Harrison Parker was considering bringing against McCormick for failure to pay his taxes. Ickes, of course, took a keen interest in it, and over several years Parker and the secretary exchanged information and words of encouragement, while the case was heard and reheard in the Illinois courts.

The warfare between Ickes and the "reactionary" element of the press continued until the end of his thirteen years in office. It was the kind of battle for which Harold Ickes was ideally suited: He had an ideal villain in the wealthy, elitist, inbred right-wing publishing community (the McCormicks and the Pattersons were cousins), he had the tacit support of the president in going after this segment of the press, and it was principally a war of words and of wit. Those features of his intellect were among his most outstanding qualities, and he used them liberally against Hearst, the Pattersons, Gannett, and especially Colonel McCormick.

By the end of 1935 Ickes had become a seasoned political executive. He understood that administering a vast public works program entailed putting up with enormous pressures from both friends and associates who wanted their pet projects given special consideration, and from his enemies, who were always ready to throw brickbats designed to knock him out of his position. He took a lot of this in stride, but the more serious issues with which he grappled in 1935 and 1936—involving problems with personnel, the continuing battle with Harry Hopkins and his WPA, and a serious confrontation with FDR—nearly cost him his career.

Through most of 1935 Ickes had one principal staffing problem, and his name was Louis Glavis. Ickes had hired him shortly after taking office in 1933 and made him director of the Division of Investigations in the Interior Department. Glavis's responsibilities were far-ranging; in fact, they paralleled Ickes's. When Ickes was made public works administrator and oil administrator under the NIRA, Glavis's division became the primary investigative unit for these functions as well.

Early in 1935 the story was leaked to the press that the White House had ordered Secretary Ickes to fire Glavis because his unit had gotten out of hand. The worst accusation was that certain telephones, not only in the Interior Department but also outside of it, had been tapped by Ickes's investigators. Both the White House and Ickes denied the story, but Ickes believed that a number of people, including Mrs. Roosevelt, were actively seeking the resignations of Glavis and Assistant Secretary of the Interior Ebert Burlew.

Through most of 1935 Ickes tried to save Glavis, although he was extremely unpopular and the secretary was under tremendous pressure to get rid of him. At first he tried reining in Glavis, hoping that that would be sufficient. But Glavis didn't want to be reined in, and toward the end of the year Glavis threatened to resign. But Ickes, who still wasn't prepared to lose his valuable, albeit unpopular, assistant, talked him out of it.

Problems with Glavis continued into 1936. Ickes gradually became aware that he had made a big mistake in giving his investigations director so much authority. In April he wrote:

I am willing to continue him as Director . . . but only under clearly defined and restricted powers. I will no longer put up with his highhanded methods. He has raised up a veritable Frankenstein's monster. These investigators have become persecutors, man hunters, and they are just as eager to hunt and drag down members of my staff as they are lobbyists and crooked contractors against whom we are trying to protect the Department and PWA.[34]

Circumscribing Glavis's activities still didn't work. On July 18, 1936, Louis Glavis resigned his position, and Ickes, along with many others in Washington, breathed a large, collective sigh of relief. By this time relations between Ickes and Glavis had become exceedingly strained. Ickes said that when he began exercising some oversight, Glavis became "surly and recalcitrant" and completely forgot how much he owed Ickes for bringing him back into public life.[35] The situation was very ugly for several months leading up to his resignation, as Glavis looked to others in the department to help him retain his position. He also tacitly threatened to expose Ickes by telling all he knew about the affair with Marguerite. Early in July Ickes wrote that "Glavis is busy spreading poison against me in all directions," but that he finally was able to convince him that it would be in both their interests not to wash any dirty linen in public.[36]

So ended Louis Glavis's three-year "reign of terror," as departmental employees called it only half in jest. By this time Glavis was, by his own account, a mental basketcase.[37] While the Division of Investigations admittedly went to extremes, it did succeed in implementing one of Harold Ickes's primary objectives, that of reducing graft and corruption in the PWA to a bare minimum. The fact that there was only one well-documented instance of fraud within the PWA (other allegations were made, of course, but nothing was ever proven) was perhaps reason enough for Ickes's reluctance to let Glavis go.

It was the case of the phony CCC camp.[38] A few years into the popular employment program known as the Civilian Conservation Corps, an enterprising employee of the National Park Service's budget division decided to set up an illusory camp in one of the parks and populate it with fictitious young men. For nearly a year the official received the paychecks that were delivered to him through the Department of the Army (but whose funds ultimately came from the PWA), and proceeded to endorse and cash them at several locations in Washington. Several thousand dollars, out of the hundreds of millions that passed through departmental hands, were siphoned off by this Park Service employee.

The man made the mistake of calling in sick on a day that the courier from the Army delivered the checks to the Interior Department. The scam was discovered and Secretary Ickes hit the roof. He immediately asked to see a young Park Service official named Conrad Wirth, whose many responsibilities included overseeing the CCC camps within the National Park Service. It was a job unto itself: At the height of the program in 1935 Park Service personnel were managing some 600 CCC camps with an enrollment totaling 120,000 young men.[39]

"I was called into the Secretary's office, and he was working at his desk, with his sleeves rolled up," Wirth recalled fifty years later. "He barely looked up at me when he asked whether I was the person responsible for CCC oversight." When Wirth replied, "Yes sir," Ickes said, "You're fired." Wirth turned around and left the office.

While the young man made his preparations to leave the agency, higher-ups within the Park Service pleaded his case with the secretary. Four days later Wirth was called back in to see the secretary. This time he asked him about his workload, and Wirth mentioned that he was simultaneously running three offices. This hit home. A more sympathetic Ickes replied, "I think you've got too much work on your hands." Conrad Wirth was rehired, and Ickes took responsibility for the theft when he was called to testify about it on the Hill. Wirth would later direct the agency for thirteen years under presidents Eisenhower, Kennedy, and Johnson.

"He [Ickes] was a gruff sort of person, but I enjoyed working for him very much," Wirth wrote in his memoirs.[40] "He was unequivocal in his instructions and could be depended upon to back up an employee who got in trouble carrying out his orders."

The most serious problem Ickes had in running the PWA through 1935 and 1936, however, concerned his own resentment toward his rival, Harry Hopkins. It almost cost him his career. Ickes never was comfortable with FDR's Hyde Park settlement of September 1935, and he continued to see Hopkins as the villain. Around Thanksgiving he wrote in his diary that "the pressure for money for PWA projects still continues."[41] The trouble was that he just didn't have funds, thanks to Hopkins, to consider the many worthy and durable proposals still flowing into his agency.

Compounding the money shortage was the recognition that an unusually deep friendship had developed between Roosevelt and Hopkins. A number of people around the president, including Harold Ickes, recognized that as FDR's long-time associate and personal friend Louis Howe became sicker and sicker, the president turned increasingly to Hopkins. Louis Howe died in April 1936, and with his death Hopkins's enviable position vis-à-vis the president was established. The friendship inevitably aroused feelings of jealousy and even fear among several of Roosevelt's other friends and aides.

Ickes continued as PWA administrator through the early months of 1936, allotting what little money he had, but the whole festering issue came to a head in May. The president was working on an additional $1.5-billion budget request to Congress. In a meeting with FDR, Ickes learned that the president was inclining heavily toward giving the whole sum to Hopkins's Works Progress Administration. As originally drafted, the bill did not earmark monies for Ickes's PWA or for any other agency of government. Thus it was an even worse situation than what he'd had to endure the previous fall. Ickes concluded that Roosevelt "was prepared to help Harry Hopkins carry out the desire he had had at heart for the last two years to scuttle PWA and salvage from it whatever he can for the benefit of his own administration." He vowed that he would not, under any circumstances, work under Hopkins and his relief program.

One week later, at a cabinet meeting on May 14, Ickes came perilously close to losing his entire public career when both the president and Ickes reached their boiling points. As the two men discussed whether Ickes would be allowed to testify before the Senate Appropriations Committee about the PWA, tempers flared. "We hammered back and forth at each other on this subject and it was plain to see that the president was not in the best of tempers. Neither was I," Ickes wrote. "I was pretty angry by this time. It was as clear as day that the President was spanking me hard before the full Cabinet and I resented that too. All the other members appeared to be embarrassed, but I could see Henry Morgenthau stealing a covert glance at me from time to time. Doubtless he enjoyed the spanking very much," Ickes concluded.

A humiliated Harold Ickes felt he had no other choice than to resign. Within a few days of the "spanking," Ickes wrote the president a polite but cool letter telling him that, since he had repudiated Ickes's PWA for all the world to see, he was tendering his resignation. As it happened, Ickes had a luncheon appointment with Roosevelt the next day. When he was ushered in to the president's office, FDR gave him a quizzical look and handed him a handwritten note addressed to "Dear Harold." The note said that neither he nor the PWA was repudiated. "Resignation not accepted!" FDR wrote, then signed it, "Your affectionate friend, Franklin D. Roosevelt."

Over lunch Roosevelt proceeded to charm his prickly friend back into the fold. Ickes noted that he was "quite touched" by the president's "undoubted generosity and . . . evident sincerity of tone." The meeting, Ickes went on to say, "undoubtedly cleared the sky." He was back in, but it was a close call. Had FDR been endowed with even a slightly more vengeful, less patient, nature, Harold Ickes's New Deal career would have been finished in 1936.

OVER THE NEXT few weeks the PWA was brought back to life, and in the emergency appropriation bill for the 1936–37 fiscal year, Congress earmarked $300 million for public works. Harold Ickes's appointment as public works administrator continued well into Roosevelt's second term. But because it was an election year, and because other issues were coming to the fore, Harold Ickes found himself concentrating less on the PWA after the May crisis. He threw himself back into the fight for a Department of Conservation, and he began to think about the marvelous political battle shaping up between liberals and conservatives. In his personal life, too, things were beginning to look up, as his romance with Jane Dahlman became increasingly serious.

CHAPTER 10

"I STRUCK A REAL NOTE"

THE LIBERAL

LIGHTNING ROD

IN 1934 SEN. ROBERT WAGNER received a handwritten letter with a postmark from Georgia. It read:

> In Georgia thay Ar Killing the Colored Woman and Saturday Night Oct 27th they mobed a Negro man he is Not Dead but looking to Die Any Day i Want you to Do your best to Stop this. . . . i wont Rite my Name fer that it Would be Publish and thay Will Kill Me as i A Negro.[1]

Whether it was through a radio broadcast, a newspaper article, or by word of mouth, a terrified citizen from Georgia somehow learned that the senator from New York was a friend. This person then did a courageous thing: He or she found a scrap of paper, an envelope, a two-cent stamp and wrote Wagner a letter describing some of the unspeakable atrocities that were happening to blacks in the South as the country focused on economic recovery.

In fact the German-born senator, who emigrated to the United States as a boy and who grew up in a working-class section of New York City, was doing his best to end the outrageous practice of lynching, which had swept the Depression-ridden country like the plague. Lynchings had occurred from time to time in all parts of the nation but only in the South did they become an accepted form of social control. White Southerners initially used lynching to keep their newly freed slaves in line, and for half a century the barbaric practice waxed and waned, largely in response to economic conditions. It was never altogether abandoned. Blacks attempted to keep track of the incidence of lynchings that occurred from the end of the Civil War until the 1930s and they found that, from a low point in 1930, the number crept up yearly as the economic crisis worsened. By 1933 the Negro community had become deeply alarmed and they looked to Washington for help.

A handful of men and women of principle, in positions of power, joined the battle. Foremost among them was Robert Wagner, the stocky, plain-speaking champion of liberal causes, who was first elected to the Senate in 1926. After his reelection in 1932 Wagner became a key man in Roosevelt's New Deal. He helped draft a number of precedent-shattering bills, including old-age assistance and the working man's right to collective bargaining. He also introduced, in 1933, an antilynching bill. From 1925 to 1932, not a single bill on this subject was considered by the Congress of the United States, but as the situation worsened and the practice spread, a movement developed to make lynching a federal crime.

In 1933 two bills were introduced in Congress, one of which was the Wagner-Costigan bill. Wagner's bill was reintroduced in 1934, 1935, 1936, 1937, and 1938. Despite substantial public support, no antilynching legislation was ever passed, testimony to the Southern legislators' stranglehold on that institution during the Roosevelt era. In the Senate's 1938 session, South Carolina's Sen. James Byrnes told the president's son that he and his fellow Southerners would filibuster "until the year 2038, unless the bill is withdrawn before then!"[2]

Edward P. Costigan of Colorado was another legislator for whom lynching was an evil reminder of the Dark Ages. Born in 1874, the same year that produced Harold Ickes, Costigan came of age during the Progressive Era and helped found the Progressive Party in 1912. He was elected to the Senate in 1930 as a Progressive Republican but served only one term. In the midst of his reelection campaign Costigan suffered a complete physical breakdown and was forced to withdraw his nomination. "This is really dreadful news," Harold Ickes wrote on April 11, 1936, "because Costigan is one of the outstanding men in the Senate, both from the point of view of ability and of single-minded devotion to the public interest."[3]

But during his one term in the Senate Costigan joined forces with his fellow liberals on both sides of the aisle in order to rid the country of mob violence. Interestingly, the Rocky Mountain region, which could be described as the nation's geographic backbone, produced and sent to Washington certainly its share of individuals with sturdy backbones. From Montana came both Thomas Walsh and Burton Wheeler, the latter having come, "so to speak, out of a mining camp, and [with] the temperament and passion of a vigilante."[4] Montana also sent the first woman ever to be elected to Congress, Jeannette Rankin, and she distinguished herself as a dedicated pacifist. Idaho sent William Borah, Colorado produced Costigan, and New Mexico had, until his tragic death in a plane crash in 1935, Bronson Cutting. Most of these western legislators strongly supported the antilynching bills introduced by Wagner and Costigan.

What helped spur liberal congressmen to action was the publication in 1933 of a book, Arthur F. Raper's *The Tragedy of Lynching*. The immediate occasion for this exhaustive and carefully researched history was "the marked increase in lynchings early in 1930," coupled with the fear that the number would escalate as hard times deepened. Raper's book began with a description of the lynching of James Irwin at Ocilla, Georgia, in 1930. He was one of twenty-one men who were lynched that fateful year. All but one were, like Irwin, black men:

> Mobs are capable of unbelievable atrocity. James Irwin at Ocilla, Georgia, was jabbed in his mouth with a sharp pole. His toes were cut off joint by joint. His fingers were similarly removed, and his teeth extracted with wire pliers. After further unmentionable mutilations [to his genitals], the Negro's still living body was saturated with gasoline and a lighted match was applied. As the flames leaped up, hundreds of shots were fired into the dying victim. During the day, thousands of people from miles around rode out to see the sight. Not till nightfall did the officers remove the body and bury it.[5]

Lynching was the most depraved way in which white Southerners caused blacks to suffer during the Depression, but they were denied their basic rights in countless other ways as well. No other minority group, except perhaps the American Indians, had a harder time finding work, sustenance, and shelter than did blacks in the 1930s. This was true for all regions of the country—north, south, east, west— although no other region outside of the South went to such extremes in its cruel and callous treatment of blacks. Nor did their social and economic status improve dramatically with the changing of the guard in 1932. At the time of Franklin Roosevelt's stunning victory over in-cumbent Herbert Hoover, most blacks who could vote supported the candidate of Abraham Lincoln's party, and so they rallied around the slogan "Who but Hoover?" [6] Roosevelt's record on civil rights, up to and including the 1932 campaign, gave Negroes no reason to hope that a President Roosevelt would give them a new and better deal.

When the new First Family moved into the White House in March 1933, and the new administration took over the various power centers of the executive branch of government, the black community discov-ered a few civil libertarians among the incoming entourage in Wash-ington. The president himself had delivered a stirring message of hope in his inaugural address on March 4, when he told the American people, "The only fear we have to fear is fear itself." Most Americans were badly shaken by the economic crisis enveloping the nation and thus they welcomed FDR's self-confident message. Few whites, how-ever, could identify with the absolute terror that many blacks felt at the time over violence in general and lynching in particular. The white majority never knew the awful despair that came with realizing that there was no recourse to established authority. Thus when FDR promised to rout fear and panic from his fellow citizens' lives, the mes-sage had a unique significance for blacks.

Of much greater import than the president's address, however, was the fact that the nation's First Lady became a tireless and extremely effective champion of the black community. Through her own expe-riences with emotional deprivation as a child—a poignant sense of rejection that never quite left her, and a host of childhood fears with which she constantly struggled—Eleanor Roosevelt was able to iden-tify with the black experience. Once in the White House she devel-oped close friendships with several black leaders, especially Walter White of the NAACP and Mary McLeod Bethune, president of the National Council of Negro Women. It took Mrs. Roosevelt a year— in which she took a "crash course" on issues of race discrimination, lynching, and methods of political disenfranchisement—before she began to speak out publicly on civil rights. [7] But once she did, Negroes and other minorities had no better or more powerful friend in Washington.

In Secretary of the Interior Harold Ickes, though, blacks had as good a friend. His ties to their community extended back into the Chicago of the 1920s, when he served briefly as president of that city's chapter of the NAACP. He continued his membership in the NAACP and joined in its struggles through the Roaring '20s. When his big break came in February of 1933 Harold Ickes was ready for action.

He wasted no time in pressing forward his commitment to equal rights. The "Whites Only" and "Colored" signs immediately came down, and he followed up his executive order integrating the public facilities in the Interior Department with the establishment of an Office on Negro Relations. It became known as the Black Cabinet, and it served as the lead unit that pressed the other executive departments and agencies in Washington not to forget about blacks. Ickes knew, of course, that it would take considerable time to end racial discrimination in the hidebound federal bureaucracy, which included his own department, but to his credit he began the slow process and tenaciously kept at it throughout his thirteen years in power. When he learned, for instance, that there wasn't a single black employee in the Mormon-dominated and rapidly expanding Bureau of Reclamation, he promised that that would change as soon as vacancies occurred.

When Roosevelt gave him the Public Works Administration to run in June of 1933, Ickes recognized that an even better opportunity to effect changes in governmental and social policy had come his way. This was a totally new organization with the potential to put back to work millions of unemployed Americans—whites, blacks, Indians, Hispanics—and to pay them all the same wage. That was as radical a policy as was attempted during the decade. As administrator he saw that he could also provide minority groups with their fair share of new school buildings, hospitals, and affordable housing. Although Ickes's actions on civil rights were compromised rather considerably by bumping against the bedrock of racism in American society, "to at least a minimum extent, Ickes . . . proved that anti-discrimination orders and racial quotas could work," historian Harvard Sitkoff concluded.[8]

Harold Ickes began his appointment as PWA administrator by prohibiting all forms of discrimination in that organization. Walter White of the NAACP and other black leaders wrote him congratulatory letters. The secretary replied by assuring them that "I have not lost interest in the Negro problem, and I am happy to have such a close contact with several phases of it under the administration of the Department of the Interior." [9] Nevertheless, rooting out discrimination proved extremely difficult, even in a new organization. One of Ickes's advisors on race issues, Clark Foreman, pressed him in 1933 to appoint black supervisors to any all-black Civilian Conservation Camps that fell under the jurisdiction of the National Park Service. Ickes readily agreed. He told Foreman to discuss it with Arno Cammerer, the Park Service's new director, and to get the ball rolling. Cammerer, however, was characteristically cautious.

In a memo that probably irritated Ickes and helped form his low opinion of the director, dated November 23, 1933, Cammerer apprised him of some of the difficulties pertaining to that policy. He pointed out that there were nine black CCC companies at various locations in the East: Four companies at Colonial National Monument in Yorktown, Virginia; two companies at Gettysburg National Military Park in Pennsylvania; two companies at Chickamunga-Chattanooga National Military Park in Georgia; and one company of World War I veterans at Shiloh National Military Park, Tennessee. The problem, Cammerer noted, was:

> The supervisory work organizations for all of these Camps are white men, generally local residents, who have been appointed on the recommendation of Senators or Members of Congress, or have secured the proper endorsements from the County Democratic Chairman. The principal difficulty at this time in giving some of the supervisory positions to negroes is that we would have to discharge white men who have political backing. However, in the event that any of the supervisory positions in these camps become vacant we might then promote enrolled colored boys who have merited such promotion and are qualified for the work. [10]

Patronage wasn't the only barrier to giving blacks equal opportunity within the CCC, however. In his lengthy memo on the subject of race relations, Arno Cammerer did a lot—probably unintentionally—to illuminate what blacks and their white supporters, like Ickes, were up against in the 1930s. The memo deserves to be quoted in virtually its entirety:

> One forestry and one historian foreman position in the second CCC camp at Gettysburg, and one forestry foreman position at Shiloh have not yet

been filled. We are having difficulty in finding qualified white foresters for these two forestry positions and know of no negro who has had the necessary forestry training to qualify. We might consider a qualified negro for the historian position at Gettysburg where the man could find other accommodations in the event he did not want to eat with the negro enrollees. As I understand the situation the question of making some of the CCC companies 100 per cent colored has been discussed by Mr. Fechner with representatives of the Army, the Forest Service and this Office from time to time in the ECW meetings, but because of the Army's unsatisfactory experience with negro officers in command of negro troops, it has been the opinion of a majority of the representatives that white officers and white work supervisors would get better results from negro enrollees in work and discipline than would negro officers and negro supervisors.

Fully two years later Secretary Ickes was still trying to crack the hard nut of racism within the CCC. In a letter dated September 26, 1935, to Robert Fechner, director of Emergency Conservation Works (ECW), Ickes wrote:

For my part, I am quite certain that Negroes can function in supervisory capacities just as efficiently as can white men and I do not think that they should be discriminated against merely on account of their color. I can see no menace to the program that you are so efficiently carrying out in giving just and proper recognition to members of the Negro race.[11]

Through Roosevelt's entire first term in office Harold Ickes, in his various capacities, did more to further the rights of minorities than did any other official in the administration. And while it cannot be said that FDR shared Ickes's concern for the rights of blacks in particular, as opposed to the rights of all disadvantaged Americans in the 1930s, the president allowed his subordinate very wide latitude. By never silencing or otherwise reining in Ickes on the extremely touchy issue of race relations, Roosevelt in effect lent tacit support to these efforts. It was not an inconsequential strategy on the president's part.

FDR's behind-the-scenes support for Ickes's principled stand on civil rights extended into 1936, the presidential election year. In January Roosevelt received a letter from Clyde T. Ellis of Bentonville, Arkansas. Chairman of Bentonville's Young Democratic Club, Ellis wrote the president to complain about a black employee who was in town to investigate some ongoing PWA work. The specific complaint was the fact that Mr. M. J. Chisum had a job with the Interior Department. Ellis wrote, "We do not object to the negroes working in their places but we do object to an outrage like this, especially when so many able and efficient white people are out of employment." [12]

A copy of Ellis's letter was sent to Ickes from the White House with the customary "for your information" designation. Mr. Chisum retained his position with the Division of Investigations. He was, Ickes observed, a good worker, and that was the end of the matter.

"WE WILL WIN easily next year but we are going to make it a crusade," the president buoyantly proclaimed in November 1935. This was music to Ickes's ears, for there was nothing he loved more than a political crusade on behalf of liberal principles. He also recognized, after nearly three years in the administration, that he was pivotal among the liberal faction that vied continuously with the conservatives for influence over FDR's policy direction. Roosevelt himself inclined toward liberalism, not out of dogmatism but rather, as the journalist John Gunther put it, "out of what was basically an emotional and personal approach, his sense of fellowship and profound regard for all human suffering." The defining experience for Roosevelt, the one that deepened him and awoke his sympathies for the downtrodden, was, of course, his paralysis. In his thirty-ninth year, Roosevelt was stricken with polio and learned that he would never walk unaided again. "The supreme experience of his life was to beat Death off, and then conquer indomitably the wounding traces that Death left," Gunther wrote.[13]

All the people closest to Roosevelt recognized the irony. Had it not been for this tragic experience, Franklin Roosevelt would never have achieved the heights of greatness that he did, and he would not have become the adored, compassionate leader of the ordinary American. No twentieth-century president, and quite possibly no president in all of American history, was more loved than he was.

However, FDR was also a supreme pragmatist, a believer in politics as the art of the possible. So his first administration was a motley collection of liberals, conservatives, and centrists. On the conservative end was Budget Director Lewis Douglas, who everyone agreed was brilliant but who also was utterly unyielding on the subject of the balanced budget. "The Director of the Budget is a young man . . . of Arizona," Sen. Hiram Johnson observed, "born to the purple, loves the English and their ways, and has a heart of stone." [14] Douglas lasted about a year. Although Roosevelt shared Douglas's belief that deficit spending was bad, he found no way other than through Keynesian economics to rout the Great Depression and end the panic.

Cordell Hull, at State, also represented political conservatism, and Homer Cummings at the Justice Department represented middle-of-the-road politics. Roosevelt's vice-president, the good ol' boy from Texas, John Nance Garner, was liberal on some issues and conservative on others. Ickes found himself pleasantly surprised on more than one occasion by Garner's enlightened, that is, liberal, views on certain subjects. The president's good friend and Treasury secretary, Henry Morgenthau, was a moderate. On the liberal side of the table were Frances Perkins, Henry Wallace, and Harold Ickes. Harry Hopkins did not have a cabinet appointment until he became secretary of commerce during FDR's second term, but he, too, was definitely of the liberal persuasion and influenced the president in that direction through his various administrative appointments.

Harold Ickes was well aware that he was as thoroughgoing a liberal as could be found in the administration, and so when it came time to think about the 1936 election he took the president at his word and proceeded to do his part to make the campaign a crusade. Ickes, Arthur Schlesinger Jr. wrote, "assumed the role of hatchet man with grim relish." [15] In December 1935 Ickes seized the moment when he made a speech in Detroit to a large crowd of about 2,500 people. "It was," he wrote in his diary, "a well-fed, well-dressed, prosperous crowd, mainly Republican, I should judge." [16] The theme of the speech was "a plea for a return to the America of the Founding Fathers, where the great majority of the people would actually own some property and would have the means of sustaining themselves and their families in reasonable comfort and of living in economic security." At the conclusion only a smattering of polite applause was audible in the large hall.

Despite its cool reception, Ickes was pleased with the speech. He felt that it would have an impact on the upcoming campaign. Shortly after delivering it he wrote, "As I see it now, I have put it up to the Administration pretty hard to follow along the same lines or to repudiate me, and I don't think they will want to do the latter. I find that I struck a real note."

Actually he struck several notes, some of which were alarm bells. Conservative newspapers began labeling Harold Ickes a radical. The *Washington Herald* even called him a Communist after having read his Detroit speech. How it interpreted a speech extolling the virtues of Jeffersonian democracy as communism was difficult to understand,

Ickes noted, but then he never expected much from a certain segment of the press. Nevertheless, such epithets served mainly to convince Ickes he was on the right track, and early in 1936 he pressed the president for a "frontal attack" on two of the most vociferous critics of the New Deal administration, Roosevelt's political mentor from New York, Al Smith, and newspaper magnate William Randolph Hearst.[17]

At the time the president was discussing with his cabinet and others what should be done not about Smith or Hearst but about the Supreme Court, which was well on its way toward making a clean sweep of all New Deal legislation. The Court issue was inextricably bound up with the presidential election, and Ickes, true to form, pushed for a "second front" on the institution that he said had become "a third branch of Congress." At a cabinet meeting held early in 1936 the administration's approach to the problem of the Court's conservatism was debated, and Secretary Ickes observed with slight annoyance that Miss Perkins was the only cabinet member to think "that we ought to pussyfoot on the Supreme Court issue." He supposed that that was to be expected of a woman.[18]

While the Court continued its remarkable session in which it tried to demolish the New Deal, Roosevelt kept his counsel. He decided— as Frances Perkins had argued—against making the Court a direct issue in the 1936 campaign. Once reelected, he then would tackle that formidable political problem. Ickes's preference was of course otherwise, but he, too, kept a low profile on the issue in accordance with FDR's overall strategy. He found it hard to keep his mouth shut, however, especially after the Court handed down its decision in May 1936 on the Guffey Coal Act, a piece of legislation that Ickes, John L. Lewis of the United Mine Workers, and many others had fought for. Of that thoroughly conservative decision Ickes wrote:

> The Supreme Court yesterday handed down a five-to-four decision which, in effect, held that neither the nation nor a state may pass any law interfering in any respect with the right of an employer to come to such terms as may please him with any employee as to wages and hours of employment. The sacred right of contract again—the right of an immature child or a helpless woman to drive a bargain with a great corporation. If this decision does not outrage the moral sense of the country, then nothing will.[19]

WITH THE ADVENT of the new year, a presidential election year, it was becoming apparent that a vast movement was underway among the American electorate. It was the political equivalent of a tidal wave—a fluid, not clearly defined, shift of major proportions in the sentiments and party allegiance of a great mass of the voters. President Roosevelt and his New Dealers were in the process of creating a new and powerful political coalition in America, the composition of which would become solidified by the end of 1936. As champion of the underdog, Ickes, a nominal Republican, made important contributions to the emerging Democratic majority.

The major division in this political realignment was economic. With his good grasp of history, Roosevelt was quick to recognize that 1936 bore resemblances to previous defining elections, and he capitalized on that fact through 1936. He set the tone for the upcoming election in his annual State of the Union address before Congress in January. It was a fighting speech. Arthur Schlesinger Jr. called it a "slam-bang attack on the 'resplendent economic autocracy'; phrased with felicity and delivered with evident relish, [it] transformed the State-of-the-Union message into a campaign harangue." [20]

A few days later, as keynote speaker at the annual Andrew Jackson Day dinner, Roosevelt repeated the performance. He vigorously attacked the business interests that were impeding the New Deal and slowly but surely aligning themselves against his reelection. Borrowing an idea that Harold Ickes said he gave him in 1935, the president proceeded to cast himself as a contemporary Andrew Jackson. "It is the fight of Jackson against the U.S. Bank all over again with concentrated capital in the place of the Bank," Ickes had noted,[21] and FDR agreed. Thus the memory of the rough-hewn, fiercely independent frontiersman who became the country's first president of the common man, and who took on the vested interests of the time, was resurrected for the 1936 election.

The fight over the recharter of the Bank of the United States had taken place just a little over 100 years prior to 1936, and it figured prominently in Jackson's bid for reelection in 1832. In his fine history of the period, Vernon Parrington in 1927 called Jackson's veto of the recharter bill perhaps the most courageous presidential act in all of U.S. history, for "he knew how fiercely it would be defended." [22] FDR's own determination to press forward the New Deal despite bitter opposition from business, the press, and the Court was hardly less bold in 1936.

Through the first half of 1936 Ickes was an enthusiastic supporter of Roosevelt's renomination but he continued to fear that the election in November would be close. As Ickes saw the political situation in January, the Republicans were still powerful and could align themselves with Southern Democrats—the group FDR was trying mightily to contain within his party. Roosevelt wouldn't speak out publicly, for instance, in support of the antilynching bill because he needed Southern Democratic support to win in 1936. It would have amounted to political suicide to have done so. As he told the NAACP's Walter White, "I did not choose the tools with which I must work. But I've got to get legislation passed by Congress to save America." [23]

Despite Ickes's penchant for not wanting to underestimate the Grand Old Party, he nevertheless sensed what a lot of people were, that the Republicans were on the verge of tripping themselves up. In January he wrote his longtime Progressive Republican friend, Max Rutter of Philadelphia, a letter discussing the upcoming election:

> If the Republican campaign, except to the extent that it may be modified by the efforts of [William] Borah, will not be directed toward the reestablishment of the social and economic system that prevailed prior to March 4, 1933, then I miss my guess. The altruistic heights that can be expected of the Republican party can be gauged from the lyrical ecstasies that, with . . . Hearst as cheer leader, are going up from the throats of the reactionaries today with respect to Governor Landon, of Kansas. We are asked to throw our hats in the air in our enthusiasm over the discovery of the "Kansas Coolidge." I have always felt that, spiritually, America scraped the bottom when Coolidge was in the White House, and I say this even with Harding in mind. [24]

As summer and the national conventions approached, it looked more and more as if the Republicans would turn to the "Kansas Coolidge," Alf Landon, to be their party's standard bearer against a certain-to-be-renominated Franklin Roosevelt. With his popularity at an all-time high, the president acted as though he cared little whom the Republicans nominated in Cleveland that June. He was confident of a big victory in November. (The endlessly fascinating question among his campaign staff was "How big?") Since Harold Ickes was still a registered Republican, the president asked him to deliver a radio address on the eve of the Republican National Convention. Ickes was delighted to be in the thick of things, and he and his staff of speechwriters proceeded to work on it.

On Sunday evening, June 7, Harold Ickes spoke on national radio about the Republicans. Rather than make it an all-out attack, Ickes claimed that he chose a more subtle approach in which he "gently" poked fun at the party's leadership. His old friends William Allen White, Gifford Pinchot, and Frank Knox came in for some of the Ickes-style kidding, but he reserved his heaviest blows for William Randolph Hearst, who could boast of being, as Ickes delicately put it, "the discoverer of Governor Landon . . . the dictator of the Republican platform and the absentee boss who will determine the deliberations at Cleveland as successor to former Republican bosses." Ickes also pointed out to his radio audience that the Republicans were about to select, as they frequently did, "the man who is the least troubled by views on any subject and who is least qualified, on the basis of experience, to be President of the United States." [25]

"It was a peach," a chuckling president told Ickes after he had read it. Then, while the Republicans opened their convention in Cleveland on Monday, June 8, the president and his party boarded a train that carried them to the Lone Star State to attend the Texas Centennial.[26]

While Roosevelt campaigned in Texas and en route, the Republicans opened their deliberations over who would be their sacrificial lamb on the altar of the 1936 presidential election. All assembled recognized that it would be, to put it mildly, an uphill battle. The members of the press who were covering the convention were quick to note that the atmosphere in the great hall where the party faithful were assembled was like a religious revival. "The delegates were solemn and dedicated. The band roused them less with gay tunes like 'Oh! Susanna,' the Landon song, than with 'Onward, Christian Soldiers' and 'The Battle Hymn of the Republic.' " [27]

The climax of the convention occurred on Wednesday, not when Alf Landon and Frank Knox were nominated as presidential and vice-presidential contenders (that occurred the next day), but when Herbert Hoover spoke before the earnest assembly. As the Great Engineer made his way to the platform, the pent-up emotions of a crowd verging on desperation burst forth, and for over fifteen minutes Hoover was greeted with cheering and yelling, clapping and foot-stamping. Once order was restored, the former president made his speech—and his last-ditch attempt at being his party's nominee. Hoover lambasted Roosevelt and the New Deal, likening it to European collectivism and calling it the first phase in the establishment of American fascism. In a decade when the conflict of "-isms" was raging, Hoover gave voice to the fear that many Americans felt when they heard about events overseas: That the foreign "-isms"—fascism, collectivism, socialism, and communism—might invade America. The only hope, Hoover proclaimed, was to return to a homegrown "-ism," to the "old safe ground of American individualism."

It was what the Republicans wanted badly to hear but they chose instead to repudiate their former chief executive, and to nominate the bland governor of Kansas, Alf Landon, and the Theodore Roosevelt Progressive from Illinois, Col. Frank Knox. A ticket more dedicated to America's conservative heartland and homegrown values was hard to imagine.

Two weeks later it was the Democrats' turn to revel in party loyalty and hero worship. But the big difference between the revival in Cleveland and the festivities in Philadelphia later that month was the overwhelming scent of success that hung in the air, tickling the nostrils of convention delegates, in the city that gave birth to the Republic in 1789. The Democrats knew they had a winner, and nothing, seemingly, could ruffle the happy conventioneers—not Al Smith's exhortations in the press to nominate a "genuine Democrat," nor Father Coughlin's use of the Nazi-inspired tactics of black armbands and flag-waving to protest the renomination of the country gentleman from Hyde Park.

Selected as a delegate-at-large from Illinois, Harold Ickes left Washington promptly at 9 o'clock on Monday morning, June 22. His driver, Carl Witherspoon, made the trip to Philadelphia in four and a half hours, just in time to deposit the secretary at the Franklin Hotel for the Illinois delegation's caucus, which was postponed because Illinois governor Horner and Chicago mayor Kelly were fighting, "as they have been fighting ever since Kelly undertook to defeat Horner for renomination as Governor," Ickes wrote.[28] The caucus finally met on Tuesday afternoon, and for the next few days Ickes attended, off and on, various sessions and meetings of the DNC.

"The first session of the convention was no more interesting than I had expected it to be," Ickes wrote. Some complained that Jim Farley, chairman of the Democratic National Convention, spoke too long in calling the convention to order on Tuesday afternoon. Ickes was sitting with his friend, Sen. J. Hamilton Lewis of Illinois, who didn't like the fact that a Catholic bishop, resplendent in scarlet robes and a scarlet cap, delivered the opening invocation. Farley was a Catholic and FDR was frequently criticized for courting the Catholic vote as well as the

Jewish vote. The high point of the convention, as the delegates awaited Saturday and the president's acceptance speech, was the keynote speech given by Sen. Alben Barkley of Kentucky. The border-state orator was in good form as he attacked both the "fat hogs of Republican plunder" and a Supreme Court that cared not a whit for the "tortured souls and bodies of its working men, women, and children. . . . Is the Court beyond criticism? Barkley asked the delegates. May it be regarded as too sacred to be disagreed with? The crowd roared back: *No! No!*" [29]

But it was the president's acceptance speech on Saturday night, June 27, for which the delegates had been waiting all week. The crowd of over 100,000 began filling the Franklin Field stadium early on that evening, even though Roosevelt wasn't scheduled to speak until after 9:30. Ickes arrived before 7 o'clock and since he had a seat on the speakers' platform his place was secured. But he also had several tickets for reserved seats for his friends, and these, like many others in the reserved and box sections, were completely overrun even at this early hour. Although the skies threatened rain, the crowd continued to swell and was treated to classical music played by the Philadelphia Symphony Orchestra as it awaited the appearance of the president of the United States. [30]

Finally, the orchestra broke into "Hail to the Chief," and the crowd went wild as spotlights illumined its hero, Franklin Delano Roosevelt. The president emerged from his limousine, and with the help of his son, James, shuffled through the crowd toward the speakers' platform. A buoyant Roosevelt shook hands and exchanged greetings as he moved through the well-wishers. Then he caught the eye of his old friend, the 84-year-old, white-bearded poet Edwin Markham. Markham came forward to shake hands but the crowd pushed him just as he neared the president and his son. James lost his balance and so did the president, whose right leg brace snapped out of position. Roosevelt began to topple over and would have ended up sprawled on the rain-soaked ground had it not been for a Secret Service man who got under him to break the fall.

The president was mortified. Pale and shaken, he snapped to his aides, "Clean me up!" He then saw the pages of his carefully prepared speech scattered on the muddy ground where he had nearly fallen. "Keep your feet off those damned sheets," he ordered, while James helped to wipe the dirt off his father's suit. A few minutes later, with his speech back in his hands and his composure restored, Roosevelt said simply, "Okay, let's go." They proceeded toward the platform and toward FDR's own rendezvous with destiny.

"It was the most frightful five minutes of my life," Roosevelt recalled of that night.[31] Yet he went on to deliver what Harold Ickes called "the greatest political speech I have ever heard." In a strong, sonorous voice, brimming with confidence, Roosevelt told his fellow Americans that "there is a mysterious cycle in human events. To some generations much is given. Of other generations much is expected. This generation of Americans has a rendezvous with destiny."

How Franklin Roosevelt managed to deliver his stunning, historic address after those frightful five minutes is a mystery in itself. But, as personally unsettling as the incident was to FDR, it gave to those few who actually saw it, or later read about it, the true measure of the man. In that moment the most important feature of Roosevelt's character, the ability to overcome adversity, was permanently illumined. Only the most obtuse would continue to wonder why the American people held this particular president in such high esteem, or why they rewarded his courage and leadership with a victory of history-making proportions in November of 1936.

CHAPTER 11

THE NEW DEAL TRIUMPHANT

THE 1936 ELECTION

FOR HAROLD ICKES, attending the Democratic National Convention in Philadelphia and hearing his chief's acceptance speech was a high point of the summer. Moreover, once the members of the administration returned to Washington, Roosevelt made it clear that he wanted his secretary of the interior to be active in the campaign. On July 1, Ickes lunched with Roosevelt at the White House and complimented him again on making the greatest political speech he had ever heard.

I asked the President what part he expected me to play in the campaign and he said he wanted me to attack. Later, just as I was leaving after luncheon, I told him that I hoped he would feel free to call upon me for anything that I could do at any time and he said again that I made such a grand attack that that was what he wanted. He discussed with me several sections of the country where he thought I ought to go, particularly New England and the Middle West.[1]

Ickes was both happy and relieved to hear this. His friendship with the president had been severely tested due to the rows that he'd gotten into earlier that year with Henry Wallace over Forestry and Harry Hopkins over the WPA, so FDR's comments could be construed as a presidential vote of confidence. Moreover, Roosevelt's speech served to validate in Ickes's mind his own actions and pronouncements on behalf of liberalism. He had decided in 1935 to go as far out as he could on a liberal limb, but he was never sure that the president wouldn't saw it off. FDR's words, however, cleared up those concerns. Ickes wrote, "There is no doubt in my mind that he stated the fundamental issue that must be decided in this country sooner or later, and that is whether we are to have real freedom for the mass of people, not only political but economic, or whether we are to be governed by a small group of economic overlords."

So impressed was he by the words Roosevelt spoke in Philadelphia that Ickes unabashedly told the president, "I would have to support you even if you should fire me." But by July 1936, dismissal had become a dim possibility. Roosevelt had forgiven his secretary's peevishness with respect to his rivals; his position vis-à-vis the president was secure at this time. With his public career in good order, and with the prospect of a good fight looming ahead, Harold Ickes found a third reason to be optimistic that summer: He was very much in love with a young lady named Jane Dahlman.

Harold Ickes had known Jane since she was a child, for she was the youngest sister of Betty Dahlman Ickes—Wilmarth's wife. After Wilmarth and Betty married in 1923 the two sisters, Ann and Jane, would occasionally accompany their sister, brother-in-law, and their three young children to the Ickeses' Winnetka home. Jane was then a red-headed, freckle-faced girl who ran around the house and yard at Hubbard Woods with the other kids. The Dahlman girls' visits were lively and pleasant times in the Ickeses' ménage, and Harold remembered Jane with fondness. Perhaps those visits also served to relieve some of the strain between Anna and Harold.

Jane was graduated from Smith College with honors in 1935 and decided to look for work in a city alive with career possibilities, the nation's capital. She contacted Harold that fall to tell him of her impending arrival, and he met her train at Union Station. Harold had seen her only occasionally since she was a child; in March 1934, he mentioned that Raymond, Ann, and Jane Dahlman were all in Washington to spend a few days at his and Anna's house.² But Harold had been married then. Now he was a widower. He wrote that when she stepped off the train he saw, for the first time, a very attractive, slim, young woman with beautiful red hair. Jane was then 22 years old; Harold was 61. Although he didn't admit it to himself at the time, he acknowledged later that it was love at first sight.

Jane wanted an interesting job, so Harold found her a position with the history division of the National Park Service. Through the fall of 1935 he and Jane saw one another, but he also said that he realized, largely because of the forty-year age difference that separated them, he had to keep his distance and allow Jane to meet people her own age. He tried not to monopolize Jane's time during her initial months in Washington. He also kept himself occupied by seeing Cissy Patterson occasionally that fall.

His good intentions notwithstanding, Harold figured in Jane's social life from the minute she arrived in Washington. They were together for Thanksgiving Day, when he "had for dinner Jane Dahlman, Bill McCrillis, Fred Marx and his bride, and a girl guest of the latter. It rained hard from noon on. I took Jane to the movies at night to see [George] Arliss." On the last night of the year Harold and Jane had New Year's Eve dinner at the apartment of two of his closest friends, Ruth Hampton and Bess Beach. After spending a pleasant evening together, and learning that Ruth was "enthusiastic" about Jane, the couple departed for home. "Jane was spending New Year with me and we went home at a reasonably early hour and went to bed," Ickes wrote, "although I heard the whistles and the revolvers at twelve o'clock."³

Harold's own enthusiasm for Jane deepened as he got to know her better. On her birthday, January 27, 1936, which was coincidentally Anna's birthdate as well, Harold hosted a dinner party at which several important people were present. He invited the president's two secretaries, Marguerite (Missy) Le Hand and Grace Tully, Tom Corcoran, who then was in full favor with FDR, a young and eligible attorney who worked in the PWA named Edward J. Foley, and the Rollin Larrabees. "We had a very good time," Ickes noted. "Practically everyone knew everyone else and it was a jolly party. Tom Corcoran brought his accordion and guitar and kept things going after dinner."⁴ It was one of those raw January days, when a fierce wind whipped outside and the temperature plummeted. Inside Harold's house, however, a well-tended fire and a bunch of young, happy guests helped to make Jane's twenty-third birthday a memorable occasion for both her and Harold.

The festive atmosphere continued. Harold had prevailed upon the First Lady's social secretary for an invitation for Jane to a musicale at the White House set for January 28, the day after her birthday. (Harold explained in his diary that she "ranked this sort of thing" because her uncle was John Cudahy, the American ambassador to Poland, and also because of her close connection to the Ickes family.) Jane, naturally, was excited about meeting the president and Mrs. Roosevelt and insisted that Harold accompany her to her first soirée at the White House. He agreed to be her date, although he claimed, somewhat disingenuously, that he shunned such affairs whenever he could.

With the degree of self-satisfaction that only an older man accompanying an attractive, much younger woman can display, Ickes recorded in detail what a great hit Jane made that evening:

> She had bought a new evening gown for the occasion and, unlike most red-headed women, she has a real sense of color in clothes. I don't think I am exaggerating at all when I say that she was the most striking-looking woman at the White House last night. She has the freshness of youth and her coloring is superb. Her hair is really beautiful. She was happy and it was evident that many people found her interesting. I took malicious pleasure in introducing her to Mrs. Homer Cummings, Mrs. J. Fred Essary, and one or two other women who I knew would be burning up with curiosity as to who she was and why I happened to have her at the White House. . . . Captain Brown, the naval aide of the President, whom I ran across at the White House today, commented upon Jane's appearance, and so did the President when I was in with him. Both of them thought that she was not only very good looking but that she was sweet and attractive. They were right on all of these propositions. She is with me a good deal and I have never had anyone in the house, man or woman, who creates such a genuinely happy atmosphere, who is so companionly and so pleasant to get along with.[5]

Harold was utterly in love. He courted Jane through the spring of 1936 and several times asked her to marry him. By this time Jane, too, was very much in love, yet she had substantial doubts over marrying a man who was not just old enough to have been her father but her grandfather. Her own reservations about the relationship were compounded by the fact that her parents, particularly her father, were tell-

ing her in the strongest terms not to marry Harold. Her sisters Ann
and Betty also counseled against it.

The Dahlmans were a conventional, middle-class Catholic family
from Milwaukee who viewed with alarm Harold's courtship of their
youngest daughter. They knew from Wilmarth and Betty of his Washington affair with a younger woman while his wife was in Illinois and
New Mexico. Wilmarth for years had badmouthed his stepfather to his
in-laws and others. His resentment probably developed at the time of
his grandmother's death in 1919, when he was a young man of about
20. Shortly after the end of the war, Wilmarth returned home and
enrolled at Northwestern. In the process of complaining to his stepfather of his small allowance, Wilmarth blurted out that he felt Harold
"had cheated him out of his grandfather's estate." That estate, Ickes
explained, left everything to Anna after the deaths of her mother and
sister. When Anna inherited her parents' estate, Harold renegotiated
the lease on the State Street property from a five-year to a fifty-year
term. By doing so, the family received a much greater income, but
Wilmarth believed that the renegotiation cut him out of his inheritance.[6] Over the ensuing fifteen years the two men occasionally fought
for control of Anna's money, but the last straw came when Anna's will
left everything to Harold. Wilmarth's resentment grew to dangerous
proportions after September 1935.

During the year after Anna's death Wilmarth complained often to
his father-in-law, who was sympathetic. The Dahlmans' picture of
Harold Ickes thus was not an attractive one. They considered him a
womanizer and far too old to be their future son-in-law.

The Dahlmans' religion added further weight to their reservations
about Harold. Mrs. Dahlman attended mass every morning and often
took the girls with her. Divorce was rare among most groups of
Americans in the 1930s but it was almost unheard of among Catholics.
The fact that Harold had been married to a divorcée, and in their eyes
(via Wilmarth) partly responsible for the break-up between James and
Anna Thompson was another mark against him. Mr. and Mrs. Dahlman were living proof of the idea that Catholic couples were expected
to persevere through the worst of marriages.

"My grandmother [Jane's mother], I think, was unhappily married,
Roman Catholic . . . and instead of them being able to separate and
divorce she kind of retreated into semi-madness," Elizabeth Ickes recalled in 1991. "So she had regular stays at a sanitarium." However,
she "recovered fully from all her indispositions when her husband died

[sometime in the 1940s]! So I think she was much more accepting, probably, than her husband, after that, even during that [period of courtship]." Her unspoken attitude, Elizabeth believed, was "if you love the guy, honey, go do it!"[7]

Jane's father, however, was unalterably opposed to the marriage. "Her father disowned her," Elizabeth flatly stated. The Dahlmans had never been a close-knit family, and over the years they dealt as best they could with problems common to many families. But the courtship between Jane and Harold served to deepen the estrangement between parents and children and among the three sisters. Although Jane displayed more independence than did many women of her generation, nevertheless, at age 23, she was deeply affected by her family's opposition to Harold. She decided to spend the summer of 1936 in Europe. She said that she always wanted to see Ireland and Germany, the countries of her ancestors, but it is clear that she also needed time for reflection, far away from her lover.

Jane and Harold saw each other up to the point of her departure in June. On Memorial Day weekend, with his chauffeur driving, Jane and Harold went on an excursion through the countryside of Altoona, Pennsylvania, in search of Ickes's childhood. On their way through Hollidaysburg they decided to look for his Grandfather McCune's farmhouse and grist mill, and situated about three miles outside of town along the banks of the Juniata River. It was in this house that Harold LeClair Ickes had been born. After some difficulty they found the homestead, but, like the great novelist of the 1930s, Thomas Wolfe, discovered, Harold also found going home to be disappointing:

> Only the stonework that had comprised the lower part of the mill was left, and the covered bridge had entirely disappeared. The old farmhouse looked quite run down and disreputable. The farmhouse had been cut in half years ago . . . so that it had long ceased to be the capacious, comfortable, and respectable farmhouse of my boyhood's recollection.[8]

June was a bittersweet month for the couple. Jane's departure for a three-month tour of Europe was imminent, and so they saw a great deal of each other before she left for New York to board ship. It was apparent that the young woman had a noticeable effect on Harold, as was evident in his description of their activities on June 9:

> I played hookey from the office yesterday. This is the first time I have done this since I came to Washington and I am going to try to do it again during the next few days. Jane and I drove down to the Blue Ridge Mountains,

not far from the Hoover Camp on the Rapidan, where we had a picnic lunch, and then home again.[9]

Then she was gone. Harold couldn't bring himself to see her off in New York, so on the dock to wave goodbye were her sister, Ann, and two male friends, Ed Foley and Lawrence Morris.[10]

TRUE TO HIS NATURE, Harold threw himself into his work. The ability to work under even the most trying personal circumstances was one of Ickes's great strengths, and he found plenty to keep him occupied during that summer Jane was away. First and foremost was the election. After spending the week in Philadelphia attending the convention, Ickes returned to Washington at the end of June hoping that the president would immediately begin campaigning. Ickes, certainly, was more than ready to attack. Roosevelt, however, had already decided on another strategy. After reassuring Ickes that he would be used in the campaign, he also told him "that there would be little doing until after Landon had made his speech of acceptance, and he advised me to close up my office and go away for a vacation."[11]

FDR was determined to relax and enjoy himself during July and August, thereby conserving his energies for the exhausting campaign trail in the fall. He dragged Ickes, and others, along in his wake. Over the Fourth of July weekend the secretary of the interior joined the president's party for a trip to dedicate Shenandoah National Park in Virginia, a region of subdued, impressionistic beauty. After the ceremony, they drove to Monticello, where FDR made a nationwide radio speech extolling Jeffersonian ideals. From Monticello, part of the group then drove to Richmond with the Roosevelts and boarded the Potomac for a leisurely fishing trip down the James River and into the Chesapeake Bay.

Ickes accompanied them on the entire trip. He said that he enjoyed getting away from the oppressive heat that smothered the East Coast that summer, and since it was fresh and cool aboard the yacht, he had a few nights' undisturbed sleep, a rare event for the lifelong insomniac. The trip also gave Ickes the opportunity for an extended discussion with the powerful political chieftain Jim Farley. Farley helped to fill the vacuum left by the death in April of FDR's close friend and premier political strategist, Louis Howe, so Ickes was anxious to talk over the upcoming election with him.

In addition to campaign strategy, Farley and Ickes mulled over the composition of the cabinet after Roosevelt's reelection, a subject of vital interest to the Interior secretary. Farley told Ickes that he was going to give up the postmaster generalship because "he felt he had to go into business to make money for his family." [12] As for the other cabinet members, Farley thought that Hull would stay on as secretary of state, and "so far as Morgenthau is concerned, he . . . couldn't be blasted out with a cannon." Ickes was not elated with that bit of news since he still felt resentful toward the Treasury secretary—whom he began referring to as "the satellite, Henry Morgenthau."

Other possible changes, according to Farley, included Secretary of War George Dern, whose health was so bad that he had no idea of what went on in his department, and Homer Cummings at Justice. Cummings, like Farley, wanted to go back into business for financial reasons. Moreover, the postmaster general observed, the attorney general was lazy. He had refused to make any campaign speeches for the president, which was unfortunate because he was an effective campaigner. "As to the Secretary of the Navy," Ickes related, "Jim thinks that the state of Swanson's health is such that he may drop off at any time."

The two men agreed that Henry Wallace probably would stay on at Agriculture, and Farley thought that both Commerce Secretary Dan Roper, the "Pollyanna of the Cabinet," and Labor Secretary Frances Perkins would want to leave the cabinet during Roosevelt's second term. Then there was Harold Ickes. "I tried to draw him out with respect to myself by saying that there were a good many rumors to the effect that the President wouldn't retain me, but Jim said that he had never heard any such suggestion from the President."

Farley was being honest. Despite the fact that Ickes was a controversial figure in the administration, Roosevelt was more than satisfied with his performance and wasn't thinking of replacing him. A little later in the summer Farley canvassed prominent Democrats in every state in order to gauge the president's strength, and he found that the principal objection they raised to Harold Ickes (and also to Harry Hopkins) was that far too many good PWA and WPA jobs had gone to Republicans. Detroit's Congressman John Dingell wrote Farley in August complaining that "the head of the PWA, Mr. Pierson, is a Republican. The new director of the PWA for Wayne County, Democracy's stronghold, is . . . a Republican." [13]

Sen. Pat McCarran of Nevada echoed Dingell's complaint about Ickes, an official whom he didn't much like for other reasons as well. Early in August McCarran wrote Jim Farley that he had howled about this state of affairs for three years but to no effect. "In other words, Mr. Chairman, we must now face the results of the Ickes-Hopkins regime, both of whom openly declared that their departments should be without political atmosphere, but nevertheless seemed to favor the party of the opposition." [14]

Although it was clear from Farley's survey that Ickes had stepped on several influential toes in administering Interior, PWA, and Oil, these objections were, in Roosevelt's view, overshadowed by Ickes's contributions—not least of which was that he served as FDR's lightning rod. As the saying goes, Harold Ickes was loved, by Roosevelt and others, for the enemies he made.

The president continued to shower attention on Harold Ickes that summer. Perhaps it was because he knew how much Ickes missed Jane, and perhaps it also was because he himself recently had lost his friend of many years, Col. Louis Howe. Shortly after the Fourth of July excursion, FDR paid his secretary a high compliment by inviting himself to dinner at Ickes's home on the outskirts of Washington. Roosevelt didn't like eating out and rarely did so, for the obvious reason that his paralysis made it awkward for him to get around. He almost never dined in restaurants, and food didn't particularly interest him, but occasionally FDR would enjoy an informal evening spent at a friend's house.

When Missy Le Hand telephoned Ickes on July 7 to tell him that the president would like to come the following night, Ickes called in extra help to prepare for an outdoor dinner party. When the president arrived around 6:45 on a balmy Wednesday evening, everything was ready for the party of eight. "The party was a great success," Ickes related.

> We started with honeydew melon, then had cold salmon with mayonnaise dressing, as well as cucumbers and tomatoes, bread and butter, then squab with peas and potatoes. Then followed a green salad with a choice of cream, Swiss, or Roquefort cheese. For dessert there was my own special ice cream, black raspberry, with cookies and coffee to finish with. . . . I served Chateau Yquem, a good claret, and a good vintage champagne.
>
> Tom Corcoran brought his accordion with him and he played and sang practically the whole evening. . . . The President seemed to enjoy himself

hugely and he entered into the fun very naturally and spontaneously. I kept them supplied with their favorite highballs. The President certainly carries his liquor well. He must have had five highballs after dinner . . . but he never showed the slightest effect. . . . He must have had a good time because he didn't leave until half past twelve and then only after Miss Le Hand prodded him two or three times and insisted that he must go home and to bed.

As FDR was leaving, Ickes said that he "started in again to tell me . . . that I must go away. He thinks I ought to take a boat and go to Europe for three weeks and he almost made me promise to do that." Although he longed for Jane, and admitted that he was feeling very much out of sorts, Harold did not take the president's advice and dash off to Europe and to Jane.[15]

Harold spent a good deal of the remainder of the summer campaigning for his boss. He was here and there, giving both live speeches and radio broadcasts, and feeling that he, together with a few other stalwarts, was actually keeping Roosevelt's campaign alive. In mid-July an exasperated Ickes wrote, "Day after day the newspapers headline the defection of some prominent Democrat to the Landon camp. Meanwhile, the President smiles and sails and fishes and the rest of us worry and fume." [16] The situation got worse before it got better. Toward the end of July Ickes was beside himself with worry over the latest polls:

With even our own private polls showing an alarming falling off in the President's vote, the whole situation is incomprehensible to me. . . . Mrs. Roosevelt is worried and so is Farley, but the President himself seems to be up in the clouds with his mind fixed on more spiritual things than that of his own reelection. I am in an unsettled state of mind. I do not mind taking a licking, because I have been through lots of those, but I do hate to take a licking lying down.[17]

The summer was fraught with anxiety. Harold worried about Jane being in Germany with the extremist Adolf Hitler in power, and he fretted over the possibility of a Landon victory in November. Ickes noted in his diary that he had to rely on "soporifics" practically every night to get to sleep. When Cissy Patterson called in late July to invite him to dinner at her mansion at 15 Dupont Circle, he quickly accepted. They saw a lot of one another over the next two months.

Eleanor "Cissy" Patterson was a wealthy, powerful and socially prominent woman whom Ickes had met in his first few months in

Washington. She was the editor of the Hearst-owned *Washington Herald,* and about as well-connected to the newspaper business as anyone could be. Her brother Joe Patterson ran the *New York Daily News,* and her cousin was none other than Robert McCormick, publisher of the *Chicago Tribune.* When she first invited Harold Ickes to one of her soirées in the spring of 1933, Cissy was an interesting-looking woman "of a certain age," as the French delicately put it. She was twice divorced and a grande dame of the Republican Party. She also was quite interested in the Interior secretary.

They saw each other socially over the next few years, but the relationship intensified after Anna's death and during the summer of 1936 as Cissy actively pursued Harold. A few days after their dinner together in Washington Cissy left for her 65-acre estate on Long Island. Harold joined her there on the weekend. At first he had decided against going, he said, and so he telephoned Cissy on Friday to tell her that he couldn't make it. "But she was so insistent that I said I would go. . . . It didn't seem fair to let her down. Moreover, I decided that it would do me good if I went." [18]

On Saturday evening, July 25, Cissy and Harold attended a dinner party at the home of her neighbors, the Herbert B. Swopes. The guest list of fourteen included many of the most famous names of the era. Harold found himself *à table* with Henry and Clare Booth Luce of *Time* magazine fame, Mr. and Mrs. William Randolph Hearst Jr. (the son and daughter-in-law of the legend), and "a young Vanderbilt," who, Ickes hoped, "is not as dumb as he looks and acts." The guests talked politics. Certainly one of the attractions Cissy held for Harold was the entree it afforded him to the Republican rich and famous. He learned a lot about the opposition to FDR and the New Deal that he otherwise wouldn't have known. At this party, he heard that "it isn't anything that Roosevelt has done or proposes to do to hurt business directly but simply the fear of increased taxes that has made such a bitter enemy out of practically everyone in the class with which I was associated over the weekend." This information in turn was relayed to the president and his political advisors.

Cissy showered Harold with attention at precisely the time when his true love, Jane, was in Europe. After another dinner party in mid-August—this one at her residence in Maryland called Dower House—they had a long conversation by the swimming pool. "She told me how foolish she thought I was to work so hard and allow things to worry me, and of course I had to admit the force of everything she said," he wrote.

That evening they also discussed the possibility of his resigning from the cabinet after the election. Cissy evidently found his association with FDR and the New Deal uncongenial, for she told him on several occasions that he should quit. Although Ickes easily dismissed that advice, he didn't so easily dismiss her concern about his well-being. After their tête-à-tête at Dower House he wrote:

> I was impressed again with Cissy's gentleness and friendly understanding. I have come to be very fond of her. I have found in her the best friend I have made in Washington. . . . She doesn't see why I stay on in the Cabinet considering the difficulties under which I have had to work during the last year or more. I have wondered myself why I do it.

WITH THE APPROACH of autumn Harold found himself occupied with his official responsibilities. The campaign finally went into high gear, and Ickes spent a lot of time beating the bushes for FDR. Jane returned to Washington in September and the couple took up where they left off. She continued to be tortured by indecision over whether or not to marry Harold, so he found himself riding an emotional rollercoaster through the winter of 1936–37. As a consequence he had little time or emotion left over for Cissy, and he gradually withdrew from that affair. Although initially Cissy put on a good show, Harold reaped the consequences of her unrequited love when she, as the new owner of the *Washington Times-Herald,* took every opportunity to publicly smear him and the New Deal. As late as 1942, the headline "Old Harold in a Lawsuit With His Son Over First Wife's Will" appeared in Cissy's paper, and it was typical of the attacks she leveled at him from about the time that he and Jane decided to marry.[19]

ON THE FIRST anniversary of Anna Ickes's death, August 31, 1936, her son, Wilmarth Thompson Ickes, shot himself with a service revolver at the family home in Winnetka. The caretaker found him "lying on the bed in the downstairs bedroom in a pool of blood . . . just before eight o'clock Monday morning."[20] He left behind a suicide note for his wife, Betty. Harold Ickes was in Washington when this latest tragedy occurred. He recorded his laconic reaction:

> Monday morning I reached the office a little before eight and had barely started on my work before H.L. Woolhiser, the village manager of Win-

netka, called me to tell me that Wilmarth had been found dead. Mike
Straus wanted to go to Chicago with me, so we took the twelve o'clock
plane out of Washington.[21]

Several factors contrived to bring Ickes's 37-year-old stepson to this
degree of desperation, where he saw death as the only way out. Because of his love of gambling, liquor, women, and nightlife, his marriage for years had been tenuous. Financial pressures, undoubtedly exacerbated by his expensive pastimes, mounted. Years of dissolute living
were taking their toll as well. Wilmarth recently had learned that he
had tuberculosis. Finally, the loss to his stepfather of his mother's entire
estate at a time when he needed the money produced a resentment
that grew, rather than diminished, with time.

Although Harold Ickes felt that he had done right by his children—
he set up Wilmarth in business in the 1920s by purchasing the General
Printing Company, and as late as 1936 found Robert a minor job in
Massachusetts working in the PWA—it was in their view too little and
too late. Rather than feeling grateful, Wilmarth had for years felt
cheated by his stepfather, whose least endearing trait was penurious-
ness. Throughout his life Ickes kept track of practically every nickel
and dime he spent or earned, including money given to the children.
An entry in his expense journals for November 18, 1919, for instance,
recorded a cash outlay to Wilmarth Ickes for 75 cents.[22] This occurred
at the same time as Wilmarth complained about his stepfather's handling of his mother's inheritance.

In his suicide note to his wife, Wilmarth referred to his strained
relationship with his stepfather. "Sure I know it's a dirty trick but I'll
be damned if I can take anymore from H.L.," he wrote.[23] It surely
wasn't the only, or even the primary, reason that Wilmarth killed himself, but that reference, coupled with the obvious symbolism of destroying himself in the family home on the first anniversary of his
mother's death, cannot be ignored. It indicated a profound anger with
his stepfather, if not also with his mother.

As Wilmarth contemplated killing himself in Winnetka, his wife,
Betty, vacationed on Mackinac Island with their children and her sister
Ann. But she, too, was worried over finances and Mike's (Wilmarth's
nickname) condition. She wrote her father-in-law a special delivery
letter in which she underscored the family's desperation of August
1936. She told Harold that their daughter Ann was sick, that Wilmarth

had TB, and that they were having severe money problems. "If we only can have it [their house] clear, so that we can rent or anything if Mike has to go away and so that we won't be so worried if he is well enough to stay home," Betty asked. She added that she thought "Mrs. Ickes" would have wanted them to have the house.

Harold said he wrote Betty back immediately, telling her that he would help them in any way he could, but that he didn't understand what she meant by "free and clear." He also mentioned that the reference to Anna "frankly . . . rubs me just a little the wrong way." Then after receiving his letter Betty sent him a telegram dated Sunday, August 30, telling him that she and Ann were leaving for Chicago that day: "Will be at Hubbard Woods with Wilmarth. Hope to see you. Letter follows. Love, Betty." Betty didn't return home in time to save Wilmarth.

When he arrived in Winnetka on August 31, Harold Ickes had much to do. He had to make funeral arrangements, help Betty and the children, and keep Wilmarth's violent death from becoming a full-blown scandal. If his suicide note were made public, Ickes realized, it "would make a front page sensation." So he called in political IOUs and asked the chief of police of Winnetka and the county coroner not to mention Wilmarth's last letter. The two men agreed. At the inquest, Ickes wrote,

> The Lieutenant . . . who had found the note, was put on. Walsh . . . asked him whether he had made a search for letters and notes. The Lieutenant, looking the Coroner straight in the eye, told him that he had searched carefully, but had found nothing. I think that Chief Peterson denied that anything had been found. They perjured themselves magnificently and I have always felt tremendously grateful to them. Nor has my conscience bothered me about this matter.[24]

After a simple and private ceremony, Wilmarth Thompson Ickes was interred next to his mother at Winnetka's Memorial Park Cemetery. Harold Ickes and Mike Straus then returned to Washington, where Ickes could bury whatever remorse he felt at Wilmarth's tragic end under mounds of work.

THE CAMPAIGN WAS now in full swing. After fretting nearly the entire summer over the president's inactivity, Ickes was pleased to see some movement. The two lunched together on September 8, just after

FDR returned from his western campaign trip and just before he left on another swing through the country. The president, Ickes observed, continued to be very friendly toward him and expressed his condolences over Wilmarth's death. "He was most kind and understanding," Ickes wrote. "He has a very real touch in his human relationships."[25]

During the luncheon the president told Ickes that he was approving over $7 million for PWA projects, an action he had postponed for several months because he was trying to keep down the budget deficit in the election year. Roosevelt was especially pleased with the PWA-financed housing projects for minorities, and the two men discussed their impact on the upcoming election:

> [FDR] spoke especially of a housing project for Negroes that we are building in Indianapolis. He said that this was fine. He remarked also that he had driven through several streets in the Negro section near the housing project and that his picture was in the window of every house. . . . He also told me that . . . he would like to go ahead with the housing projects in Bridgeport, Connecticut, and Lackawanna, Pennsylvania. He thought these projects would be of great advantage politically, and I said, "Hardboiled Harold understands."

In fact, as Ickes noted in his diary, he had been urging the president for months to move ahead with the low-income housing program. Now, in September, it was "rather late for the President to come to a realization of the political benefits that would flow from housing projects. This is quite aside from the social desirability of such projects." However, the old campaigner vowed, "I will not overlook any opportunity to start two or three more projects if we can do so."

But by the middle of September these last-minute attempts to influence the election were inconsequential: The president was being greeted by enormous and enthusiastic crowds everywhere he went, while the Landon-Knox campaign appeared dead. When Ickes read Landon's speech given before the Kansas Legionnaires in Wichita, he remarked that "it was as flat as ditch water." Even the pessimistically inclined Ickes had to admit that "I cannot now see how Landon can win unless there is a sudden and decided change in the situation."[26]

"For Roosevelt, October assumed the aspect more and more of one long victory parade," a historian wrote.[27] It was an extraordinary campaign, both for FDR and for the country. Such a spontaneous outpouring of emotion for a presidential candidate was rarely seen, and even the professional politicians were awestruck at the spectacle. On October 15, Ickes's man in Chicago, James Denvir, wrote him about the president's recent reception in the Windy City:

> President Roosevelt was here. "Veni Vidi Vici."
>
> The welcome parade, the meeting, the thronged thoroughfares combined to make this the greatest political spectacle of all times. In all my time I not only never witnessed its equal or any near approach to it. . . . There is one point in connection with this demonstration at the Stadium that I wish called to your attention. Ordinarily 25,000 people packed the hall. This 25,000 was augmented by . . . an additional 5,000, so you will know that they were packed in the Stadium like "sardines in a can." . . . One of the Stadium managers informed me that 5,000 were assembled in the Stadium as early as 2:30 in the afternoon. They brought their luncheon and remained through the hours awaiting the President's appearance.
>
> The point I want to make, Harold, is this; while the [Democratic] Organization performed brilliantly in its arrangement, advertising, and creation of enthusiasm, the audience was almost entirely composed of the common people and free from the job holders and political workers.[28]

Roosevelt's speech on October 31 at New York City's Madison Square Garden was final proof of the victory that loomed just over the horizon. "The Garden, packed to the rafters, erupted into 13 minutes of cheering and shrieking when Roosevelt appeared, with the band blaring 'Happy Days Are Here Again,' and cowbells, horns, and clackers adding to the uproar."[29] Time and again his speech was interrupted by roars of applause, and the audience was on its feet for practically the entire address. Despite the uproar, the buoyant president managed to convey to the frenzied crowd what the election was about. "In 1932," Roosevelt said, "the issue was the restoration of American democracy; and the American people were in a mood to win. They did win. In 1936 the issue is the preservation of their victory." The New Deal, he said, could not go ahead without a bitter struggle, for the "forces of selfishness" were seeking to regain their power. "They are unanimous in their hate for me—and I welcome their hatred," FDR said defiantly.

After the thundering applause died down, he spelled out what still needed to be done. The New Deal administration would continue to improve conditions for the workers and for the farmers of America, it would fight against monopoly and unfair financial practices, it would wipe out the slums and rehabilitate the cities, and it would continue to enlarge opportunities for all our young men and women. "For all these," Roosevelt declared, "we have only just begun to fight."

THE EMOTIONS THAT translated into Roosevelt's margin of victory over Hoover in the 1932 election were largely negative. The American people were fearful. They were angry at political and economic leaders who had allowed the Wall Street debacle to occur in 1929, and who then made matters worse by responding so ineffectually to the depression that followed. By 1936, however, the mood was transformed, and so was the American electorate. Instead of fear, an exhilarating optimism greeted Roosevelt wherever he went. Ordinary men and women went out of their way to hear the president speak or just to see him pass by in his car. No president for decades, certainly none since Theodore Roosevelt, had inspired this kind of enthusiasm from the people.

The photographs of FDR in the windows of Negroes' homes in Indianapolis told a large part of the election story. Breaking with tradition, blacks voted overwhelmingly for FDR in the 1936 election: The Gallup polls estimated that over 75 percent of blacks living in the North voted Democratic in that election.[30] The efforts of Eleanor Roosevelt and New Dealers such as Harold Ickes, Harry Hopkins, and Frances Perkins to end discrimination were handsomely rewarded.

Organized labor lined up solidly behind Roosevelt and the New Deal, too. Labor leader John L. Lewis broke with tradition and helped to forge the new Democratic majority. Lewis, a life-long Republican who had voted for Hoover in the 1932 election, led the CIO in pouring some $770,000 into the president's campaign coffers. He also helped organize "Labor's Non-Partisan League" to reelect FDR. The Supreme Court's decision striking down the Guffey Coal Act was the last straw for Lewis. Years later, Lewis told his biographer that his union, the United Mine Workers, paid "cash on the barrel for every piece of [New Deal] legislation that we have gotten."[31] Organized labor stuck with Roosevelt's Democratic Party for decades.

From the urban Northeast to the Pacific Coast support for Roosevelt was enormous. Voters in California, with its influx of poor migrants from the parched heartland, gave FDR the biggest majority of any state in the country; he won by nearly one million votes over Alf Landon.[32] The efforts of Sen. Hiram Johnson and other California leaders to attract federal monies for relief were instrumental in creating this landslide.

Harold Ickes was at home in Washington when the election results were broadcast on November 3, 1936. He was in bed suffering from an attack of lumbago and therefore content to listen to the radio to get the latest news. Although he sensed victory, he admitted that he wasn't prepared for the surprising results that crackled over the radio throughout the evening:

> It is all over now, but even in retrospect the result is astonishing. Landon carried only two states—Maine and Vermont, with eight electoral votes between them. . . . The President's popular majority is well over ten million. There has been nothing like it in the history of American politics.[33]

Anna and Harold Ickes at Hubbard Woods, 1930.
(Courtesy Raymond Ickes.)

Hubbard Woods, 1930 (*left to right*): Anna, Wilmarth ("Mike"), Frances, Harold, Raymond, and Robert Ickes. *(Courtesy Raymond Ickes.)*

The president and his cabinet, December 1933. *Clockwise from left of FDR:* William H. Woodin (Treasury), Homer S. Cummings (attorney general), Claude Swanson (Navy), Henry A. Wallace (Agriculture), Frances Perkins (Labor), Daniel C. Roper (Commerce), Harold L. Ickes (Interior), James A. Farley (postmaster general), George H. Dern (War), and Cordell Hull (State). *(Courtesy Raymond Ickes.)*

Inauguration day, March 4, 1933 *(left to right)*: Anna, Harold, Raymond, and Robert Ickes. *(Courtesy Raymond Ickes.)*

John Collier, Bureau of Indian
Affairs director, 1933–45.
(Courtesy Grace Collier.)

On a tour of CCC camps, President Roosevelt arrived in Harrisonburg, Va., on August 12, 1933. *Left to right:* FDR, Harold Ickes, Henry Wallace, and Robert Fechner, director of the CCC. *(Courtesy Elizabeth Ickes.)*

First Lady Eleanor Roosevelt (partially obscured) and Harold Ickes with Blackfeet Indians, August 1934, at Two Medicine Lake, Glacier National Park. *(Courtesy Glacier National Park.)*

President and Mrs. Roosevelt on Going-to-the-Sun Road, Glacier
National Park, August 1934. Sen. Burton Wheeler at left. *(Courtesy Glacier
National Park.)*

Temperamentally and physi-
cally these two Bull Moose
Progressives—Sen. Hiram
Johnson (*left*) and Harold
Ickes—resembled one another.
*(Courtesy Bancroft Library,
Berkeley, Calif.)*

" . . . and then [I] blew up another house." *Left to right:* Gov. Eugene
Talmadge of Georgia, Public Works Administrator Harold Ickes, and
Deputy Administrator Horatio Hackett, in Atlanta for the first PWA slum
clearance project, September 29, 1934. *(Library of Congress.)*

Harry Hopkins and Harold Ickes on a shopping spree in Panama, October 1935. *(Library of Congress.)*

Dedication ceremony of the Outer Link Bridge, Chicago, October 2, 1937, where Roosevelt made his famous "quarantine" speech. Ickes at podium. *(Library of Congress.)*

Secretary of the Interior Harold L. Ickes, March 1938. *(Harris & Ewing.)*

Harold Ickes on his first trip to
Alaska, at Mt. McKinley's
Muldrow Glacier, August 1938.
(Library of Congress.)

Panoramic view of the Marian Anderson concert at the Lincoln Memorial,
Easter Sunday, April 9, 1939. *(Library of Congress.)*

The famous FDR smile wins the audience. Ickes is seated behind him.
(Library of Congress.)

The caption to this June 1938 newspaper photograph read: "Secretary Ickes Returns with Bride, N.Y. Photographed aboard the *Ile de France* as the ship docked . . . is Secretary of the Interior Harold L. Ickes and his bride, the former Jane Dahlman of Milwaukee." *(Courtesy Elizabeth Ickes.)*

PART THREE

THE SECOND TERM

CHAPTER 12

"A FIRST CLASS FIGHT

ON HIS HANDS"

COURT ATTACKS AND

HEART ATTACKS

FRANKLIN ROOSEVELT'S second term began on a nearly perfect note. His astounding victory in November 1936 should have been accompanied by the celestial playing of Beethoven's "Ode to Joy," such was the sweetness of his personal and political triumph over the Republican opposition to the New Deal. But such a spirit proved to be short-lived for Roosevelt and his administration. That year, 1937, which one logically would have predicted to be his most successful year in office, turned out to be his worst. By the fall of 1937, "Roosevelt appeared to be a thoroughly repudiated leader."[1] Fault lines and stress fractures began appearing in the grand New Deal coalition.

Of all the critics of Roosevelt and the New Deal none was more important or effective than the Supreme Court of the United States. As early as 1935 the Court began invalidating much of the economic recovery program by declaring its key provisions unconstitutional. By the fall of 1935 a frustrated

President Roosevelt began thinking about possible solutions to the judiciary's conservatism. In mid-November, over a nondescript lunch at the White House, Ickes and the president discussed the Court and what could be done. Ickes revealed that the origins of FDR's controversial court reform legislation were British. In his diary he wrote:

> The President's mind went back to the difficulty in England where the House of Lords repeatedly refused to adopt legislation sent up from the House of Commons. He recalled that when Lloyd George came into power . . . under Edward VII, he went to the King and asked his consent to announce that if the Lords refused again to accept the bill for Irish autonomy . . . he would create several hundred new peers, enough to outvote the existing House of Lords. With this threat confronting them, the bill passed the Lords.[2]

Through the election year, Roosevelt kept his counsel on the question of the Supreme Court. He made monopoly capitalism, not the judiciary, the primary election issue. Ickes noted that the president privately hoped that the Court would make a "clean sweep of all New Deal legislation," however, for this would clearly force the constitutional issue in the new year, a year that FDR confidently felt would be his.

The president's second term began auspiciously enough. He retained nearly all of his key officials, including his secretary of the interior, who had tendered his resignation after the election in the event that the president wished to replace him. It was a courteous act on Ickes's part, and was appreciated by the president, who told Ickes in confidence that he wished a few other cabinet members had followed suit: He was having a difficult time telling Secretary of War Harry Woodring, who replaced George Dern when he died in 1936, and Commerce Secretary Dan Roper that he intended to replace them.[3]

Roosevelt valued continuity and friendship, the reasons that, in the end, he kept intact his cabinet from the first term. There was much unfinished business to attend to in 1937. Although clearly vindicated by the American electorate in November, the New Deal was under severe attack by the Supreme Court and other powerful elites in American society. Roosevelt needed the men and women who had helped fashion the economic and social recovery programs in this important first year of his second term for a counterattack. "We have only

just begun to fight!" he promised the American people at the end of
the presidential campaign, and he meant it.

The other reason for retaining the same political executives was that
FDR was personally fond of most of his top officials. Roosevelt's difficulty in firing anyone was a source of annoyance for less gentle souls
such as Harold Ickes. The Interior secretary related his irritation at this
aspect of his boss's character when, at the annual White House dinner
for the cabinet in January 1937, 76-year-old Secretary of the Navy
Claude Swanson "began to weaken in his legs and . . . fell into a dead
faint." Ickes observed with amazement that once Swanson was taken
away, the dinner went on as if nothing unusual had happened.

"I am not very much enamored of the idea that the impression
should go out to the country that the Cabinet is a group of senile, old
people," Ickes wrote. "Swanson's continued membership in the Cabinet, when everyone knows that he is neither physically nor mentally
qualified to serve, must create a bad impression." [4] FDR, however,
could not bring himself to relieve Swanson of his job, a position he
held until death claimed him in 1939, just before World War II erupted
in Europe.

On January 6, 1937, the president delivered his State of the Union
address to an overwhelmingly Democratic and pro – New Deal Congress. Roosevelt's coattails in the November election gave Democrats
impressive three-to-one margins in both chambers. The president put
on a virtuoso performance, one of his most ardent admirers, Harold
Ickes, said. "The President delivered his message as well as I have ever
heard him speak," Ickes wrote. "He had a great reception . . . and
there was more enthusiasm shown during the delivery . . . than I have
ever seen on any similar occasion. . . . I found myself yelling on one
occasion and that is something that I do not often do." [5]

The secretary of the interior found himself shouting approval because the president addressed the issue of the Supreme Court, which
Ickes had been urging FDR to do for at least a year. Roosevelt, supporting himself at the podium in the Senate chamber and looking relaxed and robust, began by reviewing the accomplishments of the last
four years. He lauded the spirit of cooperation between legislative and
executive branches that made recovery possible. "The broad objectives
of the National Recovery Act were sound," Roosevelt said. He added,
however, that "we now know that its difficulties arose from the fact

that it tried to do too much. . . . It was unwise to expect the same agency to regulate the length of working hours, minimum wages, child labor and collective bargaining on the one hand and the complicated questions of unfair trade practices and business controls on the other." He concluded, "The statute of NRA has been outlawed. The problems have not. They are still with us."

"There are those who, sincerely or insincerely, still cling to State action as a theoretical hope." But, Roosevelt told Congress, experience has shown that it will take "Federal laws supplementing State laws" to solve the problems of an industrialized and urbanized nation. Finally the president raised the issue of the judicial roadblock.

> During the past year there has been a growing belief that there is little fault to be found with the Constitution of the United States as it stands today. The vital need is not an alteration of our fundamental law, but an increasingly enlightened view with reference to it. Difficulties have grown out of its interpretation; but rightly considered, it can be used as an instrument of progress, and not as a device for prevention of action. . . . Means must be found to adapt our legal forms and our judicial interpretation to the actual present national needs of the largest progressive democracy in the modern world.[6]

A month after giving his State of the Union speech the president acted on the most critical issue of 1937. Harold Ickes noted in his diary entry for February 6 that "at last the rains have stopped. The floods are receding and here in Washington during the last two or three days we have had clear and cold weather for practically the first time this whole winter."[7] With the parting of the clouds came the lightning bolt from the White House: On February 5, FDR sent his bill calling for a reorganization of the federal judiciary to Congress. "The President's message was read at noon yesterday in both Houses," Ickes excitedly wrote, "and there has been little else in the newspapers since, thus proving its sensational nature."

The great battle of 1937 was on. For the next several months the fight between a liberal president and a conservative Court, with Congress serving as referee, captured headlines, held the attention of the populace, and consumed a lot of the time and energy of Washingtonians as they chose up sides. The pitched battle was fought on many fronts. Not surprisingly Harold Ickes again managed to place himself in the thick of things. Although he had plenty of other activities to keep himself occupied—in early 1937 the president named him chairman of a reconstituted National Power Policy Committee, and at the same time Ickes decided to make another attempt at realizing his dream for a Department of Conservation—the lifelong crusader nevertheless found time to jump into the Court-packing fray.

Ickes felt strongly about the Court issue. No novice when it came to legal-judicial issues, he disapproved of the Supreme Court's behavior on both constitutional and political grounds. The fight was, after all, about both the correct interpretation of the role of the Court in the legislative process, and the Court's refusal to sanction the newly emerging powers of the federal government under Franklin Roosevelt's leadership. Because some of his own powers had been declared off limits by the Court, and with other programs threatened in 1937, Ickes, like FDR, decided to counterattack. It was time, the secretary declared, not to pack the Court but to unpack it.[8]

Ickes was especially critical of 75-year-old Chief Justice Charles Evans Hughes who, Ickes wrote shortly after the fight began, "has not shown either the strength or the adroitness to control his court and make it an instrument for social and political progress."[9] Also reinforcing Ickes's negative attitude was the fact that in the 1920s Hughes had been employed as counsel to the American Petroleum Institute. In his capacity as a lobbyist for the oil industry Hughes vigorously attacked the conservation movement. He argued in 1926 that mineral extraction was not "commerce" and therefore that no conservation restraints could be imposed on the industry.[10] As Chief Justice, he continued on his reactionary course, according to Ickes, and helped to strike down in 1935 Petroleum Administrator Ickes's energy conservation program.

Ickes's efforts to line up outside support for the president's Court reform bill began immediately after the bill was introduced. He combed academia, and in February he discovered Leon Green, dean of Northwestern University's School of Law. The two men exchanged several letters on the subject on which they saw eye to eye. In a letter to Professor Green on March 8, Secretary Ickes wrote that "I showed to the President today your letter to me of March 3 and he wondered whether it might be possible for you to get *Liberty* or *Colliers* to publish an article by you on the constitutional issue. This would be a fine thing to do and very effective."[11]

The attempt to line up academic support for the controversial plan moved ahead with difficulty. By the middle of March Ickes wrote that a number of excellent witnesses had appeared before the Senate Judiciary Committee. "It is surprising how many law school deans have come to the front. [Senators] Connally and Burke and King have tried their best to break down these witnesses and their inability to do so testifies to the effectiveness of the witnesses." [12]

Overall, however, only a handful of academics publicly supported the president's Court-packing plan. It proved to be about as popular with this group as with congressmen, who defected from the liberal New Deal coalition in substantial numbers. Barely a week after the bill was introduced a number of prominent senators, many with long-standing Progressive credentials, pulled away from the president. Ickes wrote about his "distinct disappointment" at seeing Burton Wheeler of Montana and Hiram Johnson go on the attack. He felt especially upset by his old ally's defection:

> Hiram Johnson got back from quite a long stay in Florida on Monday morning and he hardly alighted from the train before he gave out an interview condemning the President's plan. . . .
> I am very sorry that he should have done this and I can't understand it. Surely a man who stood, as Johnson did in 1912, for Theodore Roosevelt's plan to recall judicial decisions, which would permit the people on a referendum vote to override a decision of the Supreme Court on a constitutional issue, ought not to balk at the comparatively mild reforms suggested by the President. [13]

Ickes suggested to himself a number of reasons for Johnson's perplexing position: Poor health, old age, the opportunity to retire from public life "in a blaze of glory," and, perhaps beneath it all, "a real respect for the courts as such." William Warne, one of Ickes's public information officers in the 1930s, suggested another reason. He spoke with his fellow Californian around this time, and Senator Johnson told him, "You know, Mr. Warne, I've always been a president-hater. It's hard for me not to be. . . . I don't know how long I can remain friendly to this man down in the White House!" Soon after their conversation, William Warne noted that Johnson and Roosevelt indeed parted company over the Court-packing issue. [14]

That FDR's unprecedented electoral victory in the 1936 election actually worked against him in 1937 is seen in the attitudes of a number of seasoned congressmen on the Court issue. Many on the Hill resented or even feared Roosevelt's growing power, Sen. Burton Wheeler among them. When FDR's political liaison Tom Corcoran came to him in 1937 to discuss the Court bill, Wheeler burst forth with invective: "Now I've been watching Roosevelt for a long time," he angrily told Corcoran. "Once he was only one of us who made him. Now he means to make himself the boss of us all. . . . Well, he's made the mistake we've been waiting for for a long time—and this is our chance to cut him down to size." [15] Wheeler even intimated to Corcoran that he suspected Roosevelt of having had a hand in Huey Long's assassination in 1935. No evidence has ever been uncovered to support that view, but Wheeler was one of a handful of senators who genuinely liked the Kingfish, who was shocked and disturbed by his death, and who tried to find a rational explanation for Dr. Carl Weiss's act, an act that puzzles some to this day.

Wheeler, who had done much to enact important elements of the New Deal during FDR's first term, became in 1937 the acknowledged leader of the congressional opposition to the Court-packing bill. As with Hiram Johnson, there were a number of reasons for Wheeler's opposition. But for Burton Wheeler, an important one was, according to their daughter, his wife.

"Lulu White Wheeler was the force behind the Senator throughout his twenty-four-year-career in Washington," Elizabeth Wheeler Coleman wrote in her memoirs. Mrs. Wheeler plainly did not like Franklin Roosevelt. She never forgave him for one of his first acts in office, that of repealing Prohibition, and from 1933 onwards she viewed him as lacking integrity. "She thought him an opportunist of the worst kind," her daughter recalled.[16]

When Roosevelt sent Tom Corcoran to make Senator Wheeler an offer—in exchange for his support of the Court-packing bill, FDR promised that the senator could name one or two of the new justices—Mrs. Wheeler "was outraged. In private discussions with her husband, she made it clear she would not permit the Senator to play Roosevelt's game of backroom politics."

After Wheeler told the president of his opposition to the Court-packing proposal, the president, Mrs. Coleman wrote, "was furious, all the more so when he . . . found out who had helped Wheeler make up his mind." Not long afterwards, the president referred to Mrs. Wheeler as "Lady MacBeth" as he chatted with a group of reporters. It was an off-the-record remark but naturally was relayed immediately to Lulu Wheeler. "Coming from the President, I consider it the highest compliment," Mrs. Wheeler retorted. She continued to counsel wariness to her husband for the next eight years while both Roosevelt and Wheeler remained in office.

Influential people outside Washington, such as the wealthy San Francisco businessman Rudolph Spreckels, found it "very strange that so many members of Congress are making war upon President Roosevelt's Court proposal." Spreckels wrote Ickes that he found Senator Wheeler's opposition especially perplexing because it was at odds with what Wheeler himself had just said in a radio address: The senator claimed that it was "undeniable" that the Court had usurped the legislative power of the Congress. Spreckels, a Progressive Republican like Ickes, could only conclude that such behavior on the part of liberals in Congress sprang from "the malign influence of predatory interests."[17] The sugar magnate probably didn't have Mrs. Wheeler in mind.

The immediate reaction to the Court-reform legislation was more negative than positive. By the middle of February Roosevelt knew, as Ickes put it, that he had "a first-class fight on his hands." Practically all of the newspapers were against him, even those of the Scripps-Howard chain, which had supported him in the election. Worse yet, Ickes observed, several liberals both inside and outside Congress were "lining up with the reactionaries."[18]

It became apparent that if the president was going to win on this issue, he would need the active and vocal support of the American people demanding that Congress pass the legislation. In addition to using his weekly press conferences to inform the public about this highly charged issue, the president delivered on March 9 one of his most dramatic and finely crafted Fireside chats. "This plan of mine is no attack on the Court," Roosevelt told his audience. "It seeks to restore the Court to its rightful and historic place in our system of constitutional government and to have it resume its high task of building anew on the Constitution 'a system of living law.' The Court itself can best undo what the Court has done." The president concluded with a promise: "You who know me will accept my solemn assurance that in a world in which democracy is under attack, I seek to make American democracy succeed. You and I will do our part."[19]

Roosevelt also sent several of his aides, including Ickes, out to the country's grassroots to beat the bushes for the Court-reform plan. For some time the secretary had been scheduled to visit Texas, thus making him the first sitting secretary of the interior ever to set foot in the Lone Star State.[20] The trip had two official purposes: Ickes was scheduled to address the annual meeting of the Associated General Contractors of America in San Antonio, and, at the urging of Congressman James Paul "Buck" Buchanan, he was to dedicate the newly constructed Marshall Ford Dam on the outskirts of Austin, the state's capital. Since the Court dispute was raging so ferociously, Roosevelt and Ickes decided to use the Texas trip to address that issue as well.

On Monday, February 15, Ickes spent an hour with the president at the White House before he left Washington aboard the *Pennsylvania*. Ickes wrote that Roosevelt "outlined several things which he would like to have me say when I speak before the joint session of the Texas Legislature on Friday. He insisted that he would win his fight and I told him that he simply had to." Ickes also told him that "unless he won he might as well resign, because he could not hope to realize the objectives he has in mind or to accomplish what the people elected him to accomplish by such an overwhelming majority last November."[21]

Ickes's train pulled into San Antonio on Wednesday. He arrived, appropriately enough for his whirlwind trip through Texas, during a severe dust storm. "From the time I struck San Antonio, and in fact all the way to that city . . . ," Ickes wrote, "the air was thick and beclouded with dust that was blowing in from Oklahoma. . . . It is interesting that during the last few years these tremendous dust storms have made the country aware of our valuable topsoil by wind erosion, whereas they were not heard of . . . until quite recently."

His first speech was delivered that evening at San Antonio's St. Anthony Hotel to the contractors' trade association. Wearing his PWA hardhat, Ickes began by congratulating them on their record of keeping graft to a bare minimum in the public works construction program. The speech was very well received, Ickes said, adding that "I suspect that every contractor there retained a . . . vivid recollection of the speech that I had made on a similar occasion in Washington in 1933, when . . . I had told them that many contractors were crooks and chiselers and that we were not going to permit them to get away with that sort of thing in carrying out the PWA program."[22]

Ickes also managed to work in a reference to the Supreme Court fight in his speech. He defended the emergency works program as being in the national interest, but pointed out that the courts still could not decide whether key components of the public works program were constitutional. In 1937 the test case on the provision of public power, *Duke Power Company v. Greenwood County*, was making its way through the federal court system. That decision would determine the outcome of over ninety other such suits brought against the government's program of providing low-cost electricity to Depression-ridden municipalities.[23]

The following day the secretary was up at dawn for his scheduled appearances at the construction sites of three dams on the Lower Colorado River. Accompanied by Gov. James Allred and Austin's Congressman Buck Buchanan, Ickes bounced over central Texas's dusty, rough roads as they headed for the dams. In one sense, the visit was timely: The dedication of Marshall Ford Dam on February 18 came just four days before Congressman Buchanan suffered a massive coronary and died. At least the politician had the satisfaction of witnessing the culmination of many years of work aimed at rejuvenating the economy of his native Texas hill country.

On the occasion of Secretary Ickes's historic trip to Texas to dedicate dams, an editorial in the *Austin Statesman* predicted that the secretary "will touch off a dynamite blast . . . whose reverberations in the cedar hills will echo fulfillment of a half-century dream of Texas."[24] Perhaps. But what produced more immediate reverberations was Ickes's speech before the Texas legislature in Austin on the evening of the eighteenth. Although he was "dead tired" after the long day he had spent on the road, Ickes nevertheless geared up for his 8 o'clock speech before a joint session of the legislature. As he put it, he "waded right into the constitutional issue [of the Court] with both feet."

> I could hear a gasp go up as I disclosed my purpose to discuss the issue. . . .
> In my first sentence I asked where had the Supreme Court gotten its supposed power to pass upon the constitutionality of acts of Congress. I read the Tenth Amendment and then I said that this power had been usurped. I then went on to discuss the supposed checks and balances in our tripartite Federal system, pointing out that while there were ample checks and balances with respect to the legislative and executive branches, there wasn't a single check on the judiciary except that of impeachment, which was slow and cumbersome and of doubtful efficacy when it came to a court of nine men. I remarked in passing that one could not be impeached for being too old, that that was not a crime but merely a misfortune.[25]

To his surprise, Ickes observed that his speech was "exceedingly well received. The audience got the points quickly and there was a good deal of applause." After his speech, "several young members of the lower House were among those who expressed themselves as being in accord with what I had said." Ickes particularly enjoyed the mentoring role he played for the younger generation.

After discussing the judicial issue at two forums in Texas, the secretary returned to Washington via a circuitous route that took him to St. Louis, Missouri, to dedicate a hospital for blacks built with PWA funds, and then through New York City to make a speech on the government's low-income housing program. But the Court fight left him little respite. In early March Sen. Millard Tydings of Maryland made a demagogic speech about "foreign dictators" that the administration deeply resented. Jim Farley suggested that Ickes go to Raleigh, North Carolina, where Tydings just had spoken, to make the rebuttal. Reluctantly he acquiesced, "although," he noted, "it throws a pretty heavy extra burden on me."[26]

Roosevelt's judicial reform bill was nowhere more bitterly contested than in the South. Southern leaders such as Byrd, George, Smith, and Glass attacked the legislation as being "the first step toward the destruction of white supremacy." A more liberal Supreme Court, they feared, would reverse decisions such as *Plessy v. Ferguson* which, Virginia's Carter Glass boasted, had "saved the civilization of the South."[27] These Southerners could discover no hyperbole too extreme to describe what President Roosevelt, listening to "political janizaries" such as Harold Ickes, was attempting to do to the South. Passage of the bill would mean another tragic Era of Reconstruction. It amounted to Sherman's Second March, with "Nigger-loving" New Dealers carpetbagging their way through Southern culture and cutting a wide swathe of social destruction. Harold Ickes cogently summed up their views when he wrote, "Some southern leaders affect to believe that an enlarged and more liberal court would lift from the southern Negro some of the weight of oppression that he has carried since the Civil War."[28]

When Senator Tydings spoke about Mussolini and Hitler, the European dictators who were undermining democratic institutions, the inferences were clear. The president sent his most strident civil libertarian, Harold Ickes, to North Carolina to respond to the suggestion that Roosevelt was seeking to become a dictator. Shortly before leaving Washington for Raleigh, FDR told Ickes that he hoped he would take Tydings's hide off and rub salt in it. Harold did. In a speech titled "Tidings of Victory," Ickes said he went after the "gentleman from Maryland" with "hammer and tongs." The half-hour speech was given at Raleigh's Municipal Auditorium on March 12 and was also broadcast throughout the South and as far north as Washington.

It was sweet revenge for the Interior secretary, who vividly remembered Tydings's efforts to smear him and his officers in the 1935 Virgin Islands investigation. Ickes claimed that the "crowd loved it. I have never made a speech that was so enthusiastically received. . . . The applause was . . . prolonged and frequent . . . and afterward many people crowded up to congratulate me."

Despite the grand reception in Raleigh, the Washington newspapers ignored the speech. Ickes concluded, "This means . . . that the opposition newspapers are not going to give a fair break to the supporters of the Court reform plan." He was disgusted, but not surprised, by their obvious bias.[29]

Traversing the eastern half of the nation to speak out on the Court battle, along with everything else he was doing, took its toll. A person half of Ickes's age would have been exhausted. On March 15, 1937, his birthday, he found himself in bed, prostrate with exhaustion. The speech in Raleigh, he said, left him "hanging over the ropes." Reluctantly, Ickes canceled his scheduled trip to Boston to make yet another speech on the Court controversy:

> I . . . hate like the devil to break an engagement not only because I am scrupulous about that sort of thing but because I do not want word to get out that I have had any kind of a break. But the fact is that my tail is dragging the ground and I haven't any steam left. I have no energy or ambition, or even much care about anything.
>
> I am sixty-three years old today.[30]

ROOSEVELT WAS solicitous. Once the secretary was back on his feet, after having spent two full weeks in bed, the president "ordered" him to take a vacation in the Florida Keys and the Everglades, and also to cut back on his speechmaking. This time Ickes accepted the order, and while in southern Florida he renewed his interest in the Everglades. "When Audubon . . . came into this country years ago apparently there were then a thousand birds for one that survives today. It is particularly appalling to me how people can kill these beautiful birds and more astonishing still that the state and the nation haven't found some effective way of protecting them." [31]

Through the remainder of the spring Ickes gave himself over to his official responsibilities: Running the Interior Department, managing the Public Works Administration, and chairing the National Power Policy Committee. He directed some of his energies to blocking what his director of the Grazing Service, Farrington Carpenter, was trying to do. When Carpenter was appointed head of the new division in 1934, Ickes described him as a "typical cow man." The manner in which Carpenter proceeded to run the Grazing Service validated that view. In 1937 Ickes realized that the director was in bed with the grazing interests: He was trying to amend the Taylor Grazing Act so as to give the local advisory committees, which were dominated by ranchers, legal status. "This movement I am opposed to," Ickes wrote. The committees will become a "Frankenstein that I will not be able to manage." In March he convened a conference of his top officials, and with Carpenter present, "raised particular hell." Ickes scolded him for going around both himself and Solicitor Margold on the advisory committee issue, and wondered whether the time had not come to "take the bull by the horns and abolish all of them." [32] Privately, he said he wanted to get rid of Carpenter, too, but when he moved to do that, the secretary discovered the power of the Western ranchers' lobby. Ickes was unable to take either action in 1937.

The secretary also found time early that year to pound the table and engage in a shouting match with Agriculture Secretary Henry Wallace over the possible transfer of the U.S. Forest Service to Ickes's department. Ickes came back to this issue time and again, and found he could never completely abandon it.

After two years of fruitless efforts to gain control of the agency, Ickes recognized by 1937 that the president's support was absolutely necessary to tip the balance in his favor. Roosevelt, however, continued to steer a neutral course between Ickes and Wallace, which only served to infuriate Ickes and sometimes frustrate Roosevelt. One of those occasions occurred when Prof. Charles Merriam stopped in to visit Roosevelt. Entering FDR's office, he saw the president slouched forward on his desk holding his head in his hands. "Professor," Roosevelt said, "did you notice who just left the office?" Merriam replied that, yes, he had just said hello to his good friend Harold Ickes in the anteroom. "Did you see the other fellow who was in here?" FDR asked. "No,"

Merriam replied. "Wallace," Roosevelt responded. "He and Ickes were in here for an hour arguing as to who should have a couple of sticks of timber along the Cumberland River. And do you know— neither of them controls a single vote!" [33]

Harold Ickes's obsession about control of the Forest Service notwithstanding, through the spring and into the summer of 1937 the Court issue continued to be the focus of national attention. Grassroots organizations sprouted up on both sides of the issue. In March some Roosevelt supporters set up the Chicago Committee for the President's Court Proposal. William F. Clarke, Charles P. Schwartz, and James L. Houghteling comprised the Executive Committee. At the same time opponents set up the Chicago Citizens Court Defense Committee, while newspaper magnate Frank E. Gannett chaired the National Committee to Uphold Constitutional Government.[34]

Harold Ickes corresponded with many people with views similar to his own on the subject, including businessman Rudolph Spreckels and attorney Bruce Johnstone, both of San Francisco, as well as attorney Marshall Solberg of Chicago. To Ickes's pleasure, his old Progressive Republican friend, Raymond Robins, began writing him about the issue. Robins and Ickes were both active in the municipal reform movement in Chicago in the early 1900s, together with Jane Addams, John Harlan, Anna Thompson, and others. For many years Ickes counted Raymond and Margaret Robins among his most intimate friends; he named his first-born son after him. Then, however, the Robinses "strayed after the false gods of Harding, Coolidge, and Hoover," Ickes wrote with dismay.[35] The two couples went their separate ways for some fifteen years, until Raymond broke the long silence and wrote Harold in 1937.

After retiring to Chinsegut Hill, their farm in Florida, Robins spent most of his time tending his garden. Tragically, one day he fell out of a tree he was pruning and broke his back. From 1935 until his death in the 1950s Raymond was bedridden. But his mind was unaffected and he remained vitally interested in politics, so he and Ickes carried on a voluminous, oftentimes touching, correspondence for some fifteen years. In his initial letter Raymond told Harold that he was not only "one hundred percent" in favor of the Court-reform plan, but he accurately predicted that "the third person in the Great American Triumvirate is now determined. History will record 'Washington-

Lincoln-Roosevelt' as the master statesmen and political leaders in the Saga of America."³⁶ Raymond Robins would have been pleased to learn that by the 1980s historians considered Franklin Roosevelt to be the second greatest president the United States has had, trailing only Abraham Lincoln.

By mid-March it looked like a standoff between the president and the Supreme Court. Then, on March 29 the Supreme Court handed down three decisions of vital importance to the New Deal program. One concerned the power of the states to pass a minimum wage law for women. The Court upheld that power, despite the fact that nine months earlier it had struck down such legislation. On the same day the Court handed down a second decision sustaining the new Railway Labor Act. Third, it upheld a slightly revised Frazier-Lemke Farm Bankruptcy Act.

In April, the Court, by a five-to-four margin, sustained the constitutionality of the National Labor Relations Act. In the middle of May 78-year-old Justice Willis Van Devanter announced his retirement, to become effective at the end of the Court's session in June. Finally, at the end of the session, the Court announced its verdict on the centerpiece of the New Deal: The "nine old men" validated the historic Social Security Act. "It would be a little naive to refuse to recognize some connection between these 1937 decisions and the Supreme Court fight," Roosevelt coolly observed a few years later.³⁷ He also wrote that he, at least, was convinced that the about-face would never have come about without "this frontal attack . . . upon the philosophy of the majority of the Court."

These events obviously changed the complexion of the battle. While the president continued to press Congress to pass the judicial reform bill, it was becoming a moot point. The bench was changing its views without it. Moreover, President Roosevelt was losing some of the key people leading the charge, including Harold Ickes and Arkansan Joe Robinson, the Senate's majority leader.

On May 27, Ickes rose early, as he always did, but he said that he was feeling awful. Because he had an appointment with the president that morning he went to the office. By two o'clock, however, Ickes was in the hands of two physicians who told him he had just suffered a mild coronary thrombosis. They immediately sent him home and on May 31 he checked into the Bethesda Naval Hospital, remaining there until July 2. Although he tried to do as much work as he could, there was little that the ailing Ickes could do about the Court battle from bed.

On July 13, Senator Robinson was found dead on the floor of the bathroom of his apartment, the victim of a fatal coronary. In his hand he clutched a copy of the previous day's Congressional Record.[38] Heart attacks thus claimed two of FDR's supporters in 1937—first Buchanan and then Robinson—and sidelined a third, Ickes. But with the majority leader's passing any hope of getting the Court bill through Congress became merely fantasy. When the final vote came at the end of July, defeat of the bill came as no surprise.

THAT THE PRESIDENT suffered a major defeat by Congress on this issue is incontestable. While Roosevelt was not at all pleased by the defection of liberal support—it figured into his attempted purge of the Democratic Party in 1938—he nevertheless took it in stride and emphasized the positive aspects of the conflict. FDR's own assessment of the great struggle of 1937 was that he lost the battle but won the war. "The Court changed. The Court began to interpret the Constitution instead of torturing it," he wrote.[39]

There was also a pleasing symmetry between his thinking back in the fall of 1935 and the outcome two years later. In discussing with Ickes the political dilemma England's Prime Minister Lloyd George faced with a stubbornly conservative House of Lords over the Irish issue, Roosevelt discovered what the prime minister had learned: The threat was sufficient.

CHAPTER 13

"FACING THE COMMON ENEMY"

CIRCLING THE WAGONS

ON THE LAST DAY of 1936 Tom Corcoran stopped off at the Interior Department to chat with Harold Ickes who, despite it being New Year's Eve, was working. The two men had developed a close friendship over the last few years, and the frequent visits from Tommy "the Cork" were pleasing to the secretary because Tom was, by this time, an insider *par excellence* in FDR's White House. He could be counted on to bring some interesting gossip along with his Irish sense of humor.

Ickes also liked the young man because he was, like his close friend, Ben Cohen, a "true liberal." For their part, the young liberals in Washington sought out Harold Ickes because of his liberal credentials. The older and powerful Interior secretary prided himself on being able to further the careers of a number of progressives of the younger generation, including Cohen and Corcoran. A freshman congressman by the name of Lyndon Johnson, who came to Washington in 1937, also benefited substantially from his friendship with the Interior secretary. He not only received money for projects in his district, but through Ickes he met the brilliant and ambitious protégé of William O. Douglas, Abe Fortas. LBJ and Fortas soon developed an intimate and mutually supportive friendship that endured for the rest of their lives.

On this cold winter's afternoon, Corcoran and Ickes discussed the upcoming Court fight, whether Ben Cohen would go to the Justice Department as assistant attorney general, and the recent thaw in relations between Harry Hopkins and Ickes. Since the election, Ickes noticed that Harry had become very friendly toward him which, given their well-publicized rivalry over control of work relief funds, made the secretary more than a little curious as to the motive. Tom Corcoran was able to provide an explanation. Harry, Tom said, was "made to realize that the Progressives in the Administration should not fight each other; that they should stand in a circle with tails touching and horns facing the common enemy." [1]

It was appropriate imagery for 1937, a year in which there seemed to be no end to the fights in which the administration, and Ickes, became embroiled. Through 1937, however, one-time adversaries Ickes and Hopkins decided to work together. There developed a genuine friendship between them, strengthened probably by the fact that both men wrestled that year with illness and death: Harold Ickes's heart attack in May was followed in October by the death of Barbara Hopkins, Harry's wife, from breast cancer. Not long after her funeral Harry was hospitalized and had a large part of his cancerous stomach removed. The cancer never recurred, but, biographer Robert Sherwood observed, "the operation [in 1937] produced nutritional maladjustments which made him prey to various weird diseases afflicting him over and over again, and which ultimately proved fatal." [2]

Virtually any way one turned in 1937, a battle was looming or being waged. Of course the most celebrated was Roosevelt's Supreme Court fight, but it in fact was the tip of the iceberg. There also was the fight in Congress over passage of the president's seemingly innocuous reorganization bill. Conflict also raged over the government's authority to provide public power from the network of hydroelectric dams built under the emergency works program. A number of suits were being heard in federal courts challenging that policy. There developed, too, a serious split in the ranks of the administration over how to respond to the fearful economic recession that developed in the fall of 1937, while a deepening rift over policy and politics separated the president and his vice-president, John Nance Garner. By May it was agreed that Garner was "off the reservation."[3] What if anything to do about him produced further dissension within the cabinet.

Finally, in 1937, ominous storm clouds gathered on two horizons, across the Atlantic and the Pacific. The "three bandit nations," as FDR referred to Germany, Italy, and Japan, were hell-bent on pursuing a fateful belligerence vis-à-vis their neighbors.[4] Whereas during the first term the president and his advisors paid very little attention to foreign affairs, in the difficult second term international conflict increasingly consumed them.[5] Even the Interior secretary felt the pull of foreign affairs in 1937 and indeed through his entire second term in office.

In January President Roosevelt sent to Congress not only his bill to reorganize the federal judiciary but a bill that would give the president considerable authority to reorganize the executive branch of government. One effect of the New Deal's swift response to the Great Depression was that the administrative branch had grown haphazardly over the first term. It was a public administrator's nightmare. Although not a man to worry needlessly over the neatness of organization charts, Roosevelt nevertheless wanted to straighten things out, and so he appointed three political scientists—Louis Brownlow, Luther Gulick, and Charles Merriam—to study the matter. Their work came to be known as the "Brownlow Report." A number of their recommendations, including the establishment of a new Department of Public Welfare, and a reorganized Department of the Interior to be called the Department of Conservation, were contained in the president's January message to Congress on the subject of reorganization.

Reorganization of the executive branch hardly seemed like the stuff of which battle royals are made. But the battle over the Supreme Court had a deleterious effect on FDR's reorganization proposal. Despite its overwhelmingly Democratic composition, Congress was in no mood to blindly follow the president where he was trying to lead. It didn't legislate on this issue until a full two years later, and only after a lot of spleen had been vented over which federal agencies would be transferred where.

But at the beginning of 1937 a stalemate in Congress was about the last thing New Dealers expected to encounter, and so Harold Ickes was excited over the reorganization proposal. The introduction of the bill gave him the opportunity to make a fresh attempt at rounding up the various conservation activities of the federal government and housing them all under one roof—his. Ickes's two main targets for a reconstituted Interior Department were the U.S. Forest Service and the Army Corps of Engineers. But Ickes's colleagues in the cabinet, Agriculture's Henry Wallace and Secretary of War Harry Woodring, didn't see things in quite the same perspective. This battle thus became one of the two most divisive for Ickes during an unusually divisive year.

On January 8 Henry Wallace came to Ickes's office to discuss holding a Governors' Conference on Conservation later that month. FDR thought well of the idea, and so he instructed Ickes to talk it over with Wallace. Frederic Delano, the president's conservationist uncle, was also in attendance, as were the city planner Charles Eliot and Ickes's assistant, Harry Slattery. The proposal had originated with Slattery.

Henry Wallace didn't like the idea. "He insisted that conservation had passed the propaganda stage," Ickes related, "and that if there was to be a conference on anything, it ought to be on the constitutional situation or the international situation. None of the rest of us agreed with him, but he was as stubborn as a mule." When Ickes "good-naturedly" twitted him for being a "standpatter," Henry, Ickes wrote, "turned on me savagely."[6]

At this point the meeting degenerated into a shouting match between the two principals, with Delano, Eliot, and Slattery looking on with acute embarrassment. Wallace on two or three occasions accused Ickes of being disloyal to the president, and Ickes pounded his desk for added effect while castigating Wallace for convincing Roosevelt to take the Soil Conservation Service away from him while he was in Florida. "Not an hour of grace was given me," Ickes fumed.

After the shouting went on for several minutes, Wallace introduced the real issue dividing the two Progressive Republicans in the cabinet, the possible transfer of Forestry to Interior under the reorganization bill. "Henry said that if the President proposed to transfer Forestry to me he would, of course, make vigorous protests." Ickes replied that that would be his privilege. He argued that "Agriculture was already so big and cumbersome that if all conservation activities were sent there, it would only be a question of time until the department would be split into two and out of it would come a Department of Conservation. It seemed to me to be a waste of time and effort to wait for that event rather than to set up a Department of Conservation now."

Once both men got past grievances off their chests, the fireworks died down. As he was leaving, Wallace extended his hand and Ickes shook it cordially. Nevertheless, both men were embarrassed by some of the verbal abuse they had hurled back and forth, so later that day Ickes wrote Wallace a short note. It read:

January 8, 1937
My dear Henry:

I regret the unfortunate incident of this afternoon. After all, as members of the Cabinet, our first consideration must be for the President. Our personal differences must not be allowed to count as against the loyalty to our Chief. I have regarded you as a friend, even when we have differed on policies and principles, and I shall continue to do so regardless of whether the President shall add, subtract, or divide as between our two Departments.

Sincerely yours,
Harold L. Ickes

The next day Ickes received a memo from Wallace:

Dear Harold:

I am glad to have your note. . . . Our frank speaking seems to me to have been fortunate, not unfortunate.

It was and is my hope that we can perfect a co-operative formula for the general welfare between our Departments. After the President has obtained the powers which we both hope he will get, I trust the problem will be carefully examined from every point of view and that the solution found will serve the public interest in the long run.

With good wishes,
Sincerely yours,
H. A. Wallace[7]

While the exchange of letters between Ickes and Wallace helped to smooth some ruffled feathers for the moment, both men recognized that battle lines were drawn. The fight over the Forest Service would continue at least until Roosevelt made up his mind over where the Forest Service should be housed.

EARLY IN 1937 Ickes believed, for good reason, that his goal of establishing an expanded conservation department might soon be realized. Not only had the president included the notion in his executive reorganization bill, thus strongly suggesting to him that he finally was supporting the transfer of Forestry, but a related issue, that of water resources development, was in a considerable state of flux. Ickes, as the chairman of the National Power Policy Committee, was strategically situated to launch an assault on one of the most powerful agencies of the federal government, the U.S. Army Corps of Engineers. His ultimate goal here, as with the Forest Service, was to incorporate it into his new department. Since the Bureau of Reclamation was in Interior, it seemed only logical to him that the Corps should be there also.

The government's water development activities were being reconsidered in 1937 for two reasons. Mother Nature was one. Severe flooding during the winter of 1936–37 prompted, as it always has, demands for increased flood control activity by the federal government. The flooding, moreover, dovetailed with the second reason, the Roosevelt administration's unprecedented commitment to water resources development during the first term. It was a program embarked upon during the economic emergency, and it, like some other New Deal measures designed to rout the Depression, was hardly well thought out at the time. The president, in his second term, wanted to bring some order out of the chaos of the piecemeal pork-barrel approach. He hoped to impose greater executive-level control over the agency that was once described as the construction and engineering arm of the U.S. Congress.[8]

Late in January Tom Corcoran spoke to Harold Ickes about the possibilities inherent in the situation. Ickes noted,

> Corcoran developed the idea that out of this flood situation there might come a great opportunity for the new Department of Conservation. He thinks that all of the great watersheds in the country should be considered from a broad conservation point of view and he thinks that this is a good time to sound such a note.[9]

Of course Tom Corcoran was only relaying to his friend the president's own thinking on the subject. On the following day, January 26, Ickes and the Power Policy Committee met with FDR to discuss the plan that he and the acknowledged water expert in Congress, Nebraska's Sen. George Norris, had been working on to reformulate the government's water-related activities. It was a grand, long-range, functionally integrated plan. As outlined by Roosevelt at the meeting,

> The country would be divided roughly into eight great districts. Some agency would be set up for each district along the lines of TVA. These districts would be—first, the Atlantic Coast; second, an enlarged TVA; third, the Ohio River watershed; fourth, the Mississippi watershed; fifth,

the Missouri watershed; sixth, the northwestern area; seventh, the area running from Colorado down through Texas to the Gulf of Mexico; and eighth, the Pacific coast.

"It is the President's idea to have all of these areas do whatever sound conservation policies demanded," Ickes related, "and all of them are to head up through the new Department of Conservation."

With plans like these being discussed by FDR and by powerful members of Congress, Harold Ickes's ambition of heading up a strong and enlarged department of conservation was understandable. No wonder that he expended so much effort at realizing it in the months ahead. No wonder, too, that he experienced so much distress and frustration over seeing the dream vanish by the middle of the year.

In March 1937 the opposition surfaced. At the president's request Ickes's Power Policy Committee had just drafted the Bonneville Power Authority bill. It was introduced in the House by Martin Smith of Washington. However Oregon's powerful Republican senator, Charles McNary, hesitated in cosponsoring it because the bill provided for an administrator who would be named by the secretary of the interior. "From information that we get," Ickes wrote, "the power interests in the Northwest are opposed to the administrator who is to make contracts for Bonneville power, to be named by . . . Interior. They want the War Department to have charge of this phase of the administration."

After some effective lobbying on the part of the Corps's chief, Gen. Edward Markham, and others, the president was persuaded to accept an alteration in the bill in favor of the Corps of Engineers. Ickes was not pleased. In early May he wrote,

> This committee [NPPC] finds itself rather out on a limb. . . . I do not trust the Army engineers on power and, moreover, I do not think that . . . they ought to be permitted to extend their powers and jurisdiction as they would if this bill should pass as amended. . . . We are going to try to hold the thing until he [FDR] gets back from his trip and see whether we cannot swing him back to his original views.

They couldn't swing it. The Army Engineers thus gained control over the powerful Bonneville Power Authority that straddled the Columbia River between Oregon and Washington and that helped to bring cheap electricity to the Northwest.

At the same time that the Corps and its supporters were working to defeat Ickes on the Bonneville Power bill, the secretary learned that "the organized forestry interests are busy opposing that part of the President's reorganization bill which will rename this Department and make possible the transfer to it of the conservation activities of the Government. They and the farm interests are doing a lot of talking and resoluting."

Naturally the "father" of American forestry, Gifford Pinchot, jumped back into the fray. The longstanding friendship between Ickes and Pinchot had been strained since 1934, due mainly to the Forest Service issue, but in 1937 their relationship reached its nadir. Ickes became outraged when the conservation organization, the Izaak Walton League, asked the former chief forester to address its annual meeting in Chicago in late April. It then adopted his position on reorganization.

In his speech Governor Pinchot took off the gloves. The *Chicago Tribune's* headline for May 1 read, "Ickes, President Grab for Power, Pinchot Charges," and quoted him as saying:

> The Brownlow report . . . proposes to dislodge, dislocate and break up certain most important parts of the government conservation work and divide them between the agriculture department, where they are now well handled, and the interior department, whose handling of publicly owned natural resources is one of the blackest scandals of our history.
>
> If I were not in Chicago, the home of Secretary Ickes, I would say that the man who has been my friend for more than a quarter of a century has allowed his ambition to get away with his judgment; that great power has bred the lust of greater power, and it would be just as good for Secretary Ickes to be beaten in this raid as it would be for the conservation policy to be protected against him. He needs it.[10]

Furious, Harold Ickes responded in kind with a press release on May 2, in which he accused Pinchot of merely using the reorganization issue to get back at Roosevelt for not supporting him for senator in 1934: "If Gifford Pinchot had been substituted in 1934 as a candidate for Senator from Pennsylvania for Senator Guffey, he would not have made the speech that he did before the Izaak Walton League."[11]

Ickes's public announcement that Pinchot personally came to see him "to beg for support that was denied him" was a pretty low blow. But he had been prepared to go even further. Several months prior to this vituperative exchange Ickes asked his executive assistant, Leona Graham, to go through the files and find something that would "get"

Pinchot.[12] Her investigation found nothing, and she wrote the secretary a memo pointing out that "after going through the . . . correspondence very carefully, I truly do not see anything that could be used to discredit the Governor—at least not without embarrassing you at the same time."

The public name-calling continued. Pinchot addressed the American Forestry Association in Cincinnati in late May at which he called Ickes a "conjurer." By November the Bull Moose Progressive was referring to the secretary as "hot-spot Harold," a "former friend," the "irritable Interior Ickes," and "glum and grumpy Harold."[13]

Ickes was as angry with the Izaak Walton League as he was with Pinchot. He threatened to cancel his membership. He also began a lengthy correspondence with its officers over their stand on the reorganization issue. In November, Ickes wrote the vice-president of the league and sent some fifty copies of his letter to influential members. Contrary to what the secretary expected, most of the replies he received back supported the league's stand, not his. That Ickes by this time had lost the proper perspective on the issue is suggested by a letter he received from Dr. Robert Dixon of Denver, objecting to his original letter to the vice-president. Dr. Dixon wrote Ickes in December that "I do not hesitate to say that I was very much surprised to receive a letter with the sarcastic tone and implications from an individual of such high standing in our National Government. I could not write letters of that kind and maintain prestige in my [medical] profession."[14] Dixon sent copies of his letter to Colorado's congressional delegation.

The interdepartmental conflict among Agriculture, Interior, and War ground on through the spring, taking its toll on Harold Ickes's health. In early May a replay of the fight in January with Henry Wallace occurred, except this time it was with Secretary of War Harry Woodring, whom Ickes characterized as a "midget General MacArthur," who "struts about with inflated chest . . . and [is] more disagreeable and dictatorial than any man I have met in the Government."[15] This was also a turf battle, fueled by a presidential request to review a Corps of Engineers proposal for a substantial increase in flood control funds. Woodring wanted to appoint a committee of engineers drawn from the Corps and the Bureau of Reclamation, while Ickes, who greatly mistrusted the Corps, wanted an independent engineering review. "What's the matter with the Army engineers?" Woodring asked Ickes during their heated meeting. Ickes retorted that that was beside the point, adding a non sequitur, "What is the matter with the Reclamation engineers?" [16]

Afterwards, Ickes admitted that the fight upset him very much; he had to go to his doctor's office and was kept there for two hours. "When I got home I was pretty dead to the world," Ickes wrote. These struggles, coupled with anxiety over the Court fight, were simply too great a strain for the 63-year-old Ickes. Later that month his heart gave him that severe reprimand, though fortunately it was no more than that.

ONE BATTLE, HOWEVER, Ickes had won by this time. It turned out to be far more important to him in the long run than the numerous political conflicts he found himself embroiled in that year. Sometime during the winter of 1937 his young sweetheart, Jane, decided to marry him. [17] Although they did not wed until May of the following year, keeping their engagement a secret all the while, nevertheless her decision settled Harold's personal life.

Looking forward to his life with Jane, in the spring of 1937 Ickes purchased a new home near Olney, Maryland, and called it Headwaters Farm. The several hundred–acre estate had a ten-room main house built in the colonial style, a separate lodge for the servants, and yet another for the farmer-in-residence. It was heavily wooded, quiet, and cool, with acres of fertile land to work. He loved it as soon as he saw it that spring. A deep attachment to nature that originated in his rural Pennsylvania boyhood had impelled Ickes to return to the countryside.

In buying the secluded estate, he repeated the pattern of his first marriage. After marrying in 1911 Anna and Harold built Hubbard Woods some twenty miles north of Chicago in the then-sparsely populated town of Winnetka. They moved to the country about 1915 and raised their children while Harold indulged his interest in horticulture. Working in the city and living in the country as he did, Harold Ickes thus was among the first group of Americans to experience the pleasures of suburban living. Both his need to be at the center of things and his love of nature were satisfied by the arrangement.

When he came to Washington in 1933, Ickes lived in three different residences, each one a little further out of town than the last. Then, once he and Jane decided to get married, he bought Headwaters Farm.

Just as he was getting ready to move in, however, the heart attack confined him to Bethesda Naval Hospital. Jane was constantly at his bedside during the month he spent recuperating.

Ickes finally settled in his new home in mid-July. On July 16 he wrote,

> At last I have been able to dispense with the constant care of both the doctor and the nurse. I am at my new home on my farm. . . . I came out yesterday afternoon through a heavy thunder storm which cleared the air and made the temperature delightfully cool. Jane came with me, and [her sister] Ann, who has been in Washington since Monday. . . . I am sure that I am going to like it here and be quite happy and comfortable.

Through the summer and fall the couple kept up appearances. Jane did not move in with Harold—that would have been unthinkable in the 1930s—but they were together, naturally, a great deal. In early December Ickes went to New York to deliver a speech before the Civil Liberties Union and was met by Jane. "I stayed in New York over Wednesday night and on Thursday morning Jane and I went shopping again," Ickes wrote. "Our excursion . . . was to Wanamaker's where we found some very lovely lamps, of which I bought six for the house. . . . These lamps are of old Chinese, French, or English pottery and they were very attractive." His impending marriage was all that was needed to give him, at last, the kind of domestic situation for which he had yearned all of his life.

That Harold Ickes's personal affairs were resolving themselves so nicely in 1937 certainly caused him great satisfaction. That was fortunate because Ickes was taking a beating on several political issues about which he felt very strongly. First, the Supreme Court fight did not turn out the way Ickes hoped it would. At the president's bequest he had worked hard at putting the Court into its proper place, and it was a disappointment when Congress refused to do it. Ickes also lost the battle on the Bonneville Power Authority that spring when Congress and FDR decided to give the Corps, and not the Interior secretary, management control. Worst of all, though, he saw that he was losing the battle for Forestry for the third straight year. That distressed him more than anything else because, by this time, Ickes had become obsessed with getting control of the national forest system.

There has been considerable speculation about the origins of Ickes's obsession with the Forest Service, which, at the time, was a matter to

joke about—when Ickes wasn't around. An exasperated but still playful President Roosevelt said in November of 1937 that he might divide
responsibilities along the Mason/Dixon line.[18] Ickes said the president's nonchalance made him "uneasy."

The secretary's intensity on the subject can be explained in purely
political and organizational terms. The Forest Service was in the 1930s
one of the most powerful, well-run agencies of the federal government. It had a good image with the public, and it wasn't tarnished by
scandals the way some other resource-managing agencies were. It was,
in short, quite an organizational catch, and the desire for more power
wasn't then or now an orphan disease among political executives.

Moreover, according to Ickes, its mission of managing the expanding national forest system clearly placed it within the domain of the
Interior Department. The Interior secretary never accepted Pinchot's
view that forestry was tree farming, that trees were a crop—albeit a
slow-growing one—like any other crop and thus were best managed
by the Agriculture Department. In arguing against this conception of
forestry, Ickes concluded that the logical place for the Forest Service
was in the Interior Department, along with the other land-managing
agencies. Many others have made that argument, including the natural resource scholar Marion Clawson. In 1987, Clawson said that
"all things being equal, the Forest Service probably does belong in
Interior." [19]

But the organizational explanation doesn't quite encompass the
near-fanatical nature of Ickes's quest. When he thought that FDR was
reneging on his promise to give him Forestry, Ickes came close to giving up a career in public service that, until that time, had been the
most important and rewarding element in his life. More than once he
resigned or threatened to resign because of frustration over the forestry
issue. In view of this, one needs to consider certain personality and
character traits of Harold Ickes.

Why did Ickes latch on to the Forest Service and refuse to let go?
There seem to have been conscious and, perhaps, unconscious drives
operating in the secretary which would account for this. All of his life
Ickes had a compelling need for control and order in his life. As secretary, he organized his work day down to minutes, and would remain
(or return) to his office at night in order to clear off the day's work
from his desk. Sloppiness and laziness disturbed him greatly. He maintained a carefully groomed appearance—his children remembered that

even at home he frequently wore a tie and white shirt—and he kept the most careful track of his pocketbook as well as his calendar. He allowed himself little slack time, and expected the same behavior from others.

Harold Ickes was an individual who respected authority and always opted for a single, hierarchical chain of command (unlike his boss). Relationships with his superiors and subordinates were, on the whole, less conflict-ridden than with his colleagues—that is, fellow cabinet members and others, like Harry Hopkins, who occupied an organizational level on a par with him. These aspects of his personality impelled him toward the capture of the Forest Service. Ickes became convinced—or convinced himself—that this agency logically belonged in his department, and that its being in Agriculture was simply a historical aberration. He needed to correct this anomaly.

The other aspect of his personality that bears on his obsession has to do with Ickes's need for, and identification with, political heroes. The fact that the career of one of his first idols, Theodore Roosevelt, was bound up with the creation of the Forest Service further explains why Ickes was so desirous of getting control of that agency. Roosevelt was not only an outstanding "public steward," but he epitomized nineteenth-century conceptions of masculinity. As complete a man as was fashioned in his generation, Ickes thoroughly identified with him and his accomplishments.

Another of Ickes's mentors, Gifford Pinchot, was cast from the Theodore Roosevelt mold. He combined a remarkable intellect with a thoroughly civilized demeanor, yet he was fearless when it came to exercising political power. In his capacity as first chief of the U.S. Forest Service Pinchot created a powerful, professional, highly respected organization that transcended partisan politics. During his political coming of age, Harold Ickes also greatly admired Pinchot, a man who was ten years older than Ickes but who, unlike Ickes, enjoyed great influence during the first two decades of the twentieth century.

Once Ickes had a chance to exercise power, he tried to step into Pinchot's shoes by becoming the custodian of the valuable national forests. The chief forester, however, refused to relinquish either his role or his creation. Although he was getting on in years by the 1930s, Pinchot had lost none of his fighting spirit, and he succeeded in beating Ickes on this issue. That there existed a deeply personal element in the Ickes-Pinchot feud seems clear. It was not simply differing conceptions of forestry that caused both men to hurl the kind of epithets they did at one another for several years.

Finally, Harold Ickes was well aware that one other individual was deeply interested in trees and forests, and his name was Franklin Roosevelt. The president's lifelong interest in nature and forests rivaled that of the previous Roosevelt in the White House. Both before and after becoming president FDR experimented with tree planting on his Hyde Park estate, in the nation's capital, and elsewhere in the country.

Some of Roosevelt's pet New Deal projects involved trees, such as the Forest Service's Great Plains Shelterbelt, the extension of the national forest system east of the Mississippi River, and the preservation of old-growth forests through their incorporation into national parks. Even when he was burdened by poor health and the need to conclude the Second World War with an Allied victory, President Roosevelt thought about trees. After returning to Washington from the conference with Winston Churchill and Joseph Stalin in Teheran in 1943, FDR considered suggesting to the Iranian government that it embark on a reforestation program. He was much bothered, he said, by the barren hills he saw on his trip to the Middle East. They were not natural.

Roosevelt's interest in forests was not lost on Harold Ickes, and his consuming desire to get the Forest Service transferred to his domain had very much to do with his relationship with the president. By entrusting Ickes with this valuable resource FDR would be adding significantly to the secretary's stature vis-à-vis his colleagues. An element of sibling rivalry compounded Ickes's desire to be given this particular agency by the president.

The public lives of three men—Theodore Roosevelt, Gifford Pinchot, and Franklin Roosevelt—were all linked to forests and the Forest Service. They were all men whom Ickes admired and emulated in his own public career. Ickes, a boy raised by an emotionally absent father, was drawn to these men because they were everything that he felt his own father was not. His acceptance by this vital group would be assured if the president, whom he practically worshipped, gave him stewardship over the nation's forests. Harold Ickes needed that prize in order to feel secure about his relationship with Roosevelt and about his place in history.

But in 1937 Roosevelt still was not prepared to give Ickes the Forest Service. From his bed at the Naval Hospital Ickes noted ruefully that the battle for a conservation department was again being lost. With mounting frustration, he blamed the president. In June he wrote:

> The tactics of the Administration this session have been very poor. The reorganization bill could have been put through Congress in a month or six weeks. Everyone was for it at the beginning, Republicans as well as Democrats, Chambers of Commerce and big business organizations as well as New Dealers. With added prestige resulting from the passage of this bill, the President could have gone forward with his Court plan, but that in turn was badly handled—just as badly as possible.[20]

Once back on his feet, Ickes continued to press for a conservation department, but issues not foreseen at the beginning of 1937 began intruding on the Roosevelt administration's agenda. New battles with more impersonal and more distant adversaries were building, as fanatics at home and abroad began running amok. Harold Ickes thus found himself speaking out with increasing frequency in defense of civil liberties. It was a role with which he was very familiar, and one at which he excelled.

CHAPTER 14

"NATIONS IN NIGHTSHIRTS"

RECESSION AND RACISM

EVENTS FOR THE Roosevelt administration went from bad to worse as 1937 wore on. Even in areas where the president appeared to have scored some points, as in the battle with the Supreme Court, the victory turned sour. Roosevelt's choice of Sen. Hugo Black of Alabama to replace the 78-year-old Willis Van Devanter, first hailed as a masterful political stroke, turned into an embarrassment. In FDR's calculations, the Senate could hardly fail to confirm one of its own, even if the one had turned out to be a lot more liberal on social and economic issues than were most of his Southern colleagues. "Even 'Cotton Ed' Smith, of South Carolina," Ickes happily wrote, "who 'God-damned' the nomination all over the place when it was first announced, didn't have the courage to stand up and vote against a fellow Senator from the Deep South." [1]

But no sooner had the senator donned the regal black robe of a justice of the Supreme Court than rumors began circulating about the skeletons in his closet. It turned out, much to the president's chagrin, that Hugo Black not only had been elected to the Senate with the help of the Ku Klux Klan but had been himself a member at one time. Through the fall of 1937 Roosevelt was pressured to investigate the matter by Sen. Burton Wheeler and others, but by then the appointment was a *fait accompli*. The president told Wheeler that he wouldn't do it. The issue now was entirely up to the Senate. That body, FDR argued, and not the president, had the constitutional prerogative of investigation.

There was some support in Congress for the president's position, most notably from the powerful Progressive Republican from Idaho, William Borah. Shortly before Borah left Washington for Idaho at the end of September, Harold Ickes went to his office to discuss the Hugo Black situation. Ickes said that the senator agreed that

> Black could not be impeached and he particularly agreed that the President had no more right to investigate a member of the Supreme Court than he had to investigate a Member of the Senate. . . . Borah also agreed that Black could not be impeached for membership in an organization at the time of his nomination and confirmation as a member of the Supreme Court.[2]

The Interior secretary stopped short of asking Borah to try to rein in his colleague from the neighboring state of Montana, Burton Wheeler, but, Ickes said, "as I told Tom Corcoran afterward, I am willing to ask him if Wheeler repeats this statement and Borah does not voluntarily take him to task." He added that "Borah said he was willing to help in any way that he could."

Roosevelt nevertheless took a beating in the short run on the Black appointment. Most Republicans, some Democrats, and the conservative press crowed with delight at FDR's faux pas—and eagerly looked to the 1938 midterm elections, just a year away, in order to further excoriate the president.

Adding substantially to Roosevelt's difficulties, the economy went into a tailspin. The hard-won gains of Roosevelt's New Deal recovery program, which reached their apex in May, became threatened by an ominous downturn in business activity. On October 19, "Black Tuesday," the stock market began a precipitous drop and although it leveled out by the end of the month, Roosevelt acknowledged that he had a major problem on his hands. Some two million people were thrown out of work in the last three months of 1937, and steel production fell to one quarter of what it had been.[3] The American people's confidence was shaken.

Until this point the economic indicators had all been positive. Roosevelt's awesome popularity sprung in good measure from the public's perception of him as "Dr. New Deal." He and his advisors had resuscitated in a few short years a nearly prostrate economy that, while still a bit wobbly on its feet, showed signs of complete recovery. National income had gone from $46 billion in 1932 to $68 billion in 1936; gross farm income climbed from about $4.5 billion to $8.5 billion; wages and salaries went from $31 billion to $42 billion; and, significantly, the net profits of corporate America went from $4 billion in the red to $6.5 billion in the black. "By the spring of 1937," historian William Leuchtenburg reported, "the country had finally pulled above 1929 levels of output." [4]

But then the "Roosevelt Recession" hit. The administration was divided over what to do about the economic calamity, and the president himself was openly perplexed. However, he drew himself up and on October 12 gave an upbeat, substantive Fireside Chat outlining his intentions to the American people. He told them he was calling Congress into a special session that would begin on November 15 in order to consider measures that it hadn't yet passed and that the president felt were urgently needed. In his speech Roosevelt dwelt on the problems of huge agricultural surpluses, the need for regional, TVA-like conservation authorities to do long-range planning, a renewed antitrust effort, and minimum wage and maximum hour laws. He said:

> American industry has searched the outside world to find new markets, but it can create on its very doorstep the biggest and most permanent market it has ever seen. A few more dollars a week in wages, a better distribution of jobs with a shorter working day will almost overnight make millions of our lowest-paid workers . . . buyers of billions of dollars of industrial and farm products. . . . I am a firm believer in fully adequate pay for all labor, but right now I am most greatly concerned in increasing the pay of the lowest-paid labor.[5]

Although the president knew what he wanted, which was what nearly every president wants—economic prosperity and some degree of equity in its distribution—FDR found himself whipsawed in two different directions on how to achieve those objectives. At the end of October Ickes observed that instead of taking the advice of liberal newspaper publisher J. David Stern to invite John Maynard Keynes to the White House, the president "has turned first to one man and then to another." [6] Both Stern and Ickes worried that Roosevelt was making a mistake in not seeking out truly competent advice on the recession. In his memoirs, "Brains Truster" Raymond Moley characterized Roosevelt's economic theories with acidic imagery: "To look on his policies as the result of a unified plan . . . was to believe that the accumulation of stuffed snakes, baseball pictures, school flags, old tennis shoes, and the like in a boy's bedroom were the design of an interior decorator." [7]

Roosevelt's cabinet was as divided as was the country and its economists and business leaders over how to proceed. On the one hand Secretary of the Treasury Henry Morgenthau, along with Postmaster General Jim Farley and Commerce Secretary Dan Roper, pushed for a conciliatory approach to the business sector, while Labor Secretary Frances Perkins lined up with Henry Wallace, Ickes, and Harry Hopkins to urge an expansion of New Deal pump-priming measures. Public works expenditures were cut back by the president in early 1937 as a result of an improved economy, Perkins observed, and a retrenchment policy was put into effect. "The recession of 1937 was undoubtedly the result," she wrote.[8]

Although the causes of the 1937 recession were plain to some, they were not plain to the president. In November Ickes recorded that a "plainly worried" Roosevelt devoted almost the entire meeting of the cabinet, some two and a half hours, to discussing the deepening recession. Ickes wrote that it was one of the few cabinet meetings where they really got down to serious business:

> While at Hyde Park the President saw some important businessmen. He thinks that the stock market break was due to several causes. The foreign situation has had a good deal to do with it, there was much overspeculation which forced prices much higher than earnings would justify, and there has been an abnormal lull in business. The recession in employment, according to figures given by Miss Perkins, was much greater than the average for this time of year over a considerable period. The result has been that a psychosis of fear has been engendered, resulting in cancellation of orders and nervousness on the part of business, especially the smaller businessmen. . . .
>
> The President feels that the big money interests are in an "unconscious conspiracy" (I think this was his exact expression) to force the hand of the Administration. They want concessions in taxation . . . they want a lightening of the laws and regulations of SEC; they want the President to take a strong stand against sit-down strikes and especially against the CIO. . . .
>
> Henry Morgenthau started in to tell the President that he ought to re-

assure business that he is not against business as such. The President almost jumped down his throat. He said . . . that he has taken this position publicly time and time again. Henry looked and acted like a spanked child. Jim Farley supported Morgenthau after the President had quieted down. He thinks that the President ought to do a little backslapping with business. And then he turned to me and said, sotto voce, "That's right, isn't it?" In the same manner, I said to Jim that I didn't think it would make a particle of difference.[9]

Through a dreary November the economy continued its downslide and the president, unable to decide what to do, drifted. The reconvened Congress showed itself equally at sea. Shortly after Thanksgiving FDR gathered up some of his closest associates to accompany him on a fishing trip to the Dry Tortugas Islands in the Gulf of Mexico. Filing aboard the *Potomac* in Miami were Roosevelt, Ickes, Assistant Attorney General Robert Jackson, Harry Hopkins, Dr. Ross McIntire, the president's son James, and military aides Captain Woodson and Col. "Pa" Watson. Such was the camaraderie between Hopkins and Ickes by this time that, Ickes noted, "Harry . . . and I were given the largest of the cabins to share."[10] At other times in their thirteen years working together it could have been expected that one of them would have thrown the other overboard.

The week-long trip was a welcome change of scenery but a worried and sometimes seasick Ickes observed that the president was not his usual cheery and playful self. He didn't join his guests in the first night's poker game, although he did come in for the last hour or so on the succeeding nights—and was "extraordinarily lucky . . . the biggest winner on the trip," Ickes noted with envy. Most of the time, however, the president kept to himself. Even when he was out on deck, he passed his time reading or working on his stamp collection. "He seemed to me to have the appearance of a man who had more or less given up," Ickes related.

Toward the end of the trip Roosevelt perked up, to the relief of his friends aboard ship. Perhaps the president's poor spirits were primarily the result, after all, of a badly infected tooth that had bothered him for some time. But deep down Ickes and others acknowledged that it was more than an infection draining away his usual happy and optimistic demeanor.

It was at this time that several of the New Dealers decided to go on the offensive with respect to the economic situation, intending to proceed, if necessary, without the president's backing. Worried about Roosevelt's indecision and recognizing that he needed help, in December Tom Corcoran, Ben Cohen, Ickes, Robert Jackson, and a few others unleashed an all-out attack on the "economic royalists" who were bent on destroying the New Deal. Corcoran and Cohen drafted speeches to be delivered by Jackson and Ickes over the holiday season. The speeches turned out to be not the kinds of Christmas presents that big business was expecting.

The recently appointed assistant attorney general, Robert Jackson, opened the December campaign. Ickes, who got to know Jackson on the fishing trip, liked him. "Jackson is a quiet person and sometimes his reactions seem slow," Ickes wrote. "But he is thoughtful and well-poised and fundamentally very sound from my point of view. . . . There is no doubt he is a real liberal." Best of all, he was ready to fight.

In a nationwide radio address in early December Jackson laid the blame for the recession on the doorstep of corporate America. "By profiteering the monopolists and those so near monopoly as to control their prices have simply priced themselves out of the market, and priced themselves into the slump," he charged.[11]

A few days later Harold Ickes fired his first salvo in a speech given in New York before the American Civil Liberties Union. Its provocative title, "Nations in Nightshirts," was undoubtedly chosen to deflect some of the criticism of the Hugo Black nomination, and its content lived up to its billing. It was a broad-gauged volley assailing "international Ku Kluxism," the denial of civil liberties in some parts of America, the conservatism of the Supreme Court, and the increasing concentration of economic power in the United States.

Ranging far and wide, Ickes's words were broadcast over national radio and were intended to stomp on as many toes as possible. He began by lambasting the "madness of men in night shirts," who "riding forth at night in the anonymity of cowardice . . . dragged men from their beds, tarring and feathering, assaulting, and, in some instances, even killing their victims." The menace, he said, now has spread throughout the world. "Where benighted men of our own country at one time indulged in a moronic exhibitionism which disgraced the nation, we now find nations that boast of their civilizations committing deeds of unprovoked violence against their neighbors."[12]

After castigating the Klan and the fascist regimes of Germany, Italy, and Japan, Ickes then trained his sights on corporate America. In a section of the address that was, Ickes noted, "frankly Ben Cohen's and . . . was one of the strongest sections of the speech," the Interior secretary discussed how the rise and concentration of corporate power threatened the civil rights and liberties of the common man and woman.[13] Ickes railed against the "fascist-minded men of America," describing them as

> the real enemies of our institutions. . . . They have solidarity, a common interest in seizing more power and greater riches for themselves, and ability and willingness to turn the concentrated wealth of America against the welfare of America. It is these men who, pretending that they would save us from dreadful communism, would superimpose upon America an equally dreadful fascism.

"Comments that have come in to me since I made the speech have been more numerous and more enthusiastic than after any other speech I have ever made," Ickes wrote. "I really think that this speech had a great air-clearing effect."[14] When Supreme Court Justice Harlan Fiske Stone told Ickes, after the annual Gridiron Club Dinner on December 11, to "make some more speeches like that," the secretary was convinced that he was on the right track. The liberal Ickes-Jackson duo thus kept after corporate America, with Tom Corcoran and Ben Cohen doing much of the initial speech-drafting.

At the end of December, Robert Jackson gave a rousing address titled "The Menace to Free Enterprise" in Philadelphia before the American Political Science Association. Rather than trying to subvert the New Deal, Jackson argued that big business should do everything it can to save it, since it turned out to be its major beneficiary. Comparing the business profits under Hoover with those under FDR, Jackson concluded, "The unvarnished truth is that the government's recovery program has succeeded nowhere else so effectively as in restoring the profits of big business. Labor has had no such advance. The small merchant has had no such prosperity. The small manufacturer has had no such advantage."[15]

The very next night, December 30, 1937, Harold Ickes was on the air to put an exclamation mark at the end of this conflict-ridden year with his speech, "It Is Happening Here." In this attack on monopoly capitalism he succeeded in "stirring up the animals," as he put it, as never before. Singling out certain great business tycoons (the so-called Sixty Families) such as Henry Ford, the duPonts, Girdler, and Rand, as well as certain "kept newspapers," Ickes warned the nation that if the monopolists won the current battle with New Deal liberalism, "it meant a fascist state with an end to our liberties." [16]

"Nothing I have ever done before has been the cause of so much publicity," Ickes wrote on New Year's Day, 1938. This was quite an admission from an individual whose public life, especially since coming to Washington, had been nothing if not sensational.

The public harangues had their intended effect. A businessman coming in to see FDR after the fusillade told him, "For God's sake call off that man Ickes!" The president was pleased with the reaction they provoked among the business community. He told his cabinet early in 1938 that, before the speeches and while the recession was still severe, a number of men had refused his invitation to the White House to discuss the economic situation. Afterwards, they were "only too glad to come." [17] The effect on FDR was noticeable as well. The liberal faction's assault on the monopolists pushed the president more in the direction of their camp, as he continued in the new year to grapple with an economy that refused to stir out of its doldrums.

FDR gave up, for example, efforts at balancing the budget, which Henry Morgenthau and the budget director pushed forcefully in 1937. The Treasury secretary was so upset by this that he considered resigning, but he simply couldn't bring himself to forsake Roosevelt, his lifelong friend, at this perilous time. The ability to engender that kind of loyalty among his associates was one of FDR's great strengths.

The president also began working on plans to stimulate the housing construction sector of the economy and a federal budget that not only continued but significantly increased public works and work relief expenditures for another year. The much criticized public housing component of the Public Works Administration was reorganized, and a new administrator, Nathan Straus, was appointed—over Secretary Ickes's loud objections. As a last resort, FDR turned again to pump-priming in 1938 in order to end the recession.

But some of the biggest increases in federal spending in the new year were tied to the steadily deteriorating international situation. Events in Asia and Europe during 1937 had the inevitable result of progressively rearming the United States during FDR's second term. It was not a policy necessarily chosen by the president or by anyone else. Rather, it was the product of the force of circumstances.

AS BAD AS THE domestic political situation was for Roosevelt in 1937, foreign affairs caused him and his cabinet even greater concern.

Civil war engulfed Spain, and the governments of other European nations jumped into the bloody conflict. The expansionist designs of Hitler and Mussolini were unfolding across Western Europe while French and English leaders seemed unable to grasp their significance. A militant Japanese government began its incursions into China by the summer of 1937, and in December it eliminated any doubts about the seriousness of its intentions by sinking the American warship *Panay*. President Roosevelt, along with other leaders of the European democracies, searched for policies that sought to avoid what appeared to be an increasingly inevitable world war.

As secretary of the interior and public works administrator, Harold Ickes had had very little to do with foreign policy during his first four years in office. With the exception of having responsibility for the Division of Islands and Territories, which was then under Interior Department jurisdiction, Ickes's duties largely stopped at the Atlantic and Pacific shores. That ended in 1937, when he was drawn into the vortex of international politics. It was a measure of their seriousness that a secretary of the interior would find himself in the midst of foreign policymaking. But it was also a measure of the respect Ickes had won in Roosevelt's eyes that he would be allowed to contribute to the terribly difficult decisions confronting the president in the international arena. Although Ickes sometimes exasperated Roosevelt, the president did consider, usually, the Interior secretary's opinions on foreign affairs.

Helium and the *Hindenburg* disaster of May 1937 introduced Ickes to international politics. Few events were more sensational that year than was the spectacle of the German dirigible suddenly bursting into flames and burning to death all those aboard as it stood tied to its moorings at Lakehurst, New Jersey. It was a shocking tragedy, made real for millions of Americans who listened to a tear-choked eyewitness account that described the *Hindenburg* exploding and plummeting to earth, engulfed in fire. To some, the disaster must have symbolized the growing dangers abroad.

After the accident, the German government asked to buy 10 million cubic feet of the less volatile gas, helium, from the United States in order to avoid another hydrogen-caused tragedy. At the cabinet meeting held a few days after the *Hindenburg* explosion, Ickes brought up the German request. He explained, "We are afraid that if we begin to sell helium to foreign countries it may be used for war purposes." [18] After discussion, the president, following Ickes's suggestion, told the secretaries of the interior, war, Navy, and commerce to formulate a governmental policy on helium.

A week later a committee report was sent to Congress and a bill based on it was drafted. Helium, the bill proposed, could be sold abroad for commercial purposes provided that the United States could be assured that it was not being used for military purposes. Another clause in the legislation that passed Congress in August 1937 provided for the creation of a government monopoly for this valuable natural resource. A board of appraisers (one of whom was to be designated by the Interior secretary) would fix a fair price for the purchase of the American Helium Company, which had to this time enjoyed a virtual worldwide monopoly on the gas's production and distribution. The strategic nature of certain mineral resources, in an increasingly dangerous world, was becoming apparent. And the Interior secretary controlled many of them.

The passage of legislation generally would have marked the end of the debate. A full year after its initial request for helium, however, Germany still hadn't received one cubic foot of it, due to Secretary Ickes's distaste for the ugly dictatorship in Germany. Harold Ickes had always cast a jaundiced eye on Germany. Despite being of German descent on his father's side, he displayed a lifelong antipathy toward that country. Jesse Ickes had been a keen disappointment to him and consequently Harold identified strongly with his Scotch ancestry, the McCunes. When America entered the First World War in 1917 Ickes managed to find his way into the conflict. Stationed in France for some six months, he did his little part in fighting the Germans. He came home proud to have helped beat back German aggression.

Germany's politics in the 1930s served to validate Ickes's innate dislike of that country. With respect to its neighbors and to its Jewish minority, it was behaving in precisely the way calculated to deepen Ickes's disgust. After having heard an especially belligerent and obnoxious speech by Hitler, Ickes quipped that the "goose step" was the perfect expression of the German national character. Given Ickes's values and attitude, it is clear why the secretary of the interior was not anxious to sell helium to Germany.

Nothing Germany did while the sale was pending settled Ickes's doubts. On May 31, just as Congress was given the administration's recommendations regarding a helium policy, Ickes noted in his diary that German warships shelled the Spanish seaport of Almeria. A number of civilians, "including women and children," were killed. The attack, Germany explained, was in retaliation for the Spanish shelling of the battleship *Deutschland.* "If Germany is to set the pace for modern civilization," Ickes warned, "we will soon be back in the days preceding the Dark Ages."

Further aggression on the part of the three bandit nations followed in December. Most of the president's cabinet meeting on December 17 was devoted to a discussion of Japan's deliberate sinking of the *Panay* in the upper Yangtze River. Ickes found it interesting that Secretary of the Navy Claude Swanson was, "in his feeble old voice," shouting for war. He also was mildly amused that "the one member of the Cabinet who is least fit of all physically is the one who is strongly urging war. . . . Undoubtedly he is talking for the admirals."

Whether Swanson was speaking for himself or the admirals, or both, Ickes nevertheless confessed that "Swanson's point of view cannot be lightly dismissed." Further aggression from the Fascists seemed inevitable, the president and his cabinet concluded.

> The President believes that between . . . Germany, Italy, and Japan there exists a secret agreement delimiting their spheres of influence. Germany is to be left free to wreak her will against Austria, Hungary, Poland, Czechoslovakia, Lithuania, etc. Italy is to have no restraints imposed upon her so far as the Mediterranean is concerned, and this includes Spain, Egypt, Greece, Turkey, and various French and British colonies. . . . The consideration moving to Japan is the right to use a free hand in Asia.

Discussion of the international situation at the last cabinet meeting of 1937 foreshadowed further tragedy that was to take place in the new year: Roosevelt announced that Romania had just gone Fascist and that Yugoslavia was on its way. Worst of all, he said, "Romania has followed the pattern set by Hitler by virtually outlawing the Jews."

By this time Ickes decided that it would be very unwise to sell helium to Germany. So had America's Jewish leaders. During the next several months Ickes utilized a number of strategies to block the sale. It amounted to a one-man crusade within the government, and a weaker person could not have withstood the enormous pressures to go forward with the sale. But Ickes's tenacity was never in much doubt, and in this case it became one of his most successful endeavors.

Toward the end of February 1938, Ickes held a meeting of Interior Department officials regarding the helium issue. "I told the solicitors to stiffen up considerably on our terms, putting in certain stipulated safeguards to prevent helium from being used for military purposes. I also indicated that our asking price for helium should be $10 for

10,000 cubic feet instead of $8.50. I have not been satisfied with the way the Bureau of Mines has been handling this helium matter," he added.

The contract then was ready to go. It had the approval of the Munitions Board, which was created by the helium statute, as well as the approval of the State, War, and Navy departments. The president in March had signed the considerably stiffer regulations suggested by Ickes. Even so, the secretary refused to sign off. "In view of Germany's ruthless and wanton invasion of Austria I doubt whether it is right for us to sell any helium gas to Germany under any pretext. Moreover, a bill has been introduced in the House . . . preventing any such sale."

It was the middle of April and Ickes still hadn't signed the contract. The issue by now had become a minor sensation, and the secretary was pleased to see that public opinion was with him: "The editorials that I have read have all been in favor of refusing," he wrote. He therefore continued to lobby the president on the subject and believed that he finally had won him over to his viewpoint.

But FDR was being lobbied by individuals on the other side of the debate, too. These included Secretary of State Cordell Hull, Hull's assistant, Sumner Welles and the secretaries of war and Navy. On May 5, Roosevelt convened a high-level conference to try to resolve once and for all the helium issue. The crux of the issue was whether or not helium had "military importance." At the meeting were FDR, Ickes, Solicitor General Robert Jackson, Army Chief of Staff Gen. Malin Craig, and Adm. William Leahy of the Navy.

Roosevelt himself took the lead, Ickes noted, and went to great length to explain why he thought that the helium desired by the German Zeppelin Company had no military importance. "He argued quite effectively," Ickes admitted, noting the heads of the military backed him up. Then Ickes took the floor and proceeded to raise one legal technicality after another, until they got to the heart of the matter.

> The President said that in any event we would not ship the helium unless we had a guarantee from Hitler that it would not be used for military purposes. My reply . . . was that the statute did not turn upon whether it might be used for military purposes but whether it had military importance. Moreover, I inquired: "Who would take Hitler's word?"

After raising a further objection about the handling of the contract by the Munitions Board, which the solicitor general backed up, Ickes reported with satisfaction that "the President gave up."

Cordell Hull was livid. At the cabinet meeting following the conference, the matter was raised again. Hull, whose "voice was tense and [whose] hands trembled as he read from documents in support of his position," proceeded to lead the charge against Ickes's intransigence. Even the president showed signs of exasperation when he asked Ickes whether a letter from him, as "Commander-in-Chief of the Army and Navy," would do. Despite the fact that not one other cabinet member voiced support for Ickes's position (Perkins and Morgenthau remained silent, Ickes noted, while everyone else supported Cordell Hull), the secretary stood his ground. The helium contract was never signed. Germany never received any helium from Roosevelt's government.

Harold Ickes provided his own assessment of the helium controversy at his weekly press conference some years later. On January 8, 1942, a month after Pearl Harbor was bombed and shortly after Hitler declared war on the United States, it was reported that the Axis powers might use zeppelins to bomb East Coast cities. The secretary allowed himself the luxury of saying, "I told you so."

> Well, they won't have any helium. That little chicken is coming home to roost after all. It was a very worn little chicken with no tail feathers left and only one wing working, but they have no helium, and if they come over here . . . in zeppelins inflated with flammable gas . . . one little pot-shot will send them where they ought to be.[19]

CHAPTER 15

THE CALM AFTER THE STORM

DEPARTMENTAL WOES AND

A DUBLIN WEDDING

"The Department is pretty well shot as the result of this Burlew incident," Ickes wrote in January of 1938. "Burlew himself has had little time for Department work and he hasn't been in condition to do real work. Harry Slattery was in the hospital for . . . a week and returned only Thursday. West is away and would be of no use if he were here. I have been in bad shape during the last week . . . largely because I have been sleeping so very badly."[1]

The "Burlew incident" referred to the Senate confirmation hearings on Ickes's aide, Ebert K. Burlew, to become first assistant secretary of the Department of the Interior. Burlew had the president's backing; he had Ickes's; he was a career civil servant who had worked in the Interior Department since 1923; he was a Republican nominated to a higher position by a liberal Democratic administration. Under normal circumstances the appointment would have breezed through Congress. Instead, a senior member of the Public Lands Committee, Sen. Key Pittman of Nevada, used the hearings to conduct a lengthy, thorough, and quite nasty investigation of Harold Ickes's management of the Interior Department, the Public Works Administration, and the Oil Administration.

By the time Pittman and his allies were finished the "Burlew incident" was anything but that. The hearings continued for two months and produced over 600 pages of testimony.[2] At the conclusion nearly everybody's nerves were frayed, and a number of reputations were tarnished. The confirmation hearings on Ebert Burlew turned into the second comprehensive congressional investigation of Ickes's various authorities. The first took place in 1935 when Sen. Millard Tydings was appointed to investigate Ickes's and Governor Pearson's administration of the Virgin Islands. To Ickes's chagrin, many of the allegations raised during those hearings were looked into again in 1938.

Key Pittman's antipathy for Harold Ickes, which was glaringly evident in 1938, went a long way back. Actually neither Pittman nor Nevada's other senator, the distinguished-looking Pat McCarran, applauded the way Harold Ickes ran the department in which westerners claimed a proprietary interest. A first skirmish occurred over the Taylor grazing bill, which was introduced at the outset of the New Deal and was intended to bring some order to, and federal control over, the public domain. The senators were instrumental in ensuring that the grazing interests in the West lost little of their power over the newly created Grazing Service. Ickes initially favored stricter federal regulations and more centralized authority but he had to content himself with a compromise bill that set up powerful, locally controlled advisory boards. Under this structure, the Grazing Service became identified as a "captured agency."

McCarran and Pittman also were unhappy with Ickes's staffing policies. Shortly before the 1936 presidential election, McCarran wrote fellow Democrat Jim Farley to complain about Ickes's and Harry Hopkins's presumed nonpartisanship. He told Farley that in fact both the WPA and the Grazing Service employed a preponderance of Republicans, and that this could only hurt the Democrats' prospects in the upcoming elections—a prediction that, incidentally, was not borne out by the 1936 election returns.

By 1938 Pittman and Ickes were irreconcilable adversaries. In January, just before he was to testify, Ickes privately described the Nevadan as "an objectionable person. He is under the influence of liquor most of the time and no one can ever tell what he is going to do. . . . He looks like a heavy soak and he acts like one." [3] At the same time as Ickes expressed his disdain for the senator, Pittman had the public forum he needed to express his unflattering opinions of Ickes. He was determined to topple the secretary, if not from his cabinet position, then at least from his pedestal.

The eight-week hearings ranged far and wide. In his six years in office Ickes had managed to accumulate a number of enemies. Some of them were called to testify and some worked behind the scenes. The overall picture looked like it had been drawn from the pages of Machiavelli. Ickes was fairly certain that Vice-President Garner was working behind the scenes along with his friend, the powerful and very wealthy Texan Ralph Morrison; that Gifford Pinchot was involved; that his undersecretary Charles West was stabbing him in the back; that his former director of investigations, Louis Glavis, played a part; and that perhaps even Farrington Carpenter of the Grazing Service, Alaska's territorial governor Ernest Gruening, and Assistant Secretary Oscar Chapman were members of the cabal. [4] The hearings, Ickes noted, were less about Ebert Burlew, although he came in for his share of criticism, than they were about Ickes. A result was that he and Pittman went after each other "pretty savagely."

Among other topics, the committee spent considerable time looking into the "Stitely case," the one documented case of fraud in Ickes's Public Works Administration. A Park Service employee named Reno Stitely managed to embezzle $70,000 from the War Department, $13,000 from the National Park Service, and $11,000 from Agriculture's Bureau of Public Roads by setting up a nonexistent CCC camp and cashing the "workers' " checks. "Altogether," Ickes noted, the responsibility was divided between War, Interior and Agriculture. . . . But Pittman didn't want it this way." [5]

Although overall Ickes and his staff accumulated a genuinely estimable record of managing the PWA, the administrator was aware that his and Glavis's persistent rooting out of graft had threatened some powerful individuals. During the Burlew hearings Ickes said he was told that "it was to save [Ralph] Morrison . . . that [Vice-President] Garner expressed the hope that both Burlew and I would be blown up." The PWA files for the Lower Colorado River Project in Texas "does not show Morrison up in a very enviable light," Ickes wrote, and since Morrison and Garner were close friends it was plain to the secretary that both men were helping Pittman in his vendetta. [6]

Harold Ickes also tried to run a scandal-free Oil Administration during the early New Deal years. When he discovered that some of his field men in Texas had accepted rides aboard an oil company airplane, he immediately issued a memo instructing his employees not to do that. Although it was not illegal, he said that such activity looked bad, especially if the press got hold of it. He cautioned them to avoid all situations in which they might be charged with "impropriety." He also dismissed two employees of the Oil Administration in 1935 for conflict of interest but upon further investigation had them reinstated.[7]

The Senate Public Lands Committee, with Pittman leading the charge, managed to find time in their two-month hearing to review Ickes's record on oil. They didn't come up with much, although they looked into the Department of Justice files, especially with regard to the management of the problematic East Texas oil field. Justice and Interior had clashed on a number of occasions in 1934 and 1935 over the government's oil policy. Several witnesses were called by the committee, including the two fired employees. They claimed that they had been "jobbed."[8] Ickes pointed out that they had been rehired.

The activities of Ickes's former director of investigations, the controversial Louis Glavis, naturally were of great interest to the committee. Glavis knew as much as anyone about what had gone on in the Interior Department, the PWA, and the Oil Administration for six years, so he was called in January as a key witness. Ickes knew that he would be in trouble if Glavis divulged everything he knew, and he did a lot of politicking to keep him from testifying—to no avail. However, the worst case scenario did not materialize. "Glavis, who never even liked Burlew, refused to throw him to the dogs," Ickes wrote with relief. "The total result is that no real damage was done" although Louis Glavis finally admitted for the record that he had tapped some telephone wires when he was director. He also told the congressmen that Ebert Burlew knew about it but that he hadn't authorized it. With regard to his boss, he said that Ickes didn't know about the illegal wiretaps but when he learned about them, he took full responsibility for Glavis's overstepping his authority.[9]

Although the committee came close to delving into the one area where Ickes was most vulnerable, to its credit it steered clear of his personal life. Rumors about the secretary's sexual indiscretions first surfaced as a public issue during the 1935 Tydings Hearings. They began circulating again in 1938, in part because the nominee, Ebert Burlew, had been accused of covering up his boss's amorous trysts and related questionable behavior. Copies of a document written by a former employee of the Interior Department who made the original charges were sent in January to all of the members of the Senate's Public Lands Committee. They contained some shocking allegations. No member of the committee went so far as to introduce the document as evidence, and Sen. Pat McCarran, who wasn't fond of Ickes, told Burlew that "he wouldn't let it get into the record if he could help it." But at least one senator, the conservative Republican from Oregon, Frederick Steiwer, considered including it in the investigation. "Slattery [however] says that Steiwer hasn't anything to boast about so far as his own personal conduct is concerned," Ickes wrote. Interestingly, Senator Steiwer resigned on January 31, 1938, in the midst of the hearings and before his six-year term was up in 1939.[10]

In the end, the committee kept within the bounds of examining Burlew's and Ickes's official conduct, although it did that with great thoroughness. Once the hearings were over, the Senate overwhelmingly voted to confirm Burlew. Only Key Pittman and Pat Harrison voted no. For Harold Ickes, no less than for Ebert Burlew, it represented a significant victory.[11]

Harold Ickes had reason to be infuriated with a number of people in connection with the hearings. Not only had he been put through the wringer, but Ebert Burlew came out of them a nervous wreck. Ickes was concerned that he might break under the strain, unaccustomed as he was to political hardball. A novice to this kind of politics, Burlew had made, the secretary noted, "an astonishingly bad witness."[12] Ickes therefore feared that he would lose perhaps his most hard-working and trusted assistant. Although he had plenty of legitimate targets, like the vice-president, some of his anger was directed, justifiably or not, at Roosevelt. In the midst of the messy hearings he wrote, "Nothing can convince me that the President couldn't have stopped these hearings, or at least kept them within reasonable bounds, if he had taken hold at the beginning when I told him what dangers were involved."[13]

It seemed to Ickes that it was a replay of the 1935 hearings during which Senator Tydings did all he could to smear him while Roosevelt maintained a safe distance from the melee. But in fact, by intervening just as the committee received documents about Ickes's extramarital affair, Roosevelt saved the secretary's career. Ickes never grasped the import of FDR's eleventh-hour compromise, which involved reassigning both Governor Pearson, the administration's appointee, and Judge Wilson, the favorite of certain senators.

The president's apparent nonchalance throughout the latest ordeal aggravated Ickes. On one occasion Roosevelt assured his beleaguered cabinet officer that Pittman would let up after "one more Roman holiday." This was not the response Ickes wanted, and he deliberately stayed away from the cabinet meeting on January 28 to indicate to FDR that he had "at least one foot off the reservation. I don't like the way he has acted and I don't propose to make any bones about it," Ickes wrote.[14]

Where was the president in all of this? He was being "the prince." Around the end of January, as the hearings continued and as he was being pressured by Ickes and others to intervene, an annoyed Roosevelt said to Missy Le Hand, "I wish Tommy [Corcoran] would quit nagging me about that matter."[15] For one thing, the president respected the congressional right of inquiry. He wasn't about to alienate unnecessarily important members of Congress, like Key Pittman, by trying to tell them how to proceed. For another, Roosevelt knew that his combative secretary was quite capable of defending himself when attacked—that, in fact, he relished a good political fight.

Finally, the record suggests that Roosevelt considered the hearings worthwhile, even, perhaps, a desirable airing of what went on in the corridors and offices of the Interior Department. For, while the president was personally fond of Harold Ickes, and greatly admired his executive skills, he was not totally uncritical. FDR surely knew about the allegations concerning Ickes's behavior with his mistress in 1933 and 1934. In fact, in March 1934 Ickes had a heart-to-heart talk with the president about the gossip: "I spoke about my lifelong acquaintance with Mrs. Brumbaugh and her family and said that I had resumed my old friendship with her in Washington. . . . I told him that I saw her on occasion and that I didn't see any reason that I shouldn't. He agreed with me."[16]

Roosevelt may have agreed that Ickes's affair was his own affair, but he also took measures in 1935 to keep an eye on what went on in the Interior Department. Shortly after the Tydings hearings ended, the president persuaded Ickes to appoint his man, Charles West, to the newly created undersecretary's position.

What appeared to bother FDR the most about Ickes's administration concerned the deputy director of the PWA, Col. Horatio B.

Hackett. Hackett was appointed to that position in 1934, and in 1935 Roosevelt confided to Treasury Secretary Henry Morgenthau that he thought that Hackett was on the take.[17] By August of 1937 the president told Ickes that he had to get rid of Hackett. Ickes wrote that Roosevelt "has no possible use for Hackett," so he told Budget Director Daniel Bell, while Ickes was in the hospital convalescing from his heart attack, "to set up a separate organization, if necessary, and check everything PWA did." Not long after making this threat, Ickes got Hackett out of the PWA. Roosevelt's distrust appears to have been justified. In March 1938 Ickes noted that a grand jury was looking into a Buffalo, New York, sewage treatment project to ascertain whether "Colonel Hackett might be indicted on the charge of having solicited a bribe."[18]

There was little that President Roosevelt didn't know about his administrators and their domains. He had a passion for information, and created a variety of methods to acquire it, often unbeknownst to others. It is quite possible that the Burlew hearings proceeded generally as the president wanted.

Burlew's nomination to first assistant secretary was part of a much needed general overhaul of the Interior Department, which Harold Ickes undertook in late 1937 and continued implementing through 1938. Much of the secretary's time and attention had been deflected from the department per se as a result of the other responsibilities heaped upon him during FDR's first term. But now, with the PWA functioning smoothly, with oil not being a critical domestic issue, and with no presidential election to worry about, it was time to make some personnel changes in Interior. This effort was also linked to Ickes's continuing desire to get an enlarged conservation department that year. He knew that Roosevelt intended to push his reorganization proposal during the 1938 legislative session, and Ickes wanted his existing department to be in the best possible shape when it took on added activities.

There were some more immediate reasons for making changes at the top. One was the death of Assistant Secretary Theodore Walters in November of 1937. A native of Idaho and a Democratic Party stalwart, "Walters was," Ickes noted on the occasion of his unexpected death, "strictly a political appointment. At first he was very disappointing to me. Since that time, however, I have never had any reason to complain of him. He was loyal, he never shirked any task, and he tried to do his duty the best he knew how." [19] Ickes rarely gushed in his praise of any individual, so his comments about Walters were significant.

This was the position the secretary wanted to fill with career bureaucrat Ebert Burlew, but the fact that he was neither a Democrat nor a westerner constituted two strikes against him when it came to the Senate confirmation hearings. Ickes and Roosevelt thought that it would be in the spirit of the president's executive reorganization proposal to recognize merit in the filling of this traditionally political post, but since Congress was none too pleased with the reorganization bill, it also balked at Burlew's nomination.

Patronage had its place and purpose, many congressmen felt. When news of Walters's death became known, the White House was inundated with telephone calls from Capitol Hill. Roosevelt's aide, Marvin McIntyre, sent the president a memo on December 13 noting that Sen. Dennis Chavez of New Mexico wanted to see him to discuss the Interior vacancy. Roosevelt jotted down a handwritten reply, saying, "I can't do it. I have had 96 requests from Senators on the same subject." [20]

A second personnel change that Ickes sought in the fall of 1937 involved the important undersecretary position. The man filling this post was the second-in-command at Interior. When the position was first created in 1935, FDR suggested that it be filled by Charles West, a former Democratic congressman from Ohio. Because West was pleasant, a liberal, and reputed to be the president's man on the Hill, Ickes told FDR that he'd be "very glad to take Mr. West." [21]

He turned out to be, in Ickes's words, "an utter flop." At a staff meeting in May 1938 Secretary Ickes shared with his top assistants his assessment of Undersecretary West, with whom he had worked for three years:

> Administratively he was no good; he couldn't make up his mind to anything; he was afraid to sign anything. . . . Stuff would pile up on his desk until we would have to go down and raid his desk and take it away from him. . . . He wasn't worth one good tinker's damn. He couldn't say No, and he couldn't even say Yes on [routine] stuff that went over his desk. [22]

Worse yet, West turned out to be disloyal to his immediate superior, the Interior secretary. When Ickes discovered this, in November 1937, he wrote that he was "a slimy, slinking son-of-a-bitch," and then wrote a long letter to Roosevelt. [23] In his letter he pleaded with the president to get West's resignation because the undersecretary had leaked a vicious story to David Friendly of the *Washington Daily News*. The story charged Ickes with continuing the Louis Glavis "reign of terror" by tapping the telephone lines of certain officials in the Interior Department, including West's. Ickes flatly denied the allegation and told Roosevelt that he had called in the Chesapeake and Potomac Telephone Company to examine all the lines in question. It found no present taps, or any evidence of previous taps. What the company did find was that the line into Ickes's private office had a dictaphone connection. Ickes insisted that this was entirely proper, and that, moreover, he had used it on only a handful of occasions, when the telephone conversation dealt with sensitive and/or legal questions. In his diaries he noted that he had recorded, for example, a conversation about the government's purchase of the American Helium Company in early 1937.

A furious Ickes ended the letter to FDR by noting that his department could ill afford another scandal at precisely the time when he was making herculean efforts to have the Forest Service transferred to Interior. Charles West's machinations threatened to undermine all this. In fact, Ickes implied that West was working with his opponents on the reorganization issue to further his own ambition to become Interior secretary. He had to go.

Shortly before their fishing expedition to the Dry Tortugas in November, Ickes suggested to the president a replacement to the objectionable West. He wanted to offer the position to the chief of the Forest Service, Ferdinand Silcox. In addition to admiring Silcox's intellect and professional demeanor, Ickes's strategy was obvious: If he could lure Silcox to Interior with the offer of the undersecretary's position, then perhaps his entire organization would be inclined to follow in his wake. Ickes thought that it was worth a try.

But Roosevelt demurred. On the train returning from Florida to Washington, FDR and Ickes discussed personnel matters and the president suggested Harry Slattery, Ickes's personal assistant, for the undersecretaryship in lieu of Silcox. Roosevelt felt that this would be a good appointment because the position was "more or less a political job," and Slattery was nothing if not political.[24] Ickes subsequently agreed to Slattery in a typical pattern of resolution between the president and his Interior secretary when making appointments in the Department. "The President has never forced anyone on me," Ickes proudly told his top staff in 1938.[25] Roosevelt didn't need to; a suggestion usually was sufficient, although Ickes did have the right of rebuttal.

Burlew's name went to the Hill in December, but Harry Slattery's did not. Roosevelt, who hated firing anyone, searched for another position to offer Charles West instead of asking for his resignation. But another reason for FDR's hesitation in not removing West immediately was that the undersecretary was a conduit for information about what was going on in the Interior Department and in the Public Works Administration.

Along with other sources, Henry Morgenthau's diary entries indicate that West performed this function for FDR. Morgenthau had a standing invitation to lunch every Monday with the president, and their conversations not only covered official business but many other topics as well. They were old friends and so they gossiped about this and that person or issue. On October 31, 1935, the Treasury secretary recorded an interesting conversation with Roosevelt:

> For the first time he [FDR] started to run down Ickes. He said with all Ickes' snoopers Colonel Hackett, Deputy Administrator of PWA, has an engineering firm in Chicago and I didn't quite understand what the President meant but I gather that the firm had been splitting fees with somebody. Charlie West told me that the head of PWA housing, Mr. Clas', statement to the President and Ickes on the progress of slum clearance had been found to be incorrect.[26]

A few months later Morgenthau wrote, "At lunch the president said that Ickes had gone south in a very brown mood implying that he was sulking." Ickes was feeling slighted. He complained to West that the president didn't have time to see him but that he lunched every Monday with Henry Morgenthau. Ickes also said that FDR saw the five assistant secretaries of state all the time. Ickes's feelings of rejection were promptly relayed to FDR. Morgenthau then asked the president whether "Ickes wept on his shoulder and the President said, 'no.'"[27] Obviously, though, Ickes's weeping on West's shoulder went directly to the White House, as did other bits of useful information.

While Roosevelt took his time in finding another job for West, Ickes decided to turn on the pressure to force his undersecretary out of the department after he learned that West was providing ammunition to Sen. Key Pittman for use in the Burlew hearings. "This was the most despicable thing of all [that West did]," Ickes said. It was the last straw. Ickes proceeded to fire West's administrative assistant, who happened to be the undersecretary's brother-in-law. He transferred West's secretary and his stenographer to another agency, with the expectation that "leaving him with [only] a receptionist" would be sufficiently humiliating to force his resignation. But Ickes was taking no chances. William Warne, who at the time was working for the Bureau of Reclamation, remembered that Ickes had West's desk moved out in the hall while he was away to make sure that he got the message.[28]

West took the hint. He stopped showing up for work sometime after the Christmas holidays, but he refused to resign. Much to Ickes's dismay this situation continued through the spring of 1938. The secretary's scorn was palpable. "He has been drawing down his $10,000 a year," Ickes complained to his staff in May. "I told him at the last interview I had with him that if he had any self-respect he would resign. But he didn't. He lived up to my estimate of his character."[29]

Finally in May West gave up his position. An incredulous Ickes noted that Roosevelt was considering appointing him comptroller of the currency. That proposal was short-lived, however, because Morgenthau refused to take him into the Treasury Department.[30] In any event he was no longer causing trouble for Ickes, and the secretary immediately sent Harry Slattery's name to the Senate for confirmation. Slattery didn't encounter the kind of opposition that Burlew had and by mid-year, at long last, Ickes had his top staff in place: Harry Slattery as undersecretary, Ebert Burlew as first assistant secretary, and Oscar Chapman as second assistant secretary. It was a hard-working team that Ickes felt would accomplish far more than his previous one had. He could, he felt, work with them all and be reasonably sure of their loyalty.

In May the former director of the Park Service, Horace Albright, wrote Ickes a congratulatory letter, calling the Slattery and Burlew appointments "magnificent." He added:

> It seems to me that now you are in a position to overcome much of the Forest Service opposition to the Interior Department on two grounds: first, that you will not recognize men who have been in the Government in high places in previous Republican administrations; and, second, that appointments in the Interior Department in high places are made as matters

of political preferment. I know that . . . there was much genuine fear in the Forest Service and Biological Survey that if they should be transferred to . . . Interior . . . they would be replaced by outsiders, and probably politicians.[31]

THE STRUGGLE TO MAKE personnel changes at the top of his department was but one activity that occupied Ickes well into 1938. He also tried to effect a few changes in the behavior of some of the agencies under his jurisdiction. The National Park Service and the Grazing Service again came under Ickes's scrutiny, each for somewhat different reasons, but with the same general objective: to strengthen his department in preparation for its becoming, finally, the premier conservation department of the federal government.

In the 1930s a number of efforts were underway both to enlarge the country's national park system and to create new types of park experiences. Certain areas were designated "wilderness" for the true nature lover, and scenic parkways were constructed for the motoring public. Both the president and Harold Ickes worked hard on behalf of the Park Service during the New Deal years; they were two of the best friends the agency ever had. But Ickes felt that the Park Service, under Arno Cammerer's leadership, could push a bit harder. So he tried to light a fire under it, and Cammerer, whenever he could.

On August 26, 1937, the secretary wrote Cammerer a curt letter asking him to explain the delays in calling for bids on the North Carolina link of the Blue Ridge Parkway. Authorized by Congress in 1933, and enthusiastically supported by FDR and Ickes, the Blue Ridge Parkway proposed to link the Shenandoah and Great Smoky Mountains national parks with a spectacularly scenic 470-mile road. However the plan engendered a bitter political battle between North Carolina and Tennessee over alternative routes. North Carolina won, in part due to some effective lobbying by Roosevelt's former boss, Navy Secretary Josephus Daniels. In the summer of 1937 Ickes wanted construction to start before the lobby for the Tennessee route made another attack so he told Cammerer: "I have tried to make it emphatically clear to the National Park Service that I wanted such sections of this parkway completed in North Carolina as would settle once and for all the question."[32]

In January 1938 another brief memo went from the secretary's desk to Cammerer's: "Has anything ever been done to bring in the Quetico

National Forest as a national park? What would you advise?" [33] Not long afterwards, Ickes held a meeting with the top staff of the agency and told them that he thought the Park Service organization was "soft in spots. . . . I especially criticized it," Ickes wrote after the meeting, "because there was no one in the Washington office who has ever had any actual experience in the field. I told them that I wanted this system changed." [34]

In fact, the organizational model Ickes had in mind for the Park Service to emulate was the Forest Service. As the agency's first chief, Gifford Pinchot instituted a rotational system for personnel and he insisted on recruitment to executive posts from within the agency. Foresters were expected to gain field experience in their early years with the agency and have the opportunity to work themselves up to executive positions in Washington if they desired. It was a system that would work very well for some eighty years, a period during which the Forest Service enjoyed the reputation of being one of the most powerful and professional of all federal organizations. However, policies imposed on the agency in the 1980s by the Reagan administration significantly altered the agency's positive image.

In the midst of the battle over FDR's reorganization bill, an exasperated Ickes sent yet another memo to the Park Service director. The April 1938 memo asked Cammerer, rhetorically, if any good had come from the attendance of Park Service officials at the annual meetings of the Izaak Walton League. Ickes could see none, given the league's position on the Forestry transfer: "I question the advisability of our representatives attending merely in the role of spectators of a Forest Service holiday." [35] In other words, as Ickes might have put it, Get out there and do some lobbying like the Forest Service, goddamn it!

Despite the Park Service's timidity on some issues, several substantial victories were made in expanding the park system. After a two-year fight, with the Forest Service and the timber industry in the Pacific Northwest on the one side, and the Park Service, numerous conservation organizations, Ickes, and FDR on the other, Congress passed the Olympic National Park bill on June 29, 1938. The new park incorporated Mt. Olympus National Monument and transferred jurisdiction of some majestic old-growth acreage from the Forest Service to the Park Service. A popular recreation area, the Chesapeake and Ohio Canal that ran from the District of Columbia into Maryland, also became a national park in 1938. Finally that year battles over establishing new parks in California—to save some of the remaining stands of magnificent sequoias and sugar pines from multiple-use management—began in earnest. All in all, the Park Service was not doing badly, and Ickes's pestering helped to produce results.

Harold Ickes's watchful eye also focused on the Grazing Service in 1938, an agency created by the Taylor Grazing Act some four years earlier. His effort to shake up that agency had to do with the continuing battle to pass the reorganization legislation. Some of the Grazing Service's most vociferous critics happened to be officials of the Agriculture Department, and in particular Forest Service personnel. The two agencies, the Forest Service and the Grazing Service, had overlapping functions, leasing some of the lands under their jurisdictions to cattle and sheep ranchers. But the Forest Service claimed that it had the better permit system, in that it charged stockmen a fairer market value for the privilege of having their animals roam the public lands.

On March 15, 1938 (Ickes's sixty-fourth birthday), the secretary sent a memo to the director of the investigations division. It read:

> I want a complete investigation made of the Grazing Administration with a view to determining—
> (1) Whether a fair deal is being given to the small stockman;
> (2) Whether there has been any discrimination against the small stockman; and
> (3) How many small stockmen there are compared with big stockmen?[36]

The previous year Ickes set up an Advisory Committee on Grazing in order to "keep a closer watch and a better control over the Grazing Division." In 1938 he was at it again, but the Grazing Service proved difficult to rein in. In May, therefore, Ickes decided he had had it with his Grazing Service director. He asked Chief Forester Silcox to find a Forest Service man to replace Carpenter. "I don't want a stockman again," he flatly stated.[37]

"Black Friday" for Harold Ickes occurred on April 8, 1938. After narrowly passing the Senate by a five-vote margin, the president's reorganization bill was defeated by a mere eight votes in the House of Representatives. Dashed again were his hopes for a reconstituted department, despite everything he'd done over the previous months to realize the dream. In his diary Ickes wrote, "The defeat of this bill was a severe blow to me because I had been hoping that, under whatever name, I would have a real Department of Conservation. I had an extremely bad night after Burlew telephoned me that it had been defeated and I got up yesterday feeling tired and bedraggled, but fighting mad." [38]

He then called Missy Le Hand and asked for ten minutes with the president to discuss the defeat. She was able to get him in to the Oval Office around noon on Saturday, and Ickes blasted away:

> I have never talked to him as I did yesterday. I hit him with words, telling him that he couldn't accept such a defeat; that if he did this Administration was through. I begged him to go along with the fight. . . . And then I said: Mr. President, if I were you I would call a special meeting of my Cabinet. I would say to them: "God damn you, I am not going to be satisfied with lip service with respect to this bill. I want every one of you to get out and line up every vote you can. We have got to win this fight. Henry Wallace (and here I shook a vigorous admonitory finger at an imaginary Henry Wallace), how about your farmer votes?"

But Roosevelt did not share Ickes's anguish. After listening to the secretary's harangue, the president told him that "the most pressing matter now is a measure to bring about economic recovery." Roosevelt, unlike Ickes, felt that he had no choice but to table for the time being the contentious reorganization issue. However, he helped to calm Ickes down by signing off on a list of 222 PWA projects at the very moment that the reorganization bill was being voted down in the House.

IT WAS GOOD that Harold Ickes had something grand to look forward to, and that was his marriage to Jane. Shortly after suffering the defeat on the reorganization bill, and with Harry Slattery's appointment still hanging, Ickes prepared to sail on the *Normandie* for England. His ultimate destination was Dublin, Ireland, where his lovely Jane was awaiting him with their marriage license in her purse.

Harold worked until the very moment of departure. Keeping everything as secret as possible, he flew to New York on May 18 and boarded ship under the assumed name of John L. Williams (a deceased cousin). Ickes felt that there would be an avalanche of adverse publicity due to the forty-year age difference and so he told only a handful of people about the arrangements. But shortly before leaving, he did confide in FDR about his impending marriage. He was, Ickes noted, "perfectly fine about the whole thing." [39] Roosevelt observed that his own father was almost 60 years old when he married his mother, who was a young woman, "and that it did not matter if I was over sixty." Although Ickes was pleased with the president's response nevertheless he noted that "generally speaking, the feeling [among family and friends] is not one of approval."

Arriving late in Southampton because of foggy conditions, Harold had to make a beeline to catch the boat train for Liverpool, which he boarded with less than five minutes to spare. From Liverpool he caught another boat that took him across the Irish Sea and deposited him in Dublin at 6 A.M. on May 24. If there were any doubts about his physical stamina at age 64, they were dispelled by his getting to the Adelaide Street Presbyterian Church on time. Jane met him when he arrived, and the couple was married at 9 A.M. the same day, by Rev. R. K. Hanna.

It was a simple ceremony, he wrote: "There were only three witnesses present, in addition to the minister, the organist, and the sexton. Dr. Hanna did not know whom he was marrying and continued in ignorance until the newspaper correspondents descended on him late that afternoon."

The young and attractive Jane Dahlman was now Mrs. Harold Ickes, and Harold undoubtedly was as happy as he had ever been in his life. The couple proceeded on a storybook honeymoon that took them to County Cork, London, and Paris, before they sailed back to the United States aboard the *Ile de France* on June 15.

The couple was treated royally in both London and Paris. Joseph Kennedy, the ambassador to Great Britain, "was most cordial and hospitable," Ickes related, even though Kennedy probably was aware of Ickes's low opinion of him. (When FDR had appointed Kennedy head of the Securities and Exchange Commission, Ickes expressed his displeasure at having a "typical Stock Market plunger" in the position.) On their second night in London they were invited to dinner at the American embassy, after which they attended a Toscanini concert. A few days later, Kennedy invited them to the "big Embassy dinner for this social season . . . in honor of the Duke and Duchess of Kent."

Harold thought that Jane looked "stunning" in her new evening gown and Chinese jacket as the couple sat down to a formal dinner with some of the most famous people in America and Europe. Among those present, Ickes noted, were Prime Minister and Mrs. Neville Chamberlain, the Belgian Ambassador, Viscount and Viscountess Astor, Mr. and Mrs. Winston Churchill, Mr. and Mrs. John D. Rockefeller Jr., Mr. Arthur Sulzberger of the *New York Times,* and Joseph Kennedy's 21-year-old son, Jack.

While Jane retired to the drawing room after dinner with the ladies, Harold was introduced to England's prime minister. Ickes said that he asked Chamberlain what he thought about his government's refusal to sell helium to Germany. "The Prime Minister was guarded in his remarks," Ickes said, "but it was clear that he . . . approved of our action in not selling this helium to Germany."

Harold Ickes also met Winston Churchill for the first time at the embassy dinner, and his initial impression of this man of destiny was not particularly flattering: "He is a dumpy-looking person with decidedly bowed shoulders but with a very alert expression," Ickes wrote.

After a week touring London and the English countryside, Jane and Harold flew to Paris. Harold's good friend and the ambassador to France, William Bullitt, met the couple at the airport. He whisked them away to his leased chateau in Chantilly. They spent one night at this "perfectly charming old chateau . . . that is situated in ten thousand acres of woods with beautiful streams," and from this fairy-tale setting the honeymooning couple was driven to Paris. Bullitt had selected the Hôtel de France et Choiseul on the fashionable Rue St. Honoré for their quarters. It turned out to be more than adequate, and with much lower room rates, Ickes pleasantly observed, than he had to pay in London.

Harold Ickes loved good cuisine and during their ten "delightful" days in the city of lights the couple gorged themselves on wonderful French food. "We were so charmed with Paris that we just lived in it without doing too much sightseeing," Ickes wrote.

As Joseph Kennedy had done in London, Ambassador Bullitt invited the Ickeses to an embassy dinner given on June 8 in honor of the president of the French Senate. Harold and Jane again found themselves in the company of a number of distinguished Europeans and Americans. Among those attending this gala were Le General and Mme. Gamelin, Sen. and Mrs. Henry Downe, M. and Mme. Camille Chautemps, S.E.M. and Mme. Henry Berenger, and Ickes's cabinet colleague, Frances Perkins, who happened to be in Paris at the time.

The three weeks the couple spent in London and Paris were personally delightful, but Ickes also learned a lot about the tense European situation first-hand from his conversations with the American ambassadors and others. Joseph Kennedy remarked that he thought all "hell might break loose at any time over Czechoslovakia." In March 1938 Hitler had annexed Austria, and it looked as though his next move would be against the Czechs. Chamberlain, however, continued to follow his policy of appeasement, a policy that Kennedy supported.

In Paris, Ickes found Bill Bullitt "even more jittery over the European situation than was Kennedy." Bullitt thought that a catastrophic war in Europe was "inevitable sooner or later," and he envisioned, at the war's end, a Europe completely and totally in ruins. His one hope, Ickes remarked, was that the United States stay out of the war "so as to be in a position to assume the burden of rebuilding what this war will have left of Western civilization."

Bullitt, like Kennedy, adhered to isolationism during this critical period. Although Ickes respected Bullitt's opinions, if not Kennedy's, he was inclined toward a more aggressive stance toward Germany's expansionism. However, none of the opinions of these three men really mattered. Reflecting public opinion, the governments of England, France, and the United States were overwhelmingly committed in that fateful year of 1938 to avoiding another war with Germany.

On June 15 Harold boarded the *Ile de France* at Le Havre with his bride, and the couple sailed back to the United States. They ran the gauntlet of reporters and photographers both in New York and in Washington. On the whole, Ickes was pleased with the press they received. "The newspapers have really been quite decent and I think that their pictures and stories have conveyed . . . a very favorable impression of Jane." Certainly that was his own impression of his new bride: "I have thanked God more than once that I had not married a flapper or a flibbertigibbet," he wrote. "Jane is young but she is not immature. Both of us since our marriage have been perfectly sure that we did the right thing. There has not been so much as a flyspeck to mar our happiness."

Harold's delight with his wife knew no bounds. He wrote his sister Mary on June 27 to tell her how happy he was. "In brave caveman fashion I have dragged my red-headed bride into my habitat at Headwaters Farm and now I am ready to exhibit her to all comers and so receive the acclamations on my judgment and taste that I am entitled to."[40] Perhaps his blatant sexism can be excused by later generations in light of the many years of misery he had endured until he found Jane.

CHAPTER 16

"TO SAIL, NOT DRIFT"

THE CHALLENGE

OF 1938

THE PIVOTAL YEAR of 1938 increasingly defined itself in terms of polarization. Both at home and abroad an angry spirit of divisiveness threatened to destroy the hard-won gains made by liberal democratic leadership against the Great Depression. That year the House of Representatives set up its committee to investigate un-American activities and it appointed the Democrat from Texas, Martin Dies, to chair the committee. The journalist David Brinkley once described Dies as "one of the great buffoons of his time," while Harold Ickes noted with a sigh of resignation that the newly created "Dies Committee . . . is on one of the periodic Red hunts that Congress is addicted to." [1]

The situation in Europe, however, caused the greatest concern. The "rape of Austria," as Ickes put it, was only the first of Hitler's moves. The dismemberment of Czechoslovakia a few months later produced a wave of fear throughout the world that had not been matched since the Great War. Europe was disintegrating. Its democracies appeared frail, headed as they were by a cadre of "clammy conservatives."[2] But isolationist sentiment in the United States also overwhelmed the few voices that dared call for firmer action against the Fascists. Once the appeasement policy of England's Neville Chamberlain and France's Edouard Daladier became evident, a historic opportunity to avert a cataclysmic war was lost—if it could have been averted at all. By September it was clear that there was little of substance that America's president could do to alter events in Europe. Roosevelt became, in Frank Freidel's words, a "powerless witness to Munich." It was not a position with which he was ever comfortable, and as soon as he could he broke out of it, but the fact remains that FDR's influence in European affairs in 1938 was largely symbolic.

Although Roosevelt and his administration were stymied in foreign policy during most of 1938, there was much they could do domestically. The economic recession that began in the fall of 1937 grew worse in 1938. At the outset of the new year, "many Americans once more neared starvation. In Chicago, children salvaged food from garbage cans; in Cleveland, families scrambled for spoiled produce dumped in the streets when the markets closed."[3] With unemployment approaching 11 percent, and serious labor unrest occurring in many parts of the country, Roosevelt was forced to fall back again on pump-priming and other emergency measures. In a Fireside address delivered on April 14, 1938, the president described at length what he was planning to do with Congress's help. "To abandon our purpose of building a greater, a more stable, and a more tolerant America, would be to miss the tide and perhaps to miss the port. I propose to sail ahead," FDR said. "For to reach a port, we must sail—sail, not lie at anchor—sail, not drift."

At the same time as he addressed the nation, the president sent to Congress a massive emergency relief bill. Ickes's PWA, and Hopkins's WPA, which just a year earlier had begun winding down, again became the principal organizational weapons used to rout the "Roosevelt Recession." The president's long-range plans were to reorganize the whole public works/welfare tangle of organizations, but the recession forced him to put that idea on the back burner and for the time being work through the existing agencies. Harold Ickes was pleased that his PWA was getting a new lease on life. It came at a time when he was still smarting from the reorganization defeat. In fact, less than a week after he barged into the White House to tell FDR in very blunt language that he must continue that fight with Congress and with members of his own administration, he learned that FDR was thinking about a reorganized public works program. Ickes wrote that over lunch with the president he "asked him how the program would be administered and he said he had not made up his mind. In any event he will want to use the present PWA organization but his mind is turning to a corporation." Ickes leapt at the prospect: "I told him that we could incorporate." [4]

Afterwards Ickes confided to his diary that "I intend to make a fight for the retention of this new PWA program. With little prospect remaining for the satisfaction of my ambition to head a real Department of Conservation, I see no reason why I should give up PWA without a struggle." [5] Another reason for not wanting to give up the PWA was that he admitted that he had derived a greater sense of accomplishment from that title in his seven years in Washington than from being Interior secretary. It appealed both to his pragmatic nature and architectural inclinations.

While Ickes was abroad for his marriage, Congress debated and passed, on June 21, 1938, the PWA Extension Act. The statute set up rigorous deadlines for Ickes's agency. First, all applications for PWA-sponsored projects had to be into the hands of agency officials by September 30. Then, their review had to be sufficiently telescoped so that project construction began no later than January 1, 1939. Finally, the public works projects embarked upon under this authority had to be completed by July 1, 1940. [6] The legislators thus recognized the necessity of responding to the current harsh economic conditions with additional government spending, but they also spelled out a definite conclusion to the program. It was acknowledged that a permanent federal work relief program was unacceptable, at least as it was conceived in the midst of the extraordinary conditions of the 1930s.

On his return from his honeymoon, Ickes jumped back into his administrator of public works role. Roosevelt had just approved a list of some 2,000 PWA projects so, as Ickes wrote, "as soon as I got back to the office I began to gather up the threads so far as PWA is concerned and I find that we are in good shape. My only fear has been that within the limitations imposed by the law we would not be able to get out all of our money. However, it begins to look as if this fear is a groundless one." [7]

From the end of June to the end of July Ickes's organization spent money at a record pace, belying his reputation as "cautious and conservative" Harold. On July 27, Ickes reported to the president that a total of 3,816 new projects for permanent public improvements had been approved by his agency, involving approximately $1 billion of construction-related activities. Moreover, he said, additional applications from every part of the country were streaming into the offices daily.[8] Clearly, the program remained very popular with states and localities, whose public officials found in these projects a satisfying alternative to having their citizens rummaging through garbage cans in search of a daily meal.

Public works spending proceeded at this pace until the congressionally mandated deadline of September 30. Roosevelt held a press conference at Hyde Park on October 7 to announce that he recently authorized PWA allotments for the construction of 113 additional sewage disposal projects, thus pumping some $19.5 million into local economies around the country. The president was particularly proud of the New Deal's record in the area of pollution abatement. He pointed out to the press that never before had the federal government taken such an active interest in water quality: "Since 1933 PWA loans, not counting what WPA has done, [which] I approved have carried through approximately 500 sewage disposal plants at a total construction cost of over a billion and a quarter of dollars in five years. That is pretty good."[9]

On the eve of Congress's January 1, 1939, deadline to have all construction begun, Ickes wrote FDR a detailed letter announcing that the PWA program was on schedule. In six short months the "PWA has put a $1,574,769,686 program completely under contract. It has achieved the purposes intended by Congress. It has aided in building up employment in private industry. Its progress has been accompanied by a constantly accelerated recovery in business and industry." All totaled, the agency processed some 7,853 projects under the 1938 Extension Act, with the full economic effects to be realized in the coming year.[10]

Like the president, Ickes felt that he had reason to be proud of this accomplishment. He added a caveat, however: "Our economic framework is so complex that no single agency carrying out its share of your national program can accurately estimate its contribution to the recovery that is now so obvious. Nevertheless, there is sufficient evidence to warrant the claim that the Public Works program has made a substantial contribution."[11] He concluded his letter by noting that a substantial backlog of worthwhile projects existed, should Congress or the president find it necessary to prime the pump in the future. Everyone hoped not.

WITH HIS PWA functioning smoothly—"I am holding two or three staff conferences a week in order to keep steam up in my PWA boiler," he wrote on July 23—Harold Ickes turned his attention to politics and a vacation in the congressional election year. As 1938 wore on, the midterm elections began to look suspiciously like a referendum on the entire Roosevelt recovery program. The president himself decided to define the Democratic Party's primary elections in that manner, as he sought to purge the Democratic Party of some of its anti-New Deal members. A number of his aides, Ickes among them, thus took to the campaign trail that summer and fall to publicize the New Deal and to speak out on behalf of liberal candidates.

At the end of July Harold and Jane left Washington for a month-long trip to the Pacific Northwest and to Alaska. Their itinerary took them by train to Chicago, then through North Dakota and across Montana for a brief stop at Glacier National Park. In the small ranching community of Shelby, just to the east of the park, Secretary and Mrs. Ickes were met by Congressman Jerry O'Connell and Fred Martin, secretary of the Montana Council for Progressive Political Action.

"O'Connell had won out in a hard-fought primary contest," Ickes wrote. "He is very anxious for me to make a speech in his district before election day. Senator Wheeler is bitterly opposed to him and O'Connell has frankly accepted the Wheeler issue. . . . O'Connell anticipates that Wheeler will do everything he can to help his [O'Connell's] Republican opponent, and this is probably true." The secretary told O'Connell that what he could do for him would be determined by the president, and if he could, he "would be glad to return to Montana later in the year for a speech."[12]

Boarding the train at Shelby to accompany the Ickeses to Glacier Park were the president of the transportation concession for the park and a "fine-looking" representative of the Blackfoot Indian Tribe. On the short trip to East Glacier the two men lobbied the secretary on behalf of establishing two Indian museums, one at Browning, some twenty miles east of the park, and one at Two Medicine Lake in the park. Ickes wasted no time, he said, in wiring back to Washington to see whether these museums could be put through as a PWA project. He added, "I will try to interest the President when I return to Washington." The Museum of the Plains Indians at Browning was built with PWA funds. Its construction began shortly after Ickes's trip.

At Glacier Park the secretary and his wife were met by a delegation of Blackfeet Indians, and Jane was made an honorary member of the tribe under the name Princess Mountain Bird Woman. Four years earlier the secretary had been designated a member of the Blackfeet and given the name Big Bear. But the Ickeses were met not only by a delegation of Indians at Glacier Park but by the powerful senior senator from the Big Sky state. "To my surprise Senator Wheeler was at the station. He didn't say anything to me of a political nature, but he did some complaining to Jane about Jerry O'Connell's proclaiming during the primary fight that the President had told him to go out and lick Wheeler. Wheeler must know that I am with the President in the political line-up," Ickes wrote, adding that Wheeler "has a very bitter tongue but for some reason he has never turned it against me."

After their brief stop at Glacier to take in the beauty of nature and the nastiness of the primaries, the Ickeses headed for Seattle. They were met by the president's daughter, Anna, and her husband, John Boettiger. A genuine friendship between the Ickeses and the Boettigers began developing when, shortly after Harold and Jane returned from their European honeymoon, the Boettigers dropped in to chat with Ickes at his office. It appeared to be an impromptu visit, Ickes believed, since he didn't know them very well. Moreover, John Boettiger had worked for Colonel McCormick's *Chicago Tribune* before taking over the publishing job for the Hearst-owned *Seattle Post Intelligencer,* and Ickes's rows with both those newspaper magnates were well known. Boettiger, when he still worked for the *Tribune,* had interviewed Ickes about his financial dealings. Nevertheless, the Boettigers were extremely friendly during their visit in June and suggested that the Ickeses visit them on their trip to the Pacific Northwest later that summer.

The foursome got along well. They did some sightseeing in the Seattle area, which included an aerial tour of the recently acquired Olympic National Park. The Interior secretary observed that "it did not require more than a superficial glance to determine that these mountains should be in a national park where they could be preserved for all time." Harold and Jane also attended a political speech that Anna

Roosevelt Boettiger made before a group of Seattle "builders and representatives of labor, banking, and business; she did very well indeed," Ickes said. "She is a delightful person—simple and unaffected but interesting and attractive. She and Jane seemed to fall for each other from the very start."

After spending a few enjoyable days with the Boettigers on the Olympic Peninsula, the Ickeses left for Ketchikan, Alaska, aboard the *Mt. McKinley*. Neither Harold nor Jane had been to Alaska, so the trip served to give the Interior secretary and his wife some first-hand knowledge of America's last frontier—and also some understanding of what federal officials were and were not doing in this distant northern outpost.

Much of what Ickes saw in the Alaskan territory he did not like. He had several objectives in mind in visiting Alaska: He wanted to look over the controversial Matanuska resettlement project before accepting Harry Hopkins's "generous" offer to transfer responsibility for this political hot potato from the WPA to the Interior Department. He also wanted to check up on what the Indian Bureau was doing for the Alaskan tribes. In addition, he hoped to get some ideas for national park expansion in this vast resource-rich region.

But he recognized at once that before anything of enduring value could be accomplished in Alaska, the settlers had to give up the "wrong psychology" of the mining camp. He wrote:

> The chief drawback to Alaska . . . is that the people here, generally speaking, think of everything in terms of mining, and those of us who do not live in Alaska think of mining too when we think of this Territory. Mining is more or less a gamble . . . , and a gambling spirit does not make for the building up of a normal American community with a background of agriculture or industry. . . . Alaska has reached the point . . . where it ought to build up its agricultural, forest, and other stable resources for the long pull. . . . I have taken occasion to talk along these lines to people whom I have met here. I have told them that their psychology is wrong. I very much doubt whether they have understood what I was talking about.

The Matanuska project, outside of Anchorage, was one of the New Deal's attempts to do what Ickes was talking about. It was an effort at grafting the stable and productive society of the family farmer onto the boom-and-bust activity of the prospector. The Ickeses visited it in August, and what the secretary saw in the Matanuska Valley was an attempt at farming that hadn't lived up to its potential. It was definitely a fertile area, one which "ought to be a very prosperous section of Alaska," but it was just as obvious to Ickes that it had been mismanaged. The $4.5 million of taxpayers' money thus far expended on the colony involved a lot of waste, Ickes saw. For one thing, the barns on the forty-acre tracts given to each settler were far too large. They looked "big enough to take care of a farm of one hundred and fifty acres," Ickes surmised.

But the biggest problem with the Matanuska project was

> due to the fact that poor judgment has been used in selecting settlers. When this project was first discussed . . . in my office, I insisted that settlers ought to be selected on the basis of their farm experience. . . . I thought, and I said, that Scandinavians and other hardy, industrious, and self-respecting people were the kind of stock that should be sent into the Matanuska Valley. Apparently some communities saw a chance to get rid of their ne'er-do-wells and the sentimental social-service people in charge of selecting the settlers allowed their sentimentality to run away with their judgment. . . . Almost fifty per cent of the original lot have had to be sent back.

Despite its several problems Ickes felt that he could whip the colony into shape. "I am willing to accept it [from Hopkins] but only on certain conditions," he wrote after his visit. "I will want all outstanding expenditures taken care of and I will want an over-all sum of . . . $350,000 to put the colony firmly on its feet. I will want the right to weed out the drones and replace them with men and women who are willing to work when they have such a fine opportunity."

Nothing he saw in Alaska disturbed him more, however, than the plight of some of the Native peoples, peoples whose well-being very much depended upon the performance of the Interior Department's Indian Bureau. While the Indians living around Ketchikan seemed to him to be doing reasonably well, Ickes admitted to becoming "very depressed" when he visited the Hooniah village further to the north, home to members of the Thlinget tribe. "It was ramshackle, squalid, dirty, and apparently poverty stricken," he observed. Tuberculosis was rampant; so was alcoholism, thanks to some white traders who dominated the economic life of the village and who supplied the Indians with liquor, "the worst possible thing for people who are tubercular."

Moreover, Ickes was displeased with the local Indian Bureau official. Although Hooniah had a new school building for the Thlinget children, Ickes's brief tour revealed that it was "dirty and disorderly," and had flammable materials stored in the basement. "I do not see how our man in Hooniah could expect to impress his Indian charges with the importance of cleanliness and order when he permitted his school building to fall into such a state as this one was in," Ickes wrote. He immediately alerted the head of Alaska's Indian Bureau to the conditions in Hooniah, and sent a radiogram to Bureau Director John Collier in Washington. "This Indian situation . . . needs immediate and forceful attention," Ickes said. "Collier has never been in Alaska and I am sure that he can do something about it if he comes."

Although Secretary Ickes found plenty to complain about on his trip to Alaska, he was pleasantly surprised, toward the end of his week's visit, when he toured Glacier Bay with a Forest Service officer named Heintzleman. This official actually proposed that the existing national monument be turned into a national park by adding adjacent national forest land to it. Ickes was delighted to find at least one forester with the proper perspective, that is, his. "Since it [the park] would be extended at the expense of the Forest Service, his attitude in the matter is all the more noteworthy and praiseworthy," he wrote. It took over forty years, but when Pres. Jimmy Carter signed the legislation on December 1, 1980, the idea of Glacier Bay National Park was realized.

The Ickeses returned to Seattle on August 23. Before leaving for Washington the secretary worked in a speaking engagement in Tacoma on behalf of its congressman, John Coffee. "Coffee is one of our liberals in Congress and we do not want to lose him," Ickes said. In his extemporaneous speech the secretary took a few jabs at the Dies Committee which, Ickes learned, was busy investigating child star Shirley Temple for "Red" affiliations. "In general," Ickes wrote, "I made a New Deal speech, putting in some boosts for Coffee at intervals, and there is no doubt that the speech went over well."

Ickes was back in Washington at the end of August, at about the same time that FDR returned from his latest fishing trip off the coast of Florida. It was the height of primary season, and much of the conversation and activity in Washington concerned who was knocking off whom. Roosevelt made a stand for his New Deal in many of the Democratic primary races, and he called on a number of his aides to help him out. Harry Hopkins, who, Ickes observed, was closer to the president than he'd ever been, was "up to his neck in the President's effort to defeat some of the Democratic candidates."[13]

The administration made a special effort at unseating Maryland's

Sen. Millard Tydings (who had been such a bane to Ickes's existence), and one of New York City's congressmen, John O'Connor. The president himself campaigned over Labor Day for Tydings's opponent, the liberal congressman David Lewis. When Tydings overwhelmed Lewis by 60,000 votes Ickes fretted that "the candidates opposed by the President in the various Democratic primaries continue to win." In Georgia, Roosevelt's candidate ran a poor third against his primary opponents, Walter George and the state's former governor, Eugene Talmadge. Ickes disliked both men, but he had especially nasty words to say about Talmadge. He, Ickes wrote, "looks more like a rat than any other human being that I know and he has all of the mean, poisonous, and treacherous characteristics of that rodent." Ickes found the Georgia defeat unsettling, too. By the middle of September Ickes hoped that at least the administration could unseat the powerful chairman of the House Rules Committee, New York's John O'Connor, who had been instrumental in bottling up a number of liberal bills during the previous session.

The defeats in Maryland and Georgia notwithstanding, Ickes admired Roosevelt's audacity. Once again the president proposed to sail and not drift. "I think the fight that the President has been making was necessary and proper," Ickes wrote on September 15. "After all, we do not want to go into 1940 without the issue having been drawn between the New Deal and the Old Deal in the Democratic party. It has been a courageous course for the president to pursue. With only two years more until the end of his term, he could simply have stood by and let nature take its course."

At least one primary turned out well for the New Dealers. With Tom Corcoran leading the charge against his own cousin, O'Connor went down in defeat. However, O'Connor had run in both the Republican and Democratic primaries, and he proceeded to win the Republican nomination. Such a bizarre outcome reflected what the purge was all about: FDR hoped to "remake the Democratic party in his own image." [14] Conservatives such as O'Connor thus were being forced into the Republican camp. Ickes was delighted with O'Connor's loss and noted that, even if he were to win the November general election as a Republican, "he will lose his place as Chairman of the Rules Committee. I think this victory in total effect offsets the defeats that the Administration suffered in South Carolina, Georgia, and Maryland." [15]

Three weeks prior to the November general elections Roosevelt sent his Interior secretary on another trip to the West Coast to show-case the New Deal and campaign for liberal candidates. With Jane ac-companying him, Ickes headed for California. They made a brief stop in St. Louis to speak at the dedication ceremony of a state park, and another in Reno to speak before the Reclamation Association.

They arrived in San Francisco on October 13 and spent a few days relaxing at the fashionable Mark Hopkins Hotel before departing for Southern California. On October 17 Ickes dedicated a PWA power plant at Brawley, in California's Imperial Valley. The next day he was present for the historic moment when Colorado River water began flowing into cement channels bound for Los Angeles to the west and the scorching Arizona desert to the east. "Here [at the Imperial Dam]," Ickes wrote,

> everything was set to press the buttons that would start the water into the irrigation ditches of this project. These ditches are the biggest that have ever been built. . . . I pressed the button that let the water into the canal on the California side . . . and Jane pressed the button that let the first water into the canal serving the Arizona side.[16]

After parting the waters at the Imperial Dam, the Ickeses headed for Los Angeles to meet some of Hollywood's most famous personages. His host, Philip Dunne, took the secretary to lunch at Twentieth Century–Fox Studios before his scheduled afternoon address to the Hollywood Council for Democracy. The secretary was placed be-tween Darryl Zanuck, whom he characterized as "a hard-boiled, ag-gressive, thirty-eight year-old man," and Louis B. Mayer, "one of the big producers." Other celebrities in attendance included Sam Katz, Melvyn Douglas, John Ford, Frank Tuttle, Adolph Zukor, and Hal Wallis. Ickes spoke only briefly at the luncheon before going off to the main show at the Shriners' Auditorium.

Ickes addressed a huge crowd of 5,000 people who, he noted with surprise, actually paid money to hear someone make a political speech. But that was Hollywood. Along with the secretary on the speakers' platform were two California congressmen and Culbert Olson, the lib-eral Democratic candidate for governor. Ickes observed that Olson seemed very popular and was in the lead in his race, but that the liberal candidate for U.S. senator, Sheridan Downey, was having a rough fight. "From all appearances his declaration for $30 a week for every-one in California has reacted to his disadvantage," Ickes wrote.

It was in San Francisco, however, before the elite Commonwealth

Club, where Ickes intended to give his most important speech of the trip. The audience was conservative businessmen and so the secretary chose to speak principally about broad economic issues in a speech titled "Sixty Families Revisited." Reiterating many of the points he had made in a previous, highly controversial speech, Ickes changed the tone to one that was more low-key. He wanted, he said, to impress his audience with the dangers inherent in the current inequitable distribution of wealth in America, and he hoped to accomplish this by not igniting the usual fireworks that characterized an Ickes speech. The secretary quoted Alexis de Tocqueville, Daniel Webster, and Andrew Jackson on the concentration of wealth and its danger to democracy. He cited statistics:

> A recent report by the National Resources Committee revealed that there are 12,482,871 families . . . in this country with incomes of less than $750 a year. That is less than $15 per week per *family*. The total of the income of those 12½ million families was a little under $5,700,000,000. The same report shows that there were a top 178,058 families . . . whose total income is a little over $5,800,000,000.
>
> The disparity may be seen even more vividly in the figures . . . which show that there were 327 families . . . with incomes above $500,000. The total of their income was slightly less than $300,000,000. There were 2,123,534 families . . . with incomes of less than $250, and the total of their income was likewise slightly less than . . . $300,000,000. That is, approximately 300 families on the one side and approximately 2,000,000 families on the other received the same total share of our wealth.[17]

He concluded with a warning: "The disparity in that situation, gentlemen of the Commonwealth Club, must be corrected, if not as a matter of justice, then as a matter of common sense. It must be corrected, if for no better reason, than to prevent those highest bracket people from destroying themselves and ourselves along with them."

Harold and Jane returned to Washington from their marathon West Coast trip just in time to hear the election returns on November 8. As the results rolled in for the congressional and gubernatorial races, the question everybody was asking was, "Did this mean a repudiation of Roosevelt and the New Deal?" The Republicans made substantial gains in the elections: the Democrats' huge majority in the House of Representatives plunged from 322 to 262, a sixty-member swing. Staunch New Dealers, such as Texas's Maury Maverick, had been knocked off in the primaries. A number of people in the administration believed that Maverick's defeat was due to a stab in the back by his fellow Texan, Vice-President Garner. Garner was quite active in the 1938 elections because he intended to run for president in 1940. The more "Roosevelt New Dealers" who were defeated, the better it was for him.

The most serious defeat, Ickes thought, was Michigan's Gov. Frank Murphy. A former mayor of Detroit, Murphy had served as high commissioner to the Philippine Islands, and was governor of one of the most populous states in the country. He was also a devout Catholic who detested his fellow Catholic, the demagogic priest from Royal Oak, Father Coughlin. The combined attacks on Murphy by Father Coughlin and by the Dies Committee, which accused him of giving "aid and comfort to communists . . . in connection with the sit-down strikes [in Detroit]" undoubtedly hurt him a great deal, Ickes concluded. Roosevelt, too, was disturbed by Murphy's loss. But the next year he took the sting out of the defeat by appointing him attorney general. In 1940 Frank Murphy became a justice of the Supreme Court.

Ickes noted that, of course, the newspapers "hailed the [election] result as a serious setback for the President." Ickes himself "could not read in the returns any conclusive repudiation of the President or his policies. . . . To me, the result means that the voters are still independent and this I regard as a good thing." [18] As much as Ickes supported FDR and the New Deal, he still considered himself an "independent." He thus found comfort, he claimed, in election returns that indicated that voters had not allowed themselves to be manipulated, even by a president who remained personally very popular with them in 1938. [19]

If Roosevelt was either disappointed or worried about the elections, he didn't share those concerns with his cabinet. Throughout the fall, when partisan bickering at home was at its peak, and when events in Europe were proceeding from bad to worse, Ickes had been impressed with how well the president looked. He also admired the fact that FDR took in stride the defeat of most of his candidates. At the Friday cabinet meeting following the November election, the results were mentioned, and Ickes related that "the President remarked that he did not think it had done us any damage."

On that same Friday, Harold Ickes captured a few headlines when he discussed the election at his weekly press conference. The secretary told reporters that if the president had been a candidate, "he would have won easily because the people have no doubt as to his liberalism." [20] Ickes had said much the same thing back in July, but this time the press seized on it, he said, as proof that FDR intended to run for an unprecedented third term in 1940. Although Roosevelt certainly had not made up his mind as early as November 1938 to run for a third term, Ickes's offhand remark brought that issue to the forefront of public speculation. It remained there until the Democratic Party convened in Chicago in the summer of 1940.

Whether or not the 1938 elections were a repudiation of Roosevelt, they did mark a turning point. For all practical purposes, the New Deal had run its course, and the net result of the political equation between 1937 and 1939 was "stalemate." [21] While the days of precedent-shattering domestic policy initiatives were largely behind the New Dealers, defense of those reforms was not. Tremendous effort was expended at consolidating and maintaining what had been won.

Also by 1938 the president and his administrators found themselves increasingly turning their attention to the serious events abroad. The vacuum of power, on the side of the democracies, inexorably pulled them in. So did FDR's determination to sail, not drift.

"FRANCE AND ENGLAND are apparently willing to throw Czechoslovakia to the dogs," Ickes wrote on September 15, 1938. For two weeks everyone was on tenterhooks as heads of state scrambled to avert a war with Germany. President Roosevelt sent a first, then a second, communiqué to Hitler urging all the interested parties to sit down at a conference table to work out a peaceful solution to the Sudetenland. After receiving the first message, Hitler made a speech that was broadcast live throughout Europe and in the United States. Ickes said,

> I did not hear him, but, according to common opinion, he ranted and raved for over an hour. . . . He shrieked his defiance to the whole world, bragging of the prowess of Germany and its ability on the basis of its own resources not only to withstand any assault from without but to reach its objectives beyond its borders. . . . War seemed to be inevitable, with every tick of the clock bringing it closer.[22]

The day after Hitler's speech Roosevelt called a special meeting of the cabinet to discuss what to do. Ickes wrote that the president "had received a reply from Hitler to his communication. . . . This reply covered eighteen full pages and was truculent and unyielding in tone."

The president asked whether he should send one more message to Hitler urging him to convene a conference, and whether the United States should send someone to it as an unofficial observer. "This [latter suggestion] was promptly ruled out," Ickes noted, "because we all felt that the country would take exception to this as an effort on our part to mix into a foreign affair that did not concern us." After more discussion, the general feeling among cabinet members was that Roosevelt should make one more effort at talking reason to Hitler.

"The second note to Hitler was a masterpiece," Ickes wrote, adding that FDR also wrote to other European leaders urging negotiation. "Just what influenced Hitler I will not attempt to say, but the fact is that a few hours after receiving the President's message he announced that he had called a conference to meet in Munich the following day to which he had invited Mussolini, Chamberlain, and Daladier."

Ickes was doubtful as to whether these efforts would avert another European war, "Hitler being the maniac that he is," but he nonetheless wholeheartedly supported Roosevelt's efforts. During the September crisis he took some public works books over to the White House for the president's approval, and FDR spoke about the European situation, telling his Interior secretary that he wanted to avoid the mistake that President Wilson had made in 1914. "He felt that if Wilson had expressed himself vigorously then, war might have been averted. First Wilson wanted to wait to see what Russia would do, then what France would do, and then what England would do." Roosevelt said that when Wilson "finally expressed himself, he did not allow for the difference in time between Washington and Berlin, with the result that the German troops were already across the Belgium frontier."

Hitler's moves in the fall of 1938 not only drew Roosevelt into the sphere of active diplomacy, but they stiffened the president's resolve to strengthen the United States' military arsenal. After listening to the Fuehrer's Nuremburg speech on September 26, the president immediately dispatched Harry Hopkins to the West Coast to survey the aircraft industry with an eye to its expansion. "The President was sure that we were going to get into war and he believed that air power would win it," Hopkins wrote about his mission. "About this time the President made his startling statement that we should have 8000 planes and everybody in the Army and Navy and all the newspapers in the country jumped on him." [23]

The particular number of aircraft that FDR said America needed was not pulled out of the air. It was based on information that was being supplied to the president by, among others, his ambassador to France, William Bullitt. Bullitt shared those figures with the Ickeses over dinner at Headwaters Farm in December of 1938, some two months after FDR made his sensational statement. Bullitt told Harold and Jane about the enormous disparity in aircraft existing between England and France on the one hand and Germany and Italy on the other. Germany, Bullitt reported, had over 5,000 first-class planes and almost 4,000 second-class ones. Italy had a total of about 5,000. England and France together, he said, had only about 1,500 and most of these were in England. Ickes was shocked. "Of course," he wrote, "if these figures are anywhere near accurate, Chamberlain and Daladier had no option except to yield to Hitler's demands." [24]

War had been averted, temporarily, by the Munich conference. But the German nation-state shocked the civilized world again on November 9, 1938, when Germans took to the streets to express their virulent hatred for the Jews. Men and women of Jewish heritage throughout the country were beaten up, their businesses were ransacked after mobs shattered storefront windows, and synagogues were defaced and defiled during a night of rampage that came to be known as *Kristallnacht*. The next morning, reflected in the shattered glass strewn about Germany's streets and sidewalks was the awful face of anti-Semitism. The destruction of the European Jews had begun.

Harold and Jane Ickes were visiting Colonial Williamsburg with Mr. and Mrs. John D. Rockefeller Jr. when they learned about Germany's latest outrage. Ickes, naturally, was alarmed, but he was also disturbed by the indifference of his host. He wrote, "The news from . . . Europe was especially bad . . . and I felt a considerable degree of shock that Mr. Rockefeller seemed to be so little interested in grave world affairs and knew so little about them." However, Ickes continued, "I can overlook a lot in a man who has done the wonderful restoration job at Williamsburg and who has contributed so generously to public enterprises." Moreover, the secretary discovered a political ally in Mrs. Rockefeller. "She has a deep sympathy for Negroes and Jews and other underprivileged people who do not get a fair chance in life. She feels very strongly on the German situation." [25]

While many Americans and even Europeans tried, like Rockefeller, to ignore the unfolding tragedy in Germany, Harold Ickes could not. Through most of 1938 he kept a low profile in matters of foreign policy, largely because it wasn't his domain and because he didn't want to further aggravate his colleague, Secretary of State Cordell Hull. Ickes had made Hull his enemy earlier in the year over their widely publicized disagreement on selling helium to Germany, and Ickes correctly sensed that he had better tread carefully on international issues. But *Kristallnacht* and its aftermath were simply too much for him to stomach. In the middle of November, CBS asked him to participate in a half-hour broadcast sponsored by the Federal Council of Churches to discuss Hitler's treatment of the Jews. After checking with the president, Ickes accepted, because

> the Nazi government during the last . . . three days has issued a series of decrees especially aimed at the Jews. They are forbidden to go to places of amusement; Jewish students are barred from the universities; the threat is made that Germany proposes to establish ghettoes for its Jewish citizens; passports issued to Jews permitting them to leave Germany have been revoked; worst of all, Germany has levied a fine of $400 million on the Jews of Germany as a penalty for the assassination of a minor German diplomatic official by a Polish Jew in Paris recently.[26]

Ickes had Ben Cohen prepare a draft of his brief speech, which then went to Roosevelt and to the State Department for approval. "The draft as submitted was approved," Ickes wrote, "except that the President wanted us to cut out all references to Germany by name as well as references to Hitler, Goebbels, and others by name. Fortunately we could do this without weakening the speech," Ickes said. That evening Ickes joined with Herbert Hoover, Alfred Landon, Senator King of Utah, a bishop of the Methodist Church, and the president of Catholic-affiliated Fordham University in condemning Germany's violence against the Jews.

Ickes found it ironic that on the same day as he was preparing to go on the air to criticize the persecution of the Jews, Congressman Martin Dies gave a statement to the press

> listing the people of the world who incite race antagonisms and inspire hate. He included Stalin, Hitler, John L. Lewis, Miss Perkins, Harry Hopkins, and myself. He listed me as No. 2 United States aide after Lewis, with Miss Perkins No. 3 and Harry Hopkins next in line. . . . Apparently, Dies is not aware of the fight that I have made, particularly since I became a member of this Administration, against all manifestations of racial and religious prejudice.[27]

Ickes's November 14 remarks on anti-Semitism were followed by an address he gave on December 18. The secretary of the interior was the featured speaker at the Annual Hanukkah Banquet of Cleveland's Zionist Society and he proceeded to make one of the strongest speeches of his career. Titled "Esau, the Hairy Man," Ickes began with this observation:

> Recently it has come to be believed . . . that we must go back to the middle ages to find a pattern into which the political life of present European dictatorships will properly fit. But this is an insult to the middle ages. . . . To seek a true comparison it is necessary to go back into that period of history when man was unlettered, benighted and bestial. . . . The intelligence and culture of a humane people, by a sudden and swift revulsion, has been sunk without trace in the thick darkness of pre-primitive times.[28]

The secretary then lambasted two famous and popular Americans, Henry Ford and Col. Charles A. Lindbergh, for having accepted

> a decoration at the hand of a brutal dictator who, with that same hand, is robbing and torturing thousands of fellow human beings. . . . It would seem to me that any American who accepts such a trinket, defaced as it is by the sufferings and miseries and degradation of helpless and innocent people, automatically forswears his American birthright.

The Interior secretary concluded his speech by reiterating his support for a change in the immigration laws of the United States and for the creation of an independent Jewish state in Palestine. Both policies were unpopular with the majority of Americans. The relaxation of quotas to allow European Jews easier entry into the United States was especially divisive. Not only was anti-Semitism a factor but the continuing high unemployment rate added to the opposition. Vice-President Garner underscored the dilemma facing American leaders when he said at a cabinet meeting in March that "if the matter were left to a secret vote of Congress all immigration would be stopped." [29]

Nevertheless, through 1938 Ickes at least kept thinking about the plight of the Jews and talking with others about it. In July he spoke with Ambassador Kennedy and Britain's Lord Halifax about the deteriorating situation. "Both Joe Kennedy and I thought that there ought to be plenty of room in some of the British Colonies to take care of all the Jews who need a new home, and it would also seem that there must be plenty of room in South America," Ickes wrote.[30] In visiting Alaska later that summer Ickes had in the back of his mind the possibility of peopling that vast territory with European refugees. When he went public with the idea, a little later, it produced a terrific furor.

Harold Ickes's Hanukkah speech in Cleveland had the intended effect. He managed to create "an acute diplomatic situation" between the United States and Germany. The German chargé d'affaires filed a formal protest with the State Department in which he demanded that it disavow the secretary of the interior's remarks. Sumner Welles, the undersecretary of state, "sternly and categorically refused," Ickes related with relish. "I don't care very much for Welles," he wrote, "and the State Department has not been very friendly to me, but I must say that it did a good job on this occasion." [31]

"Esau, the Hairy Man" also created a row domestically, in that Ickes criticized the father of the American automobile and the handsome young aviator-hero for their friendship with members of the German regime. As he had in 1937, Harold Ickes managed to create some year-end fireworks with which to celebrate the New Year. Although he came in for an avalanche of criticism, overall he considered the controversy he stirred up to be "not bad for this country." Frank speaking, Ickes insisted, was almost always a good thing, a precondition of democracy. It was especially necessary when the lights of civilization were dimming.

The genuine tragedy of 1938 was that there was no way that liberals such as Harold Ickes and Franklin Roosevelt could have predicted what was to happen to 11 million Europeans, to Jews, Gypsies, Catholics, Communists, atheists, and others deemed undesirable by the Fascists. The Holocaust was, simply, unimaginable.

CHAPTER 17

BATTLE FOR THE BIG TREES

FORESTS VERSUS PARKS

WHILE EUROPE and the Far East hurtled toward Armageddon, trees were much on the minds of both the president and his secretary of the interior. In the middle of November 1938, as Roosevelt dealt with the agonizing issue of Jewish emigration, the fate of a few cherry trees around the Tidal Basin provided some comic relief in a worried Washington. A second tree fight, that over some marvelous, ancient sequoias and their habitat in California, also began in earnest that winter. Through most of 1939, both Harold Ickes and FDR pushed strenuously for the creation of a Kings Canyon–General Grant National Park. The opposition emanated principally from the U.S. Forest Service, since the park would be carved out of its holdings in the Sierra Nevadas.

At his November 18 press conference, after having discussed the serious international issues, the president was queried about what he was going to do about the "ecoterrorism" of Cissy Patterson, and a number of other women who had threatened to chain themselves to some cherry trees on the banks of the Tidal Basin. Mrs. Patterson and company were protesting the imminent construction of a memorial to the third president of the United States, Thomas Jefferson. After nearly two decades of public debate over the project, Roosevelt took action and authorized the spending of public works funds to construct what was to become one of the most impressive monuments in Washington. Its construction, however, entailed the removal of eighty-eight cherry trees from the site. (Cissy Patterson had put the number at well over 300 in her Washington newspaper.) No matter: To Mrs. Patterson and her fellow tree lovers, the loss of one cherry tree was one too many for the purpose of memorializing that great democrat, Thomas Jefferson.

At the press conference, the president fielded questions from the reporters in consummate Rooseveltian style. First he told them that the cherry tree issue was just a "flim-flam game," created by local newspaper editors. Then he lectured them on the subject of trees:

> Well, I don't suppose there is anybody in the world who loves trees quite as much as I do, but I recognize that a cherry tree does not live forever. It is what is called a short-lived tree; and there are forty or fifty cherry trees that die, or fall down, or get flooded out, or have to be replaced [each year]. It is a short-lived tree and we ought to have, in addition to the 1,700 trees we have today, I think another thousand trees. There are lots of places to put another thousand trees. Let us plant 2,700 trees instead of 1,700. . . . That net loss will be made up, not only those eighty-eight, as I hope, but 912 others.[1]

What if the ladies physically obstructed the tree removal process? someone asked. FDR said that he had a solution for that eventuality: "The action has been taken by Congress; and if anybody wants to chain herself to the tree and the tree is in the way, we will move the tree and the lady and the chains, and transplant them to some other place." His response was greeted with laughter.

Harold Ickes's public relations officer, Michael Straus, had an even better idea, one that would have been appreciated by the legendary eighteenth-century statesman himself. On the cold November day when the women confronted the bulldozers, Straus was down at the Tidal Basin with many large urns of hot coffee and plenty of food for the protesters. Through the morning he was zealous in refilling their paper cups and peddling doughnuts. When Nature took its course, he quickly called in the bulldozers and the deed was done while Patterson and her troops were hunkered down elsewhere.[2]

THE CHERRY TREE flap was merely prelude for the battle over the big trees of California. Once again, it was internecine warfare between the two primary conservation agencies of the federal government—the Forest Service and the Park Service—and their respective departments, Agriculture and Interior. By the end of 1938, officials in the Forest Service began to resist mightily the nibbling away at the national forest system whereby new or expanded national parks were formed. Too often, they felt, what the National Park Service won, the U.S. Forest Service lost. The most recent instance had been the creation, on June 29, 1938, of Olympic National Park in Washington. Over bitter opposition from the state's timber industry and the Forest Service, Congress, after years of negotiation, transferred hundreds of thousands of acres of national forest land to the National Park Service to create the park.

Later that year, Secretary Ickes and the Park Service's officialdom began casting covetous eyes on tracts of Sequoia National Forest in California's Sierra Nevada mountain range. Their objective was to expand the existing General Grant National Park—already under Park Service jurisdiction—into a larger Kings Canyon National Park. Again, the additional 460,000 acres for the park was going to come out of the Forest Service's hide, or, in this case, its terrain.[3]

By year's end the regional forester for California, S. Bevier Show, had had enough. On December 5, 1938, he issued a strongly worded press release declaring war on the proposed Kings Canyon National Park. Show said that "the Forest Service will fight any proposed extension of national parks in California that will lock up national forest resources vital to the welfare and prosperity of the people and the State." California already had more national parks and monuments than any other state in the country, he argued, with a total of four million acres permanently closed to uses other than public outdoor recreation.

"The Forest Service," the regional forester continued, "long acknowledged as the outstanding conservation agency of the Federal Government, challenges the implications that the Kings River area is not fully protected for the best public interests." Even in the area of wilderness preservation, he argued, the Forest Service was breaking new ground. "In 1931 the wildest and most rugged parts of these mountains were set aside as the High Sierra Wilderness, to be held perpetually in a primitive condition."[4] In the view of many officials of the Forest Service, including the outspoken regional forester, this latest park proposal emanating from the Interior Department was simply an issue of self-aggrandizement. It had to be fought.

Secretary Ickes paid no attention to Show's objections and moved ahead with the proposed park. The Interior Department planned to introduce the bill in Congress early in 1939. In this battle, Ickes had two powerful allies: President Roosevelt and the newly elected governor of California, Culbert Olson. It was a formidable executive trio that championed the park.

Just after the new year Ickes began his campaign by releasing to the press his idea for a wilderness park system, which would include not only the Kings Canyon area, if he could get it, but also Olympic Park and the Isle Royale National Park in Lake Superior. He told the press that he intended to ask Congress for permanent legislation that would establish uniform standards for wilderness management among all of the federal land managing agencies. "There is a need . . . for greater stability in policy than can be obtained by administrative orders," he noted in his press release.[5]

Although Governor Olson favored the park, many others in California were opposed. Two weeks or so after the secretary issued his press release, several members of the state Senate called a meeting in Sacramento to discuss the issue. Regional Forester Bevier Show was invited to attend. When Ickes heard about the meeting, he immediately went to FDR to complain that the Forest Service was "sponsoring" a meeting to derail park plans. The president at his next cabinet meeting asked Agriculture Secretary Wallace to look into Ickes's allegations.

On January 16, Wallace wrote FDR a short letter pointing out that it was the state legislators, not the Forest Service, who called a meeting to adopt a resolution "memorializing the president and the Congress against the creation of the park." Wallace added:

> I am told that your instructions to the Forest Service to refrain from public opposition to the proposed park have been conveyed to the Regional Forester at San Francisco, and I have no reason to believe that they are being violated. Of course, you know . . . that for many years there has been widespread opposition to this movement [for a park], and the Forest Service is bound to be asked for facts and opinions which it cannot appropriately avoid supplying.[6]

The meeting in Sacramento took place on January 16, at which a defiant Regional Forester Show sent his lieutenant to speak out against the establishment of the park. When Ickes learned about this latest outrage, he again went to Roosevelt, and a few days later FDR sent Henry Wallace and Chief Forester Silcox a curt memorandum: "How long are the orders of the President, the Secretary of Agriculture and the Chief Forester to be disobeyed?" he asked.[7]

Henry Wallace was as exasperated as everyone else with the continued wrangling between the two agencies. By nature a more easy-going individual than Ickes, Wallace nevertheless felt pushed to the limits of his endurance on the question of the Forest Service. By 1939 it appeared to him that his cabinet colleague was determined to rob him of his premier agency one way or the other—either wholesale or piecemeal. Ickes, it has been said, "ran his department like a Chinese warlord who coveted the contiguous lands of other border ruffians."[8] And Wallace, despite his relaxed management style, could be as stubborn as a mule when it came to protecting his vital interests. So he, like the regional forester, fought back.

Roosevelt found himself caught in the middle. He liked both men and tried not to alienate either one over the latest park proposal. Therefore when Wallace proposed a solution to Ickes's latest strategy of getting the Forest Service a sizable chunk at a time, Roosevelt seized upon it.

In a carefully reasoned letter, Wallace wrote FDR that what was needed to solve these "border disputes" was the creation of an "impartial committee, composed of people in no way associated with either the Department of the Interior or this Department." He suggested that the president appoint four members, two of whom would be proposed by the Interior secretary and two by Agriculture. The four members would then select a fifth person to serve as chairman. He continued:

> Within a reasonable period the Park Service would submit to this committee a list of all national forest areas which it feels should be established as national parks . . . , while the Forest Service would submit a list of converse proposals. The committee could then investigate each proposal . . . considering . . . the economic, social, and aesthetic factors and the local sentiment. From this investigation it would be possible to reach an impartial conclusion much more basically sound than any derived from present procedures.[9]

"I think well of the idea," the president told Ickes in a memo. "What do you think?" Obviously Ickes did not like the idea, because there is no record that he ever responded to the president's memo or to Wallace's proposal. This was no oversight. The secretary was utterly compulsive about responding to *every* piece of mail that came into his department, even to postcards if they carried a return address. The secretary's lack of response to a presidential memo meant that he felt he could better accomplish his objective of expanding the park system at the expense of the Forest Service without the creation of a disinterested committee to review border disputes.

Henry Wallace's suggestion in January 1939 for the creation of a land exchange committee was prompted not only by the Kings Canyon park proposal, but also by the fact that Ickes, together with the committed park enthusiast and editor of the *St. Louis Star-Times,* Irving Brant, were lobbying for new national parks in Alaska. On his trip in 1938 Ickes discovered the Park Service's Glacier Bay National Monument. When his tour guide, an official of the Forest Service no less, suggested that it ought to be expanded to protect wildlife and several more glaciers, Ickes leapt at the prospect of wresting additional acreage from the foresters in this glorious area.

Admiralty Island was located also in the vicinity of Glacier Bay, and Brant had suggested, back in 1932, that it ought to be transferred from the Forest Service to the Park Service. The Forest Service, Brant charged, was logging on Admiralty Island at the expense of the Alaskan brown bear. In 1939 Brant and Ickes teamed up to push for that public land transfer, as they had done the previous year in connection with Olympic National Park.

January was a frenetic month for Harold Ickes. He was not only working on the Kings Canyon and Glacier Bay park proposals but also Admiralty Island. Toward the end of the month Ickes suggested to FDR that this huge, heavily forested island in Alaska's southern peninsula be turned into a national wildlife refuge (under Park Service jurisdiction, of course). He gave the president material supplied by Irving Brant, who argued that Alaskans not only had an "implacable hostility to the grizzly bear," but that lumbering operations sanctioned by the Forest Service were threatening bear and other wildlife habitat.

Ickes was not reluctant to suggest a solution. "From an administrative point of view," he told Roosevelt, "I am inclined to think that Admiralty Island could be included in the proposed enlargement of Glacier Bay in one national park, since Juneau is the natural center for both areas."

Roosevelt loved forests, parks, *and* wildlife. He wrote Wallace inquiring about the situation on Admiralty Island:

During the Hoover Administration an attempt was made by certain large timber interests to get the cutting rights on Admiralty Island, Alaska. It is my recollection that you and I blocked this early in the Administration—partly because it looked like a bad bargain and partly because Admiralty Island has a wonderful growth of virgin timber and a wonderful growth of very large bears on it.

Would you be good enough to let me know the situation today? Is there any thought of selling timber? If we decide that it should be preserved as a permanent wildlife virgin forest tract, how can we make such a status permanent?

On the contested lands in Alaska—Glacier Bay and its environs, and Admiralty Island—Roosevelt did what he often did on administrative issues: He compromised. Later that year he signed an executive order that increased the Park Service's Glacier Bay National Monument by a substantial 905,000 acres. But FDR didn't follow up on Ickes's suggestion to incorporate Admiralty Island into the expanded national monument. To the relief of Henry Wallace and the foresters, it remained under Forest Service jurisdiction. It was, however, a conditional relief; everyone knew by this time that Harold Ickes was never going to give up on his quest to get control of the national forests.

In February 1939, Congressman Bertrand Gearhart of Fresno, California, introduced H.R. 3794, a bill to establish Kings Canyon National Park. As it began winding through the committees of Congress Secretary and Mrs. Ickes once more headed to California, this time to lobby in person for the park. The issue deeply divided the state. On one side, the popular governor and several Democratic members of California's congressional delegation were strongly supportive. Groups such as the "Women of California" and the DAR were pro-park, as was the influential former senator William McAdoo. John Muir's Sierra Club, then a relatively small organization with only 3,000 members, wavered. It "would have given in to Forest Service decisionmakers about the Kings Canyon High Sierra had Secretary Harold Ickes not come out to stiffen the board's resolve," a former director of the club recalled.[10]

But there was no dearth of opponents either. The state legislature went on record in February as opposing it, and a number of pressure groups including "Farmers, Incorporated," the Central Valley Reclamation Association, timber companies, the California Mountaineers, and the State Chamber of Commerce lined up with Regional Forester Show to block park expansion. A few Republican congressmen also had their doubts, and Ickes called on several people of mutual acquaintance to do some arm-twisting.

In San Francisco, the secretary personally presided over a public hearing to debate the issue. It was well attended, Ickes noted in his diary, by both opponents and proponents. The leader of the opposition was a man from the organization called Farmers, Inc., which the secretary delicately described as that "labor-baiting, fascist-minded group that constitutes a front for the antilabor bankers and businessmen of [t]his state." Ickes said that he allowed everyone at the meeting to say their piece. He then provided a summary of the debate, which included why he favored the park. "Since the facts were with me, it wasn't difficult to meet these arguments, and . . . I had the distinct impression that we made a good deal of headway," he concluded.[11]

Later that day Ickes met with another group of Californians, supporters of the Central Valley reclamation project, and one of the most ambitious water diversion projects ever contemplated by the federal government. Since no reporters were present, he read them the riot act:

I told these people very frankly that I was tired of handing things out to California, when this state showed such a reluctance to do anything that I asked of it. . . . I indicated . . . that while I was in favor of their project, my chief concern was getting the park, and a little support from them for the park might stimulate my interest in the Central Valley project.[12]

All in all, it was a worthwhile trip. Ickes felt that he had accomplished his objective of garnering support for the park in the face of local opposition. However, just as the bill appeared to be making headway in Congress, due in large part to Congressman Gearhart's efforts, some new snags emerged to imperil its progress. In March, shortly after returning to Washington from his West Coast trip, Ickes was apprised of a report that claimed that "apparently some people in the Park Service had been in a conspiracy to defraud the Government, not for personal profit, but to build up the park system."[13] A scandal was just what Ickes needed at the height of his efforts to get the park bill passed, and just as Congress was reconsidering reorganization legislation. Although most of these questionable dealings occurred during the Hoover administration—deals in which park officials knowingly inflated the value of properties to be purchased for park expansion in order to get around Congress's requirement that the property owner contribute half of the land's value—nevertheless, the 1939 report had Ickes very worried.

The secretary immediately spoke with several people in the Park Service about the allegations. "Apparently there was general knowledge down there of what was being done," Ickes learned, but no one brought it to his attention or to anyone else in his executive office. An irate Ickes wrote:

> Ever since I came here I have been trying to pound it into the heads of members of the staff that they should come to me direct with any information that reflected upon the administration of the Department. I have had particular difficulty with the Park Service because the bureaucracy there is so well established that no one down the line dares to go over the heads of his immediate superiors and bring to me important information.

While Ickes was thinking his way through this potential scandal, Assistant Secretary Burlew told him of a similar instance occurring with respect to General Grant National Park—the very area targeted for expansion. The General Accounting Office, Burlew related, was investigating some land transactions that commenced in 1931 but were completed by the Park Service in *1936*. Now, in March of 1939, the GAO had, without informing Ickes or anyone else in the Interior Department, "presented the evidence to a Federal Grand jury." True bills were voted against former director Horace Albright, the agency's appraiser (a man by the name of Solinsky), the park's superintendent, Colonel White, and the title owner of the property, who was a good friend of Herbert Hoover's.

The secretary immediately sent for Horace Albright. Ironically, he had just returned from California where he had been lobbying for the Kings Canyon Park. The two men went over the whole issue. "Albright was pretty worried . . . ," Ickes wrote, "but he protested that he had acted in good faith in every instance." The former director said that perhaps the land appraisals had been high, but he doubted whether they were double the fair value of the property as alleged by the GAO. Ickes said that he retained confidence in Albright's personal integrity, but that he feared that Albright and Solinsky "did arrive at an understanding which in law constituted a criminal conspiracy."

The top officials of the Park Service were called on the carpet for the second time in the space of a week. Ickes said that the lawyer who passed on the transactions appeared "so dumb that I asked him whether his conception of his duties was that of a legal robot." He also unleashed on Director Cammerer who, Ickes wrote, "sat by my desk vigorously chewing gum in an openmouthed manner." By this time Ickes was thoroughly disgusted with Cammerer. He liked neither his demeanor nor his managerial style, and in this session the secretary accused him of not having any idea about what was going on in his agency.

After this latest incident blew over, Ickes vowed he would do some considerable shaking up in the Park Service. "It has become too stereotyped and there are too many incompetent people down there." In the meantime, Ickes sent for his talented public relations officer, Mike Straus, to handle damage control. At the first sign of negative publicity, Straus was to "let out a blast that the whole thing went back to the Hoover Administration, which is the fact," Ickes said.

To the secretary's relief, the Park Service's inflated land deals turned out to be a tempest in a teapot and not another Teapot Dome. On March 20, U.S. Attorney Ben Harrison wrote the attorney general suggesting that the case against Horace Albright et al. be dismissed. "After a review of the case there is serious doubt, in my estimation, as to the guilt of any of the parties mentioned in the indictment and I feel it would be manifestly unfair to force them to trial under the circumstances. I therefore request your authority to dismiss this indictment." [14]

Although Ickes recognized that officials in the Park Service had been shockingly negligent in this matter—a condition he was determined to change by getting rid of Arno Cammerer—he also felt that politics was behind the allegations. It seemed too much of a coincidence that charges of Interior Department impropriety were raised precisely when the department was involved in the battle for the big trees of California. The issue smacked of Forest Service involvement. Ickes also noted that the "Acting Comptroller General [of the GAO] is a former Republican Congressman from Indiana and we have suspected for some time that he was out to do anything he could do to smear the New Deal." [15] If politics was behind the GAO investigation, it didn't work. The Justice Department decided that it was not a matter worth pursuing.

The second snag in getting the park bill through Congress arose on the heels of the first. It dealt with hydroelectric power and whether the Kings Canyon Park would threaten California's growing appetite for huge supplies of both water and power. A related issue was public-versus private-sector power development. As the state's population swelled, and its agricultural economy blossomed, thanks in large part to New Deal programs, numerous Californians objected to locking up a watershed area by creating another national park. In this attack on the park bill, the chairman of the Federal Power Commission (FPC), Clyde Seavey, took the lead. Entering the public debate in March 1939, Seavey and the FPC joined forces with the Forest Service by supporting its more flexible, multiple-use philosophy, which allowed for hydropower development in some areas.

In testimony before the House Public Lands Committee in April, an official of the FPC told the congressmen that he didn't think a new national park was necessary, that the Forest Service's management of the area "was adequate and satisfactory." [16] With victory practically in sight, the opposition by the FPC made the bill's sponsor, Congressman Gearhart, "mad as a March hare," Ickes related. Through the spring Ickes, Gearhart, and other park proponents thus were forced to re-double their lobbying efforts. The secretary personally contacted Hiram Johnson to ask him to sponsor the bill in the Senate, despite the fact that their friendship was no longer what it used to be. Too many policy differences during their seven years together in Washington had taken their toll.

Chairman Seavey's opposition stalled the bill for a few months. He and his allies pushed for a clause in the legislation that would retain power production rights both for the federal government and the state of California. Ickes and Gearhart were opposed. They wanted a Kings Canyon Park that was as pristine as possible. However, in the midst of the battle over power, California's Congressman Elliott charged that Ickes had ulterior motives for opposing the Seavey amendment. Speaking in Tulare on April 14, Elliott claimed that the secretary was in a "conspiracy" with the private power interests "to establish a na-tional park in order to prevent public power development within its boundaries." [17] Ickes had been for decades such a public power enthu-siast that it is hard to believe Elliott's allegation. But it underscores the complexity of the issue and its divisiveness. It wasn't "simply" a matter of whether this or that federal agency be given the authority to manage a tract of land in the Sierra Nevadas.

By June the impasse had reached the White House, and although the president had made it clear to Seavey that he did not favor the amendment, the FPC chairman was proving to be stubborn. On June 1, FDR's administrative assistant, James Rowe, wrote Edwin Watson, another presidential assistant, suggesting ways to break the deadlock between Ickes and Seavey.

> The argument has now reached the technical stage about whether the power potentialities of the region are worth saving. The President should not be bothered with this technical disagreement.
>
> The practical point involved is that several Congressmen opposed to the bill want a report from the Power Commission on the subject. Seavey wants to give them this report and Secretary Ickes does not. . . .
>
> Although there has been some animosity on both sides, it is my judgment that a compromise satisfactory to both could be reached if only they would sit down together.[18]

It isn't known whether the two men were locked in a room together to thrash things out—a half-serious threat FDR used in order to get agreement among his warring administrators—but the outcome was in Ickes's favor. After two more months of wrangling over some big issues—power development versus park, multiple-use versus wilderness, public versus private power—the House passed the Kings Canyon bill on July 18, 1939. The power production clause was deleted.

The Senate then took its time in considering the legislation. Reconvening after a summer recess, Nevada's Sen. Key Pittman wasn't about to let the bill go through his chamber unscathed. Due to his deep dislike for Ickes, Pittman stalled for several months, but in February 1940, he too succumbed to the overwhelming pressures to pass the bill.

In March 1940, Kings Canyon National Park became reality. The secretary could take pride in the fact that he had done much in his first seven years in office—with the invaluable assistance of people like Bob Marshall, Horace Albright, and Irving Brant—to further the creation of a wilderness system in America.[19] Through those years he put considerable pressure on officials of the National Park Service to consider wilderness values, limit roads, build more hiking trails, and keep concessions to a minimum, as they planned and managed the nation's crown jewels. He worked with sympathetic congressmen to enlarge the park system. He hounded the president on behalf of conservation. He won many turf battles against Henry Wallace and the Forest Service. In sum, Ickes had vision. He also had the temperament and stamina to get things accomplished.

IN THE MIDST of winning the Kings Canyon fight, Ickes was, however, sick at heart over President Roosevelt's reorganization orders. It was an unfortunate character trait—Ickes always felt more strongly the sting of defeat (real or imagined) than the sweetness of victory. So at a time when he should have been feeling a great degree of satisfaction, he was grousing about Roosevelt. "He has operated on me without even giving me an anesthetic," a dispirited Ickes complained in May 1939. When Tom Corcoran came in to see him, the secretary told him that "the chances are . . . eighty out of one hundred that I will be resigning shortly. My morale is already at such a low ebb that, unless there is an improvement in it, it would not be fair to anyone concerned for me to stay on." [20]

After two years of stalling, Congress had finally allowed an executive branch reorganization bill to squeak through its chambers, which gave the president authority to propose to Congress the transfer, consolidation, and abolition of federal agencies which, if not disallowed by Congress within sixty days, would take effect. Acting with dispatch, in late April FDR sent his first reorganization order to Congress. Ickes was stunned with the changes.

> This order hit me harder than any other man in the Administration. It took from me PWA, the National Resources Committee, the Office of Education, the management of Federal buildings in the District of Columbia and the United States Housing Authority and it gave me nothing. Of course, I understood that this was only the first of the orders and I took it for granted that the President probably intended to send something to Interior. However, admitting to myself the maximum that he might send, I still could not see that I would not be a heavy loser.

Of course, the one agency that Harold Ickes wanted most from Roosevelt was the Forest Service. All through the winter and spring of 1939, as Congress debated the reorganization bill, hardly a day went by when Ickes wasn't talking to someone about getting that agency transferred to his department. He spoke frequently with Roosevelt about it, but the president resorted to his famous stalling technique. Ickes became increasingly frustrated. He would hear one thing from one person as to the president's intentions, and something quite different from someone else. One week he was hopeful, the next week he was despondent.

It probably wasn't Roosevelt's intention to torment his secretary of the interior to the point of distraction, but that nevertheless was the effect. It was clear to others that the political costs of transferring Forestry in 1939 were simply too high for the president to bear. For example, Roosevelt wrote a brief letter to Senator Pittman on March 21 in which he said, "In regard to the Forestry Bureau, I have no hesitation in telling you that I have no thought of transferring them to the Interior Department." [21]

But Roosevelt did hesitate in telling his valuable assistant, Harold Ickes, that. On June 21 the two men had a long conversation over lunch at the White House, and inevitably Ickes asked, "How about Forestry?" FDR replied, "I will give you Forestry." Ickes asked, "When?" The president said, "At the same time I give you TVA and on the same principle." "Mr. President," Ickes replied, "I have been hearing for five years that I was going to get Forestry and I am getting older every day." Roosevelt replied, with what Ickes thought was sincerity, "I intend to give you Forestry." [22]

Through the spring and summer Ickes had to come to terms with a deep disappointment in the man he admired to the point of adulation. Ickes continued to plead with the president to transfer Forestry, but Roosevelt told him that he simply couldn't get away with it at this time. In reaction, the secretary began to do little things to indicate his dissatisfaction: He stayed away from a cabinet meeting, he refused Henry Morgenthau's invitation to a poker game with the president, and he told a number of people he was considering resigning. Influential men surrounding the president, such as Felix Frankfurter, came running over to his office to urge him not to leave the administration.

The newly appointed Supreme Court justice was very flattering, Ickes recounted. Frankfurter told him that "next to the President, I was the one man in the country who stood for a better civilization and whose voice carried farthest in behalf of a civilized way of living." He also reassured Ickes that Roosevelt was very fond of him. According to the president Ickes was one of two men in the administration able and willing to fight (the other one was Assistant Attorney General Robert Jackson).[23] It was difficult not to be influenced by such praise, so Ickes held in abeyance his latest resignation letter.

Roosevelt's second reorganization order, which came out in May, also helped to heal the secretary's bruised ego. Nothing further was taken from Ickes's domain, and he received several agencies to replace what was lost: The Bureau of Fisheries came from the Commerce Department, the Biological Survey from Agriculture, the quasi-independent Coal Commission was to become a bureau in the Interior Department, and the Bureau of Insular Affairs—meaning the administration of the Philippine Islands—was transferred from the War Department. "As a result of this order," Ickes wrote, "Interior is undoubtedly much further on its way to becoming a real Department of Conservation." Of course he had to add that "only Forestry is now needed to make it such a department." [24]

Through the summer of 1939 Roosevelt continued to rearrange functions and activities of the executive branch. Ickes applauded few of those moves. With his hope for the Forest Service dashed, at least for the time being, the secretary transferred his ambitions to holding on to the title of public works administrator, the position that he said had given him more satisfaction than any other. With Ickes's encouragement, an intense lobbying campaign was mounted, urging FDR to reappoint him to the reorganized public works organization (now called the Federal Works Agency). Hundreds of telegrams and letters flooded into the White House from all over the country extolling the excellent work that Ickes had done with the PWA. Roosevelt's reply was that there was no one who appreciated the work that Ickes had done more than himself, but that he couldn't in good conscience continue to saddle the man, now 65 years old, with two full-time jobs.

Ickes himself made a last-minute effort to convince Roosevelt to keep him on as public works administrator. On June 26 he wrote the president a letter which he referred to as his "valedictory as PWA Administrator." Maudlin and self-indulgent, the five-page letter read in part:

> For six years I have been Administrator of PWA. A newly born child was laid on my doorstep and I have taken care of and loved that child as if it were my own. I had hoped that I would be permitted to continue a relationship that was prized by me, at least until there should be entrusted to my care other interests [read: Forestry] that would make up the loss. . . .
>
> Word comes to me that the members of my PWA staff are badly broken up. Not only do they not know what is to be their fate, but, strange as it may seem—with exceptions, of course—they do not want to leave me. I have bullied them and driven them to a degree that, at times, I have been

ashamed of. Yet I do not doubt that if I could take all of them with me, practically everyone would volunteer to follow. . . .

You have the right to issue orders, and . . . I will continue loyally to obey. But, however much better an Administrator you may consider Mr. Carmody to be, I honestly do not think that in preferring him to me for the Federal Works Agency, you have acted with your usual wisdom. . . .

But instead of complaining, I ought to be thanking you for allowing me to be Public Works Administrator during the past six years, even if, as I have always suspected, you haven't thought a great deal of PWA.[25]

"My dear Harold, will you ever grow up?" an exasperated Roosevelt replied three days later. "Don't you realize that I am thinking in terms of the Government of the United States not only during this Administration but during many Administrations to come[?]" After the stick came the carrot. The president concluded his two-page letter with the promise of better things to come:

Work with me, please, to build up the Interior Department into a real Conservation Department. . . . Incidentally, I am entirely confident in my own mind that oil and coal will both be taken more and more under Government supervision in the near future and that, of course, is a definite function for you to add to Interior. And for the hundredth time, I am not forgetting Forestry.[26]

How could he?

The appointment in July of John Carmody to head the Federal Works Agency marked a low point for Harold Ickes. On July 17 he wrote Raymond Robins a three-page letter complaining about the Carmody appointment, the appointment of Paul McNutt to the newly created Social Service Agency, and the general eclipse of liberals in the administration. He confided to Robins:

I have become very disheartened. I believe that I am capable of loyalty in following my leader but I like to be led, not moved about like an unreasoning and unimportant pawn. I told the President not long ago that one of his great troubles was that he could not talk frankly even to those whom he trusted and who were loyal to him; that he played his cards close to his belly instead of putting them on the top of the table.[27]

WHILE ICKES WAS smarting from what he perceived as a cavalier attitude on the part of the president, and although he felt he was a big loser in the game of musical chairs that FDR had just orchestrated, nevertheless 1939 was a year in which victories outnumbered defeats. Evaluating it objectively, Ickes scored some major triumphs that year. He succeeded in enlarging the national park system and getting Americans thinking about wilderness, he emerged as a leader in denouncing the growing threats of fascism and anti-Semitism, and he was instrumental in bringing a young black woman with a remarkable voice to the steps of the Lincoln Memorial on Easter Sunday. Marian Anderson's historic concert in April of 1939 must be considered one of the country's defining moments, and Secretary of the Interior Harold Ickes did all he could to help realize America's dream, never quite abandoned, though often ignored, of equality for all.

CHAPTER 18

HIS FINEST HOUR

IN DEFENSE OF CIVIL

LIBERTIES AND RIGHTS

MARIAN ANDERSON HAD the most beautiful voice of her generation. She also had dark skin. Born in Philadelphia in 1902, she began her pathbreaking musical career the way most blacks did at the time, by singing gospel music in a church choir. During the 1920s she studied in Europe, and by the end of the decade had achieved international recognition for her unusually rich contralto voice. By 1939 Marian Anderson was known worldwide, having performed in some of Europe's most distinguished concert and opera halls. But when plans were launched for her first public concert in Washington, D.C., it appeared that Miss Anderson was not welcome. Both the Daughters of the American Revolution (DAR), a private organization, and the District of Columbia school board, a public entity, refused to allow her to sing in their halls.

Eleanor Roosevelt invited Miss Anderson to sing at the White House in 1936 and upon hearing that lovely voice became one of the singer's most enthusiastic supporters. She not only endorsed Howard University's efforts in March 1939 to bring Miss Anderson to the capital for a concert, but later that year she invited her to sing at a state dinner honoring King George VI and Queen Elizabeth of England on the royal family's historic first visit to America.[1]

Officials of the all-black Howard University, working in conjunction with Sol Hurok, Miss Anderson's agent, began looking in February for a hall large enough to accommodate what would surely be a huge crowd.[2] Inasmuch as the First Lady was a member of the DAR, university officials felt that their request for the use of Constitution Hall was not inappropriate. Located on tree-lined 18th Street near Constitution Avenue, the hall was only a few blocks from the White House, across the street from the newly constructed Department of the Interior, and within walking distance of some of the nicest neighborhoods in the city. It boasted a gracious interior and excellent acoustics.

They asked. And the DAR refused. The organization's president, Mrs. Henry Robert Jr., made the refusal worse by gratuitously telling a reporter that no Negro would ever sing in Constitution Hall. When her statement became public, Mrs. Roosevelt, like many others, was aghast at the organization's blatant racism. After careful consideration, the First Lady unleashed a bombshell by resigning her membership and explaining why in her "My Day" column. Mrs. Roosevelt said that she usually preferred to work from within an organization to change that group's policy, but since she didn't have the time to be an active member in the DAR, she had no choice but to resign. "To remain as a member implies approval of that action, and therefore I am resigning," she wrote.

After the District of Columbia school board also refused the use of a high school auditorium for the concert, Interior Secretary Harold Ickes, and his assistant secretary, Oscar Chapman, became involved in the growing controversy. With the halls closed to Miss Anderson, the idea of holding a free, open-air concert in a public park emerged. Walter White of the NAACP, a good friend of Mrs. Roosevelt's, went to Assistant Secretary Chapman with the idea. White asked him, "What can you do?" Chapman asked White whether he had given any thought to the effect it might have "if we used the Lincoln Memorial on Easter?" "Oh, my God," White responded, "If we could have her sing at the feet of Lincoln!"

An enthusiastic Oscar Chapman checked with Felix Cohen in the

Interior Department's solicitor's office, who told him that he would gamble his reputation "that there is nothing [of a legal nature] that stands in your way except courage." Chapman next took the idea to Secretary Ickes. Ickes was so excited by the prospect that he immediately raced over to the White House to catch the president before he left on his Easter vacation to Warm Springs. With FDR's agreement, Harold Ickes added his signature to the application. Marian Anderson's historic concert at the base of the Lincoln Memorial was set for April 9.

With only a few days remaining before Easter Sunday, the Democratic congresswoman-at-large from New York, Caroline O'Day, began mailing out invitations to prominent Washingtonians asking them to cosponsor the concert. Concert organizers felt it vital to have as many members of Congress, members of the cabinet, and justices of the Supreme Court as possible publicly support this unprecedented event. Having helped to secure what turned out to be the ideal location for the concert, Ickes assisted Mrs. O'Day in lining up sponsors, not only because he was in a good position to do so, but also because he spied an opportunity to make some of his less courageous colleagues on the civil liberties issue squirm.

When Ickes learned that no replies had been received from Vice-President Garner or from Postmaster General Farley, he took a certain delight in having follow-up telegrams sent to them again requesting their support. "I am trying to smoke these two men out on this Negro issue and probably they find it embarrassing," Ickes noted in his diary. As of Wednesday afternoon, April 5, Mrs. O'Day still hadn't heard from Garner or Farley. She also had no reply from Agriculture Secretary Wallace. Another round of telegrams was sent from Interior Department offices, along with telephone calls to these gentlemen. Only excuses were forthcoming. Ickes related that Farley's excuse was "that he was ill and that the two telegrams sent to him were with a mass of other telegrams and letters and were not opened until after the concert. This sounds very fishy to me."[3]

Henry Wallace claimed that he never permitted his name to be used as a sponsor, and the vice-president's secretary told Walter White much the same thing a few days before the concert. "The Vice President had not allowed his name to be used as a sponsor of anything during the last six years," White was informed. With President Roosevelt conveniently out of town, it fell to the vice-president to make an appearance of support for Miss Anderson. But Garner neither allowed his name to be used nor did he attend the concert. By leaking the story to Drew Pearson and Bob Allen, who published it in their "Merry-Go-Round" column, Ickes believed—rightly or wrongly—that he had succeeded in throwing some sand in Garner's presidential bandwagon. By this time Ickes was committed to Roosevelt for a third term, and he hoped to embarrass other aspirants, including both Garner and Farley. The vice-president, in fact, was furious with the publicity and with Ickes.

The concert itself was among the most memorable events of the decade. It proved to be one of liberalism's finest hours. Miss Anderson had been on tour in the west during the weeks before Easter Sunday and first learned from the newspapers that, due to the First Lady's resignation from the DAR, she was involved in a *cause célèbre*. When asked whether she would perform at the Lincoln Memorial, she said she would, "but the yes did not come easily or quickly. . . . As I thought further," she recalled in her autobiography, "I could see that my significance as an individual was small in this affair. I had become, whether I liked it or not, a symbol, representing my people. I had to appear." [4]

Marian Anderson arrived with trepidation in the nation's capital on the morning of April 9. Her first stop was at the Washington home of the Gifford Pinchots. "The Pinchots had been kind enough to offer their hospitality," she wrote, "and it was needed because the hotels would not take us." She then was driven to the Lincoln Memorial where she and her accompanist tried out the piano and the public address system. It contained six microphones, not only for the people present but also for what would be a huge radio audience. For one who "didn't like a lot of show," the open-air concert was a forbidding prospect confronting the 37-year-old woman. She left the monument in a nervous state, but also with the recognition that this was something she had to do.

Dark clouds threatened rain on this unseasonably cold Easter Sunday but the people came anyway, some 75,000. The majority were black, but many whites were in the crowd that stretched down the Mall to the Washington Monument. Probably a few in this great mass of people recalled that when the Lincoln Memorial was dedicated seventeen years earlier, on May 30, 1922, blacks were forced to sit in a segregated area.

Among the dignitaries in attendance were ten U.S. senators, several representatives, and one Supreme Court justice, the former Ku Klux Klansman Hugo Black. The cabinet was represented by Secretary Ickes and Treasury Secretary Henry Morgenthau. Neither President Roosevelt nor the First Lady attended the concert. FDR was spending the holiday in Warm Springs and Mrs. Roosevelt, who, unlike her husband, would not have been hesitant to attend for fear of political repercussions, felt that her presence might detract from Miss Anderson. After having been so instrumental in staging the concert, Mrs. Roosevelt with characteristic humility withdrew to backstage. "She is one of the most admirable human beings I have ever met," Anderson later said of the First Lady.[5]

Sunshine broke through the clouds shortly before the late afternoon concert was to begin. Ickes, who had the honor of introducing the famous contralto, was thrilled. It was "one of the most impressive affairs that I have ever attended," he wrote.[6] Assistant Secretary Chapman and Congresswoman O'Day escorted Miss Anderson down the steps of the Lincoln Memorial where she was greeted by Ickes. The secretary spoke for just two minutes but made what he considered "the best speech I have ever made." In introducing the lady who needed no introduction, Ickes told the audience,

> Genius, like Justice, is blind. For Genius with the tip of her wings has touched this woman, who, if it had not been for the great mind of Jefferson, if it had not been for the great heart of Lincoln, would not be able to stand among us today a free individual in a free land. Genius draws no color line. She has endowed Marian Anderson with such a voice as lifts any individual above his fellows and is a matter of exultant pride to any race.

Marian Anderson rose to sing. Wearing a fur coat against the chill, her hair pulled back, and with a minimum of makeup on her broad, sculpted face, she approached the audience. "All I knew . . . as I stepped forward was the overwhelming impact of that great crowd. . . . I had a feeling that a great wave of good will poured out from these people, almost engulfing me."[7] She was so overcome with emotion when she began to sing the National Anthem that she thought the words would not come. But they did come, and in the space of a brief twenty minutes the opera star made history. She sang "America," an aria from a well-known opera, Schubert's "Ave Maria," and concluded with three Negro spirituals—"Gospel Train," "Trampin'," and "My

Soul Is Anchored in the Lord." Then it was over, and the crowd roared back its appreciation to Miss Anderson for her courage and for her heavenly voice.

THE MARIAN ANDERSON CONCERT, one of the most memorable events in the long struggle for racial equality in America, showed Harold Ickes at his best. From the first moment that he joined the Roosevelt administration he acted on a lifelong commitment to civil liberties and civil rights. Few others dared do so. He found, however, an invaluable ally in the First Lady, and together the two seized the initiative for the administration in this deeply divisive arena. They did it because they felt that it was a moral imperative, not because it was popular and not because it would add necessarily to their power or prestige. While Ickes devoted much of his energy to building up his own domain, whether it was the Interior Department, the Oil Administration, or the Public Works Administration, on this issue his actions were motivated almost entirely by principle. It was his finest hour.

From 1933 forward Ickes and Mrs. Roosevelt said and did things for blacks and other minorities which President Roosevelt could not do. He was constrained, as he pointed out, by having to keep his shaky New Deal coalition together if he wanted to accomplish anything. That meant placating the powerful Southern Democrats in Congress, and on the race issue most in the 1930s were unreconstructed members of the Confederacy. So he didn't speak out in favor of the antilynching bills, he didn't force the issue of integration, and he didn't attend Miss Anderson's concert. But he also didn't fire Harold Ickes who, by 1939, had become the most outspoken member of his administration on these issues. (Naturally he couldn't fire Eleanor, either.) It was Roosevelt's way of lending support to this cause.

While Marian Anderson's concert turned out to be a history-making event, at the time it appeared to civil libertarians like Ickes as one more skirmish with the forces of racism and bigotry that were gaining alarming strength not only in Europe and Asia but in America as well. Through 1938 and 1939, and indeed throughout the entire Second World War, Harold Ickes and other prominent liberals fought the civil liberties war on several fronts.

One of those fronts was located in Congress. In November 1938 the Dies Committee—one of the first committees to investigate "un-American activities"—opened its attack on liberals in general and

Secretary Ickes in particular by putting on the stand a disgruntled American Indian, Alice Jemison. She proceeded to denounce Ickes, Commissioner John Collier, and others in the Indian Bureau for being communist sympathizers. "Our tie with 'communism' was the Civil Liberties Union," Ickes noted laconically in his diary.[8] "We know that the Jemison woman is closely connected with certain pro-Nazi groups in this country," Ickes added. "She has constantly attacked the Indian Service, but, of course, has never been able to get any real publicity until the accommodating Congressman Dies came along intent on smearing the New Deal whenever he could."

The secretary wasted no time in training his sights on Dies. First, he rebutted Jemison's testimony at his press conference the day following her congressional appearance. Afterwards, he gave out a statement accusing the congressman of allowing his committee to be used as a sounding board for a "foreign dictatorship." He also accused Dies of lacking patriotism. He followed these attacks with his controversial speech on fascism, "Esau, the Hairy Man," delivered in December 1938. One of his first activities of the New Year involved drafting a speech that he playfully titled "Playing with Loaded Dies."

It was late in the day on January 2, and Ickes had just finished going over a draft of his Dies speech when he received a call from Steve Early, the president's secretary. "He seemed quite excited," Ickes wrote. Early asked him whether he intended to make a nationwide speech attacking the Dies committee, and the secretary replied that indeed he was just putting the finishing touches on it. Well, Early said, "the President has just called me . . . to ask you about it and to tell you for God's sake not to do it!"

Ickes was upset and perplexed. He had spoken with the president more than once to secure his consent, for he knew better than to launch a frontal attack on a Democratic congressman without Roosevelt's approval. The about-face put him in an embarrassing position, inasmuch as the newspapers had already announced the speech and its target. "It looked to me like quitting under fire, and that I am not accustomed to do," Ickes growled.

The next day he met with FDR and spoke frankly to him about canceling the speech. Roosevelt explained that House leaders were busily trying to rein in Dies, either by limiting the amount of money he had to spend or the length of time the committee would operate. The president told Ickes that Dies wanted $150,000 and a year's time.

The House leaders believed that at the most they wouldn't have to give him more than a few weeks' time and much less money. FDR also told him that he had been lobbied hard by Dies's fellow Texan, Sam Rayburn, to call off Ickes's speech. Rayburn was convinced that it would boomerang.

"I told the President that I did not agree with this policy," Ickes wrote. "The reason Dies has made so much headway is because we have not fought him." A few potshots had been taken at him, Ickes continued, but that was not the same thing as a "well-thought-out frontal attack." The material contained in "Playing with Loaded Dies" was just that: Ickes was prepared to call into question most of Dies's witnesses, claiming that one was a racketeer, one a psychiatric case, and three or four others had criminal records. "Moreover," Ickes told the president, "I have affidavits to the effect that Dies has been getting away for years without paying taxes in Texas which he is supposed to pay."

All this juicy material notwithstanding, the president chose the more conciliatory approach. Ickes grudgingly put the speech on hold. Just a month later, however, Ickes's analysis of the situation was vindicated. "Congressman Dies had no trouble in getting a resolution through the . . . House continuing the life of his committee to January 2, next, with $100,000 to finance its fantastic investigation," Ickes wrote on February 4. "Now we will have this pest to afflict us during the coming months." The secretary also noted that "here was another example of a complete falling down of the so-called Democratic leadership of the House."

It was a dangerous situation, in Ickes's view. He observed that Mussolini's and Hitler's paths to power were premised on the need to suppress Communists, and that Japan's invasion of China was rationalized in the same way. "Dies can put his pieces together in the same pattern. . . . The result here in that event will be fascism." He could imagine no worse evil for America.

Ickes went back to FDR and asked him for the green light to make his "Playing with Loaded Dies" speech. The president, also disgusted with Congress by this time, agreed. Ickes planned to deliver what he felt would be one of his most devastating attacks on a political enemy later that month, when he was scheduled to speak in Cleveland before the School Executive Association. An overcrowded agenda, however, caused Ickes to cancel the speech; on the day he was supposed to be in

Ohio he and Jane were instead traveling back from their Kings Canyon promotional trip to California.

On February 26 Harold and a now-pregnant Jane were aboard their eastbound train, looking out the window at burnt adobe colors and the mesas of northern New Mexico. "A romantic and lovely country," Ickes wrote. "We caught a picture of a Navajo woman, with her full skirts blowing about her as she herded her sheep. . . . I tried to pick out Casa del Navajo and the little cottage that Anna built next to it which I still own," he continued, "but I could not do it from the fast-moving train." [9] Although Ickes planned to make his attack on the dangerous Dies at a later date, his own fast-moving life overtook him. The speech was never delivered.

While ideologues such as Martin Dies were bent on exposing the vast numbers of Communists on the federal payroll, others were criticizing the Roosevelt administration from a different, but equally alarming, perspective, that of anti-Semitism. A flyer published out of New York City by Robert Edward Edmondson of the American Eagles, dated January 10, 1939, claimed in bold letters that

> The only people who want war are—the Jews! International Jew Baruch, "Fellow-Traveller" Ickes, Dorothy Thompson Levy, Kosher La Guardia and the whole "Jew Deal" crowd are "baiting" friendly nations! [10]

Harold Ickes's name cropped up in right-wing publications of this sort because by this time his defense of minority rights was well known and bitterly resented by many. Not only did he champion the rights of blacks and American Indians, but he had endorsed the Zionist movement in America and was a strong supporter of Jewish causes generally. He was a frequent speaker at Jewish events. After *Kristallnacht,* Ickes gave much thought to the possible resettlement of European Jews in the territories under his domain. He looked closely at both Alaska and Puerto Rico, but the protests were deafening. Not only were local residents opposed, but newspapers in such distant places as Las Vegas and Chicago joined the chorus in opposing what was labeled his "Alaskan policy"—a policy that supported efforts at relocating the European Jews and that offered economic assistance to Indians and Eskimos in their native lands. "Of all of Harold L. Ickes' schemes," a correspondent for the *Chicago Tribune* wrote, "none has done more to make the Secretary . . . hated and feared in Alaska than his plan to multiply the population by dumping European refugees into the wilderness territory." Against such opposition little could be done to alleviate the tragedy occurring in Europe, even by Ickes.[11]

But in the area of staffing, where he had considerably more control, Ickes did a lot. He had no qualms whatsoever about hiring Jews and giving them important positions in his administration. Michael Straus was one of Ickes's closest aides through all of his Washington years, and Ben Cohen also worked intermittently for him. Both men remained lifelong friends. He hired Nathan Margold for the important solicitor's position, and brought in Felix Cohen as an assistant solicitor. In the spring of 1939 the Interior secretary, at the suggestion of William O. Douglas, hired the young, brilliant, and ambitious Abe Fortas as general counsel to the Public Works Administration. (Fortas quickly moved to the Bituminous Coal Division within Interior since the PWA was being phased out. Fortas became undersecretary during the war.) Finally, both Supreme Court Justice Felix Frankfurter and multimillionaire Bernard Baruch were among Ickes's most intimate friends.

Harold Ickes thus gained the reputation of being as good a friend to the Jewish minority in this country as it had during this wildly anti-Semitic era. Some scholars allege that there was a trace of anti-Semitism in Ickes because, in his diaries and elsewhere, he spoke frankly about Jews and what he considered to be their positive and negative qualities. When he hired Fortas, for example, he wrote that "while he is a Jew, he is of the quiet type and gives the impression of efficiency as well as legal ability."[12] The main reason he hired Jews was because he generally found them bright and hard-working, the very qualities he admired most in people.

It is easy to misinterpret the sentiments of this blunt man. Harold Ickes spoke freely about everyone, not just about Jews. Moreover, he used the language and the concepts of the era. The 1930s was a decade when even sophisticated individuals believed in the "national character" explanation of behavior. People talked frankly about ethnic, religious, and racial characteristics (now called stereotypes). But this in itself did not necessarily make them racists or anti-Semites. If Harold Ickes had any deep-seated prejudices, they appear to have been directed toward Germans and Catholics. His appraisals of these two "authoritarian" groups sometimes bordered on the stereotypical.

The fact that Ickes was regularly vilified for his support of Jews during his thirteen years in office makes the charge of latent anti-Semitism ludicrous. Certainly his many critics would have been surprised and amused by a revisionist interpretation of Ickes's candor.

THERE WAS STILL another civil liberties front on which Ickes battled in 1939. Early that year his long-standing quarrel with the nation's newspapers heated up. The most bitter feud was with Col. Robert McCormick of the *Chicago Tribune,* but Ickes despised almost as much Frank E. Gannett, whose publishing chain had, by the 1930s, monopolized most of the daily newspapers in the heavily populated state of New York. Because he, like other liberals, was alarmed at the growing concentration of power among a handful of newspaper magnates, the secretary agreed to debate Gannett on the evening of January 12 in New York City. The forum was the popular radio show, "Town Hall of the Air." The subject was freedom of the press.

On January 11, Harold and Jane took the train to New York. They spent that evening and most of the next day socializing. They saw a play, stopped off at the home of Betsy Roosevelt (Franklin and Eleanor's daughter-in-law), and dined with Mayor and Mrs. Fiorello LaGuardia before the scheduled debate. Over a very good dinner at one of the mayor's favorite restaurants, Little Venice, the foursome talked politics. The principal subject was the 1940 presidential contest. LaGuardia, Ickes related, claimed that the president had stated flatly that he would not be a candidate in 1940. Ickes thought that LaGuardia had either misunderstood or misinterpreted him, "something that he would be the more likely to do because, in his judgment, the President would be defeated on the third term issue if he should run in 1940." [13]

Of other possible candidates, both men agreed that they could not support either Garner or Farley, but that a Cordell Hull–Harry Hopkins combination "would make a strong ticket." Hardly an admirer of Secretary of State Hull, Ickes nonetheless grudgingly acknowledged Hull's widespread popularity in 1939. But Hull was becoming more somber by the minute, Ickes thought, "and how he would wear as a candidate I do not know. His is distinctly a one-track mind and the only station on his one-track mind is 'trade agreements,' which are all right . . . but which will not solve our own economic problems, let alone the grave international problems that exist today."

Ickes himself harbored presidential aspirations in 1939, but he was also realistic enough to know that his age, as well as his well-deserved reputation for combativeness, were against him. He thus saw no alternative to FDR on the horizon. It was an alternative that certainly did not displease him, for he confessed that he had no inclination to return to "obscurity" should someone else be elected president.

After dinner with the LaGuardias, Ickes was off to the business at hand. The theater was packed, he noted, and before the debate began Ickes and Gannett were introduced to one another. "He didn't make a very favorable impression upon me," Ickes said.

The secretary of the interior was the first to speak. "My thesis," Ickes said, "was that while the press of the country is free from Government regulation and control, it is not free from financial and advertising control."[14] He gave a number of specific instances but aimed his attack at the Gannett chain. When Gannett rose to speak he seemed furious, Ickes said. "He whined that he had not seen my speech in advance, but that he had been warned that I would make just such a 'personal' attack on him as I made." He wasted several minutes air time, Ickes noted with delight, in a sputtering rebuttal. Then he began his speech, which was premised on the idea that while the press of America is free, it must continue to resist encroachments on its freedom by the government. "He didn't state specifically what these encroachments were, but he did some haranguing about the President's bill to reform the . . . Court and his reorganization bill," Ickes related.

Ickes was happy with his performance. The president also congratulated him. Ickes thought that the newspapers the next morning gave him a pretty fair break, "although the International News Service, the Hearst news-gathering agency, went pretty far to prove my case that the newspapers are not fair."[15] In any event, Ickes was glad to have debated Gannett. "I have stirred up a real public discussion," he noted. It was an activity that was becoming as natural to him as working ten-hour days.

Not one to let things ride for long, Ickes continued his critique of the newspaper industry through 1939. He gave two more speeches, in February and April, in which he ventured to tread heavily on the press's toes. Later that year his book, *America's House of Lords,* was published, which dealt with the increasing monopolization of America's newspapers by a few giants in the industry: Hearst, McCormick, the Pattersons, and Gannett. Not surprisingly, Ickes came in for a lot of criticism from the newspapers owned by these individuals. "The result [of my speeches]," Ickes wrote, "was a violent storm of editorial abuse on the one hand and a stream of popular approval on the other." [16]

Ickes regularly received laudatory letters for his stand against the press from ordinary citizens as well as from editors of small and medium-sized newspapers who felt threatened by the giants in the industry. In early February the editor of the *Rochester Evening News* wrote him a long letter describing how the Gannett chain was seeking a monopoly in his city. The editor, David Kessler, concluded by asking whether Ickes knew of any New Dealers who could invest in his newspaper.[17] In August Ickes's long-time friend and publisher of the *Chicago Daily News,* Frank Knox, complimented him on having publicly discussed the Moe Annenberg tax evasion scandal:

> I have never seen so obvious an attempt at news suppression in my life. When the biggest tax case in the history of the Internal Revenue department resulted in an indictment of a man with the largest income in the United States and the income was derived from dubious sources, the *Tribune* buried the story on the 11th page. The treatment of the Annenberg story by the press of the United States has been an amazement to me.[18]

As with his 1935 book, *Back to Work,* which described the first two years of the PWA, certain publishers and editors attacked Ickes's *America's House of Lords* when it came out in 1939. They claimed it was ghostwritten by his staff and therefore underwritten by the taxpayers of America. There was, of course, a grain of truth to this criticism. It was physically impossible to have done everything that Harold Ickes claimed to have done in his thirteen years in office. In addition to working at two or three full-time jobs during practically all of those thirteen years, he gave over 500 formal speeches, kept an incredibly detailed running account of his daily activities that numbers in the thousands of pages (the "secret diaries"), wrote an autobiography, and published several books and hundreds of articles. Naturally he had help in executing all of this work, and he acknowledged such when he said, concerning the allegations made by the press, that he availed himself of the same service that any other citizen could: The Interior Department was a vast repository of information and it was there to be mined.

But not everyone was secretary of the interior, public works administrator, and oil administrator, and the possibility of abusing his positions was real. It appears that only infrequently did he cross the line between what was appropriate to ask of his staff and what was not. Although he had a lot of help in drafting speeches, books, and articles, Ickes did do much of the work himself. On only a few occasions did he give a speech that he hadn't gone over carefully. Those turned out to be disasters, in his opinion, and so he didn't want to repeat that mistake very often. Moreover, Ickes was much too meticulous about language usage to allow someone totally to ghostwrite anything to which he put his name. His command of the English language was one of his most outstanding qualities, and he took considerable pride in it. So, like most busy government officials, Ickes took advantage of his staff in the early stages of a project, but he almost invariably completed the work himself. He was also careful to recompense his writing staff if he was paid for the book or article, which was often the case. Ickes enjoyed having a comfortable income and he supplemented his rather modest government salary with royalties from his publications (and with marketing farm-fresh eggs to Georgetown's fashionable grocery stores).

Ickes's row with the press took a nastier and more personal turn in April 1939 when Cissy Patterson, owner and editor of the *Washington Times-Herald,* decided that she would counterattack. Ickes had been criticizing her métier for months, and although Cissy and Harold were still on outwardly friendly terms she objected to much of what he had to say about the industry. She took particular offense to his reference about certain "kept newspapers," so in the middle of April she publicly attacked Ickes in what he considered to be a "catty and personal" way. She divulged certain confidences that he'd told her when they were seeing one another, and she questioned whether he had ever worked, as a young man, for her cousin's newspaper, the *Chicago Tribune.*[19]

Harold Ickes decided not to respond publicly to Cissy's speech, but a week later the two met at a cocktail party given by Drew Pearson. Jane had accompanied Harold, and by this time it was clear that she was expecting their baby. At first the Ickeses and Cissy went out of their way to avoid each other. But when Harold realized that Cissy was studiously avoiding him, he couldn't resist; he went over to her, whereupon they proceeded to put on a great show of affection by kissing and throwing their arms around each other. "Everyone was watching us and everyone was much amused," Ickes later wrote. "One guest came up and remarked that we were afraid not to have our arms around each other!" It was a *bon mot,* Ickes thought.

It took another woman to recognize the basis for Cissy's increasingly vicious attacks on her old friend and former lover. "Jane used to like Cissy but she resents her attack on me and insists that it is all jealousy on Cissy's part," Ickes wrote about the cocktail party incident. "I had never felt that Cissy had any matrimonial aspirations . . . but we were very close friends and I sincerely liked her. It is a fact that from the time Jane and I became attached to each other, Cissy has gone out of her way to hammer me in her editorials and now . . . over the air." She continued to hammer him through all of his subsequent years in office.

But Ickes didn't let up either. At one social occasion he yelled at Cissy, "I can take whatever slop you dish out!" Ickes gave as well as he got, and he was always looking for ways to get at the Patterson-McCormick publishing empire. Treasury Secretary Henry Morgenthau recorded an amusing telephone conversation he had with Ickes in July 1939. The subject was Colonel McCormick. Ickes asked Morgenthau "whether his [McCormick's] income tax returns . . . showed any earnings from his law firm." Ickes explained to the incredulous secretary that he wanted to "nail the cur." Morgenthau replied that he was sorry but he couldn't help him by rummaging through confidential IRS files.

A month earlier Ickes had made another surprising request which, since it wasn't illegal, the Treasury secretary found he could accommodate. Ickes, Morgenthau related in his diary, called him in June to complain that his official cars weren't as nice as those of some other members of the cabinet, that Congress had only given him $1,800 for a new car, and that he couldn't get the fancy big Packard that he wanted for that amount. Confusing the Treasury secretary with a car dealer, Ickes asked him whether he could find some "trade-ins" for him. Morgenthau replied that his department had a nice Buick that was only three years old and which they might be able to transfer to Interior. "Ah—if—are you—are you serious on this?" Morgenthau asked. Ickes replied that he was. So the Treasury secretary called his assistant, Captain Collins, to get together with Ickes's assistant, Ebert Burlew, to arrange the used car deal.[20]

IT APPEARS AS THOUGH all these attacks and counterattacks were getting to Ickes. A hint of paranoia, and certainly a lack of proportion, began to characterize some of his behavior by this time. It is evidenced by his unusual requests to Secretary Morgenthau, one of which Ickes had to know was illegal, and by his childish letter to the president about the PWA. But it is most clearly seen in his treatment of a liberal ally, Congressman John Coffee of Tacoma, Washington, in the spring of 1939.

On May 3, Secretary Ickes wrote Congressman Coffee a peremptory letter in which he upbraided the congressman for making some remarks at a committee hearing on oil imports. Ickes curtly told Coffee that he shouldn't have quoted him without his approval. Two days later Coffee wrote the secretary an amusing two-page tongue-in-cheek letter. Using official stationery, the congressman begged the secretary's pardon:

> I wish humbly to apologize to you for having unethically, in my zeal, made reference to a conversation had with you some time ago at which time we discussed the conservation of oil with particular reference to the Connally Hot Oil Act. . . .
>
> I want you to know that I regard you as the strongest liberal in this Administration and would feel very hurt to think that the slightest feeling of friction should interpose between yourself and myself, or cast a cloud upon the warm friendship so auspiciously begun in recent years. I will never forget the pleasant time I enjoyed with yourself and your very charming wife when you were in Tacoma in the summer of 1938, nor will my liberal friends and I forget or cease to chuckle over the magnificent dressing down you gave to Carter Glass and the Dies Committee in your speech at the Winthrop Hotel [in] Tacoma. . . .
>
> Your gracious interest in the problems of my district with respect to PWA projects . . . is deeply appreciated by all of us and I want you to feel that I am ineffably grateful for the help you have rendered me and my people, both politically and as a public official. Your forthright championship of public ownership is a comfort to me on all occasions. Your denunciation of the columnists recently by radio has enthused Mrs. Coffee and myself beyond the power of description. Your analysis of the press meets with our wholehearted support. Your extension of the public park system finds sympathetic lodgement in my make-up. Your courageous denunciation of aggressor nations and your intelligent and enlightened attitude on foreign relations and collective security has delighted me no end.
>
> For these and many similar expressions and pronouncements and attitudes of magnificent liberalism, I feel that you are by all odds the foremost progressive in public life in America today in this administration, without any invidious reflections upon any of your associates.
>
> Again I express the fervent hope that this apology will remove any unpleasant reaction you may have unconsciously acquired as a result of word

having been passed to you that I had made reference to a conversation in your office on the subject of oil conservation.

With warmest personal regards . . .

John M. Coffee [21]

Congressman Coffee had a whimsical streak but Ickes didn't get it. On May 8 he sent a brief, courteous, and formal reply to the congressman, thanking him for his "apology": "I need not say that I appreciate deeply your generous expressions with reference to myself."

Over the next six years in office, Harold Ickes occasionally fell victim to an exaggerated sense of self-importance. Although he continued to work very hard, and although he accomplished a great deal during the second half of his thirteen long years in office, just as he had in the first half, he found that he needed to guard against the corrupting influences of being in power for so long a time. Fortunately, a far more placid and happy home life than he had ever before experienced served to reduce some of the strain on him. Harold discovered in Jane the perfect mate, and with the arrival of a son in September 1939, and a daughter in 1941, Harold at last found the domestic tranquility for which he had yearned through most of his life.

CHAPTER 19

ICKES'S BOOK OF REVELATIONS

THE PERSONAL MEMOIRS

HAROLD ICKES TURNED 65 on March 15, 1939. Reflecting on that milepost, Ickes noted in his diaries that, all things considered, he felt pretty good. But he admitted that he was slowing down; he couldn't work nearly as hard as he had when he was first called to Washington in 1933. "Fortunately, I don't have to," Ickes said, "because I have more help and am better organized than I was at the beginning." [1]

His thoughts then turned to Harry Hopkins, who was now secretary of commerce and hovering on death's doorstep. Harry had just returned from South Carolina, Ickes related, and his doctor ordered him to spend several days at home in bed. Harry Hopkins was a man some fifteen years Ickes's junior, yet he was far from robust. In fact he never fully recovered from his 1937 operation for stomach cancer—the same year Ickes had his heart attack—and for much of 1939 Hopkins's life hung precariously.

Ickes sympathized with Harry's plight, despite their previous disagreements and Ickes's envy at the increasingly close relationship developing between the president and Hopkins. Upon learning in late August that Harry left for the Mayo Clinic "to be gone over again," Ickes wrote: "Harry isn't able to do any work and doesn't try to do any. I feel terribly sorry for him. I can't imagine anything worse, especially for a man at his age."

Being very fond of Harry, FDR did everything he could to improve his friend's condition through those critical years: He ordered Harry to see Navy doctors who specialized in rare diseases, he excused him from many of his official duties, and in 1940 when Harry was feeling particularly bad, the president invited him to dinner at the White House and told him to stay overnight. "He remained, living in what had been Lincoln's study, for three and a half years," biographer Robert Sherwood wrote.[2] There were a number of people who claimed that Roosevelt worked a miracle. Through force of will, FDR extended Hopkins's life by several years, thus allowing him to render invaluable service to his country throughout the Second World War, and to remain one of the president's closest confidantes during that perilous time.

Another member of Roosevelt's official family was critically ill in 1939. Harold Ickes found Navy Secretary Claude Swanson's condition disturbing, too. Swanson had enjoyed a long, distinguished political career, first as a congressman from Virginia, then its governor, and then a U.S. senator. In 1933 the president named him to head one of his favorite agencies, the Navy Department. (Navy was the agency in which FDR had served as assistant secretary during the Wilson administration.) During FDR's second term Swanson began failing, and Ickes couldn't understand why the president didn't relieve the 75-year-old man of his duties. Stories of Swanson fainting at White House functions, and of having to be helped in and out of his cabinet chair, his voice so thick that few could understand him, made everyone in the cabinet look bad, Ickes thought. "He really has presented a pathetic sight," Ickes wrote in 1939.[3]

On July 7, the 77-year-old Swanson died of a stroke. He and his wife were vacationing at Rapidan when it occurred. The president's physician, Dr. Ross McIntire, told Ickes that if Swanson hadn't died he would have been completely paralyzed, thus winding up a long and vigorous life as a helpless invalid. "I think that, in the circumstances, he would have wanted to die if he had the choice," Ickes observed as he prepared to attend his colleague's funeral.

In comparison with many others, Harold Ickes at age 65 was fortunate, and he realized it. Not only was he in reasonably good health, except for his chronic insomnia, but he was happily married to the lovely 26-year-old Jane, and she was pregnant with their first child. Ickes thus was given the opportunity to do what many mortals dream of doing at some point in their lives, and that is to start over, to do it all again, except this time to get it right. But Harold Ickes's second marriage was not just a typical second-time-around story. It was freighted with deep psychological content in that it represented for him the resolution of a life-long identity problem. Perhaps for the first time in his life, Ickes felt that he was incontestably the head of his household. In 1933 Roosevelt had given him the opportunity to begin a new public career, and in 1938 his marriage to Jane Dahlman gave him a similar opportunity to change totally his personal life. He seized on both.

While contemplating his new life and impending fatherhood, Ickes began ruminating about his past: his youth, his marriage to Anna, the birth of their son, Raymond, and the children who came with Anna to their marriage. He decided to begin dictating his personal memoirs (as opposed to his secret diaries, which he began in 1933). The result was a remarkably candid document of these often tortured years. From 1939 to about May 1940, Ickes worked with his life-long secretary, May Conley, in recalling his personal life and putting it down on paper. A heavily edited version was published in 1943 as *The Autobiography of a Curmudgeon,* and while it contains a lot of interesting information about Ickes's political and professional activities, the most sensitive personal revelations were omitted. It is to Ickes's credit that he chose to preserve the original document, for he reveals a side of himself which on occasion was distinctly at odds with his public persona. Especially in his dealings with Anna and the children from her first marriage, Harold Ickes was at times vicious, calculating, and dishonest. Self-interest and his inherently combative nature often got the best of him.

In the unpublished memoirs, Ickes passed over lightly his early childhood in Altoona, but he says enough, both there and elsewhere, to conclude that it was not a particularly happy or serene time. He was the second of seven children born to Jesse and Martha McCune Ickes, and his relationship with his father was a distant one. Jesse was neither an adequate provider nor a source of affection. Consequently, almost the entire burden of holding the family together, and managing the household on what was frequently an inadequate income, fell on Martha's shoulders. Harold was her favorite child, and he reinforced that preference by being the most helpful at home. He developed a deep affection for his long-suffering mother, and an equally deep ambivalence for his ne'er-do-well father, as well as for most of his brothers and sisters. A few of his brothers, especially the older one, regularly beat up on Harold. The psychological result was an estrangement with most family members that lasted a lifetime. Even his daughter Elizabeth observed that "friends" were much more important in the Ickeses' household than were "family." [4] He also learned to hate bullies and to identify with the underdog.

Given this home life, Ickes realized that he was in danger of becoming a mama's boy, or as he put it, a "panty-waist." However, he gave himself credit for escaping this fate, largely by learning how to fight back by using his keen intellect. Harold never became a barroom brawler or a physical abuser of others, but he did develop a thoroughly aggressive style that substituted for more traditional ways of proving one's masculinity. But that style took some time to develop, and in his personal affairs it took him a very long time to escape from being dominated by a strong-willed woman. In short, Harold Ickes struggled throughout most of his life, as many do, with an identity crisis: His father and brothers were poor role models, and his mother, whom he deeply loved, was an unacceptable one for a young boy. Moreover, he couldn't help but resent at times her goodness, her piety, her lack of humor, and her inability to understand the carefree, sociable nature of her husband. "If only she had been a little more yielding," he mused.

His mother died when he was 16, and shortly afterwards Harold and his younger sister Mary were packed off to live with Ada and Felix Wheeler in Chicago. Although Aunt Ada was one of his favorite relatives—she was his mother's sister—nevertheless he hated being sent away. "I didn't like any of it," he wrote. "I missed my mother and my friends. I longed for Altoona. . . . Here were the intangible ingredients out of which a careful architect was to build a robust curmudgeonly character."

Ada and Felix were childless, owned a drugstore in Englewood, led a lower middle – class existence, and provided a stable home for their nephew and niece. However, Harold said that he found himself again in the grip of a strong woman, one who "wore the pants in the family." It was Aunt Ada, for instance, who decided that Harold should continue his high school studies in addition to working in the family drugstore.

In the long run it was an excellent decision on Ada's part. Harold was enrolled at Englewood High School and immediately buried himself in school work. It was a characteristic he held onto for the rest of his life. He did well in his studies, and he credited one of his high school teachers for giving him the encouragement to attend college. Harold ended his high school career by being elected senior class president and was chosen to deliver the Welcoming Address at graduation.

After his father "turned a stony ear to any and all appeals for [financial] help" for college, Harold knew that he would have to make it on his own. He spent seven years obtaining a bachelor of arts degree from the University of Chicago, and although he received some financial help from the university and a little from some relatives, he essentially worked his way through school. It was an experience of which Harold was justifiably proud. It was also one that engendered bitterness. He realized that he had to look out for himself because no one else was going to look after him. "I have been glad of it [not getting any help] since. I didn't have to feel kindly towards anybody," he wrote, with unintended pathos, in his autobiography.[5]

At the University of Chicago, Harold made a number of friends who remained so throughout his life. One of those was destined to become his first wife. Anna Wilmarth was a pleasant-looking young woman who was a year ahead of Harold in school. She also came from one of the wealthiest families in Chicago, a family that was well known for its interest in liberal causes. Harold became interested in Anna, and he half-heartedly courted her, but he was painfully aware of the great disparity in social standing that existed between them. When she decided to marry a young history professor, James Thompson, Harold was disappointed but not surprised.

Harold and Anna Wilmarth Thompson remained friends even after her marriage, however. After graduation Ickes worked as a reporter for two Chicago newspapers while spending as much time as he could on what he truly loved, local politics. As a young man Harold identified himself politically as a reform-minded Republican, and two of his earliest political heroes were the Chicago mayoral candidate John Harlan and the feisty Progressive governor of New York Theodore Roosevelt. Due in part to their shared attitudes about politics Harold remained in close contact with the influential Wilmarth family.

Through the *fin de siècle* years Harold was an occasional visitor at the elder Wilmarths' comfortable Chicago home and at their vacation retreat at Lake Geneva, Wisconsin. He also was frequently invited to Anna and James Thompson's home, which included a baby, Wilmarth, born to Anna and James in 1899.

In 1903, Harold decided that a career in journalism was not for him, so he enrolled at the University of Chicago's School of Law. At about the same time, he concurred in a fateful decision that had far-reaching repercussions for everyone involved: Harold, who was still single and who was again struggling to put himself through school, accepted the Thompsons' "generous" invitation to live with them.

It turned out not to be a temporary living arrangement. Harold actually lived under the Thompson roof for several years. He, Anna, and James thus entered into a potentially explosive three-way relationship in which Harold and Anna became increasingly involved and James increasingly marginalized. Although Harold denied that he and Anna were having an affair during these years, that "detail" hardly mattered. They were falling in love. And Anna was dictating the nature of the relationships for all three of them. For a third time in his life, Harold found himself under the influence of a strong-willed woman. This time, however, he had helped to put himself there.

This bizarre *ménage à trois* lasted until 1909 when Anna finally decided to divorce the diffident James. She had been contemplating divorcing her husband in order to marry Harold for awhile, but it took a sexually charged incident involving the couple's adopted daughter, Frances, to make up her mind. Against both her husband's and Harold's protestations, Anna had decided to take into their home a young girl whose mother didn't want her. So Frances, who was three years older than Wilmarth, joined the Thompson household sometime around 1908 and was adopted by the Thompsons. Harold Ickes, by then an attorney, drew up the adoption papers.

In 1909, Anna confided to Harold that she had to end the marriage with James: Frances, a pubescent girl of 13, told her mother that she had awakened in the middle of the night and found her father fondling her between the legs. As soon as she fully woke up, James left the room, Frances said.[6] The girl claimed that it had happened once before. Although Anna wasn't entirely convinced Frances was telling the truth, she finally recognized an intolerable family situation. She filed for divorce and both Harold and James left the house.

Anna's and James's marriage ended quietly and without any scandal.

Shortly after his divorce, James Thompson married again and completely faded out of the family picture, leaving Anna with the two children, Wilmarth and Frances, and with Harold.

On September 16, 1911, Harold and Anna were married in a simple ceremony at Lake Geneva. By this time, Harold said, the bloom was off the rose, but he felt obligated to go through with the wedding anyway. The couple honeymooned in Europe, during which time Anna became pregnant. Between her morning sickness and his seasickness the three-month trip abroad turned out to be less than idyllic. They returned home in early January, and their son, Raymond, was born six months later. The Ickeses' ménage by 1912 included Harold and Anna, the teenaged Wilmarth and Frances, and the baby.

But Anna insisted on the same kind of household that she had run with James. Harold noted in his memoirs that there was almost always someone else living with them, usually some male relative of Anna's. "We had a pretty conglomerate family," he admitted (27). She also repeated the adoption experience. When Raymond was four years old, Anna, recognizing at age 40 that she wasn't likely to have any more children, decided the little boy needed companionship. Harold objected to the idea, pointing out to Anna that Frances's adoption hadn't worked out particularly well, but Anna was not to be deterred. A boy, just a few months younger than Raymond, was found in New York City and brought to the Ickeses' home. They changed his name from William Francis Jones to Robert Ickes, but, strangely, never formally adopted the child. Nevertheless, Robert remained in the household and was brought up as a member of the family. Given the extended family situation at the Ickeses' Hubbard Woods estate, it probably wasn't difficult for Robert to fit in, and he did develop an affection for his "mother," Anna, if not for his "father," Harold.

When the Great War broke out, Harold Ickes was living a materially comfortable life of not-so-quiet desperation. His relationship with Anna deteriorated quickly after their marriage. There were frequent fights, and Harold found himself withdrawing both sexually and emotionally from his wife. The one bright spot in this ocean of despair was, he said, the love he felt for his young son, Raymond. It was the only relationship that wasn't tainted in some way for him.

America's entry into the war in 1917 gave three members of the household the opportunity to escape—Wilmarth, Frances, and Harold. Frances was the first to leave, but Wilmarth enlisted in the Army not long afterwards. He was stationed in France. As a young woman of 21, Frances joined the Red Cross and was assigned to a post in the vicinity of Paris. Anna was not in favor of Frances's decision and so refused to accompany her daughter to New York City, where she was to board ship. Harold wound up accompanying Frances.

The pair went by train to New York. Arriving two days before her departure, Harold rented two rooms at one of his favorite hotels, the Belmont, in the heart of the city. As Ickes described at length in his memoirs, in the course of those days their relationship metamorphosed, with one result being a determination on Harold's part that he, too, had to get away from Chicago in order to participate in the Great War.

Harold and Frances had no familial or legal relationship, but of course they had lived in the same house for many years—first in the Thompson household, then in his own. The relationship between them, Ickes noted, had always been a formal and distant one. Because of Anna's jealousy of all other women, Harold said that he had no choice other than to keep Frances at arm's length. He wouldn't, and couldn't, show any "fatherly" affection toward her.

Frances reciprocated. Even in New York that first day together, Ickes recalled, Frances behaved stiffly. After dinner together, he saw her to her room, and he went to his. Her coldness bothered him, however, and so he said that he went back to her room and asked her if he could come in to talk with her. "We sat and talked for a long time and finally I broke down her reserves," Ickes wrote. "At the end, sitting in my lap and with her head on my shoulder, she sobbed out how profoundly unhappy she had been and how much she resented her mother's treatment of her" (34–36).

The following day was far more pleasant. Harold noted that they spent the day sightseeing in New York, and were much more relaxed in each other's company. But just one day later Frances was sailing for France while Harold was heading by train in the opposite direction. He was determined, however, that it wouldn't be for long.

He was too old, at 43, to see active service, so after searching for noncombat positions that would take him to Europe, Harold joined up with the YMCA. Interestingly, his assignment was in France, like Frances's and Wilmarth's, and so in the spring of 1918, Harold sailed aboard a "second-rate" French ship bound for Paris. Although he regretted having to leave his young son, Raymond, he confessed that he was so profoundly unhappy with Anna that he hoped "never to come back." Frances had expressed that same sentiment at her departure several months earlier (51 – 52).

Although Harold spent only six months in France, it was a liberating experience. He loved being in the center of the action, and actual warfare proved to be a satisfactory substitute for the political warfare with which he was familiar. Although he claimed that what he experienced in France seemed "tame" compared to Chicago politics, it was war nonetheless, and in his capacity of assisting the American troops in a variety of locales surrounding Paris, Ickes's life was on the line. The Germans, even at this late date, were fighting back with all they had, and Ickes experienced his share of strafing, bombing, and brushes with death at the hands of the enemy. He loved it.

Harold's assignment with the YMCA brought him to Paris on several occasions. Even in wartime he was able to appreciate the beauty, fine cuisine, and romantic ambiance of the city of lights. He was acquainted with a number of Americans who were also in France when he was, so he didn't lack for companionship. There was also Frances. She was working with the Red Cross in a suburb of Paris, and living with a French family who were acquaintances of the Ickeses.

In his memoirs he described in frank detail that he spent a lot of time with Frances when he happened to be in Paris. He noted his habit with her of renting two adjoining rooms at a small hotel called the Seville, and that they left the connecting door open. On one of these occasions the pair had a particularly close brush with death, when German bombers came buzzing through Paris and dropped their explosives on a building directly across the narrow street from the Seville. Harold, who said he was in Frances's room at the time, felt the building shake and saw glass shattering about him, while Frances ducked under the covers. After a few minutes it was over, but the thrill of being in such danger had a lasting effect on Harold. Those days and nights in Paris, as his memoirs make clear, were among the most satisfying he had experienced so far.

Harold also related these incidents to Anna, who was some 5,000 miles away from the drama and wondering what her husband was up to. During their six-month separation, they wrote each other frequent, lengthy letters in which they expressed feelings that they were unable to express at closer quarters, a familiar pattern of behavior in troubled relationships. In several of these letters, Harold protested

his continuing love and admiration for Anna, despite his leaving her
at Hubbard Woods with the two six-year-old boys, Raymond and
Robert.

With a lot of time for reflection, Anna began to imagine that Harold
was having too good of a time in France. She suspected him of seeing
other women. She also became suspicious of Frances. It strained her
credulity, as it does the reader of these memoirs, to believe that Harold
and Frances weren't romantically involved in Paris. His descriptions—
some twenty years after the fact—of the hotel accommodations, of
late evening dinners in little French restaurants, of "the good times
[we had] together when I was in Paris," more than hint at an intimate
relationship that went beyond the familial (101). It was a relationship
that probably began in New York when, as he said, he "broke down
her reserves."

Harold was in Paris when the war ended. A thrilling moment for
him was seeing a triumphant President Woodrow Wilson being greeted
like a savior by the French nation, and he felt fortunate to have shared
in that moment of triumph for his country. He also could feel that it
was a personal victory for him. Over Anna's objections he had partici-
pated, albeit in a tangential way, in the war effort, and in his personal
affairs he had demonstrated a degree of independence from his wife.
He seemed satisfied that Frances, a young and reasonably attractive
woman, had enjoyed his company. He discovered that he wasn't over
the hill yet.

But perhaps more important, they had become allies in their power
struggle with Anna. Ickes admitted that, among other "things," they
shared a deep resentment over Anna's domineering ways. While in
Paris they must have spent considerable time commiserating, thus ra-
tionalizing their own untoward behavior. With these experiences to
bolster his sense of self-worth, Harold prepared to return to his wife
and family a stronger and more assertive man.

On January 1, 1919, the ship that carried Harold across the Atlantic
came to a halt in a New York City harbor. Anna was waiting for him
on the dock. Their reunion was a disaster; no sooner had they hailed
a taxi than Anna accused him of having a mistress in Paris. He vehe-
mently denied it, claiming in the memoirs that he had not had any
"intercourse" during the six months he'd been away. He had learned
to live without it, he said (190–92). In their hotel room at the Belmont, Anna continued the accusations until finally she accused her

husband of what she had suspected all along, of his having had an affair with her daughter, Frances. "Frances has won you over from me!" Anna cried.

She became utterly hysterical at the thought of this betrayal by her husband and daughter. For what seemed like hours she raved at her husband and threatened to throw herself out of the hotel window. Harold recorded that he felt powerless; all he could do was lie on the bed and pray that she would calm down. Sometime that night Anna wore herself out, but the couple's awful reunion on New Year's Day marked the beginning of a nightmarish decade for both of them.

FOR HAROLD, THE 1920s were about as frustrating as one could imagine. He found the conservative regimes of Harding, Coolidge, and Hoover to be intellectually and morally bankrupt, and while he maintained his registration in the Republican Party he voted for Democratic candidates in the 1920, 1924, and 1928 presidential elections. Ickes thus began a political pattern that he adhered to for the rest of his life; nominally a Republican, he insisted on his independence from both parties, supporting the man and not the label. Invariably, however, from 1920 on he supported the candidates and platforms of the more liberal Democratic Party. In so doing he helped create what became Roosevelt's New Deal coalition in the 1930s.

Life at Hubbard Woods was as frustrating for Harold as was the conservative political scene. Anna, he said, continued to accuse him of having affairs while he was in France. He became weary of denying it. "The final effect on me," Harold wrote in his memoirs, "was to cause me to feel that, since I was to be accused anyhow, I might as well give some basis for the accusation" (354–55). Ickes never said just how much philandering he did during the Roaring '20s but he intimated that it wasn't excessive. He preferred "throwing himself" into his work instead, to relieve himself of the load of political and personal frustration he bore through the decade. After admitting in his memoirs to indulging in some extramarital relationships, he also noted, "When a man feels down and out as I did, hard, driving work is the only way out" (359).

But hard work wasn't the only way out. While Calvin Coolidge sat solemnly in the White House, and pronounced the paramount importance of business activity for the American people, Harold Ickes found himself, like millions of others with a little money, caught up in the stock market game. He admitted that "those were exciting days and I was spending money with a free hand." Out of some early profits he bought the General Printing Company and set up his stepson Wilmarth in the business, along with two other young men. Also during one of these heady years he gave Anna—in stark contrast to his usual Scotch-German frugality—$10,000 to spend on "indulgences." Some men turn to gambling in despair, Ickes wrote, some turn to drinking, and others to women. "I had already turned to women to the extent necessary to relieve my physical wants, but I had no disposition to throw myself into the women game regardless of consequences" (367–69). So he turned to gambling, to playing the stock market primarily with Anna's money, and for a few years he was quite successful at it.

This newfound ability to make money did nothing to change Anna's view of him, Ickes believed. Sometime during these tortured years Anna began viewing her husband as a "has-been." His law practice was nothing to brag about, he spent as little time with his wife and family as possible, and he continued to back losing candidates for public office, with the occasional exception, such as Mayor William Dever. Nevertheless, his own perception of himself, and the one he attributed to Anna, was highly negative. Harold considered himself, during the 1920s, a loser, a person who didn't care much whether he lived or died.

That self-image might have been reinforced when, in 1928, Harold helped to persuade Anna to run for the Illinois state legislature on the Republican ticket. She won. By this time life at home was intolerable for both of them. Wilmarth and Frances were married and living on their own. Raymond and Robert were about 16 and no longer in need of a great deal of parental care. Anna, an intelligent and energetic woman, therefore had a lot of time on her hands. She spent some of it nagging Harold, while he turned to stamp collecting and gardening to keep himself busy when at home. Desperate to find something to keep her occupied, he suggested that she run for office. Although at first she expressed reluctance, once she entered the race she went all out. Harold, who loved managing campaigns, also threw himself into the task of getting his 55-year-old wife elected. Anna's victory became one of his few political successes up to that point in his life.

"As a matter of fact," Harold wrote, "she did a good job" (362). Anna was bright, independently wealthy, and had a high-minded attitude toward public service. Like many individuals, Anna discovered that politics could help fill the void in her own sad personal life. Her newfound political career also helped to reduce some of the strain endured by all members of the Ickeses household by keeping her busy. When the legislature was in session Anna naturally had to be in Springfield, a day's ride from Winnetka. This gave the remaining family members, Harold, Raymond, and Robert, some breathing room from the woman who, Ickes claimed, was deeply resented by all of her children, and certainly by her husband (322–23).

But the same year in which Anna began her legislative career a new strain surfaced to take the place of the old one. The stock market suddenly toppled in November of 1929. Like millions of others who had speculated in the market, Harold's financial house of cards collapsed in 1929 and 1930. "I was more than worried; I was alarmed," he wrote. During the summer of 1930 Harold reluctantly accompanied Anna, Raymond, and Robert to their summer home near Gallup. It was a costly decision. There, out on the windswept, high desert, Harold watched in agony as the stock market sagged lower and lower. Had he been in Chicago, he believed, he might have been able to cut his losses. As it was, he lost his paper profit of a quarter of a million dollars that summer. It was not enough to ruin them but quite enough to teach Ickes to be more cautious about his future investments.

When Wilmarth learned of the heavy losses to his mother's estate he, too, became alarmed. Seeing his stepfather frittering away what he felt to be his rightful inheritance, Wilmarth in 1930 tried to wrest control of his mother's property from his stepfather. Wilmarth went to Harold and, one on one, demanded that he be given responsibility for his mother's estate since Harold had done such a poor job, in Wilmarth's opinion, of managing it. In a heated exchange, Harold flatly refused to relinquish control of the family's money. He was already taking a financial beating and was not about to take another from his stepson, whom he viewed as weak. "Like any man who is at heart a coward and not sure of himself," Ickes wrote about Wilmarth, "he went at me very awkwardly" (329).

Wilmarth then appealed to his mother, and an ugly scene ensued between the three of them. Harold, who felt trapped and on the defensive, characteristically came out fighting. In this exchange he used his ace in the hole—a personal loan he made to Wilmarth in connection with the General Printing Company—and threatened to destroy Wilmarth financially if he persisted in his demands. Anna, who was caught in the middle of this emotional and financial tangle, offered to buy out the loan from her husband. Ickes refused. Anna then begged him not to ruin her son, and Harold told her that "if Wilmarth would mind his own business I would be content to let things go on as they were" (330–31).

The issue thus uneasily settled, things went on as they were. However, Wilmarth emerged at this time as another competitor for power in the family circle. Harold found himself struggling with both Anna and Wilmarth over the next several years, although he was only partly aware of the extent of Wilmarth's opposition. On the surface, Wilmarth usually acted in a solicitous and cordial manner toward his stepfather, addressing him in letters as "My Dear Dad," and appearing as a neutral arbiter in the continuing fights between his mother and stepfather. Underneath the civility, though, Wilmarth fought against Harold's position in the household. The stock market crash and ensuing struggle over control of the family finances thus ushered in what Harold described as "the most difficult time in our lives together." It coincided with his call to serve in Washington (335).

FRANKLIN ROOSEVELT'S eleventh-hour selection of Harold Ickes to be his secretary of the interior signaled the turning point in Ickes's life. It is not an overstatement to say that FDR gave Ickes, a man known to the president-elect only for his record of supporting Democratic candidates and liberal causes, the opportunity to remake his life. In the space of a few months in 1933, Harold Ickes went from being a Chicago "has-been" to a potentially powerful man in Washington. Even Anna began to change her opinion of her husband as a result of this appointment. She enjoyed the idea of being the wife of a cabinet officer, he said.

Given this unprecedented opportunity to launch a new public career, it is remarkable that Harold Ickes would jeopardize it in any way. But he did just that when, after only a week or so in Washington, he embarked on a passionate affair with a divorced woman whom he had known for many years. It evolved into an extraordinarily messy and tangled thing, as many affairs do, yet Ickes continued seeing this woman for several years, until their passions were spent. That he would do so, knowing full well that he was jeopardizing the career chance of a lifetime, is testimony to the degree to which he felt sexually and emotionally deprived in his fifty-ninth year.

This affair with "X," as he identified her in his memoirs, was a very significant event in Ickes's life. Beginning in 1933, thanks to FDR, the middle-aged Ickes was in the midst of a period of self-actualization. It encompassed both his professional and personal lives. Many pages of the unpublished personal memoirs are taken up with a candid discussion of his initial Washington affair. While he admitted that he experienced with Marguerite Moser Brumbaugh, or X, a degree of sexual gratification that he had never before known, he also acknowledged that it came at a terrific cost.

Anna and other individuals first learned of the affair when Marguerite's fiancé, Thornton Bonneville, became suspicious. He wrote numerous anonymous letters to Anna, to Marguerite, and then to newspaper publishers. Louis Howe in the White House also received letters from individuals commenting on the personal goings-on of important people in Washington. "What's this I hear about Ickes keeping a dame on the payroll?" someone wrote Howe. "First [Hugh] Johnson, now Ickes,"[7] the writer complained. If Howe knew, FDR also knew of the affair even before Ickes told him about it. But the president considered it less important than the work Ickes was doing as interior secretary, public works administrator, and oil administrator. It was fortunate for Ickes that FDR had the priorities that he did because otherwise his Washington career would have been very brief. It was a cost, Ickes claimed, that he would have borne in order to maintain the relationship with his mistress.

Although Ickes initially denied to Anna that he was involved with someone else, he decided to tell her the truth when she came to Washington in November for the White House cabinet dinner. Anna and Harold largely lived apart during 1933. She was still serving in the Illinois state legislature, and she also chose, as was her custom, to spend the summer in New Mexico. But when Anna came to town for this important occasion, her husband "hit her between the eyes" with his confession.

The result of this revelation was about six months of complete hell in the Ickeses household. Anna flew into rages that surpassed anything Harold had seen before. Their son Wilmarth was dragged down from Chicago to referee their fights; divorce was considered and rejected. Finally Anna could bear the strain no longer. She took an overdose of prescription medicine, called her physician for help, and was hospitalized for two weeks in the spring of 1934. This marked the nadir of their marriage. After returning home Anna was resigned to the changed relationship, Harold said. "I was the head of the family. She had lost her power over me. . . . She knew that she was licked and that I had licked her, however cruel my method had been," he wrote in the memoirs (404).

Just as he made heavy sacrifices in his personal life in order to continue seeing Marguerite, Ickes did the same with his official position. His behavior concerning the affair was one of a very few instances when Harold Ickes strayed beyond the bounds of what was proper public conduct. He not only hired Marguerite, her fiancé, and her female roommate for positions within his administration, but even worse, he used his director of investigations to stop the leak about the affair. He did this after going to Louis Howe to discuss what to do about the continuing stream of anonymous letters that were surfacing in Washington and elsewhere. Howe assigned an officer of the Secret Service to track down the identity of the letter-writer but he came up with nothing.

Exasperated at the Secret Service's incompetence, Ickes in desperation turned to his own head of investigations, the infamous Louis Glavis, to disclose the source of the scurrilous attacks on him. By using Glavis in this way Ickes, of course, knew that he was further jeopardizing his career. But Marguerite's grip was strong. He refused to give her up, so he felt that the only way to end the public gossip was to get some hard evidence on the individual whom he and Marguerite had figured out was the author of the letters. That was her fiancé.

"This was one really good job that he did," Ickes brashly wrote about Glavis. Within a few days of getting the assignment Glavis had the evidence. However, it took blatantly illegal means to obtain it. Ickes first sent the fiancé down south "on departmental business," and while he was out of town Glavis persuaded a real estate agent to let him into the fiancé's rented apartment. There Glavis found the typewriter on which the letters were written, and even some used carbons in the wastebasket.

With the carbon papers in hand, Ickes called Bonneville to his office when he returned from his make-work assignment. Ickes charged him with writing the malicious letters. "He denied the accusation because he couldn't very well do anything else," he wrote in the memoirs. Then, without expressing the slightest hesitation, Ickes fired him (392–94). After being dismissed, Bonneville stopped writing the letters, and Ickes had perhaps less to worry about. But he was fortunate indeed that few people at the time learned that he had used Glavis in this manner. Had Glavis divulged this incident, for instance, during the 1938 congressional hearings on Ebert Burlew's confirmation, Senator Pittman would have had the ammunition he needed. It is very likely that Ickes would have been forced to resign.

As he recalled his first year in Washington for the memoirs, it is remarkable that Ickes survived. He was under tremendous stress from his official duties, which included running three federal agencies simultaneously, and of course, from his marital and extramarital relationships. In his passion for Marguerite he did things that obviously he wouldn't have done otherwise. Consequently he created yet more pressure for himself. One of his strengths, however, which Roosevelt almost immediately saw and appreciated, was Ickes's phenomenal ability to work under duress. That quality was very much in evidence in 1933 and 1934.

At least in his personal life, things improved marginally after the 1934 dénouement when Anna half-heartedly tried to commit suicide. They reached an accommodation, he said, in which they continued to live in the same house but didn't share the marital bed. The couple kept up appearances. Although Wilmarth, who was a frequent visitor to his parents' home during this tempestuous time, counseled a divorce, neither Harold nor Anna was in favor of that solution. A divorce would have benefited Wilmarth, but Anna was already once divorced and didn't wish at age 60 to repeat that experience. Harold, although he refused to end his affair, said that he had never been willing to divorce Anna in order to marry X (397). So, this middle-aged couple grimly persevered, as many couples do.

To Anna's credit, Ickes noted, she never complained about the other woman. "As between us, X passed out of the picture entirely" (410). When Anna died in an automobile accident in August 1935, Harold still was seeing Marguerite, although the initial passion was by then far spent and she had married her troublesome fiancé.

Needless to say, his wife's accidental death was not an occasion of grief for Harold. He felt that Anna had spent one of the happiest summers of her life in New Mexico prior to her death, and that they had straightened out their personal problems "quite satisfactorily" by 1935 (337). In fact, Anna's funeral at Hubbard Woods evoked little emotion from anyone except Robert, Ickes claimed. In her misery, Anna had turned to Wilmarth and to her un-adopted son, Robert, who apparently responded with genuine affection, despite the fact that "she had always disliked and despised" him, according to Ickes.

At Memorial Cemetery in Winnetka, with the leaves beginning to turn and a late summer wind blowing off Lake Michigan, Anna Wilmarth Ickes was laid to rest as her family gathered around. For the memoirs Harold recalled his thoughts: "There I watched the lowering into the grave of the body of the woman whom I had once loved with all of my emotions and supported with all of my chivalry, a woman, however, with whom I had never lived happily from the beginning" (416–17).

If little emotion was spent grieving for Anna at her funeral, a lot was vented regarding her sizable fortune. In the memoirs Ickes acknowledged that three of the children—Wilmarth, Frances, and Robert— were shocked by their mother's will, which left almost everything to Harold. The children were aware that Anna had made a codicil to her will after she learned about her husband's affair. But when Wilmarth called on the family's attorney, Charles Thomson, to ask about the codicil, Thomson told him that it had been destroyed. A bitter and enraged Wilmarth returned to Hubbard Woods and gave the bad news to his brothers and sister (339).

It is in the memoirs that Harold Ickes described the unusual circumstances regarding the codicil, which included its destruction after Anna's death (418–19). Whether or not Wilmarth and the other children knew these facts, the result was the same. The children received virtually nothing from their mother's estate. Wilmarth and Robert, in particular, were livid at being disinherited, and both boys sought to wreak some revenge on their stepfather.

Not long after Anna's death Harold Ickes began courting Jane Dahlman, the sister of Wilmarth's wife, Betty. At the same time Wilmarth engaged in ever more self-destructive behavior. He gambled, drank too much, was seen in public with other women, and paid little attention to his business. He also managed to turn his father-in-law against his stepfather. Mr. Dahlman liked Wilmarth, sympathized with his pain over losing what he thought was his rightful inheritance, and agreed with him that Harold Ickes was an unacceptable suitor for Jane. Mr. Dahlman referred to Ickes as a "roué." Wilmarth thus succeeded in helping to delay the marriage between Jane and Harold. Her family, especially her father, was unalterably opposed, and they put considerable pressure on her not to marry a man forty years her senior who also had a reputation for womanizing.

The two-year delay in their marriage, and the unease it caused Harold Ickes, constituted a minor victory for Wilmarth. But Wilmarth's anger was profound. Although there were several reasons why Wilmarth scrawled a note to his wife and raised a loaded weapon to his head precisely one year after his mother's death, revenge played a part. Upon learning of Wilmarth's suicide on August 31, 1936, Ickes at once recognized that aspect of the tragedy. "Even in dying Wilmarth struck a vicious blow which I was fortunate to be able to parry" (343), Ickes wrote, in reference to Wilmarth's suicide note where he said that he couldn't take it anymore from "H.L."

Ickes knew that if the note were made public, Colonel McCormick of the *Chicago Tribune,* not to mention other opponents of the New Deal, would get a lot of political mileage out of it. It was, after all, a presidential election year. His parrying of Wilmarth's final blow thus consisted of asking the chief of police of Winnetka and the county coroner to deny the existence of the note at the inquest. They "perjured themselves magnificently and I have always felt tremendously grateful to them," Ickes acknowledged in his memoirs (346).

Three years after Wilmarth's death, Robert Ickes, the child who never had been formally adopted by Anna and Harold, decided to resume the warfare. In 1939 he filed a suit against his stepfather in which he claimed that he had been deprived of his rightful inheritance. Over the next few years the suit wound its way through the courts of Illinois, while some of the nation's newspapers, Cissy Patterson's especially, fueled the controversy between stepfather and son. It finally ended in the Illinois Supreme Court. In January 1944 the Court found in Harold Ickes's favor. Ickes argued, through his former solicitor, Nathan Margold, that since Robert was never adopted by the Ickeses, he was not legally entitled to any share in the inheritance.

Harold Ickes thus won a legal decision against Robert Ickes. Whether justice was served was another matter. At long last, Harold Ickes could claim that he had established a position of dominance in his original family. But the cost of the power struggle within the family during the 1930s had been tremendous: Wilmarth was dead, and Robert Ickes became a frustrated, paunchy, middle-aged man who drank too much, was in and out of jail on DUIs, and who had trouble keeping a job for very long. Fortunately the other two children, Frances and Raymond, were far less affected.

BUT ROBERT'S LAWSUIT was little more than a minor, albeit embarrassing, irritant, for by 1939 Harold Ickes had established himself as both an important public figure and the unquestioned head of his second family. With his marriage to Jane in 1938, and the births of their two children, Harold McEwen in 1939 and Elizabeth Ann in 1941, Harold established the family he had always wanted. He found familial and personal contentment for the first time in his long life. Jane, he wrote at the end of the account, was a perfect wife and companion. She was sensual, intelligent, mature, and a devoted mother (433–34). Moreover, she assumed the traditional wifely role; unlike Anna, Jane allowed Harold to wear the pants in the family and she rarely challenged his authority. "The household definitely revolved around him," their daughter Elizabeth remembered years later.[8]

This candid document, the unpublished personal memoirs of Harold Ickes, concluded on a happy note. That is a remarkable fact in itself, given the revelations it contains. In reliving those tumultuous years with Anna and her children a more introspective or sensitive individual might have been tempted to take a revolver to *his* head. But, for all of his estimable qualities, Harold Ickes was not a soul-searcher. He preferred to live in the present and look to the future rather than to brood about the past. Whatever guilt or remorse he had about those unhappy, tragic events was buried deep within him. Perhaps that is why he had such trouble sleeping.

Ickes began dictating his autobiography in 1939 and concluded it around May of 1940. His final remarks were about how wonderful Jane was and how fine a baby they were blessed with. "Our baby at nine months of age is the happiest, healthiest and most promising child that I have ever known," the proud father wrote. "I have never been sorry that I married Jane," he added (433–34). His only expressed regret in 1940 was that he wasn't twenty-five years younger.

CHAPTER 20

"THEN IT'S HAPPENED"

WAR IN EUROPE

THE FIRST WEEKEND in September of 1939 changed the world. The president, sleeping soundly in his bedroom at the White House, was awakened at 2:50 A.M. on September 2 by a transatlantic call from Paris; Ambassador William C. Bullitt was on the telephone. " 'I've just talked to Tony Biddle in Poland. The German Army has started marching,' Bullitt said. Roosevelt's answer was calm: 'Then it's happened,' " he replied.

Lights flickered on and telephones started to ring in Washington that sultry night. Secretary of State Cordell Hull was roused by calls from ambassadors Kennedy in London and Bullitt in Paris, just after they had spoken with the commander-in-chief. By a fortuitous coincidence, Gen. George C. Marshall was sworn in as chief of staff just the previous day, and he, too, was awakened with the awful but expected news early Saturday morning.[1]

As word spread through the country that weekend, many wondered how America would respond. Most Americans were still trying to work themselves, and the nation, out of the Great Depression. The economic situation had much improved over what it was in 1933, but there was still a long way to go before prosperity again became taken for granted. There was, too, the myriad of as-yet-unanswered social and political problems that worried observers of prewar America, such as David Brinkley. As a young journalist just embarking on his career, Brinkley in his wartime reminiscences reflected on the pitiful state that characterized the nation's capital on September 1, 1939:

> Outside, Washington was suffering the heat, with its politicians and lobbyists, its clerks and mechanics, with a local economy devoted mainly to retail and service trades, with miles of slums filled with shacks without plumbing and black people in poverty, more of them every day. Was it conceivable that the leadership of the Western world in wartime could fall to a city only a few generations out of the mud? A city that still boasted fifteen thousand privies?[2]

It was a sensible question posed by the journalist, but it admitted no rational answer. The United States, despite its obvious imperfections, courageously rose to the occasion and became, as FDR memorably put it, the world's "arsenal of democracy."

On Saturday morning, September 2, Harold Ickes woke up early at Headwaters Farm to learn of Germany's invasion. It promised to be an eventful weekend: Jane was expecting their baby at any moment, he had his usual weekend work to do, and he was invited to a stag dinner and poker party scheduled for that evening at the White House. Through the day Ickes took care of his weekly dictation and spent time with Jane. Since the baby didn't arrive Harold was chauffeured to the White House for an evening with the president, who was now verging on becoming a wartime leader, and four others in the poker-playing group.

The grim news from abroad notwithstanding, it was a lively and lighthearted gathering, Ickes noted. Roosevelt loved poker and found in the game a way to relax. Moreover, some of Ickes's favorite associates were there: Solicitor General Bob Jackson, the lovable life of the party "Pa" Watson, Ross McIntire, and Steve Early. Harry Hopkins probably would have been there, too, except that he was out of town for another thorough going-over at the Mayo Clinic. Over cocktails Ickes amused the president with a joke about Ambassador Joseph

Kennedy. He said that Prime Minister Neville Chamberlain recently announced his decision to increase the cabinet so that he could give Kennedy a place in it. "The President threw back his head and had a good laugh," Ickes reported.[3]

After an "adequate" dinner, which was all one ever expected in the Roosevelt White House, the group went into the Oval Room for poker. Ickes was pleasantly surprised at being one of the winners that night, collecting a total of $53.50. "The President was the heaviest loser," Ickes said, winding up $35.00 in the hole. But he was a good sport about it, and the secretary then made a remark about Roosevelt's character which had far wider application than just to poker: "One thing about playing with the President, we do not have to curry favor by letting him win. Everyone goes after him just as hard as after anyone else, and he likes it that way."

They played until just after midnight. The game was interrupted twice as the president was handed the latest news from Europe. At 11 o'clock, Ickes noted, the president looked up after having read a communiqué and told his friends, "War will be declared by noon tomorrow." The group's reaction, according to Ickes, was that "all of us were pleased at this prospect, not because any of us wanted war, but because, believing it to be inevitable in the end, we thought that it was better for England and France to get into it as quickly as possible."

On Sunday morning, September 3, Harold and Jane drove over to Johns Hopkins Hospital in Baltimore, as their baby contemplated its arrival into the world on the historic weekend. Newspaper boys were hawking special editions of the *Baltimore Sun,* and Harold stopped the car on a streetcorner to buy one. "As the President had predicted the night before," Ickes observed, "war had been declared by England against Germany," with France immediately following suit.[4]

With Jane settled at the hospital, Harold returned home to absorb the news and get ready for what would be a busy, momentous week. A special cabinet meeting was scheduled for Monday afternoon to discuss what Roosevelt told the American people in his Sunday night Fireside Chat concerning the war. "As long as it remains within my power to prevent, there will be no black-out of peace in the United States," the president promised.[5] He informed the country that he was about to issue a Proclamation of Neutrality, in accordance with existing law, and that he was going to ask Congress for the second time that year to amend the 1935 Neutrality Act so that "our neutrality can be made a true neutrality." Roosevelt made it clear that he, together with the entire government, wanted to stay out of this war, but he also said that the American people must master "a simple but unalterable fact in modern foreign relations between nations. When peace has been broken anywhere, the peace of all countries everywhere is in danger." The president thus skillfully blended isolationism with intervention in his first radio address after Europe went to war. He followed that pattern until December 7, 1941.

The president concluded the Fireside Chat with the observation that neutrality did not preclude freedom of thought and of speech. "This nation will remain a neutral nation, but I cannot ask that every American remain neutral in thought as well. Even a neutral has a right to take account of facts. Even a neutral cannot be asked to close his mind or his conscience." Ickes was pleased that FDR included this caveat in the speech. They had discussed it before Roosevelt went on the air, and Ickes felt that in making this statement "the President went as far as he could in expressing the sympathy of our people for the democracies." [6]

The subject of the special cabinet meeting on September 4 was how to get Congress's consent to amend the neutrality laws so that America could aid England and France during the critical first months of the war. They also discussed the related question of whether the president ought to issue a declaration of emergency right away or wait until public opinion solidified with regard to the European war. Henry Wallace spoke on behalf of waiting, while Ickes took the opposite position, arguing "that the people were prepared for such a declaration now [enhancing the powers of the Executive Branch] and that it ought to be issued without delay." [7]

The secretary scarcely voiced his opinion before a messenger came into the cabinet room at 3:15 and handed Ickes the news that Jane had just given birth to a "fine baby boy." Excusing himself from the cabinet meeting, Ickes went into Missy Le Hand's office and spoke with Jane's doctor, who assured him everything was fine. Ickes told him that he'd be over on the 4 o'clock train. "In the meantime," Ickes wrote of that doubly eventful afternoon, "I went back into the Cabinet room and about three-forty I sent a note up to the president, asking him whether I might be excused. He sensed the situation at once and nodded a smiling affirmative." [8]

When the new father arrived at Johns Hopkins Hospital Jane was asleep, so he went into the nursery and saw his son for the first time. The doctors and nurses assured him that he and Jane had produced a physically perfect little baby. "I was particularly glad that it was a boy because Jane wanted a boy," Ickes related, "and with the short span of life that is ahead of me . . . I, too, very much wanted it to be a boy. . . . In anticipation that it might be . . . , we had decided to call him Harold McEwen, the second name being the correctly spelled name of my mother's family."

The press of events, both personal and political, kept Harold Ickes constantly on the go during the week that witnessed the beginning of the most horrendous war of the century. He managed to get in nearly a full day's worth of work before heading to Baltimore each afternoon to visit Jane and the baby. On Tuesday he held little Harold in his arms for the first time. "He is adorable," the father wrote. "He has fair skin and big blue eyes and apparently his hair is going to be chestnut. . . . His body and limbs are well formed and his features are good, although I have some doubts about his nose." It was a ski-slope nose that resembled Bob Hope's and his own.

With Jane and the baby doing well, Harold devoted much of his time, like others in the administration, to organizational issues arising from the national emergency. On September 8 FDR issued, as Ickes hoped he would, Proclamation No. 2352, Declaring a Limited National Emergency. This allowed the president and officers of the executive branch to undertake the twin objectives of enforcing America's neutrality and of strengthening the country's national defense "within the limits of peacetime authorizations."[9]

Not coincidentally, that day the president also issued his third executive reorganization plan, dealing primarily with overhauling the executive office of the president. A White House Office was created and a strengthened Bureau of the Budget was transferred from the Treasury Department to the president's executive office. "The President needs [more] help," Louis Brownlow stated succinctly in submitting his committee's report on reorganization to Congress back in 1937. After Congress finally allowed the president some authority to rearrange functions in the executive branch, FDR moved with dispatch to strengthen his office. The final reorganizations were effected just as the war broke out.

There was no dearth of issues competing for the attention of those in the governing establishment as the nation confronted a drastically changed international situation, but two in particular concerned the cadre of liberals in Roosevelt's administration. One was the necessity of making some personnel changes in the cabinet to provide stronger leadership in the War and Navy departments. The other was how the president could avoid making the mistake that Pres. Woodrow Wilson made some twenty years earlier in not keeping at bay what Ickes referred to as the "Wall Streeters and economic royalists" of the country during a national emergency. Ickes, of course, had firm opinions on both subjects. He, together with his fellow liberals Robert Jackson, Harry Hopkins, Tom Corcoran, and Ben Cohen, tried to form a united front to lobby FDR to adopt their views.

On September 6, Ickes had an appointment with Roosevelt.[10] Ickes began by asking FDR whether he could be very frank with him. "You can speak to him perfectly frankly, just as you have always done, and just as I have talked to you," Roosevelt replied. The two men then discussed potential candidates for what was to become Roosevelt's war cabinet. They also considered how best to handle the industrialists and bankers of the country.

The president needed three new department heads and Ickes was anxious to have his candidates considered. The death of Navy Secretary Claude Swanson in July left a vacancy in that critical position. Roosevelt also was concerned that "poor Harry Hopkins" was so badly off that he would have to find a replacement for him at the Commerce Department. Third, there was the key position of secretary of war. It was currently filled, but ineffectively so, by Harry Woodring, whom Ickes described as a "pompous second- or third-rate intellect." The president agreed that he had to clear out both Woodring and his assistant secretary, Louis Johnson. The former was weak and the latter, Roosevelt told Ickes, "talks too much."

There was also the 1940 presidential election to consider. With the dual objectives of strengthening the cabinet and making it nonpartisan, Ickes called to Roosevelt's attention his old Chicago friend and fellow Progressive, Col. Frank Knox. Ickes brought a two-page letter from Knox to show to FDR. It indicated, Ickes felt, that while Knox "was impetuous and inclined to think off the top of his head at times, he liked the President personally, he was loyal, and he would do a good job if called upon." Moreover, Ickes argued, "his attitude on the international situation has been as fine as anyone could ask for."

Another point in Knox's favor was that he had been Alf Landon's running mate in the 1936 presidential contest. Roosevelt brought up the possibility of bringing into the cabinet both Landon and Knox. The secretary thought well of the idea. "[FDR] will not only have a stronger Cabinet by including two Republicans, the two who ran for President and Vice President . . . in 1936; he would silence all criticism of having a partisan Cabinet at a time of crisis." Such a move, they agreed, would blunt the criticism emanating from certain elements of the press and from the Republican Party about excessive partisanship in the White House.

But naming Knox and/or Landon would have a further benefit, Roosevelt saw. The president thought that the newspapers' hidden agenda was building up a viable Republican challenger for 1940— Herbert Hoover, Arthur Vandenberg, Robert Taft, the young Henry Cabot Lodge, and "even Dewey" were being mentioned most often as cabinet appointments. But in naming Knox and Landon he could avoid saddling himself with another John Garner–like pretender to the throne, for no one considered the 1936 Republican presidential and vice-presidential candidates serious challengers in 1940. They had been too thoroughly trounced by Roosevelt in the landslide election of 1936. With a foxy smile, Roosevelt told Ickes, "[the press] won't like it." In 1940, in time to have an impact on the election, Roosevelt demonstrated his political acumen by appointing Frank Knox secretary of the Navy. A second prominent Republican, Henry L. Stimson, became secretary of war. Stimson had served as Herbert Hoover's secretary of state.

Continuing to speak frankly to FDR during their meeting on September 6, Ickes raised the other issue that was bothering liberals, that the principles on which the New Deal was based would be abandoned during the national emergency. The secretary told FDR that the liberal movement lost all of twenty years' momentum due to Wilson's turning the government over to big business during the world war. He said he hoped Roosevelt wouldn't make the same mistake. "You are much abler and smarter than Wilson," Ickes said, "and you have the advantage of having had experience in a world war, but the same thing could happen now." The president swiftly replied, "Don't think that I am not watching everything with an eagle eye." He showed Ickes a memorandum he had just sent to the chairman of the Securities and Exchange Commission, Jerome Frank, telling Frank to redouble his efforts at watching the activities of those on Wall Street. As Ickes left the White House the president again assured him that he intended to checkmate any nefarious attempts on the part of the banking and business establishments to use the national emergency to their financial advantage. Roosevelt still believed in the New Deal.

As a result of Roosevelt's reorganization orders Harold Ickes had, through the summer and fall of 1939, merely one full-time job to do. That was his original assignment, heading the Interior Department. Most people of age 65, and especially those few in that age category having a new baby to enjoy, would be happy with a single job. They might even be contemplating retirement. Not Ickes. The departure of the Public Works Administration from his jurisdiction left him feeling empty. He also continued to be upset with the president for transferring only a few agencies which he characterized as of minor importance to his department, while not transferring the Forest Service. In October he confided to his diaries that he was depressed:

> At various periods I have been tired during my lifetime and I have had great difficulty sleeping, but I do not think that I have ever been in as bad shape as I am now. The medicine that I have been taking for sleeping . . . , nembutal, seems to have no effect on me any more, and substitutes . . . leave me with a terrific hangover. . . . This whole situation dates from the time of the issuance by the President of his second reorganization order. I am sure that the way he manhandled my Department in that order, not so much in what he took away but in what he failed to transfer to me and the manner of his doing it, hurt my morale to a degree from which I have not yet recovered.[11]

During the brief time in which the secretary had only one major responsibility, and despite his feeling awful, he nevertheless threw himself into work bearing on the Interior Department. Strengthening Interior was one of Harold Ickes's long-range objectives, but because he often had other jobs to do he could only devote himself periodically to this aim. The fall of 1939 proved to be one of those periods.

In September Ickes began cultivating a closer relationship with the president of the United Mine Workers, John L. Lewis. He invited him to his office to discuss coal policy. Lewis was, according to Ickes, an impressive individual whose "strength is almost overpowering. [He is] a great, huge bull of a man."[12] At their meeting the labor leader told Ickes that he was reasonably satisfied with the way the Coal Division was operating since its transfer to Interior. He was glad, he said, that critical aspects of the coal industry now fell under Ickes's jurisdiction. Although a deep political chasm separated them—Lewis came to despise FDR while Ickes continued, through thick and thin, to consider the president his principal political hero—the two men nevertheless respected one another. They worked together for several years, under very stressful conditions, to assure a better deal for the nation's coal miners.

Before Lewis left the secretary's office the subject of the war in Europe came up, and Lewis said that if America was dragged into it he hoped that Ickes would chair a wartime commission on coal. "We all have confidence in you," he said. Lewis then suggested the immediate creation of a commission consisting of two coal operators and two representatives of the miners. "I am not certain but that this might be a good thing," Ickes mused.[13] One way or another the nation's mineral resources were bound to play a strategic role in the war. No one understood this better than Harold Ickes, whose department had jurisdiction over a wealth of natural resources. But fashioning an efficient, centrally controlled, well-coordinated, and smoothly running organization out of the motley collection of agencies that comprised the Interior Department was not an easy task. Ickes had been working on cleaning out his Augean stables for six years by 1939, and there still was a lot to be done. So at the same time as he discussed coal policy with John L. Lewis he called in the director of the Bureau of Mines, Dr. John Finch, to discuss operations in Finch's unit. The secretary was not pleased with Finch's leadership, and he told him in September that "I felt all right about him personally but that he had not been strong enough to handle the little clique that has been running the Bureau . . . since before it came back into my Department." Ickes ordered Finch to "clean house" and establish himself as "the real head of the bureau." Ickes subsequently confided in his diary, "I doubt whether Finch is strong enough to do this but at least I have given him fair warning."[14]

A number of positions were vacant in Interior that fall, and the secretary searched for the best talent he could find to fill them. He was fortunate, he felt, to have hired Abe Fortas in the spring of 1939 to work in the Public Works Administration. When it was transferred out from under Ickes's control a few months later, Ickes asked Fortas to stay on as counsel for the Bituminous Coal Division. Although he was an imperious man, and sometimes difficult to work with, Fortas proved to be highly intelligent, hard-working, and a strong liberal. Ickes considered him to be one of his most valuable associates, and the two men became close in the six years that they worked together.

But there were a number of other vacancies to fill, including once again the undersecretary's position, and also the coveted directorship of the Division of Territories and Island Possessions. For a second time Ickes tried to entice the chief of the Forest Service, Ferdinand Silcox, to take the post of undersecretary, but Silcox refused. Despite Ickes's asking the president himself to prevail upon Silcox, the chief forester demurred. He told FDR that he was quite content where he was. Moreover, Silcox said that he didn't like Ickes's assistant secretary, Ebert Burlew, a man with whom he would have to work closely.

While Ickes was trying to persuade Silcox to take the job in Interior the chief forester died of a heart attack at age 57. The secretary said he felt "a personal sense of loss. Silcox was not only an excellent man in Forestry, he had a fine and broad and understanding outlook on social and economic questions." Shortly after Silcox's unexpected death in 1939 Ickes selected, with FDR's concurrence, the influential Texan and political mentor of young Lyndon B. Johnson, Alvin J. Wirtz, for the undersecretary's position. Although it was another political appointment, rather than one based principally on merit (such as he had hoped to make by appointing the chief forester), nevertheless Ickes was optimistic. He thought that Wirtz would work out far better than his first two undersecretaries, Charles West and Harry Slattery.

For the directorship of the islands and territories division, Ickes turned to a man with the kind of qualifications that he admired in Silcox. He asked the handsome New Dealer Rexford Tugwell to take the position. An economist by profession, Tugwell had been one of the original members of FDR's Brains Trust. In 1933 he joined the administration as assistant secretary of agriculture. Tugwell moved up to become Agriculture's undersecretary, but in 1937 he took the position of chairman of New York City's planning board. Although the directorship was attractive to Tugwell, in October he told Ickes that he would have to decline. Over lunch he explained to the secretary that it meant too great a financial sacrifice: He was making $15,000 a year in his present position while the most Ickes could offer him was $9,000. "I could hardly expect him to make such a sacrifice," Ickes admitted. It was back to the drawing boards for this appointment.

By September Ickes also had decided to replace his Park Service director, Arno Cammerer. "I am thoroughly persuaded that I cannot go along much longer with Cammerer," Ickes wrote after having discussed with FDR the possibility of offering the directorship to Robert Moses, of all people—one of the few mortals whom the president detested. Telling Roosevelt to get a firm grip on his chair, Ickes plunged ahead and asked him what he thought about a Moses appointment. "He didn't react as violently as I expected," Ickes observed. After a moment's consideration, the president said, "Well, Bob Moses would make a great park system. He would get things done. And in getting things done he would run over anybody or any law. He pays absolutely no attention to the law. You would get awake in the middle of the night and wonder what Bob Moses was doing and how he was doing it." It was back to the drawing boards on finding a replacement for Cammerer, too.

Through the fall the secretary used a giant-sized broom to sweep through his department. No doubt some of his reputation for being a tough and exacting administrator dates from this frenzy of autumnal activity. In October he was apprised of possible illegal activities occurring in his Bureau of Fisheries and its regulation of the salmon industry in Alaska. The acting head of the agency told Ickes that some of the bureau men up there were incompetent, crooked, or both, so the secretary turned to J. Edgar Hoover's FBI to investigate the situation. Ickes followed this with a reorganization of units, in which he combined the Bureau of Fisheries (which had been transferred from the Commerce Department) with the Bureau of Biological Survey (which had come to Interior from the Agriculture Department). "I think that we can effect some real economies by doing this and certainly we will be much more efficient because there has been a good deal of overlapping between these two bureaus," Ickes wrote in December.

In another meeting with FDR to discuss departmental staffing Ickes urged the appointment of Dr. Ira Gabrielson to head the reorganized agency, called the U.S. Fish and Wildlife Service. Gabrielson was a career bureaucrat. He had been employed by the Bureau of Biological Survey since 1915, and Ickes told the president that he thought highly of him. Roosevelt, however, was being pressured by Sen. Matthew Neely of West Virginia—a good friend to the administration— to appoint a physician from his state. Ickes balked.

My objection to [Doctor] McClintock is that there is nothing in his record to show that he is qualified for this important place. My principal objection is that it would be frankly keeping the Bureau of Fisheries in politics when politics has been its bane ever since 1933, when [Commerce Secretary] Roper threw out a highly qualified man in order to appoint Frank T. Bell, the secretary of the then Senator Dill, of Washington.

Ickes prevailed on the appointment, and Gabrielson became the first director of the newly formed U.S. Fish and Wildlife Service. FDR found another position for McClintock.

The secretary's housecleaning reached its zenith in December when he ordered the soda fountain in the department's basement cafeteria temporarily closed. In an unannounced trip to the cafeteria, Ickes found

the long counter . . . crowded, three or four deep, with people smoking and drinking coffee, eating sandwiches and having a pleasant, leisurely time. . . . I was in the cafe for some ten minutes and with practically no exceptions the persons whom I found relaxing from the tediousness of their work at the soda fountain were there both when I entered and when I left.[15]

As soon as he returned to his office on the sixth floor, Ickes called in Burlew and issued the order. "For a long time I have been trying to impress upon the bureau chiefs to see to it that our Government employees do not waste Government time in this fashion. Since the bureau chiefs are either indifferent . . . or unable to control the situation, I decided to take action myself." The old curmudgeon, as he called himself, was definitely on a rampage. It was time for FDR to give him more work to do.

THE EFFORT TO amend the Neutrality Act of 1935, which speechwriter Robert Sherwood claimed had been "carefully designed to prevent us from getting into war in 1917," headed the president's list of concerns during the fall of 1939.[16] Shortly after the European war broke out, FDR called Congress into emergency session and told them to concentrate on one issue and one issue alone: They must repeal the arms embargo provisions contained in one of the most extreme expressions of isolationism ever passed by Congress, the Neutrality Act.

Its intent had backfired, the president argued. He also admitted to having made a mistake in not vetoing the legislation. What the act did was to give the edge to Germany and Russia at the expense of England, a maritime power, and of France. It created artificial distinctions between exports—between the export of cotton and the export of gun cotton, or between sheets of aluminum and airplane wings—Roosevelt informed Congress when it met on September 21, 1939. "I seek a greater consistency through the repeal of the embargo provisions, and a return to international law," the president said. "I seek reenactment of the historic and traditional American policy which, except for the disastrous interlude of the Embargo and Non-Intercourse Acts [early in the nineteenth century], has served us well from the very beginning of our Constitutional existence." [17]

Ickes completely agreed with the president on the issue. He, together with the other members of the cabinet, listened while Roosevelt "soberly and effectively" delivered his message to Congress. Since the House had already passed the Bloom Amendment at its last session, the decision now rested with the Senate. Ickes believed that it would pass by a comfortable margin.

> However, the pacifists and the subversive people are busy flooding Members of Congress with communications in the name of so-called peace, protesting against an act which isn't a neutrality act at all. . . . Under the present act, we are really throwing our weight with Germany and Russia and against France and England, just as we threw it to Franco against the Loyalists in Spain and are helping Japan at the expense of China. [18]

Public opinion was changing. With it came a slight change in Congress's rigid isolationism, or what many at the time felt was a de facto pro-fascist position. At the cabinet meeting following the president's address to Congress, Vice-President Garner told the president that the situation looked good on the Hill regarding the amendment to allow "cash and carry" sales to all countries engaged in conflict. The president, Ickes related, agreed; he said that "he hadn't had to buy a Senator yet." Earlier in the week Senator Byrnes of South Carolina came in to see the president and told him that there were three who could be bought on this issue, "but he [Byrnes] didn't think it would be necessary to buy any." [19]

A month later the Senate voted. It passed an amended neutrality act by a vote of sixty-three to thirty. "So this takes us over that important hurdle," Ickes observed. The vote was a significant victory for Roosevelt, and in the fall of 1939 many people saw a marked change in the president's stature. Joseph Lash, Eleanor Roosevelt's close friend, observed that "the crisis [in Europe] . . . disposed people to listen to Roosevelt again and he moved with the same skill that he had shown in the 1933 crisis toward preparedness, aid to Britain, and a third term." [20] Harold Ickes noted the same thing, observing that "the President is on the top of the world politically. . . . From every quarter comes word that the people have confidence in the President in this international situation to a degree that they do not have it in anyone else." [21]

Ickes, who had not only been among the first to board, but who had helped build, the president's third-term bandwagon, was excited. The Roosevelt presidency, and his own career, were being given a new lease on life from an unlikely quarter—Hitler's and Mussolini's aggression in Europe.

As soon as the war in Europe was announced Ickes, together with Ben Cohen, began lobbying Roosevelt to get firmer governmental control over power production activities, and to place Harold Ickes at the head of a reconstituted National Power Policy Committee. As was common in the Roosevelt era, there were two committees with essentially the same responsibilities. Ickes was chairman of the National Power Policy Committee, which had been set up in 1934 to coordinate New Deal activities in the area of public power production. Roosevelt created the National Defense Power Committee in 1938 in response to the growing likelihood of war breaking out in Europe. Assistant Secretary of War Louis Johnson, of legendary verbosity, chaired that committee.

Ickes's and Cohen's lobbying efforts succeeded. The president agreed that there was duplication and so he issued an executive order on power on October 13, 1939. The order consolidated the two committees and named his Interior secretary chairman. The other committee members were:

Louis Johnson, assistant secretary of war

Leland Olds, commissioner, Federal Power Commission

Jerome N. Frank, chairman, Securities and Exchange Commission

John Carmody, administrator, Federal Works Agency

Harry Slattery, administrator, Rural Electrification Administration

David E. Lilienthal, director, Tennessee Valley Authority

Paul J. Raver, administrator, the Bonneville Project [22]

Some individuals might quail at the prospect of getting cooperation from such a group, several of whom had reputations for being fiercely independent. Not Harold Ickes. With this appointment he was in his element, in the thick of a national emergency, stepping on toes and bruising egos with abandon. By now Roosevelt had great confidence in Ickes's administrative abilities, and he knew exactly how he would handle a recalcitrant subordinate. When FDR told Tom Corcoran in November 1939 that he was considering appointing Ickes secretary of war, Corcoran replied that he didn't think Ickes could get along with Assistant Secretary Johnson, who also was a member of the newly formed Power Policy Committee. The president replied, "Harold will batter down his ears and hit him two or three times in the stomach and then Louis Johnson will do what I have always felt he would do in such circumstances. He will behave himself and go along." [23]

BY DECEMBER OF the year where storm clouds became visible on the eastern horizon, Harold Ickes's state of mind had improved considerably over what it had been in September. Although Ickes continued to hound the president about transferring the Forest Service to Interior, his hurt feelings over reorganization were mollified by his appointment as National Power Policy Committee chairman. This gave him an important role to play in the unfolding international drama. Moreover, FDR was being unusually solicitous toward his valued aide throughout the fall. They lunched together frequently, they discussed critical issues, the president asked for Ickes's advice, and in November he paid him a special compliment by coming out to Headwaters Farm for dinner and a poker party. All in all, Roosevelt, the expert in human nature, easily succeeded in putting their relationship back on a firm, intimate footing that autumn.

Harold Ickes returned to his old self, to parrying hostile stories in the press and uttering *bon mots* about the political scene. When a reporter asked him in December whether he heard Thomas Dewey's speech where he announced he was running for the Republican nomination for president, Ickes shot back, "No, I did not listen because I have a baby of my own." When Cissy Patterson continued her vendetta with ugly stories about him in her Washington newspaper, the *Times-Herald,* the secretary considered suing her for libel. "I am wondering whether it is not about time to show the newspapers that there is a limit beyond which they cannot go," Ickes mused. "None of them likes a libel suit." [24]

Ickes's self-confidence was bolstered not only by President Roosevelt's cordiality but by having a warm and loving family at Headwaters Farm. He was a fortunate man indeed. After living for two-thirds of a century, often under unhappy circumstances, the pieces of his life finally fell into place. His satisfaction was poignantly evident in his description of Christmas Day 1939. "Last Monday was Christmas," he wrote in his diary. "Jane let the nurse go out so that in our part of the house she and the baby and I were quite alone. We did not go out and no one called, so that we had a quiet and peaceful day. Both of us loved it. For my part, it was the happiest Christmas that I can remember." [25]

PART FOUR

IN RETROSPECT

CHAPTER 21

THE SECRETARY AND

THE SUN PRESIDENT

AROUND 1940 A FRIEND wrote Harold Ickes that, in his opinion, it would be about fifty years before the general public fully appreciated his contributions to the political revolution of the 1930s. It was an accurate prediction. A generation of scholars born during the Second World War or shortly thereafter are in the process of discovering not only Ickes but other New Dealers as well. Of course, Franklin Delano Roosevelt remains the towering figure of the era, and scholars continue to probe why this president cast such a lengthy shadow on the politics of the twentieth century.[1] In this study of one of his most influential cabinet members I have tried to illuminate why. Only Franklin Roosevelt would have been able to keep the independent and temperamental Harold Ickes within his official family, and faithfully serving him, for twelve of the most difficult years this nation ever experienced.

Just as France had its Sun King, so America has had its Sun President. Roosevelt was a man so genuinely attractive, and so skilled at dealing with all manner of people, that he exerted something like a gravitational pull on those who came into contact with him. In ways both large and small, at close quarters and from a distance, during his lifetime and ever since, FDR has had the power to change people's behavior. The change almost always has been positive. His stature grows, rather than diminishes, with time. He has now been recognized as one of the greatest presidents in history, second only to Abraham Lincoln.

Even self-styled curmudgeons such as Harold Ickes were touched by the warmth, wit, and intelligence that radiated from FDR. A fundamental proposition of this book is that an understanding of Ickes's behavior is impossible without viewing it in relation to the most important person in his adult life—Franklin Roosevelt. In his diaries and elsewhere Ickes frequently remarked upon what was so special about FDR. Recounting his month-long fishing trip with the president in October of 1935, for example, Ickes wrote:

> On this whole trip I marveled again and again at his high cheer and at his disposition. Never once did he act self-conscious; on no occasion did he seem to be nervous or irritated. Cheerfully he submitted to being wheeled up and down the special ramps that had been installed on the *Houston* for his use, or to being carried up and down like a helpless child when he went fishing. He was an avid fisherman and, with his strong arms and shoulders, he was able to give a good account of himself if he once got a fish on his hook. . . . The President is always a delightful host, ready to laugh at a joke or tell a good story. . . . I am glad I took this trip.[2]

One cannot read Harold Ickes's accounts of FDR without being moved. Who would not want to serve this charming and unaffected individual? The clear impression, not only from Ickes but from countless other sources, is that no one ever regretted a single moment spent with Roosevelt.

Winston Churchill put it memorably when he remarked that "meeting the President was like uncorking a bottle of champagne." Roosevelt sparkled because he genuinely liked people, loved being around them, and cared what happened to them. Moreover, it was not necessary to be in close proximity, such as Ickes was, to feel the force of FDR's personality. Millions of ordinary Americans felt the same way. His warmth was transmitted to the people by various means— over the airwaves, in newsreels, in black-and-white photos showing the unforgettable smile, and in person as he went to see first-hand the ravages of the Great Depression and what his administration was doing about them. Immense crowds greeted him wherever he went. Although FDR made his share of political mistakes during his twelve years in office, few doubted his basic sincerity and humanity. The result is that no president in American history has been more loved.

Although Roosevelt deserves to occupy the sun position in the political system, he didn't effect the transformation of American society during the 1930s and 1940s single-handedly. He had, as he knew better than anyone, a great deal of help. Roosevelt was able to accomplish as much as he did in office largely because he had an extraordinary ability to elicit the best in the people who worked for him. These included the prickly Harold Ickes, one of two cabinet members who served with him for the duration of his presidency.

Sharing a deep affection for each other, the Interior secretary and the Sun President made an unusually powerful team. In the process of combating the Great Depression by creating the New Deal, Ickes became Roosevelt's lightning rod. This was a completely new role for a cabinet officer who had the stomach and the stamina to fill it. In deflecting criticism away from the president and onto himself, Ickes was enormously useful to FDR. But this was no one-way street. Ickes reveled in the role, for he loved and admired FDR. Moreover, like FDR, he loved a good fight. Finally, Ickes was convinced that he was right in the positions he took, which only made him all the more effective. Rather than being a burden, the lightning-rod role unleashed Ickes's considerable talents.

By design, then, Ickes was a controversial political figure throughout his long tenure in Washington. It is likely that he will remain so. Scholars, even with the advantage of hindsight, are not apt to agree completely on his strengths and weaknesses, his contributions and his failures. Nevertheless, certain characteristics of the man, and particular accomplishments, stand out after the passage of half a century. Ickes was anything but the stereotypical bland bureaucrat, and his participation in both fashioning the New Deal and defending it against its many critics was as important a contribution as is to be found among members of Roosevelt's governing circle.

Despite the fact that he was little known outside of Illinois when Roosevelt appointed him secretary of the interior in 1933, Ickes came to the job of "a super-cabinet officer," in Charles Merriam's words, with some finely honed skills. First, he was intelligent. It is a quality that is often overlooked in evaluating public officials. Ickes received a solid liberal arts education from the University of Chicago, after which he earned a degree from its law school. As his son Raymond observed, his father's love of language, his rhetorical skills, and his firmly held political principles all blossomed during his college years.

Ickes's innate intelligence found its expression in legal and political debate. He understood better than most the force of the well-spoken word and of its centrality to politics. When he was given the opportunity to play a part in the unfolding New Deal drama in Washington, Ickes seized upon it. He quickly became one of the most outspoken liberals in the administration, and he invariably made his public utterances colorful, interesting, provocative, and grammatically correct. He captured people's attention, especially the attention of the generation that came of age in the 1930s. "Let's put it up to Harold," the young contingent of reformers in Washington would say. "He can never say no."

Communication in its many forms was central to Ickes's governing style. Indeed, with the president and First Lady setting the standard, the New Dealers distinguished themselves by their openness and accessibility. The Fireside chats, weekly press conferences, extensive traveling, and the "My Day" column were among the devices the Roosevelts used to reach the public. Ickes hardly needed much coaching on the subject of the media, and one of his first acts upon entering office was to institute his own weekly press conference. Because he held three important titles during the early New Deal years, they were well attended. Reporters found Secretary Ickes informative, and more often than not amusing. He made good copy, as when he remarked that "Emperor Long had halitosis of the intellect," that Wendell Willkie was the "Barefoot Boy from Wall Street," and that Thomas Dewey in 1944 had "thrown his diaper into the ring."

It is safe to say that no Interior secretary in history received so much publicity as did Ickes, especially of a positive nature. One of Ickes's primary goals was to change the image of the Interior Department from a parochial, scandal-tainted agency to a professionally run organization with important national responsibilities. In that objective he succeeded. The Interior Department after Ickes's long tenure was a far more respected and more visible government agency.

Ickes held regular press conferences, made numerous radio addresses, wrote scores of articles and books, and gave hundreds of formal speeches in every part of the nation. Here, too, his speeches and writings were designed to get people's attention. He purposefully used titles like "Esau, the Hairy Man," "Nations in Nightshirts," "The Sixty Families," "After the Oil Deluge, What Price Gasoline?," "Tydings of Victory," and "Playing with Loaded Dies" to stir up interest. Unquestionably he succeeded, especially when it came to stirring up the interest of his political opponents and what he called the "reactionary elements" of the press. He received a lot of negative publicity and hate mail along with the positive.

He also insisted on a departmental policy that all written communication coming into his agencies be promptly and courteously answered. "This is the only way that ordinary citizens have of reaching their government," Ickes told his employees. "Although it is time consuming and sometimes boring," he continued, "it is perhaps the *most* essential task that we government officials have." It was a policy that was implemented, although the secretary sometimes had to go on a rampage to get his employees to take him seriously. The Ickes papers at the Library of Congress and the National Archives are as voluminous as they are partly because every postcard and letter with a return address received a reply. Usually, the reply carried the secretary's *personal* signature.

Ickes's style was direct and aggressive. "If you think someone is going to hit you in the stomach, punch him in the nose first," Ickes once told one of his associates. He relished political controversy and usually managed to gain the offensive. Even when he was acting in an area in which he was a novice, such as oil policy in 1933, he stood his ground. He was not about to be pushed around by oil magnates, oil state politicians, or cabinet colleagues, he said, in deciding what to do about the collapse of the industry. Instead, he played for time while he learned as much as he could about the situation, and then coupled that knowledge with his Progressive principles to steer himself through the dangerous cross-currents of oil politics. One of Ickes's talents was that he learned quickly, and even before Roosevelt named him petroleum administrator for national defense in 1941, he had become something of an expert on oil. Oil did not bring him down, as it did another Interior secretary whose memory was fresh in the 1930s.

Although his style was colorful, and a refreshing change from the politicians and bureaucrats who kept their fingers up, constantly testing the wind, it often got him into trouble. Ickes had a nasty temper;

he tried to keep it under control, but it regularly got loose. He had particular trouble in working with his cabinet colleagues and others, like Harry Hopkins and Hugh Johnson, who occupied the same rung on the organizational ladder as he did. He got along much better with Roosevelt, his boss, and with subordinates, although his temper sometimes got the best of him in these relationships, too. Hopkins referred to Ickes as "The Great Resigner," General Johnson told him in 1936 that he was so unpopular that he had better stay out of the presidential race, and Ickes returned the compliment by observing that he and Johnson were "two snapping turtles."

At one time or another, Ickes had rows with most of his cabinet colleagues. He even told off Frances Perkins in 1937, a person he liked very much, for monopolizing a cabinet meeting. Having to work with Ickes on an equal basis was not easy, and probably more time and energy were expended on fashioning recovery programs than was necessary due to his prickly personality. Ickes also believed that valuable time was wasted, not because of his personality, but because of Roosevelt's penchant for setting up organizations where he had to share responsibility with others. He detested most committee meetings. "That great Town Hall assembly that we call the public works board," Ickes wrote in frustration after having to sit through one of its lengthy sessions.

It is quite possible, too, that Ickes's aggressive style contributed to the fact that he never got "the prize" he so dearly desired, the U.S. Forest Service. Ickes was among the first to argue the eminently sensible proposition that the federal government should have a genuine "Department of Conservation" to house *all* resource managing agencies. The two most prominent outliers were then, as now, Agriculture's Forest Service and the Army's Corps of Engineers. Ickes was anxious to get both of them into his Interior Department, but he especially coveted the Forest Service. He went after it too aggressively. After initial polite conversations between him and Secretary Wallace, the dialogue turned contentious. There were shouting matches and table poundings. The normally easy-going Wallace became, Ickes noted, "stubborn as a mule" on the subject of reorganization. Ickes also alienated members of the Izaak Walton League with his snide remarks, and he hounded FDR about forestry to the point of distraction. Roosevelt responded by playing games with his secretary. For years the president helped to keep Ickes running at full speed by dangling the prize before him. That he never gave it to him might be due to the fact that FDR understood his valuable associate too well. Ickes was at his best when he was fighting against the odds.

On the subject of work, Harold Ickes also distinguished himself. Although he didn't assume a cabinet position until he was 59 years old, age did not slow him down. Throughout his life Ickes displayed a remarkable capacity for hard work; he was also skilled at putting together organizations. Roosevelt immediately recognized these qualities in his Interior secretary, and so he gave Ickes two additional full-time assignments in 1933, that of creating and then running the Public Works and the Oil administrations. For several years Ickes held three titles. Because FDR appreciated Ickes's physical stamina, because he insisted on keeping government spending down wherever he could, and because the Interior Department was at the time a relatively small agency with a limited portfolio, the president felt little compunction about heaping work onto Ickes's desk. Ickes responded by gratefully accepting it. Never once did he complain to FDR about having too much work to do. In fact, Roosevelt usually heard the opposite from his hard-driving Interior secretary.

Ickes habitually put in a six-day work week. His government salary was modest, and it didn't include, he liked to point out to overpaid corporate executives, additional pay for running the public works and oil authorities. He ran, as did FDR, a frugally minded administration. On Sunday he'd dictate his secret diary or take care of other correspondence. The days were long, especially during his first years in office when the national emergency was of such severity. If he hadn't achieved his daily goal of clearing his desk by 5 or 6 o'clock, he had dinner and returned to the office to finish the task. He rarely took vacations (at least until he met and married Jane, when he began to take a bit more time off), observing that he was unable to "relax, like an ordinary person does. Whatever peace of mind I am capable of," he continued, "comes from working." Although he complained in private of being physically exhausted, of not sleeping, and of the enormous nervous strain he was under, these conditions rarely slowed him down. Clearly Ickes derived a great deal of satisfaction from his work, his complaints notwithstanding.

What he expected of himself he expected from others. Ickes tolerated very little slack in his various organizations, and although he sometimes overdid it—as when he closed Interior's cafeteria because he saw people lounging there for "a full ten minutes"—most observers, including Roosevelt, appreciated his concern about not wasting taxpayers' money. "He was the best administrator I ever worked for," recalled William Warne in 1988. Warne worked with Ickes from 1935 until 1946, remained in the Interior Department through the 1950s, and then was appointed to a high administrative position in the 1960s by California's Gov. Edmund G. Brown. Even the former director of the National Park Service, Conrad Wirth, whom Ickes fired over the Stitely scandal but rehired two days later, considered him a skilled executive. "He was not particularly warm," Wirth remembered, "but he was always fair. He could be counted on to back up his subordinates when they got into trouble."

Harold Ickes earned a reputation for being not only a tough administrator but an honest one. Although he didn't like the "Honest Harold" appellation, it was deserved. He kept graft and corruption to an absolute minimum in his organizations. The Public Works Administration, which had the potential in 1933 for being nothing more than a bottomless pork barrel, became instead an agency worthy of emulation because of Ickes's insistence on running an honest organization. He came in for considerable criticism for his cautious approach, but he also earned the approval of FDR and others for not just "shovelling money out of the window," as the president told his cabinet on one of the many occasions when FDR complimented Ickes.

Nor did Harold Ickes enrich himself at the public's expense. It is clear from his personal behavior that he loved wealth, but his principles and his political sense—and the president's high standards—kept him from using his positions for personal gain. One of the outstanding features of the New Deal era generally was how few public officials had their hands in the till. The standards of conduct currently in place unfortunately represent a decline from that which was considered acceptable a generation or two ago.

There were occasions when Ickes overdid his role of protector of the public interest. More precisely the department's director of investigations, Louis Glavis, overdid it. Ickes recognized he made a mistake in initially giving Glavis so much authority to ferret out wrongdoing. He had, he said, created a "Frankenstein," a "man-eater," within his administration. Ickes eventually and reluctantly let Glavis go, but to his credit he never used him as a scapegoat. He never used anyone as a scapegoat. Before Congress and with the president, Ickes took responsibility for any excesses, such as unauthorized wiretapping, that had occurred under Glavis's "reign of terror." He also lightened up considerably after 1936 in terms of keeping a watch on his employees.

The abuses notwithstanding, Ickes's decision upon taking office to err on the side of honesty looks, in retrospect, like the correct one. His thirteen-year record in running nearly scandal-free programs is remarkable.

His personal life, however, was another matter. A long, unhappy marriage to Anna, checkered with his infidelities and her threats of suicide, and his unprincipled designs on her wealth, produce a very unflattering portrait of Ickes the husband during his first marriage. The attempt to conceal his indiscrete affair with X, for example, saw one of the few instances where Ickes strayed over the boundary of proper public conduct.

His behavior toward Anna's children was even more reprehensible, for they were not, as was Anna, worthy adversaries. Only Raymond, the son they had together, escaped unscathed. There can be little doubt, for instance, that during his marriage to Anna he had an affair with her adopted daughter, Frances; and after Anna's death in an automobile accident, he cheated Wilmarth, Frances, and Robert out of their share of their mother's inheritance. Whatever Ickes's rationalizations, and whatever other problems Wilmarth had in 1936, his suicide note placed the blame for his death squarely on "H.L." In 1939 Robert tried suing "H.L." for a share of his mother's estate, but Ickes fought him with all of the resources he had at his disposal. He won again. No one is sure what scars Harold left on Frances, for she largely drifted out of the family picture after Anna's death.

It was only after Ickes's marriage to Jane that he assumed the role of a devoted husband and father. The couple was blessed with a genuine love relationship; moreover, Harold delighted in his two children with Jane. He found great comfort in having a second family in the autumn of his life. Even then, however, his career came first. The relatively little time spent with his two children by that marriage led FDR to quip that he probably knew the youngsters as well as Harold did.

Still, despite the egregious defects of character that marred his personal life, Ickes's public life remains noteworthy for its integrity and his unyielding pursuit of the public good. He recognized, as did most of his fellow administrators and members of the press, that there existed a clear line separating one's public and one's private behavior. He was very careful not to cross it.

Harold Ickes matched his outspoken and aggressive style with substantive accomplishments. When Roosevelt assumed the presidency in 1933 he made it clear that he wanted action and results, and in Ickes FDR discovered an individual who shared his own particular blend of pragmatism and idealism. Temperamentally they were very different, but when it came to demanding speedy, concrete actions to combat the Great Depression, Roosevelt and Ickes worked unusually well together. It was an era when substance triumphed over process. Literally and figuratively, the New Dealers were rebuilders of the American Dream, even though their personal lives may have fallen short of some ideal standard.

Ickes's numerous contributions to creating, defining, and defending the New Deal can be summarized by pointing out that Harold Ickes was as thoroughgoing a reformer as was to be found in Roosevelt's governing circle. He also had the courage to publicly defend his convictions. Just as age didn't slow him down physically, neither did it attenuate his bedrock political principles. Unlike many individuals, Ickes remained firmly attached to a Progressive and liberal philosophy throughout his life: He was a committed conservationist in the Theodore Roosevelt tradition, he championed the rights and defended the interests of minority groups, especially those of blacks, American Indians, and Jews, he fought against monopoly capitalism in its various manifestations, and he was ever ready to fight for the preservation of democracy against fascist and totalitarian regimes. Isolationism, quite popular in the 1930s with many of his fellow Progressives, held no attraction for him. On virtually every important issue of the decade, Harold Ickes pushed FDR and his administration toward the liberal end of the spectrum. One of the clearest illustrations of Ickes's influence occurred during the fall and winter of 1937–38, when President Roosevelt appeared to be, in William Leuchtenburg's words, a "thoroughly repudiated" leader. The Supreme Court fight of 1937, the negative publicity surrounding FDR's nomination to the Court of the former Klansman Hugo Black, and finally the "Roosevelt Recession" that began in October and proceeded to get worse in the new year all combined to make this the president's most difficult period in office. For the first time in five years, FDR lost much of his buoyancy and seemed to have lost his political moorings. He drifted.

Harold Ickes and other members of the administration's reform faction discussed what they could do to help their beleaguered chief. Ickes, along with Assistant Attorney General Robert Jackson, Tom

Corcoran, and Ben Cohen decided to call FDR's hand: They would pressure him to reassert vigorous and liberally inclined leadership. Ickes and Jackson delivered forceful speeches in December and January in which they put the blame for the economic recession (and other societal problems) precisely where they felt it belonged—in the lap of big business and the conservative elements of the press. After one of his pugnacious speeches, Ickes confided in his diary that he had "pretty much put it up to the president to either follow my lead or fire me."

Roosevelt followed his lead. In a cabinet meeting early in 1938 FDR acknowledged that the speeches by his lightning-rod secretary and the assistant attorney general had had an effect. Before the speeches, he said, he was being snubbed by powerful businessmen. After the speeches, however, they were only too happy to come to the White House to discuss the economic situation. "For God's sake, call off that man Ickes!" one executive told FDR as he came in to discuss policy.

The Sun President broke through the clouds later that year. The leader who announced to Ickes in 1936 that "I am fighting mad!" and to whom Ickes replied, "I love it when you're fighting mad!" re-emerged after several months of vacillating. To Ickes's satisfaction, FDR decided to return to pump-priming to rout the recession, he campaigned vigorously for New Deal candidates in the midterm congressional elections, and he made diplomatic overtures to Hitler and other heads of state to try to avert war. Ickes's role in tipping the political scales toward activism thus constituted his overarching contribution to the New Deal. The once obscure Chicago lawyer who was known for backing principled but losing causes succeeded into making himself the indispensable Washington reformer, the one who was, in Roosevelt's words, "always willing to fight."

NOTE ON SOURCES

Harold Ickes kept excellent track of himself and his activities. Upon taking office on March 4, 1933, he began dictating what he called his secret diary. He continued it through his entire thirteen years in office, and into retirement. It runs into the thousands of pages. The reader will note that two versions of the diaries for the period 1933 – 40 exist, a published and an unpublished version. I have utilized both in writing this book. A three-volume edited version appeared in 1954 titled *The Secret Diary of Harold L. Ickes*. It is cited in the notes in the conventional manner, as a book.

The unedited version is housed, along with the voluminous other documents, papers, and miscellany that comprise the Harold L. Ickes Papers, at the Library of Congress. It is available on nine reels of microfilm. The unpublished and unedited version is cited in the notes as part of the Ickes papers: e.g., Ickes diary, MR 1 [or 2], [page nos.], LC-HLIP.

In addition to the secret diary, Ickes wrote his memoirs. There exist two versions of this document, too. In 1943 he published the heavily edited *Autobiography of a Curmudgeon*. The book was drawn from his personal memoirs, which also are housed at the Library of Congress and are available on microfilm. Much of the most sensitive information on Ickes's personal affairs are contained in the memoirs. This document is cited in the notes as part of the Ickes papers (LC-HLIP).

The Harold Ickes Papers at the Library of Congress are one of the most exhaustive collections of material of any public official in U.S. history. The estimated 150,000 items take up 225 linear feet of space. They are a treasure trove for scholars delving into the Roosevelt era, and it is very much to Ickes's credit that he kept and collected virtually every piece of paper that crossed his desk.

Two other vital sources of information on Ickes are the holdings at the National Archives and the Franklin D. Roosevelt Library. The Department of the Interior files pertaining to Ickes's tenure as secretary are identified in the notes as Record Group 48, National Archives (NA-HLIOF). I discovered numerous documents in this collection which were not in the Library of Congress collection.

Finally, the Roosevelt Library in Hyde Park is an invaluable source on Ickes. The president's official files (OF), Eleanor Roosevelt's papers, and Henry Morgenthau's diaries are cited in the notes with the abbreviation FDRL.

NOTES

ABBREVIATIONS

FDRL   Papers of Franklin D. Roosevelt, Eleanor Roosevelt, and Henry
            Morgenthau. Franklin D. Roosevelt Library, Hyde Park, N.Y.
LC-HLIP   The Papers of Harold L. Ickes, 1874–1952. Manuscripts Division,
            Library of Congress, Washington, D.C.
MR   Microfilm reel
NA-HLIOF   Harold L. Ickes Office Files, Record Group 48, National Ar-
            chives, Washington, D.C.
NPS   National Park Service

CHAPTER I
THE GREAT TRANSFORMATION

1. Harold L. Ickes, *The Autobiography of a Curmudgeon* (New York: Reynal and Hitchcock, 1943), 6, 7.
2. Eric F. Goldman, *Rendezvous with Destiny* (New York: Vintage Books, 1977), 20.
3. Ickes, *Autobiography,* 9.
4. Ibid., 76.
5. Raymond Ickes, interview with author, Berkeley, Calif., June 1988 (hereafter R. Ickes interview).
6. Ickes, *Autobiography,* 80.
7. Goldman, *Rendezvous,* 54.
8. Ickes, *Autobiography,* 81.
9. Edmund Morris, *The Rise of Theodore Roosevelt* (New York: Coward, McCann, & Geoghegan, Inc., 1979), 243.
10. Quoted in ibid., 17.
11. Ickes, *Autobiography,* 88.
12. Ibid., 111, 120.
13. Ibid., 161.
14. Ibid., 159.
15. Goldman, *Rendezvous,* 169.
16. Ickes, *Autobiography,* 169.
17. See Peter Gay, *Freud: A Life for Our Times* (New York: Norton, 1988), esp. chap. 7.
18. Ickes, *Autobiography,* 183.
19. Quoted in Goldman, *Rendezvous,* 184.

20. Ibid., 187.

21. Ickes, *Autobiography*, 213 – 14.

22. Ibid., 217.

23. Ibid., 229.

24. Ibid., 248.

25. Kenneth R. Philp, *John Collier's Crusade for Indian Reform, 1920 – 1954* (Tucson: University of Arizona Press, 1977), 38.

26. Goldman, *Rendezvous*, 248.

27. Harold L. Ickes, personal memoirs, 370 – 71, Speeches and Writings File, LC-HLIP.

CHAPTER 2
"IS MR. ICKES HERE?"

1. Frank Freidel, *Franklin D. Roosevelt: Launching the New Deal* (Boston: Little, Brown, 1973), 142 – 43.

2. Ibid., 154.

3. Ickes, *Autobiography*, 268.

4. Ibid.

5. Quoted in Freidel, *Launching the New Deal*, 154.

6. Ickes, *Autobiography*, 269.

7. Graham White and John Maze, *Harold L. Ickes of the New Deal: His Private Life and Public Career* (Cambridge: Harvard University Press, 1985), 98.

8. Ickes, *Autobiography*, 269.

9. John Collier, *From Every Zenith* (Denver: Sage Books, 1963), 170.

10. H. L. Ickes, *The Secret Diary of Harold L. Ickes*, vol. 1, *The First Thousand Days, 1933 – 36* (New York: Simon and Schuster, 1954), ix.

11. Linda Lear, *Harold L. Ickes: The Aggressive Progressive, 1874 – 1933* (New York: Garland, 1981), 363 – 64.

12. Quoted in Freidel, *Launching the New Deal*, 154.

13. Collier, *Zenith*, 170; Lear, *Aggressive Progressive*, 381; White and Maze, *Ickes*, 98.

14. Nathan Miller, *FDR: An Intimate History* (New York: Doubleday, 1983), 303 – 5.

15. Frank Freidel, *Franklin D. Roosevelt: A Rendezvous with Destiny* (Boston: Little, Brown, 1990), 205.

16. Miller, *FDR*, 307.

CHAPTER 3
"FORM YOUR RANKS AND FIGHT!"

1. Quoted in Freidel, *Launching the New Deal*, 193.

2. Robert E. Sherwood, *Roosevelt and Hopkins: An Intimate History* (New York: Harper and Brothers, 1948), 43.

3. Ibid., 273 – 74.

4. Philp, *John Collier*, 125.

5. Ickes, *Secret Diary*, 1 : 3.

6. Ibid., 1 : 5–6.

7. Ickes, letter to Dean Bigelow, March 27, 1933, Friends File, LC-HLIP.

8. Ickes, *Secret Diary*, 1 : 20.

9. Philp, *John Collier*, 90.

10. Ibid., 115–16.

11. Ickes, *Secret Diary*, 1 : 15.

12. Ibid., 19.

13. Ickes, letter to Henry F. Dickinson, April 29, 1933, Indians File, LC-HLIP.

14. Philp, *John Collier*, 117.

15. Vine Deloria Jr. and Clifford M. Lytle, *The Nations Within: The Past and the Future of American Indian Sovereignty* (New York: Pantheon, 1984), 62.

16. John Collier, memo to Ickes, August 4, 1933; Ickes, letter to superintendent of St. Elizabeth's Hospital, August 7, 1933; both in Indian Affairs File, NA-HLIOF.

17. Ickes diary, MR 1, p. 31, LC-HLIP.

18. Harvard Sitkoff, *A New Deal for Blacks* (Oxford: Oxford University Press, 1978), 77.

19. Ibid.

20. Gifford Pinchot, letter to Ickes, February 25, 1933, Friends File, LC-HLIP.

21. Richard Lowitt, *The New Deal and the West* (Bloomington: Indiana University Press, 1984), 30.

22. Roy M. Robbins, *Our Landed Heritage: The Public Domain, 1776–1936* (Lincoln: University of Nebraska Press, 1962), 413.

23. Lowitt, *The New Deal*, xi; Ickes, memo to Horace Albright, April 19, 1933, NPS File, NA-HLIOF.

24. Ickes, Statement on H.R. 2835, before the House Committee on Public Lands, June 7, 1933, 4, Speeches and Writings File, LC-HLIP.

25. Ickes, memo to Charles Fahy, July 28, 1933, General Land Office File, NA-HLIOF.

26. C. N. Bassett, letter to S. P. Applewhite, July 20, 1933; and secretary to the director of the Budget Bureau, letter to S. P. Applewhite, August 12, 1933, University of Arizona Library, Special Collections, Lewis Douglas Papers, Box 240.

27. Louis Glavis, memos to Ickes, July 1933, and August 8, 1933, General Land Office File, NA-HLIOF.

28. Joseph P. Lash, *Dealers and Dreamers* (New York: Doubleday, 1988), 155.

29. Ickes, letter to Edith J. Goode, March 8, 1933, Indians File, LC-HLIP.

30. Ickes, *Secret Diary*, 1 : 25–27; Horace Albright, memo to Ickes, April 24, 1933, NPS File, LC-HLIP.

31. Ickes, *Secret Diary*, 1 : 82.

32. In his unpublished memoirs housed at the Library of Congress, Ickes identifies the woman only as *"X."* But it is obvious from his unedited diaries, also housed at the Library of Congress, that X is Marguerite Moser Brumbaugh. See diary entries for 1933, MR 1, pp. 173, 224, 470–71, LC-HLIP.

33. Details of the affair are from Ickes, personal memoirs, 381, 384, 391, 393–94, 398, Speeches and Writings File, LC-HLIP.

34. This episode is detailed in chapter 19.

35. Ickes, letter to Wilmarth Ickes, August 24, 1933, General Printing Company File, LC-HLIP.

36. Ickes, *Secret Diary,* 1 : 89–90.

37. Ibid., 89.

38. Ickes diary, MR 1, p. 190, LC-HLIP.

39. Ickes, letter to Charles Thomson, March 10, 1933, Friends File, LC-HLIP; Ickes, *Secret Diary,* 1 : 723 (index entry).

40. Ibid., 94.

41. Charles Merriam, letter to Ickes, August 2, 1933, Public Works Administration File, LC-HLIP.

CHAPTER 4
"TO RIVAL CHEOPS"

1. See Linda J. Lear, "Boulder Dam: A Crossroads in Natural Resource Policy," *Journal of the West* (October 1985): 82–94, for a detailed examination of Ickes's role in the construction of Boulder Dam.

2. Ickes, *Secret Diary,* 1 : 32.

3. Gifford Pinchot, letter to Ickes, June 30, 1933, Friends File, LC-HLIP; Gov. Henry Horner, letter to Ickes, June 22, 1933, Cement File, NA-HLIOF.

4. Assistant Secretary Oscar Chapman, memo to Ickes, March 19, 1934, Cement File, NA-HLIOF.

5. Ickes diary, MR 1, p. 80, LC-HLIP.

6. Ickes, *Secret Diary,* 1 : 27.

7. Ibid., 28.

8. Goldman, *Rendezvous,* 335.

9. Ickes, *Secret Diary,* 1 : 48.

10. Lash, *Dealers,* 128.

11. William E. Leuchtenburg, *Franklin D. Roosevelt and the New Deal, 1932–1940* (New York: Harper and Row, 1963), 133.

12. Quoted in White and Maze, *Ickes,* 72.

13. James MacGregor Burns, *Roosevelt: The Lion and the Fox* (New York: Harcourt, Brace, 1956), 244.

14. Public Works Administrator Ickes and H. M. Waite, Deputy Administrator, addresses before division heads, October 3, 1933, 14, Speeches and Writings File, LC-HLIP.

15. Ickes, *Secret Diary,* 1 : 75.

16. Lash, *Dealers,* 153, 159.

17. Table, Federal Emergency Administration of Public Works, "Federal Projects Allotted from the $100,000,000 Fund as of August 17, 1933," National Recovery Administration Files, OF 466–466b, FDRL.

18. Ickes, address before the Conference of Mayors, September 23, 1933, Chicago, Speeches File, LC-HLIP.

19. Editorial, *Chicago Tribune,* July 1933, Editorials File, LC-HLIP.

20. Editorial, *Business Week,* August 26, 1933, 32, Editorials File, LC-HLIP.

21. Ickes, *Secret Diary,* 1 : 71.

22. Lash, *Dealers,* 128.

23. Ickes, letter to James Denvir, May 29, 1933, PWA File, LC-HLIP.

24. Gov. Joseph Ely, letter to Ickes, August 2, 1933, PWA File, NA-HLIOF.

25. Ickes, *Secret Diary,* 1 : 80.

26. FDR, memo to Ickes, August 19, 1933, PWA File, NA-HLIOF; Congressman McSwain, telegram to FDR, November 4, 1933, NRA Files, OF 466 – 466b, FDRL.

27. Ickes, letter to Charles Merriam, October 4, 1933, Friends File, LC-HLIP.

28. Ickes and Waite, addresses before the PWA division heads, October 3, 1933, Speeches File, LC-HLIP.

29. Ibid., 9.

30. Quoted in White and Maze, *Ickes,* 137.

31. Ickes, *Secret Diary,* 1 : 100 – 101.

32. Ickes, letter to FDR, December 14, 1933, NRA Files, OF 466 – 466b, FDRL.

33. Ibid.

CHAPTER 5
OVER A BARREL

1. Ickes, memo to Louis Glavis, September 6, 1933, Oil File, LC-HLIP.

2. Donald R. Brand, *Corporatism and the Rule of Law: A Study of the National Recovery Administration* (Ithaca, N.Y.: Cornell University Press, 1988), 176 – 77.

3. Quoted in Freidel, *Launching the New Deal,* 427.

4. Ickes, *Secret Diary,* 1 : 31.

5. R. Ickes interview.

6. E. S. Rochester, memo to Ickes, March 27, 1933, Oil File, LC-HLIP.

7. Ickes, *Secret Diary,* 1 : 11.

8. Ibid., 10.

9. Pres. Franklin Roosevelt, press release on oil conference, April 3, 1933, Oil File, LC-HLIP.

10. FDR, memo to attorney general and secretary of the interior, April 5, 1933, Oil File, LC-HLIP.

11. Ickes, letter to Senator Norbeck, April 4, 1933, Oil File, LC-HLIP.

12. Ickes, *Secret Diary,* 1 : 15.

13. E. S. Rochester, memo to Secretary Ickes, April 1, 1933, Oil File, LC-HLIP.

14. Governor Ferguson, telegram to President Roosevelt and Secretary Ickes, May 5, 1933, Oil File, LC-HLIP.

15. Ickes, letter to Roosevelt, May 1, 1933, Oil File, LC-HLIP.

16. Ickes, letter to Hiram Johnson, May 8, 1933, Oil File, LC-HLIP; Ickes diary, MR 1, p. 88, LC-HLIP.

17. Ickes, *Secret Diary,* 1 : 39.

18. Freidel, *Launching the New Deal,* 449 – 50.

19. Ickes, *Secret Diary,* 1 : 49.

20. Henry Doherty, letter to President Roosevelt, June 8, 1933, Oil File, LC-HLIP.

21. Ickes, letter to Ingraham D. Hook, June 14, 1933, Oil File, LC-HLIP.

22. Ickes, letter to FDR, August 29, 1933, Oil File, LC-HLIP.

23. David S. Painter, *Oil and the American Century* (Baltimore: Johns Hopkins University Press, 1986), 6 – 7.

24. Memo, unsigned and undated to FDR, Oil File, LC-HLIP.

25. Ickes, remarks to the Planning and Coordination Committee of the Petroleum Administration, September 18, 1933, Speeches File, LC-HLIP.

26. Louis Glavis, memo to Ickes, February 2, and Ickes, memo to Glavis, February 4, 1934, Oil File, LC-HLIP.

27. Ickes, letter to Frank Knox, August 31, 1933, Oil File, LC-HLIP.

28. Ickes, *Secret Diary*, 1 : 101.

29. Sen. William McAdoo, letter to Ickes, December 19, 1933, Oil File, LC-HLIP.

30. Organization Chart of the Petroleum Administration, August 6, 1934, Oil File, LC-HLIP.

31. Ickes, *Secret Diary*, 1 : 98 – 99.

32. Press release, November 7, 1933, Oil File, LC-HLIP.

33. Peter H. Irons, *The New Deal Lawyers* (Princeton: Princeton University Press, 1982), 62 – 63.

34. William Warne, interview with author, Sacramento, Calif., February 1988.

35. Ickes, *Secret Diary*, 1 : 110, 104.

36. Ickes, personal memoirs, 402, Speeches and Writings File, LC-HLIP.

37. Details of Anna's suicide attempt are from ibid., 403 – 5, 407.

38. A. L. Ickes, letter to Mrs. Roosevelt, April 13, 1934, Disagreeable File, Eleanor Roosevelt Papers, FDRL.

CHAPTER 6
THE JUGGLER

1. Ickes, *Secret Diary*, 1 : 144.

2. F. C. Finkle, letter to Ickes, May 19, 1933, Boulder Dam File, NA-HLIOF.

3. Harold L. Ickes, *Back to Work: The Story of PWA* (New York: Macmillan, 1935), 112, 115.

4. William E. Warne, *The Bureau of Reclamation* (New York: Praeger, 1973), 17, 35.

5. Ickes, *Back to Work,* appendix B, 256 – 59.

6. Clark Foreman, letter to W. H. Christian, October 12, 1933, Negroes File, LC-HLIP.

7. Ickes, memo to Colonel Hackett, November 30, 1934, Negroes File, NA-HLIOF.

8. Quoted in Lash, *Dealers,* 142.

9. Ickes, *Secret Diary*, 1 : 103.

10. FDR, memo to secretary of the treasury, June 11, 1934, NRA Files, OF 466 – 466b, FDRL.

11. Ickes, *Work,* 178.

12. Ibid.

13. Ickes, speech no. 31, January 27, 1934, Speeches File, LC-HLIP.

14. Ickes, speech no. 35, February 24, 1934, Speeches File, LC-HLIP.

15. Ickes, letter to Freda Kirchwey, January 31, 1938, Newspaper Criticism File, LC-HLIP.

16. Ickes, *Secret Diary,* 1 : 200.

17. Ibid., 256.

18. Harold M. Stephens, letters to Roosevelt, February 24 and 27, 1934, Oil File, LC-HLIP.

19. Freidel, *Launching the New Deal,* 429.

20. Ickes, letter to the attorney general, January 5, 1934, Oil File, LC-HLIP.

21. Ickes, letter to Jesse Jones, January 6, 1934, and letter to Gen. Hugh S. Johnson, January 6, 1934, Oil File, LC-HLIP.

22. Ickes, letter to FDR, March 24, 1934, Oil File, LC-HLIP.

23. Ickes, letter to Pierson Hall, March 27, 1934, Oil File, LC-HLIP.

24. Ickes, *Secret Diary,* 1 : 157.

25. Details on the development of a new oil bill are from ibid., 155, 158 – 59, 164.

26. Ickes, memo to Charles Fahy, June 1, 1934, Oil File, LC-HLIP.

27. Ickes, *Secret Diary,* 1 : 169.

28. Freidel, *Launching the New Deal,* 428.

29. Charles B. Ames, letter to Ickes, June 26, 1934, Oil File, LC-HLIP.

30. Ickes diary, MR 1, pp. 633, 644, LC-HLIP.

31. Charles Fahy, telegram to Harold Ickes, October 27, 1934, Oil File, LC-HLIP.

32. Ickes, *Secret Diary,* 1 : 22.

33. Ickes, speech delivered before the American Civic Association, April 19, 1933, Speeches File, LC-HLIP.

34. Ickes, *Secret Diary,* 1 : 278.

35. Ickes, letter to John D. Rockefeller, May 17, 1933, NPS Files, NA-HLIOF.

36. Senator Carey, letter to Ickes, August 21, 1933, NPS Files, NA-HLIOF.

37. *The National Parks: Shaping the System* (Washington, D.C.: NPS, Department of the Interior, 1985), 44.

38. Ibid., 24 – 35.

39. Edgar B. Nixon, ed., *Franklin D. Roosevelt and Conservation, 1911 – 45,* 2 vols. (Washington, D.C.: GPO, 1957), 1 : 190.

40. Michael Frome, *Whose Woods These Are* (New York: Doubleday, 1962), 135.

41. *National Parks,* 58 – 59.

42. Cordell Hull, letter to Ickes, October 28, 1933, NPS Files, NA-HLIOF.

43. Ickes, memo to Acting Director Demaray, June 9, 1934, NPS Files, NA-HLIOF.

44. Verne Chatelain, interview with author, Silver Spring, Md., April 8, 1988.

45. Cross-country trip is from Ickes, *Secret Diary,* 1 : 175, 176.

46. Ickes, letter to Hiram Johnson, July 30, 1934, Friends File, LC-HLIP.

47. Ickes *Secret Diary,* 1 : 180.

48. Ibid., 183.

49. Nixon, ed., *FDR and Conservation,* 1 : 321 – 24.

50. Ickes, *Secret Diary,* 1 : 185 – 87.

51. Hiram Johnson, letter to Ickes, September 17, 1934, Friends File, LC-HLIP.

CHAPTER 7
"A DASH FOR THE TIMBER"

1. Arno Cammerer, memo to Ickes, January 25, 1934, NPS Files, NA-HLIOF.
2. U.S. Department of the Interior, NPS, *The Interior Building: Its Architecture and Its Art* (Washington, D.C.: GPO, 1986), 13.
3. Ickes, *Secret Diary*, 1 : 223.
4. Details of the disagreements between Agriculture and Interior are from ibid., 250, 324, 326, 343 – 44.
5. Ickes, *Secret Diary*, 1 : 350.
6. Press release, Society of American Foresters, June 24, 1935, Conservation File, LC-HLIP.
7. H. H. Chapman, letter to Ickes, July 3, 1935, Conservation File, NA-HLIOF.
8. Ickes, letter to Chapman, July 19, 1935, Conservation File, NA-HLIOF.
9. Gifford Pinchot, open letter, July 9, 1935, Conservation File, LC-HLIP.
10. Arthur M. Schlesinger Jr., *The Politics of Upheaval* (Cambridge: Riverside Press, 1960), 529.
11. Ickes, *Secret Diary*, 1 : 208.
12. Ibid., 207.
13. Gifford Pinchot, letter to FDR, October 29, 1934, Friends File, LC-HLIP; Ickes diary, MR 1, p. 626, October 7, 1934, LC-HLIP.
14. Ickes, *Secret Diary*, 1 : 388.
15. Investigation of the Division of Islands and Territories is from ibid., 301, 332, 391, 403 – 4.
16. Ickes, letter to Frank Knox, July 16, 1942, Navy File, LC-HLIP.
17. Ickes, *Secret Diary*, 1 : 393.
18. Ibid., 394 – 95.
19. Roosevelt, letter to Paul Pearson, July 23, 1935, NRA File, OF 466b, FDRL.
20. See Miscellaneous and Navy Files. In Miscellaneous File an unsigned letter to Senator Tydings, dated July 22, 1935. In Navy File, the John Hinshaw File, 1935 – 45, LC-HLIP.
21. Ickes, *Secret Diary*, 1 : 411.
22. Ickes, personal memoirs, 337, Speeches and Writings File, LC-HLIP.
23. Anna Ickes, telegram to Harold Ickes, August 15, 1933, NPS File, LC-HLIP.
24. Associate Director Demaray, memo to Ebert Burlew, January 11, 1935, NPS File, LC-HLIP.
25. Ickes, *Secret Diary*, 1 : 430.
26. Ibid., 431.
27. Ickes, personal memoirs, 416, Speeches and Writings File, LC-HLIP.
28. R. Ickes interview.
29. Ickes, personal memoirs, 339, Speeches and Writings File, LC-HLIP.
30. Ibid., 418 – 19.
31. Ibid., 421.
32. Ickes, *Secret Diary*, 1 : 429.
33. Ickes, letter to Harry Slattery, September 30, 1935, Conservation File, NA-HLIOF.

CHAPTER 8
"I AM NOT A BOONDOGGLER"

1. Ickes, letter to Hiram Johnson, September 21, 1935, Friends File, LC–HLIP.
2. Ibid.
3. Schlesinger, quoted in *Politics of Upheaval,* 345 – 46.
4. Ickes, *Secret Diary,* 1 : 365.
5. Biographical data on Harry Hopkins are drawn from Sherwood's memorable book, *Roosevelt and Hopkins.*
6. Ibid., 8 – 9.
7. Details about Ickes and the PWA are from Ickes, *Secret Diary,* 1 : 288 – 89, 424, 425.
8. Stephen Early, memo to Marvin McIntyre, September 10, 1935, NRA File, OF 466b, FDRL.
9. Raymond Clapper, "Between You and Me," *Washington Post,* March 29, 1935.
10. Lash, *Dealers,* 247.
11. Ickes, letter to Johnson (9/21/35).
12. Ickes, *Secret Diary,* 1 : 267, 291.
13. Robert A. Caro, *The Power Broker: Robert Moses and the Fall of New York* (New York: Vintage, 1975), 426.
14. Ibid., 433.
15. Ickes, *Secret Diary,* 1 : 346.
16. Schlesinger, quoted in *Politics of Upheaval,* 250.
17. Ibid., 55.
18. Unsigned memo to Jesse Jones and Harold Ickes, September 14, 1933, NRA File, OF466 – OF466b, FDRL; Schlesinger, *Politics of Upheaval,* 48.
19. Ickes, *Secret Diary,* 1 : 400 – 401.
20. Caro, *Power Broker,* 437.
21. Ickes, *Secret Diary,* 1 : 423.
22. Carl Weiss's motives for assassinating Huey Long are explored in James W. Clarke, *American Assassins: The Darker Side of Politics* (Princeton: Princeton University Press, 1982, 1990). Clarke argues that Weiss killed Long in order to protect the honor of his wife's influential family, the Pavys.
23. Ickes, *Secret Diary,* 1 : 440.
24. Details of the vacation with Roosevelt are from ibid., 438, 449.
25. Ickes diary, MR 1, p. 1223, LC–HLIP.
26. Schlesinger, in *Politics of Upheaval,* 348 – 49.
27. Ickes diary, MR 1, p. 1230, LC–HLIP.

CHAPTER 9
"BACK TO WORK"

1. Schlesinger, *Politics of Upheaval,* 447.
2. Ickes, *Secret Diary,* 1 : 465.
3. Ibid., 487.

4. Sherwood, *Roosevelt and Hopkins,* 51 – 52.

5. Ibid., 48.

6. Don Kirkley, memo to Ickes, December 22, 1934, Oil File, LC-HLIP.

7. Ickes, *Secret Diary,* 1 : 676.

8. Warne, interview with author.

9. Chart A-4, prepared by the Public Works Administration, July 14, 1934, Newspaper Criticism File, LC-HLIP.

10. Sherwood, *Roosevelt and Hopkins,* 76.

11. *Public Building: Architecture under the P.W.A., 1933–39* (Washington, D.C.: GPO, 1939).

12. Collier, *Zenith,* 286.

13. Prof. David Wilkins, interview with author, February 16, 1995, Tucson, Arizona.

14. Ickes, letter to Lewis Douglas, January 27, 1934; and Ickes, memo to Zimmerman, February 1, 1935, Indian Affairs File, NA-HLIOF.

15. Warne, *Bureau of Reclamation,* 66.

16. Schlesinger, *Politics of Upheaval,* 360.

17. Ickes, letter to Frank Knox, July 5, 1939, Friends File, LC-HLIP.

18. Honorable Turner Battle, memo to Marvin McIntyre, December 28, 1933, NRA File, OF 466—466b, FDRL.

19. For further confirmation, see two articles published in 1969: Leonard Arrington, "The New Deal in the West: A Preliminary Statistical Inquiry," and James T. Patterson, "The New Deal in the West," in *Pacific Historical Review* 38 (1969): 311 – 27.

20. Hiram Johnson, letter to Ickes, May 8, 1933, Interviews File, LC-HLIP.

21. Hiram Johnson, letter to Ickes, October 17, 1933, PWA File, LC-HLIP.

22. Ickes, letter to Hiram Johnson, November 9, 1933, PWA File, LC-HLIP.

23. Ickes, letter to Johnson, November 9, 1934; and Johnson, letter to Ickes, November 17, 1934, Friends File, LC-HLIP.

24. Hiram Johnson, letter to Ickes, July 20, 1935; Ickes, letter to Johnson, December 1935, Friends File, LC-HLIP.

25. Robert Caro, *The Years of Lyndon Johnson: The Path to Power* (New York: Knopf, 1982), 447 – 49.

26. Ickes diary, MR 1, pp. 1546 – 47, LC-HLIP.

27. Caro, *Lyndon Johnson,* 378, 460.

28. Ickes diary, MR 1, pp. 1187 – 88, LC-HLIP.

29. Eleanor Roosevelt, memos, April 7 and April 9, 1937, Correspondence with Government Departments File, 70, FDRL-ER.

30. Robert R. McCormick, letter to Harold Ickes, July 17, 1933, Complimentary File, LC-HLIP.

31. Ickes diary, MR 1, p. 632, LC-HLIP.

32. Ibid., 366 – 68.

33. Ickes, letter to Ross Woodhull, June 7, 1935, Chicago Tribune File, LC-HLIP.

34. Ickes, *Secret Diary,* 1 : 551.

35. Ibid., 641.

36. Ickes diary, MR 2, p. 1597, LC-HLIP.

37. Ibid., 1454.

38. Conrad L. Wirth, *Parks, Politics, and the People* (Norman: University of Oklahoma Press, 1980), 132 – 34. Also, Conrad Wirth, telephone interview with author, New Lebanon, N.Y., October 15, 1987.

39. *National Parks,* 42.

40. Wirth, *Parks,* 132.

41. Problems with Hopkins and the PWA are from Ickes, *Secret Diary,* 1 : 473, 583, 589, 593 – 94.

CHAPTER 10
"I STRUCK A REAL NOTE"

1. Leuchtenburg, in *FDR and the New Deal,* 186.

2. Sitkoff, *New Deal for Blacks,* 284, 293.

3. Ickes, *Secret Diary,* 1 : 553.

4. Schlesinger, *Politics of Upheaval,* 138.

5. Arthur F. Raper, *The Tragedy of Lynching* (New York: Negro Universities Press, 1933), v, 6 – 7.

6. Sitkoff, *New Deal for Blacks,* 39.

7. Ibid., 60.

8. Ibid., 68 – 69.

9. Ickes, letter to L. F. Coles, June 15, 1933, Complimentary File, LC-HLIP.

10. Arno Cammerer, memo to Ickes, November 23, 1933, Negroes File, NA-HLIOF.

11. Ickes, letter to Robert Fechner, September 26, 1935, Negroes File, LC-HLIP.

12. Clyde Ellis, letter to President Roosevelt, January 20, 1936, Interior Department File, OF 6Q – 6S, FDRL.

13. John Gunther, *Roosevelt in Retrospect* (New York: Harper and Brothers, 1950), 48, 242.

14. Freidel, *Launching the New Deal,* 453.

15. Schlesinger, *Politics of Upheaval,* 587.

16. Comments on the Detroit speech are from Ickes, *Secret Diary,* 1 : 477, 478.

17. Ibid., 519.

18. Ibid., 496, 531.

19. Ibid., 614.

20. Schlesinger, *Politics of Upheaval,* 503.

21. Ibid., 637.

22. Vernon L. Parrington, *The Romantic Revolution in America, 1800 – 1860,* Harvest ed. (New York: Harcourt, Brace and World, 1927), 142.

23. Freidel, *Rendezvous,* 246.

24. Ickes, letter to William M. Rutter, January 2, 1936, Friends File, LC-HLIP.

25. Ickes, *Secret Diary,* 1 : 615.

26. Ibid., 615 – 16.

27. Details of both conventions are from Schlesinger, *Politics of Upheaval,* 543, 544, 579; Leuchtenburg, *FDR and the New Deal,* 182 – 83.

28. Ickes, *Secret Diary,* 1 : 621.

29. Schlesinger, *Politics of Upheaval,* 580.

30. A good description of this event is contained in Schlesinger, *Politics of Upheaval,* 582 – 85. John Gunther also discusses the president's fall in *Roosevelt in Retrospect,* 237.

31. Schlesinger, *Politics of Upheaval,* 584.

CHAPTER 11
THE NEW DEAL TRIUMPHANT

1. All material on Roosevelt's speech in Philadelphia is from Ickes, *Secret Diary,* 1 : 627.

2. Ickes diary, MR 1, p. 481, LC-HLIP.

3. Ickes, *Secret Diary,* 1 : 475, 499; Ickes diary, MR 1, p. 1324, LC-HLIP.

4. Ickes, *Secret Diary,* 1 : 527.

5. Ibid., 528.

6. Ickes diary, MR2, pp. 1724 – 27, LC-HLIP.

7. Elizabeth Ickes, interview with author, Moraga, Calif., March 15, 1991.

8. Ickes, *Secret Diary,* 1 : 611 – 12.

9. Ibid., 616.

10. White and Maze, *Ickes,* 171.

11. Ickes, *Secret Diary,* 1 : 627.

12. Discussion between Farley and Ickes is from ibid., 630 – 32.

13. Congressman John Dingell, letter to Jim Farley, August 10, 1936, Presidential Campaign 1936 File, LC-HLIP.

14. Sen. Pat McCarran, letter to Jim Farley, August 5, 1936, Presidential Campaign 1936 File, LC-HLIP.

15. Ickes, *Secret Diary,* 1 : 634.

16. Ibid., 639.

17. Ibid., 640, 645.

18. Details of relationship with Cissy Patterson are from ibid., 649 – 50, 652, 662.

19. Georgiana X. Preston, "His Life with Father" (*Washington Times-Herald,* March 28, 1942), Newspaper Criticism File, LC-HLIP.

20. Ickes diary, MR 2, p. 1713, LC-HLIP.

21. Ickes, *Secret Diary,* 1 : 672.

22. Ickes, expense journals, 1916 – 37, entry, November 18, 1919, LC-HLIP.

23. Wilmarth's suicide note and correspondence between Betty Ickes and Harold Ickes are from Ickes diary, MR 2, pp. 1705, 1706 – 7, 1709, 1711 – 12, LC-HLIP.

24. Ickes, personal memoirs, 344, 346, Speeches and Writings File, LC-HLIP.

25. Details from September 8 luncheon with Roosevelt are from Ickes, *Secret Diary,* 1 : 673 – 74.

26. Ibid., 672, 679.

27. Schlesinger, *Politics of Upheaval,* 630.

28. James Denvir, letter to Ickes, October 15, 1936, Friends File, LC-HLIP.

29. Schlesinger, *Politics of Upheaval,* 638 – 39.

30. Sitkoff, *New Deal for Blacks,* 95.

31. Leuchtenburg, in *FDR and the New Deal,* 188 – 89.

32. Lowitt, *The New Deal,* 210.

33. Ickes, *Secret Diary,* 1 : 701.

CHAPTER 12
"A FIRST CLASS FIGHT ON HIS HANDS"

1. Leuchtenburg, *FDR and the New Deal,* 251.

2. Ickes, *Secret Diary,* 1 : 468.

3. H. L. Ickes, *The Secret Diary of Harold Ickes,* vol. 2, *The Inside Struggle* (New York: Simon and Schuster, 1954), 24.

4. Ibid., 30 – 31.

5. Ibid., 32.

6. *The Public Papers and Addresses of Franklin D. Roosevelt,* vol. 5, *The People Approve, 1936* (New York: Random House, 1938), No. 235, 634 – 42.

7. Ickes, *Secret Diary,* 2 : 68.

8. Ickes, letter to Dean Leon Green, February 25, 1937, Justice File, LC-HLIP.

9. Ickes, *Secret Diary,* 2 : 67.

10. John M. Blair, *The Control of Oil* (New York: Vintage, 1978), 156.

11. Ickes, letter to Leon Green, March 8, 1937, Justice File, LC-HLIP.

12. Ickes, *Secret Diary,* 2 : 98.

13. Ibid., 69.

14. Warne, interview with author, February 1988.

15. Lash, *Dealers,* 298 – 99.

16. Details on Senator and Mrs. Wheeler are from Elizabeth Wheeler Coleman, *Mrs. Wheeler Goes to Washington* (Helena, Mont.: Falcon Press, 1989), ix, x, 151.

17. Rudolph Spreckels, letter to Ickes, July 16, 1937, Justice File, LC-HLIP.

18. Ickes, *Secret Diary,* 2 : 74 – 75.

19. Russell Buhite and David Levy, eds., *FDR's Fireside Chats* (Norman: University of Oklahoma Press, 1992), 83, 93, 95.

20. John A. Adams Jr., *Damming the Colorado: The Rise of the Lower Colorado River Authority, 1933 – 39* (College Station: Texas A&M University Press, 1990), 68 – 69.

21. Ickes, *Secret Diary,* 2 : 75.

22. Ibid., 78.

23. Adams, *Damming the Colorado,* 63.

24. Ibid., 69.

25. Ickes, *Secret Diary,* 2 : 80.

26. Ibid., 91.

27. Sitkoff, *New Deal for Blacks,* 113, 114.

28. Ickes diary, MR 2, p. 2169, LC-HLIP.

29. Ickes, *Secret Diary,* 2 : 96, 97.

30. Ibid.

31. Ickes diary, MR 2, p. 2089, LC-HLIP.

32. Ibid., 2040.

33. Gunther, in *Roosevelt in Retrospect,* 338.
34. Fliers, 1937, Justice File, LC-HLIP.
35. Ickes, *Secret Diary,* 2 : 76.
36. Raymond Robins, letter to Ickes, February 6, 1937, Friends File, LC-HLIP.
37. *The Public Papers and Addresses of Franklin D. Roosevelt.* 1937 volume: *The Constitution Prevails* (New York: Macmillan, 1941), lxvii – lxix.
38. Ickes, *Secret Diary,* 2 : 161; Coleman, *Mrs. Wheeler,* 169.
39. *The Public Papers,* 1937 vol., lxvii.

CHAPTER 13
"FACING THE COMMON ENEMY"

1. Ickes, *Secret Diary,* 2 : 34.
2. Sherwood, *Roosevelt and Hopkins,* 92 – 93.
3. Ickes, *Secret Diary,* 2 : 140.
4. Ibid., 213.
5. Gunther, *Roosevelt in Retrospect,* 299.
6. Ickes, *Secret Diary,* 2 : 39. Discussion continues to 46.
7. Ibid., 45.
8. Arthur Maass, *Muddy Waters: The Army Engineers and the Nation's Rivers* (Cambridge: Harvard University Press, 1951).
9. Material on Department of Conservation and on the Bonneville Power bill is from Ickes, *Secret Diary,* 2 : 59, 61, 86, 87, 129 – 30.
10. "Ickes, President Grab for Power, Pinchot Charges," *Chicago Tribune,* May 1, 1937, in Conservation File, LC-HLIP.
11. Ickes, memo for the press, May 2, 1937, Conservation File, LC-HLIP.
12. Ickes, memo to Leona Graham, October 1936; Graham, memo to Ickes, October 20, 1936, Ickes-Pinchot Controversy File, LC-HLIP.
13. Gifford Pinchot, address, November 4, 1937, Conservation File, NA-HLIOF.
14. Dr. Robert Dixon, letter to Ickes, December 5, 1937, Conservation File, NA-HLIOF.
15. Ickes, *Secret Diary,* 2 : 135.
16. Ibid., 134.
17. Details on Ickes's personal life are from ibid., 137, 160, 265, 267; Ickes diary, 2217, MR2, LC-HLIP.
18. Ickes, *Secret Diary,* 2 : 257.
19. Marion Clawson, interview with author, Washington, D.C., October 14, 1987.
20. Ickes, *Secret Diary,* 2 : 152.

CHAPTER 14
"NATIONS IN NIGHTSHIRTS"

1. Ickes, *Secret Diary,* 2 : 196.
2. Ibid., 217.

3. Freidel, *Rendezvous*, 250.

4. Gunther, *Roosevelt in Retrospect*, statistics cited, 290; Leuchtenburg, *FDR and the New Deal*, 243.

5. Buhite and Levy, eds., *FDR's Fireside Chats*, 96 – 105.

6. Ickes, *Secret Diary*, 2 : 229.

7. Burns, *Roosevelt*, 322.

8. Frances Perkins, *The Roosevelt I Knew* (New York: Viking, 1946), 277.

9. Ickes, *Secret Diary*, 2 : 240 – 42.

10. Details of fishing trip are from ibid., 258 – 61.

11. Goldman, *Rendezvous*, 366.

12. Ickes, "Nations in Nightshirts," speech delivered December 8, 1937, before the American Civil Liberties Union, Speeches and Writings File, LC-HLIP.

13. Ickes, *Secret Diary*, 2 : 266.

14. Ibid., 277.

15. Robert Jackson, "The Menace to Free Enterprise," speech delivered December 29, 1937, before the American Political Science Association, Interior Department File, OF-6, FDRL.

16. Ickes, *Secret Diary*, 2 : 283.

17. Lash, in *Dealers*, 325.

18. Details on international situation and helium sale are from Ickes, *Secret Diary*, 2 : 143, 150, 274 – 76, 286, 324 – 25, 344, 391 – 92, 396.

19. Ickes, press conference, January 8, 1942, Press Conferences File, LC-HLIP.

CHAPTER 15
THE CALM AFTER THE STORM

1. Ickes, *Secret Diary*, 2 : 306.

2. Betty Glad, *Key Pittman: The Tragedy of a Senate Insider* (New York: Columbia University Press, 1986), 192.

3. Ickes, *Secret Diary*, 2 : 292 – 93.

4. See Ickes diary, MR 2, pp. 1887, 1902, 1905, 2406 – 7, 2454, 2543, 2548 – 69, 2574, 2599, 2604 – 5, LC-HLIP.

5. Ibid., 2548 – 49.

6. Ibid., 2559 – 61, 2574.

7. Ibid., 2606 – 8.

8. Ibid., 2607.

9. Ibid., 2558 – 59.

10. Ickes, *Secret Diary*, 2 : 299; Ickes diary, MR 2, pp. 2568 – 69, LC-HLIP; *Who Was Who in America*, Vol. 1, *1897 – 1942* (Chicago: A. N. Marquis, 1943), 1176.

11. Ickes diary, MR 2, p. 2689, LC-HLIP.

12. Ibid., 2550.

13. Ickes, *Secret Diary*, 2 : 305.

14. Ibid., 306.

15. Ickes diary, MR 2, p. 2587, LC-HLIP.

16. Ibid., MR 1, pp. 470 – 71, LC-HLIP.

17. Henry Morgenthau, diary, October 31, 1935 entry, FDRL.

18. Ickes diary, MR 2, pp. 2226, 2671 – 72, LC-HLIP.

19. Ickes, *Secret Diary*, 2 : 255.

20. Marvin McIntyre, memo to FDR, December 13, 1937, and FDR's handwritten reply, Interior Department File, OF 6, FDRL.

21. Ickes, transcript of Interior Department staff meeting, May 11, 1938, 7, Friends File, LC-HLIP.

22. Ibid., 8.

23. Ickes diary, MR 2, p. 2454, LC-HLIP.

24. Ickes, *Secret Diary*, 2 : 263.

25. Ickes, Interior Department staff meeting, May 11, 1938, 7, LC-HLIP.

26. Morgenthau diary, October 31, 1935 entry, FDRL.

27. Ibid., January 6, 1936 entry.

28. Ickes, Interior Department staff meeting, May 11, 1938, 6, LC-HLIP; William Warne, telephone interview with author, October 3, 1990, Sacramento, Calif.

29. Ickes, Interior Department staff meeting, May 11, 1938, 8, LC-HLIP.

30. Ickes diary, MR 2, p. 2761, LC-HLIP.

31. Horace Albright, letter to Ickes, May 13, 1938, Friends File, LC-HLIP.

32. Ickes, letter to Arno Cammerer, August 26, 1937, NPS File, NA-HLIOF.

33. Ickes, memo to Arno Cammerer, January 28, 1938, NPS File, NA-HLIOF.

34. Ickes, *Secret Diary*, 2 : 319.

35. Ickes, memo to Arno Cammerer, April 2, 1938, NPS File, NA-HLIOF.

36. Ickes, memo to Director Smith, March 15, 1938, Grazing Service File, NA-HLIOF.

37. Ickes, *Secret Diary*, 2 : 101; Ickes diary, MR 2, p. 2770, LC-HLIP.

38. Meeting with Roosevelt is from Ickes, *Secret Diary*, 2 : 357 – 60.

39. All information on the wedding and honeymoon is from ibid., 401 – 10 passim.

40. Ickes, letter to Mary Hately, June 27, 1938, Family and Relations File, LC-HLIP.

CHAPTER 16
"TO SAIL, NOT DRIFT"

1. David Brinkley, *Washington Goes to War* (New York: Knopf, 1988), 17; Ickes, *Secret Diary*, 2 : 455.

2. Goldman, *Rendezvous*, 291.

3. Leuchtenburg, *FDR and the New Deal*, 249.

4. Ickes, *Secret Diary*, 2 : 361.

5. Ibid.

6. Public Works Administration Program, 1938, NRA File, OF 466b, FDRL.

7. Ickes, *Secret Diary*, 2 : 411.

8. William Hassett, telegram to Steve Early, July 28, 1938, NRA File (PWA), OF 466b, FDRL.

9. Nixon, ed., *FDR and Conservation*, 2 : 257 – 58.

10. Ickes, letter to FDR, December 30, 1938, NRA File (PWA), OF 466b, FDRL.

11. Ibid.

12. All information on the trip to the Pacific Northwest and Alaska is from Ickes, *Secret Diary*, 2 : 435 – 66 passim.

13. Details on the primaries are from ibid., 2 : 459, 466; 1 : 675.

14. Freidel, *Rendezvous*, 273.

15. Ickes, *Secret Diary*, 2 : 475 – 76.

16. Information on the trip to California is from ibid., 489 – 91.

17. Ickes, "Sixty Families Revisited," speech, October 21, 1938, San Francisco, 6, Speeches and Writings File, LC-HLIP.

18. Ickes, *Secret Diary*, 2 : 498 – 99.

19. Freidel, *Rendezvous*, 287.

20. Ickes, *Secret Diary*, 2 : 501.

21. Leuchtenburg, *FDR and the New Deal*, 274.

22. Dealings with Hitler are from Ickes, *Secret Diary*, 2 : 477, 478, 481.

23. Sherwood, in *Roosevelt and Hopkins*, 100.

24. Ickes, *Secret Diary*, 2 : 519.

25. Ibid., 502 – 3.

26. Ibid., 503 – 4.

27. Ibid., 504 – 5.

28. Ickes, "Esau, the Hairy Man," speech delivered December 18, 1938, Speeches and Writings File, LC-HLIP.

29. Ickes, *Secret Diary*, 2 : 343.

30. Ickes diary, MR 2, p. 2827, LC-HLIP.

31. Ickes, *Secret Diary*, 2 : 533.

CHAPTER 17
BATTLE FOR THE BIG TREES

1. *The Public Papers and Addresses of Franklin D. Roosevelt. 1938* Volume: *The Continuing Struggle for Liberalism* (New York: Macmillan, 1941), 605 – 7.

2. Brinkley, *Washington Goes to War*, 25.

3. *National Parks*, 46.

4. A. E. Demaray, memo to Ickes, December 7, 1938, and attached U.S. Forest Service Press Release, NPS File, NA-HLIOF.

5. U.S. Department of the Interior, memo for the Press, January 3, 1939, NPS File, NA-HLIOF.

6. Nixon, ed., *FDR and Conservation*, 2 : 290.

7. Ibid.

8. Leuchtenburg, *FDR and the New Deal*, 278.

9. Information on national park development from Nixon, ed., *FDR and Conservation*, 2 : 291 – 96.

10. David Brower, *For Earth's Sake: The Life and Times of David Brower* (Salt Lake City: Peregrine Smith Books, 1990), 436.

11. Ickes, *Secret Diary*, 2 : 578.

12. Ibid.

13. Scandals in the Park Service are from ibid., 582 – 85.

398 NOTES TO PAGES 303 - 323

14. Ben Harrison, letter to the attorney general, March 20, 1939, NPS File, NA-HLIOF.

15. Ickes, *Secret Diary*, 2 : 596.

16. Ickes, letter to William Colby of the Sierra Club, April 3, 1939, NPS File, NA-HLIOF.

17. Ickes, letter to Congressman Elliott, May 2, 1939, NPS File, NA-HLIOF.

18. Nixon, *FDR and Conservation*, 2 : 344 – 45.

19. Harold Ickes's nonutilitarian philosophy is analyzed in Mark Sagoff, "Where Ickes Went Right *or* Reason and Rationality in Environmental Law," *Ecology Law Quarterly* (1987): 265 – 323.

20. Roosevelt's reorganization is from Ickes, *Secret Diary*, 2 : 623, 629.

21. Nixon, *FDR and Conservation*, 2 : 310.

22. Ickes, *Secret Diary*, 2 : 660.

23. Ibid., 629 – 30.

24. Ibid., 631.

25. Ibid., 665 – 69.

26. Ibid., 673 – 74.

27. Ickes, letter to Raymond Robins, July 17, 1939, Friends File, LC-HLIP.

CHAPTER 18
HIS FINEST HOUR

1. Miller, *FDR*, 436.

2. There are several versions of this event. This discussion is drawn primarily from Joseph Lash, *Eleanor and Franklin* (New York: Norton, 1971), 525 – 28.

3. Ickes, *Secret Diary*, 2 : 613, 615.

4. Marian Anderson, *My Lord, What a Morning* (New York: Viking, 1956), 189.

5. Ibid., 196.

6. Ickes, *Secret Diary*, 2 : 614.

7. Anderson, *My Lord*, 191.

8. Ickes's problems with Dies are from Ickes, *Secret Diary*, 2 : 506 – 7, 546 – 47, 573 – 74.

9. Ibid., 581.

10. "The American Eagles," flyer, January 10, 1939, New York, Justice File, LC-HLIP.

11. Editorial, *Las Vegas Review-Journal*, December 21, 1939, Newspaper Criticism File, LC-HLIP; George Tagge, *Chicago Tribune*, April 15, 1941, Alaska File, LC-HLIP.

12. Bruce Allen Murphy, in *Fortas: The Rise and Ruin of a Supreme Court Justice* (New York: William Morrow, 1988), 34.

13. Ickes, *Secret Diary*, 2 : 555.

14. Ibid., 557.

15. Ibid., 558.

16. Harold L. Ickes, *America's House of Lords* (New York: Harcourt, Brace, 1939), 182.

17. David Kessler, letter to Ickes, February 13, 1939, Miscellaneous File, LC-HLIP.

18. Frank Knox, letter to Ickes, August 26, 1939, Friends File, LC-HLIP.

19. Relationship with Cissy Patterson is from Ickes, *Secret Diary*, 2 : 618, 622, 623.

20. Morgenthau diary, entries for June 16 and July 5, 1939, FDRL.

21. Ickes, letter to John Coffee, May 3, 1939; Coffee to Ickes, May 5, 1939; Ickes to Coffee, May 8, 1939, Oil File, LC-HLIP.

CHAPTER 19
ICKES'S BOOK OF REVELATIONS

1. Comments on Hopkins and himself from Ickes, *Secret Diary*, 2 : 595, 699.

2. Sherwood, *Roosevelt and Hopkins*, 173.

3. Comments on Swanson from Ickes, *Secret Diary*, 2 : 678.

4. Elizabeth Ickes, interview with author, Moraga, Calif., March 15, 1991.

5. Details of Ickes's youth are from Ickes, *Autobiography*, 4 – 5, 12, 19, 24.

6. Ickes, personal memoirs, Box 432, File 7, p. 44, Speeches and Writings File, LC-HLIP. All further citations to the microfilm version of the personal memoirs in this chapter will be cited by page number in the text.

7. F. A. Scott, letter to Louis Howe, February 3, 1934, Department of the Interior File, OF 6, FDRL.

8. E. Ickes, interview with author.

CHAPTER 20
"THEN IT'S HAPPENED"

1. Gunther, *Roosevelt in Retrospect*, 303.

2. Brinkley, *Washington Goes to War*, 25 – 26.

3. Events at poker game are from Ickes, *Secret Diary*, 2 : 712, 713.

4. Ibid.

5. *The Public Papers and Addresses of Franklin D. Roosevelt*. 1939 Volume: *War—and Neutrality* (New York: Macmillan, 1941), No. 118, 464.

6. Ibid., 463; Ickes, *Secret Diary*, 2 : 713.

7. Ickes, *Secret Diary*, 2:715.

8. Details on son's birth are from ibid., 714 – 15, 717.

9. *Public Papers*, 1939 Vol., No. 123, 488.

10. Details of September 6 meeting are from Ickes, *Secret Diary*, 2 : 717 – 18, 719, 721.

11. H. L. Ickes, *The Secret Diary of Harold Ickes*, vol. 3, *The Lowering Clouds* (New York: Simon and Schuster, 1954), 31.

12. Ickes diary, MR 2, p. 2029, LC-HLIP.

13. Ickes, *Secret Diary*, 3 : 4.

14. Changes in personnel are from ibid., 6, 9, 33, 71 – 72, 94.

15. Ibid., 83.

16. Sherwood, *Roosevelt and Hopkins,* 123.
17. *The Public Papers,* 1939 Vol., 512–25.
18. Ickes, *Secret Diary,* 3 : 18.
19. Ibid., 27.
20. Lash, *Dealers,* 401–2.
21. Ickes, *Secret Diary,* 3 : 50.
22. *Public Papers,* 1939 Vol., 544–45.
23. Ickes, *Secret Diary,* 3 : 69.
24. Ibid., 73–74, 81.
25. Ibid., 100.

CHAPTER 21
THE SECRETARY AND THE SUN PRESIDENT

1. William E. Leuchtenburg, *In the Shadow of FDR: From Harry Truman to Ronald Reagan* (Ithaca: Cornell University Press, 1989).
2. Ickes, *Secret Diary,* 1 : 449–50, 461, 460.

BIBLIOGRAPHY

MANUSCRIPT COLLECTIONS

Douglas, Lewis. Family Papers. Special Collections, University of Arizona Library, Tucson.

Ickes, Harold L. The Papers of Harold L. Ickes, 1874–1952. Manuscripts Division, Library of Congress, Washington, D.C.

———. The Office Files of Harold L. Ickes, 1933–46. Record Group 48, National Archives, Washington, D.C.

Roosevelt, Franklin D. Papers of Franklin D. Roosevelt, Eleanor Roosevelt, and Henry Morgenthau. Franklin D. Roosevelt Library, Hyde Park, New York.

PERSONAL INTERVIEWS

Max Beard, August 5, 1993, West Glacier, Mont.

Edward Bearss, March 28, 1988, Washington, D.C.

Verne Chatelain, April 4, 1988, Silver Spring, Md.

Marion Clawson, October 14, 1987, Washington, D.C.

Grace Collier, June 1, 1990, Tucson, Ariz.

Nina Roosevelt Gibson, May 15, 1995, Tucson, Ariz.

Elizabeth Ickes, March 15, 1991, Moraga, Calif.

Harold M. Ickes, June 25, 1989, New York, N.Y.

Raymond Ickes, June 20, 1988, Berkeley, Calif.

Barry MacKintosh, March 28, 1988, Washington, D.C.

Sen. Jennings Randolph (by telephone), April 18, 1988, Washington, D.C.

William Warne, February 20, 1988, Sacramento, Calif.

David Wilkins, February 16, 1995, Tucson, Ariz.

Conrad Wirth (by telephone), October 15, 1987, New Lebanon, N.Y.

BOOKS AND ARTICLES

Adams, John A., Jr. *Damming the Colorado: The Rise of the Lower Colorado River Authority, 1933–39.* College Station: Texas A&M Press, 1990.

Anderson, Marian. *My Lord, What a Morning.* New York: Viking, 1956.

Arrington, Leonard. "The New Deal in the West: A Preliminary Statistical Inquiry." *Pacific Historical Review* 38 (1969): 311–16.

Barber, James David. *The Presidential Character,* 4th ed. Englewood Cliffs, N.J.: Prentice Hall, 1992.

Blair, John M. *The Control of Oil.* New York: Vintage, 1978.

Brand, Donald R. *Corporatism and the Rule of Law: A Study of the National Recovery Administration.* Ithaca, N.Y.: Cornell University Press, 1988.

Brinkley, David. *Washington Goes to War.* New York: Knopf, 1988.

Brower, David. *For Earth's Sake: The Life and Times of David Brower.* Salt Lake City: Peregrine Smith Books, 1990.

Buhite, Russell, and David Levy, eds. *FDR's Fireside Chats.* Norman: University of Oklahoma Press, 1992.

Burns, James MacGregor. *Roosevelt: The Lion and the Fox.* New York: Harcourt, Brace, 1956.

Caro, Robert A. *The Power Broker: Robert Moses and the Fall of New York.* New York: Vintage, 1975.

———. *The Years of Lyndon Johnson: The Path to Power.* New York: Knopf, 1982.

Clarke, James W. *American Assassins: The Darker Side of Politics.* Princeton: Princeton University Press, 1990.

Clawson, Marion. *New Deal Planning: The National Resources Planning Board.* Baltimore: Johns Hopkins University Press, 1981.

Coleman, Elizabeth Wheeler. *Mrs. Wheeler Goes to Washington.* Helena, Mont.: Falcon Press, 1989.

Collier, John. *From Every Zenith.* Denver: Sage Books, 1963.

Cook, Blanche Wiesen. *Eleanor Roosevelt.* Vol. 1, *1884–1933.* New York: Viking, 1992.

Culhane, Paul J. *Public Land Politics.* Baltimore: Johns Hopkins University Press/ Resources for the Future, 1981.

Deloria, Vine, Jr., and Clifford M. Lytle. *The Nations Within: The Past and the Future of American Indian Sovereignty.* New York: Pantheon, 1984.

Ellis, Richard J. *Presidential Lightning Rods: The Politics of Blame Avoidance.* Lawrence: University Press of Kansas, 1994.

Engler, Robert. *The Politics of Oil.* Chicago: University of Chicago Press, 1961.

Freidel, Frank. *Franklin D. Roosevelt: Launching the New Deal.* Boston: Little, Brown, 1973.

———. *Franklin D. Roosevelt: A Rendezvous with Destiny.* Boston: Little, Brown, 1990.

Frome, Michael. *Whose Woods These Are.* New York: Doubleday, 1962.

Garrison, Lemuel A. *The Making of a Ranger.* Salt Lake City: Howe Brothers, 1983.

Gay, Peter. *Freud: A Life for Our Times.* New York: Norton, 1988.

Glad, Betty. *Key Pittman: The Tragedy of a Senate Insider.* New York: Columbia University Press, 1986.

Goldman, Eric F. *Rendezvous with Destiny.* New York: Vintage Books, 1977.

———. *The Tragedy of Lyndon Johnson.* New York: Knopf, 1969.

Gunther, John. *Roosevelt in Retrospect.* New York: Harper and Brothers, 1950.

Ickes, Harold L. *America's House of Lords.* New York: Harcourt, Brace, 1939.

———. *The Autobiography of a Curmudgeon*. New York: Reynal and Hitchcock, 1943.

———. *Back to Work: The Story of PWA*. New York: Macmillan, 1935.

———. *Fightin' Oil*. New York: Knopf, 1943.

———. *The Secret Diary of Harold L. Ickes*. Vol. 1, *The First Thousand Days, 1933–36*. Vol. 2, *The Inside Struggle, 1936–39*. Vol. 3, *The Lowering Clouds, 1939–41*. New York: Simon and Schuster, 1954.

The Interior Building: Its Architecture and Its Art. Washington, D.C.: GPO, 1986.

Irons, Peter H. *The New Deal Lawyers*. Princeton: Princeton University Press, 1982.

Kluger, James R. *Turning on Water with a Shovel: The Career of Elwood Mead*. Albuquerque: University of New Mexico Press, 1992.

Lash, Joseph P. *Dealers and Dreamers*. New York: Doubleday, 1988.

———. *Eleanor and Franklin*. New York: Norton, 1971.

Lear, Linda J. "Boulder Dam: A Crossroads in Natural Resource Policy." *Journal of the West* (October 1985): 82–94.

———. *Harold L. Ickes: The Aggressive Progressive, 1874–1933*. New York: Garland, 1981.

Leuchtenburg, William E. *Franklin D. Roosevelt and the New Deal, 1932–1940*. New York: Harper and Row, 1963.

———. *In the Shadow of FDR: From Harry Truman to Ronald Reagan*. Ithaca: Cornell University Press, 1989.

Lower, Richard Coke. *A Bloc of One: The Political Career of Hiram W. Johnson*. Stanford, Calif.: Stanford University Press, 1993.

Lowitt, Richard. *The New Deal and the West*. Bloomington: Indiana University Press, 1984.

Maass, Arthur. *Muddy Waters: The Army Engineers and the Nation's Rivers*. Cambridge: Harvard University Press, 1951.

MacKinnon, Janice R., and Stephen R. MacKinnon. *Agnes Smedley: The Life and Times of an American Radical*. Berkeley: University of California Press, 1988.

Miller, Nathan. *FDR: An Intimate History*. New York: Doubleday, 1983.

Morgan, Chester M. *Redneck Liberal: Theodore Bilbo and the New Deal*. Baton Rouge: Louisiana State University Press, 1985.

Morgenthau, Henry III. *Mostly Morgenthaus: A Family Portrait*. New York: Ticknor and Fields, 1991.

Morris, Edmund. *The Rise of Theodore Roosevelt*. New York: Coward, McCann, & Geoghegan, 1979.

Murphy, Bruce Allen. *Fortas: The Rise and Ruin of a Supreme Court Justice*. New York: William Morrow, 1988.

The National Parks: Shaping the System. Washington, D.C.: National Park Service, Department of the Interior, 1985.

Nixon, Edgar B., ed. *Franklin D. Roosevelt and Conservation, 1911–45*. 2 vols. Washington, D.C.: GPO, 1957.

Painter, David S. *Oil and the American Century*. Baltimore: John Hopkins University Press, 1986.

Parrington, Vernon L. *The Romantic Revolution in America, 1800–1860.* Harvest edition. New York: Harcourt, Brace and World, 1927.

Patterson, James T. "The New Deal in the West." *Pacific Historical Review* 38 (1969): 317–27.

Perkins, Frances. *The Roosevelt I Knew.* New York: Viking, 1946.

Philp, Kenneth R. *John Collier's Crusade for Indian Reform, 1920–1954.* Tucson: University of Arizona Press, 1977.

Public Building: Architecture Under the P.W.A., 1933–39. Washington, D.C.: GPO, 1939.

The Public Papers and Addresses of Franklin D. Roosevelt. Compiled by Samuel I. Rosenman. Vol. 5, *The People Approve, 1936.* New York: Random House, 1938.

————. 1937 vol., *The Constitution Prevails.* New York: Macmillan, 1941.

————. 1938 vol., *The Continuing Struggle for Liberalism.* New York: Macmillan, 1941.

————. 1939 vol., *War—and Neutrality.* New York: Macmillan, 1941.

Raper, Arthur F. *The Tragedy of Lynching.* New York: Negro Universities Press, 1933.

Reisner, Marc. *Cadillac Desert: The American West and Its Disappearing Water.* New York: Viking Penguin, 1986.

Robbins, Roy M. *Our Landed Heritage: The Public Domain, 1776–1936.* Lincoln: University of Nebraska Press, 1962.

Sagoff, Mark. "Where Ickes Went Right *or* Reason and Rationality in Environmental Law." *Ecology Law Quarterly* (1987): 265–323.

Schaller, Michael. *Douglas MacArthur: The Far Eastern General.* Oxford: Oxford University Press, 1989.

Schlesinger, Arthur M., Jr. *The Politics of Upheaval.* Cambridge, Mass.: Riverside Press, 1960.

Sherwood, Robert E. *Roosevelt and Hopkins: An Intimate History.* New York: Harper and Brothers, 1948.

Sitkoff, Harvard. *A New Deal for Blacks.* Oxford: Oxford University Press, 1978.

Ward, Geoffrey C. *A First Class Temperament: The Emergence of Franklin Roosevelt.* New York: Harper and Row, 1989.

Warne, William E. *The Bureau of Reclamation.* New York: Praeger, 1973.

Watkins, T. H. *Righteous Pilgrim: The Life and Times of Harold L. Ickes, 1874–1952.* New York: Henry Holt, 1990.

————. "The Terrible-Tempered Mr. Ickes," *Audubon* (March 1984): 94–111.

White, Graham, and John Maze. *Harold L. Ickes of the New Deal: His Private Life and Public Career.* Cambridge: Harvard University Press, 1985.

Who Was Who in America. Vol. 1, *1897–1942.* Chicago: A. N. Marquis, 1943.

Wirth, Conrad L. *Parks, Politics, and the People.* Norman: University of Oklahoma Press, 1980.

Worster, Donald. *Dust Bowl: The Southern Plains in the 1930s.* Oxford: Oxford University Press, 1979.

Zieger, Robert H. *John L. Lewis, Labor Leader.* Boston: Twayne Publishers, 1988.

INDEX